An Introduction to
Forensic DNA Analysis

Second Edition

Illustrations (including cover) and Photography by Norah Rudin

The illustrations and photos in this book are available as a PowerPoint presentation directly from the authors. Please contact:

Norah Rudin, Ph.D.
e-mail: norah@forensicdna.com
Web: http://www.forensicdna.com

1563 Solano Ave. PMB 506
Berkeley, CA 94707-2116

Fax: (510) 236-1601

An Introduction to
Forensic
DNA
Analysis

Second Edition

Norah Rudin, Ph.D.
Forensic DNA Consultant

Keith Inman, M. Crim.
**Senior Criminalist
California Department of
Justice DNA Laboratory**

CRC PRESS

Boca Raton   London   New York   Washington, D.C.

Library of Congress Cataloging-in-Publication Data

Rudin, Norah.
    An introduction to forensic DNA analysis / Norah Rudin, Keith Inman.—2nd ed.
      p. cm.
    Keith Inman's name appears first on the previous ed.
    Includes bibliographical references and index.
    ISBN 0-8493-0233-1 (alk. paper)
    1. DNA fingerprinting. I. Inman, Keith. II. Title.

  RA1057.55 .I56 2001
  614'.1—dc21
                                                       2001043472
                                                           CIP

Visit the CRC Press Web site at www.crcpress.com

© 2002 by CRC Press LLC

No claim to original U.S. Government works
International Standard Book Number 0-8493-0233-1
Library of Congress Card Number 2001043472
Printed in the United States of America   2 3 4 5 6 7 8 9 0
Printed on acid-free paper

Dedication

We dedicate the second edition of *An Introduction to Forensic DNA Analysis* to Anthony Longhetti (1928–2001). Tony was a pioneer in American criminalistics, and we acknowledge the position of DNA analysis within the field to which Tony dedicated his life.

We also honor those whose lives were lost on September 11, 2001. The identification of many remains will be achieved through the technological advances of DNA analysis described in this book, and through the determined efforts of many DNA analysts. Speaking on behalf of the profession, these services are offered to provide some small measure of relief to the families and friends of those who perished that day.

Acknowledgments

No project of this magnitude is completed in a vacuum. We are indebted to our colleagues in the field of forensic DNA typing and the greater profession of criminalistics for providing the backdrop against which the first edition of this book has found acceptance and widespread use. Some of those colleagues have provided fresh material with which to update the second edition of *An Introduction to Forensic DNA Analysis*.

Rhonda Roby, of Applied Biosystems, provided Identifiler™ data; Carol Zabit, of Promega Corporation, provided PowerPlex® 16 data; Jaiprakash Shewale, of ReliaGene Technologies, provided Y-Plex™ 6 data; Rebecca Reynolds, of Roche Molecular, provided immobilized SSO probe mtDNA data; Terry Melton, of Mitotyping Technologies, provided sequencing mtDNA data; Howard Baum and Mechthild Prinz, of the New York Medical Examiner's Office, provided Y-STR case data; Byron Sonnenberg, of the San Diego Sheriff's Office, provided Profiler Plus™ data; and Shelley Webster, of the San Diego Sheriff's Office, provided a hair photomicrograph. Kim Herd and Adrianne Day, of the American Prosecutor's Research Institute, arranged, once again to provide us with updated information about DNA cases and admissibility decisions; William Shields and Kim Kruglick provided otherwise hard-to-find information about the Crow mtDNA decision in Florida.

We must also acknowledge the editorial and production staff at CRC Press for producing yet another nonstandard book. Our acquiring editor, Becky McEldowney, has maintained both her sense of humor and composure while we found more rules to break than she knew existed. Mary Jamieson corrected all of our split infinitives and floating "whichs" without changing the style and feel of the text — an unusual trait in copy editors. Shayna Murry and Jonathan Pennell were more than patient with our multitude of homegrown graphics and exacting specifications and Pamela Morrell had the thankless task of weaving them into the text to produce a coherent document. Words cannot express our gratitude to Andrea Demby, our project editor, whose standard of quality matches our own.

Whenever you have excluded the impossible,
whatever remains, however improbable,
must be the truth -

Sir Arthur Conan Doyle
The Adventures of Sherlock Holmes
"The Adventure of the Beryl Coronet"

Table of Contents

6 Procedures for Forensic DNA Analysis   65

7 Interpretation of DNA Typing Results   97

8   Assessing the Strength of the Evidence   139

9   The DNA Databank   157

Table of Case Histories (Sidebars)

The Authors

Keith Inman holds a B.S. and M.Crim., both from the University of California at Berkeley. He is a Fellow of the American Board of Criminalistics. In his professional career he has been employed as a criminalist by the Orange County Sheriff-Coroner's Department, the Los Angeles County Sheriff's Department, the Los Angeles County Chief Medical Examiner-Coroner, and the Oakland Police Department. He was in private practice for 6 years at Forensic Science Services of California, Inc., a private crime laboratory that undertook both prosecution and defense work. Mr. Inman is currently employed as a senior criminalist by the California Department of Justice DNA Laboratory. He has co-authored *Principles and Practice of Criminalistics: The Profession of Forensic Science*, also published by CRC Press. He has taught in the Criminal Justice Administration Department at California State University, Hayward, and currently teaches a variety of general forensic science and forensic DNA courses for the University of California at Berkeley Extension as well as through the Internet.

Norah Rudin holds a B.A. from Pomona College and a Ph.D. from Brandeis University. She is a Diplomate of the American Board of Criminalistics. After completing a post-doctoral fellowship at Lawrence Berkeley Laboratory, she worked for 3 years as a full-time consultant for the California Department of Justice DNA Laboratory and has also served as consulting technical leader for the DNA programs at the Idaho Department of Law Enforcement, the San Francisco Crime Laboratory, and the San Diego County Sheriff's Department. Dr. Rudin divides her time between consulting, writing, and teaching about forensic DNA and forensic science as well as more general topics in biology. Dr. Rudin has co-authored *Principles and Practice of Criminalistics: The Profession of Forensic Science*, also published by CRC Press. She is also the author of the *Dictionary of Modern Biology*, Barron's Educational, 1997. Dr. Rudin teaches a variety of general forensic science and forensic DNA courses for the University of California at Berkeley Extension as well as through the Internet. She is active as a consultant and expert witness in forensic DNA for both prosecution and defense.

Please visit the *Forensic Education and Consulting* Web page at **www.forensicdna.com**.

Preface

The use of DNA typing as a crime-solving tool is no longer novel. However, forensic DNA analysis, which claims roots in classical genetics, biochemistry, and molecular biology, has, from its origins, found itself in an unlikely arena, a court of law. How can judges and juries, generally people with no specific scientific training, hope to comprehend the minutiae of molecular biology and population genetics, subjects that have emerged from the ivory tower of academia to appear as star witnesses in courtrooms throughout the world?

Our intention in the following pages is to translate science into English so that the layperson can gain insight into how the process works, from sample collection to interpretation of results. Key to the understanding of any analytical technique is a keen appreciation of its advantages and limitations. These concepts, even more than any specifics performed in the laboratory, aid in a determination of the appropriate application and interpretation of any test. By definition, any science becomes somewhat less accurate when simplified. We have tried to write for the person who is being introduced to DNA for the first time. To this end, we aim to clarify general principles; the exceptions that occur in every field are best left to a more advanced treatise.

The potential power of DNA typing has served to highlight issues of certification of laboratory personnel and accreditation of laboratories. Not only DNA, but all of forensic science has come under public scrutiny and the demand to show competence and adherence to proper procedures. As the underlying science becomes recognized by the legal community as generally accepted, these issues come to the front as weapons with which to refute evidence in any particular case. Appropriately, the forensic community has instituted peer-administered programs for initial and ongoing testing of both analysts and laboratories.

The statistical interpretation of DNA typing results, specifically in the context of population genetics, has been the least understood and, therefore by definition, the most hotly debated issue of many admissibility hearings. The perceived incomprehensibility of the subject, has led to a recalcitrance of the judicial system to accept DNA typing. Although this issue was virtually resolved with regard to older RFLP and AmpliType® PM+DQA1 typing systems for which a great amount of data had been accumulated, it is being challenged anew for STRs.

As predicted in the first edition of this book, DNA typing has become increasingly automated and miniaturized. The unique aspect of forensic science, however, is that each case is different. The previous history and current state of any sample must be considered when making decisions regarding the handling and analysis of samples, and this process of assessment continues throughout the analysis. These are not decisions that any analyst willingly gives up to a machine. Computer technology has become invaluable in the processing and management of large numbers of similar samples, such as those used in making a convicted offender database. Computers will also continue to be used as an aid in the evaluation, statistical analysis, and storage of data. We do not foresee the day, however, when the computer will take the stand, swear an oath "to tell the truth, and nothing but the truth," and render an *opinion* that "this sample came from that person."

Authors' Note:

Although this is formally the second edition of this book, as published by CRC Press, it is actually the fourth iteration of our continuing attempts to cogently codify the subject matter. In 1994, in the heat of O.J. mania, we self-published a 35-page, spiral-bound booklet entitled *The Forensic DNA Compendium* in a misguided attempt to educate the media. When we realized that it was mostly attorneys who were purchasing the booklet, we expanded and redirected the subject matter, resulting in *DNA Demystified*, a 128-page work, still self-published and presented in a three-ring binder. *DNA Demystified* sold several hundred copies before we decided to seek a publisher who would print, distribute, and market the book, allowing us to concentrate on the technical aspects. We expanded the book still further, resulting in a 250-page volume, now with the more traditional title of *An Introduction to Forensic DNA Analysis*, that CRC Press published for us in 1997. Major additions were an "intermediate-level" chapter detailing interpretation issues specific to various forensic DNA typing systems and also a chapter on quality control and regulation. With this additional information, we added forensic DNA analysts to our readers; these users tell us that they keep the book handy both as a resource for educating attorneys and also as a well-organized reference of basic information for themselves.

In this edition, we acknowledge STR typing as the current system of choice and greatly augment the relevant sections. We have significantly expanded the chapter on DNA databases and augmented the section on automated analysis. In previous iterations, we attempted to provide a comprehensive listing of legal decisions about forensic DNA typing. Because the use of DNA evidence has become commonplace, this has become an overwhelming task. Instead, we focus on key decisions and Appellate or Supreme Court rulings that provide precedents at the state and federal levels.

In part, because of continuing automation and computerization, and in part because the science of forensic DNA typing has, after a decade, come of age, the field has become increasingly more complex. It is our goal to continue to make this book accessible to the novice or non-expert, while addressing the growing complexity to at least some extent. As before, we address this need mostly in Chapter 7 "Interpretation of DNA Typing Results."

We sincerely hope that the current additions and refinements will increase the usefulness of this book. As always, we welcome input from our readers.

The Nature of Physical Evidence 1

I.   Science and the Law

 The application of science to the legal arena is fundamentally one of reconstruction, that is, trying to assist in determining what happened, where it happened, when it happened, and who was involved. It is not concerned with, and cannot determine, why something happened (the motivation). When science is applied in this way, the adjective "forensic" is added, which means that it is applicable to a court of law. Forensic analysis is performed on evidence to assist the court in establishing physical facts so that criminal or civil disputes can be resolved. The legal question determines the direction of scientific inquiry. It is the job of the forensic scientist to translate the legal inquiry into an appropriate scientific question, and to advise the judiciary on the capabilities and limitations of current techniques.

In forensic science, the laws of natural science are considered in making a determination about the state of a piece of **physical evidence** at the time of collection. Using the scientific method, inferences are made about how the evidence came to be in that state. These inferences then limit the events that may or may not have taken place in connection with said evidence. The law defines elements of a crime; science contributes information to assist in determining whether an element is present or absent.

The inferential aspect of the scientific contribution must be emphasized. Science used in court does not establish guilt or innocence (which are properly the province of the judge and jury). Rather, forensic science contributes information about what may have happened and who may have been involved. It does not assert whether the action was legal or illegal. The primary way in which reconstruction occurs is by establishing **associations**; a bullet is associated with a weapon, a fingerprint associated with a person, a shoe print associated with a shoe, etc.

By its very nature, physical evidence is **circumstantial**; it provides clues to a particular course of events, but does so only indirectly. It is left to the forensic scientist, and ultimately the court, to make an inference about a criminal event from the physical evidence.

II. Principles and Processes of Criminalistics

 Over the last several decades, a theoretical framework for the discipline of criminalistics has evolved. These fundamental precepts provide a philosophical and rational framework for the application of scientific knowledge to the forensic arena. They are concepts that guide a forensic analysis in a logical progression, starting with understanding the origin of evidence and culminating in a statement of the significance of the analytical result. We understand the major paradigm of their work to comprise six basic concepts:

1. **Divisible matter:** the division of matter
2. **Transfer** (*Locard exchange principle*): the exchange of material between two objects
3. **Identification:** defining the physico-chemical nature of the evidence
4. **Classification/Individualization:** attempting to determine the source of the evidence
5. **Association:** linking a person with a crime scene
6. **Reconstruction:** understanding the sequence of past events

In previous work, we (Inman and Rudin, 2000) have proposed this paradigm to organize current thinking about forensic science (Figure 1.1). In this work, we also conclude that **divisible matter** and **transfer** define scientific principles that relate to the generation of evidence; the other concepts — **identification, association** through class and **individualizing** characteristics, and **reconstruction** — are integral to the *practice* of forensic science, and are *processes* we use in our attempt to answer the various investigative questions of "who? what? where? why? when? and how?"

Figure 1.1 is a pictorial representation of the paradigm as we understand it. All of the ideas are arranged around a physical and temporal focus, the **crime**. The interactive elements of a scene, a victim, a suspect, and witnesses are not novel. However, they are usually depicted as a triangle with the victim, suspect, and witnesses as apices surrounding the physical scene. We prefer to think of these elements as overlapping domains. Regardless, the crime defines the border between the generation of evidence and the recognition and subsequent analysis and interpretation of evidence.

A. The Principles

Only two of the concepts mentioned emerge from the fundamental nature of matter: **divisible matter** and **transfer**. These principles exist independently of any human intervention, or even recognition; therefore, we accord them a different status than the processes that begin with the recognition of evidence by human beings. However, although all matter is constantly dividing and transferring, it does not become evidence until division and transfer occur in conjunction with a criminal event. Note that for some types of evidence, the contact necessary for transfer may be the force causing division. For example, a collision between two vehicles causes the simultaneous division and transfer of paint. Recognize that divisible matter does not account for a large category of evidence, that of pattern

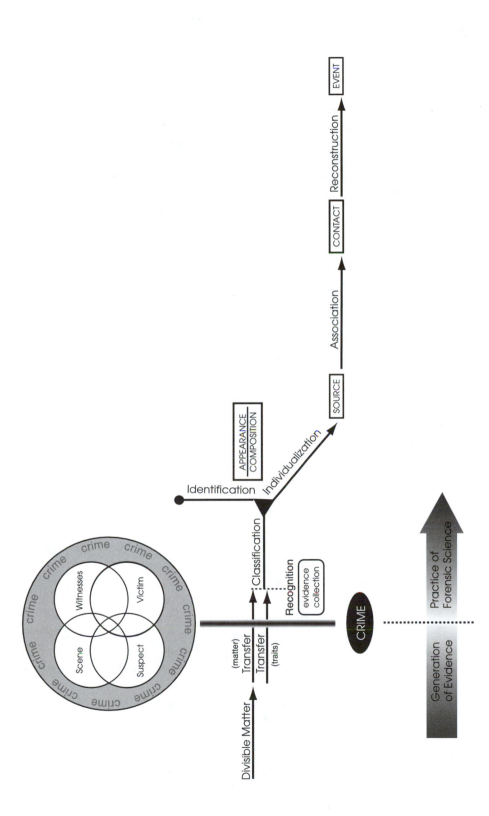

Figure 1.1 Individuals practicing a profession need a common map to guide them through their work. While never fully articulated in an organized fashion, over the years a map of the discipline of criminalistics has emerged. Numerous workers have contributed to the conceptual framework. The paradigm includes the principles of evidence formation (the origin of evidence) and the processes of analysis that describe the profession of criminalistics.

transfer evidence, such as prints and impressions. The transfer of matter requires its prior division; the transfer of *traits* may not.

B.   The Processes

At some point after the commission of a crime, evidence can be recognized as such and collected. The recognition of evidence and all of the processes that follow in a case investigation all result from decisions made and actions performed by people. We therefore separate the practice of forensic science from the fundamental scientific principles upon which the generation of evidence rests. If the crime is never discovered or the evidence is never detected, matter has still divided and transferred, and traits have still transferred. It is only when answering investigative questions about a crime that the processes of association through class and individualizing characteristics and of reconstruction are employed.

1.   *Identification*

Kirk and others emphasize the process of individualization, the reduction of a class of evidence to one. It is useful to take a step back and realize that identification, defining the physico-chemical nature of the evidence, can be an end in itself. For some purposes, for example, the recognition of illegal drugs, the forensic process stops with identification. The criminal justice system is not necessarily concerned with the marijuana field or methamphetamine lab from which the drugs originated (although sometimes they may be); simple possession of the scheduled substance fulfills the criteria of illegality. The process of **identification** answers the case investigation question of "what is it?". While we understand that the term "identification" is commonly used as a synonym for individualization, especially by workers in comparative evidence, such as fingerprints, we prefer to maintain the distinction.

2.   *Classification and Individualization*

Identification may also occur as a step leading to individualization. To distinguish it from end-point identification as discussed in the previous section, we refer to the intermediate process that may lead to individualization as **classification**. Any forensic analysis that proceeds on the path toward individualization relies on a comparison of at least two items. Physics and logic determine that any individual object is unique; this is not the question. The forensic question asks whether items share a common origin. There may be some disagreement about whether an item must be classified before it is individualized. We believe that, whether intentionally or not, the analyst will know what the item is by the time he concludes a common source. If ambiguity exists about the classification of an item, the individualization to a common source is also compromised. The process of **individualization** answers the questions of "which one is it?" or "whose is it?," depending on whether the item is animate or inanimate; it does this by inferring a common source or origin.

a. Classification.   An item is classified when it can be placed into a class of items with similar characteristics. For example, firearms are classified according to their caliber and rifling characteristics, and shoes are classified according to their size and tread pattern.

Any physical item will possess **class characteristics** that make it what it is, and these may vary, depending on what part of the item is of interest and on what scale it is examined.

Forensic scientists have classified a number of items that are routinely encountered in criminal investigations, and have developed tests based on those traits that, in their testing, have proven to be useful in identifying an item as belonging to a particular class. For example, hairs are routinely found in crimes of violence. Analysts have found that examining some of the microscopic characteristics will assist in identifying it as a hair, as opposed to a fiber, and will also serve to place it in the category of human hair, as opposed to animal hair.

One key part of this understanding of class characteristics as identifying an item is that many other items with similar characteristics exist in the world. For example, many millions of shoes that have a particular size and tread pattern exist at any one time. This means that measuring and describing class characteristics of a track found at a crime scene may have been left by one of many millions of tennis shoes manufactured in the United States. This still, however, serves to eliminate many other kinds of footwear as being responsible for the evidence shoe print, and narrows the search and comparison considerably.

b. Individualization.   An evidence item can be individualized when it, along with a reference item, can be inferred to originate from a unique common source. Individualization relies on the acquisition of traits that are so rare, either alone or in combination with other traits, that it is unreasonable to think of them being duplicated by chance alone.

A key element considered in determining whether a trait is a class or an individualizing characteristic is the origin of the trait. Those traits created by a controlled process become class characteristics. Examples include the rifling characteristics of a weapon, the tread pattern on a shoe, cocaine from a coca plant, and the blood group of a person. The first two examples result from the repetitive nature of manufacturing; the last two are biological products, under genetic control. When objects or substances are the product of a repetitive process under some direction or control, class characteristics result.

When forensic scientists look at new evidence for ways of identifying it, they look to those traits that are under some known control. Frequently, these traits are so obvious that they are difficult to articulate. For example, a fiber is first described as long and thin, and we describe it so quickly in our minds that it is difficult to reconstruct why or how we arrive at the conclusion that it is a fiber. But it is easily distinguished from a cement truck, if for no other reason than scale and shape. Class characteristics can include millions of similar items, or only two.

Individualizing traits are those created by random acts and are therefore not predictable or controlled (e.g., Figure 1.2). Traits acquired by shoes after they are on someone's foot, such as nail holes, cuts, or embedded glass fragments, qualify as individualizing characteristics. Similarly, the microscopic variations on weapon barrels that occur during manufacture, but that are not controlled because they are so small, impart individualizing characteristics to bullets fired through them. Fingerprints arise as a result of a random process during a certain stage of gestation. Because of the number of different combinations of types of traits and spatial configurations possible on a finger, it is accepted that no two fingerprints are the same. The random process that contributes to the great variability of DNA from one person to another is mutation.

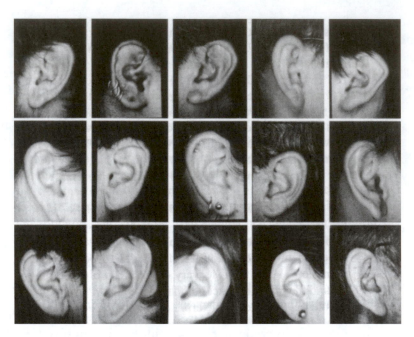

Figure 1.2 Ears — a trait that probably approaches individuality.

3. Association

The theory that makes these concepts of identification, classification, and individualization applicable in the context of criminal and civil litigation is one attributed to Edmund Locard in the early 20th century. He proposed that when two objects come in contact, traces from one will be transferred to the other, and in both directions. These traces may not always be detectable (because detection depends on the sensitivity of the method employed), but they are always present. This is known as the Locard Transfer Theory, which serves as the linchpin of all forensic examinations.

Although the word "association" is used freely in describing the results of a forensic examination, no clear definition seems to exist, at least not in the published literature. We propose that association be defined as an inference of contact between the "source" of the evidence and a "target." Such an inference is based on the detection of transfer of material or a physical match determined by complementary edges. The source and the target are relative operational terms defined by the structure of the case; if transfer is detected in both directions, for example, each item is both a source and a target.

The association process involves the evaluation of all the evidence for and against the inference of common source; in other words, competing hypotheses are compared. The probability of the evidence under competing hypotheses is an expression of the likelihood of the evidence given that the target and source items were in physical contact, contrasted with the likelihood of the evidence given that the target was in contact with a different unrelated source. This process requires combining the strength of the evidence established during the individualization process with additional information (such as may be provided by manufacturers of materials and empirical studies), as well as assumptions made by the analyst.

Note the distinction between a conclusion of common source (the evidence and reference fibers are classified or individualized as sharing a common source) and an inference of contact between a source and a target (the carpet and the deceased are associated).

The value of physical evidence lies in the ability of the forensic scientist to measure traits in evidence left at a scene and compare them to traits found in reference materials. If the traits are found to be similar, then a connection of varying strength has been created between the evidence and reference item. For example, codeine removed from a suspect's shirt (the crime scene) is compared to a reference sample of codeine in the laboratory's library, and concordance of key chemical traits confirms the identification of the material as codeine. Note that this does not, in and of itself, prove a crime. For example, if the codeine is found on a transient in the street without a prescription, a crime has been committed. If, on the other hand, the codeine is found in the shirt pocket of a pharmacist, and his other pocket has a prescription for it to be delivered to a patient, nothing illegal has occurred, although the physical evidence finding is the same.

4.   Reconstruction

We consider **reconstruction** to be the ordering of associations in space and time. Reconstruction attempts to answer the questions of "where?, how?, and when?" It should be stressed that the "when?" usually refers to an ordering in relative time only; was the sweater in contact with the couch before, during, or after the murder took place?

In summary, the organization of the forensic paradigm centers around the crime event. The principles of divisible matter and transfer interact in the generation of evidence before and during the crime. The practice of forensic science begins after the crime event with the recognition of physical evidence. Divisible matter and transfer are the two fundamental scientific principles upon which the forensic analysis of physical evidence is based. Identification, association through classification and individualization, and reconstruction form the infrastructure for the practice of forensic science.

III.   Fingerprints and DNA

 Because most people are familiar with dermatoglyphic fingerprints and are convinced of their individuality, it is useful to compare and contrast them to what were originally called "DNA fingerprints," a term that is, in fact, a misnomer. Dermatoglyphic fingerprints were first described at the end of the 1900s as possessing individualizing characteristics. Originally, their understanding and use was developed empirically, without reference to the specific genetic basis of the underlying patterns. Empirical examinations comprising tens of thousands of prints led examiners to conclude that no two prints examined were alike.

It has been thought for some time that the genetic contribution to a fingerprint (e.g., the determination of ridge count) is determined by not one, but several genes. In forensic applications, minutiae in the fingerprint patterns are analyzed. The minutiae result from a combination of genetic and nongenetic events during embryonic development; thus, even identical twins are distinguishable.

The original "DNA fingerprinting" method, developed by Alec Jeffreys, examined many locations in the DNA of a genome at once. The result was a multi-banded pattern whose complexity suggested a fingerprint, and was probably unique to each individual (excluding identical twins). Because of the complexity of the system, however, it was decided that the examination of one genetic location (**locus**) at a time would provide a more comprehensible result, and would better allow for the numerical estimation of the strength of similar genetic patterns. This method, called DNA typing or DNA profiling, was also more amenable to the examination of mixed samples because the number of bands (one or two) expected from one person was known.

In dermatoglyphic fingerprints, it is possible to obtain all of the information from all ten fingerpads; thus, there are no missing pieces of information. This was not true even of "DNA fingerprinting," and it is certainly not the case in current DNA typing methods. If we could easily obtain information about all three billion genetic units, DNA typing could be compared more directly with dermatoglyphic fingerprints. Because only a small portion, perhaps one millionth, of the three billion units of human DNA are even available for examination by current methods, the result is better compared to a partial print. Similar to a partial print, however, it may not be necessary to have all this information to be convinced of the individuality of a DNA profile.

IV.   Conventional Blood Typing

 Conventional blood typing was used to answer the most prevalent question about a biological sample; that is, "who could have contributed this sample?" After the discovery of the ABO blood typing groups, workers found that the differences among ABO blood group types between people could be exploited to determine who might be a donor of an evidentiary stain.

When it was discovered that one could exclude large percentages of the population as possible donors, genetic typing of biological fluids became a powerful technique for assisting the triers of fact in determining what might have happened at a crime scene, and in particular, who might have been involved.

The ABO blood group system was the only one used to type forensic samples for a long time. But a significant breakthrough was achieved in the early 1970s when other protein and enzyme markers, which had been known to be polymorphic for a decade or more, were also found to be useful for typing forensic evidence. The bulk of this work was performed by scientists in the Scotland Yard Laboratory in London. They found that some of the markers previously used for paternity testing could also be used on bloodstains and other kinds of physiological fluid evidence found at crime scenes. In England in particular, this was beneficial because much of the crime there was, and still is, person-on-person. With the restriction on handguns in that country, most of the assaults were of a personal nature (i.e., stabbings and beatings) where blood was shed in close proximity to the assailant. It was inevitable that the nature of the evidence would lead to the development of appropriate marker systems. The early work was performed on genetic markers such as phosphoglucomutase (PGM), erythrocyte acid phosphatase (EAP), haptoglobin (Hp), and adenylate kinase (AK).

This work was brought to the United States through a pioneering effort of the Law Enforcement Assistance Administration (LEAA) in 1976 with the publication of a book by Brian Culliford (an examiner at Scotland Yard). This book outlined methods for the examination of genetic markers on bloodstained and semen-stained evidence.

The fundamental questions about, and the approaches taken to, conventional blood grouping are exactly the same as those used in DNA typing. One can ask two general questions of a bloodstain: "How did this stain come to be in this place?" and "Whose blood is it?". The first question is properly considered a part of crime scene reconstruction, in particular, a discipline known as bloodstain pattern interpretation. That question will not be considered here. The second question is the one most commonly asked, and is the focus of the balance of this book.

If a bloodstain is found at a crime scene, it is frequently important to know if it could be from the assailant or the victim. If a stain is found on a suspect, it is important to know if the blood could be from the victim; occasionally, it is of interest to determine if a stain on the victim is from a suspect. In this way, an association might be made between the crime scene evidence and a person. A biological association between the crime scene and the donor of the blood establishes that they were in contact. This conclusion usually leads to the strong inference that this contact occurred during commission of the crime. The question then becomes: "what physical properties of the evidence can be used to make a statement about the possible association between the bloodstain and a putative donor?" The physical traits that can answer this question are genetic in nature. By choosing genetic traits that vary from person to person in the population, one can say that a stain could not be from a certain percentage of donors, and could be from another percentage. In addition, one can test particular individuals to determine if they have the same genetic type as the evidence; this establishes whether they are among the group of possible donors.

The classical ABO blood group system serves to illustrate this concept. Four common ABO types exist: type A, type B, type AB, and type O. Further, each type is known to occur with a particular frequency in any population. For example, type A occurs in about 35 to 40% of the Caucasian population. If a bloodstain is found at a crime scene and is typed as "A," several statements can be made about it. First, individuals who are *not* type A cannot be the source of the sample. These people are **eliminated** as the donors of the bloodstain. Second, anyone who is type A is a possible source of the sample; they are **included** as possible donors of the stain. Third, approximately 35 to 40% of the Caucasian population would fall into this category of individuals included as a possible source. The strength of the typing result can be expressed as the size of any reference population that might be included as possible donors of the stain. The larger the percentage of the population that can be included, the weaker the finding. Conversely, the less common the type, the stronger the inference that a person with the same genetic traits is the donor of the sample.

Clearly, the goal of genetic typing is to reduce the frequency of the profile to the smallest number possible. This is accomplished by examining more than one genetic locus (typing system). ABO is only one of numerous conventional markers that are useful for this purpose. Like ABO, these other markers have different types associated with them, and each type is present at a known frequency in any particular population. If the same bloodstain examined above is also typed in the PGM system and found to be a type 1+, then the overall strength of the finding is expressed as the frequency of ABO type A (35%) multiplied by the frequency of PGM type 1+ (19%). Another way of thinking about this is to consider what percentage of the population is ABO type A (35%), and what percentage of these type A individuals is PGM 1+ (19%). The frequency of the Caucasian population that is both ABO type A and PGM type 1+ is: $35\% \times 19\% = 6.7\%$. As more markers are added, the percentage of the population included as possible donors becomes smaller and smaller.

Forensic DNA typing seeks to attain the same goal as conventional genetic marker systems: to reduce the number of possible donors to a minimum. The advantage of DNA in this respect is that more types are present in the population at any one locus, and more loci are available to be tested. For the RFLP markers, between 20 and 80 types may be present at any one locus, and each type occurs with a fairly low frequency. This means that a genetic type determined by several loci in combination, each with many possible types, will be rare. Consequently, very few individuals in any population will have the types detected in an evidence item; the significance of finding someone who has those types is concordantly high. Markers used in PCR-based systems, such as STRs, usually have fewer types per locus than the RFLP loci, but the frequencies of these types in the population are still lower than for conventional blood typing markers. When coupled with the fact that DNA is far more stable than the conventional protein and enzyme markers, DNA typing is much more powerful than conventional typing of evidentiary material.

Further References

Ashbaugh, D.R., *Quantitative-Qualitative Friction Ridge Analysis: An Introduction to Basic and Advanced Ridgeology,* CRC Press, Boca Raton, FL, 2000.

Ashbaugh, D.R., The premises of friction ridge identification, clarity and the identification process, *J. Forensic Ident.*, 44(5), 499–516, 1994.

Balding, D.J. and Nichols R.A., DNA profile match probability calculation: how to allow for population stratification, relatedness, database selection and single bands. *Forens. Sci. Int.*, 64, 125–140, 1994.

Cook, R. et al., A model for case assessment and interpretation. *Sci. Justice*, 38(3), 151–156. 1998a.

Cook, R. et al., A hierarchy of propositions: deciding which level to address in casework. *Sci. Justice*, 38(4), 231–239. 1998b.

DeForest, P., Gaensslen, R.E., and Lee, H., *Forensic Science: An Introduction to Criminalistics*, McGraw-Hill, New York, 1983.

Evett, I.W. and Weir, B.S., *Interpreting DNA Evidence*, Sinauer Associates, Inc., Sunderland, MA, 1998.

Gaensslen, R.E., *Sourcebook in Forensic Serology, Immunology, and Biochemistry*, U.S. Government Printing Office, Washington, D.C., 1983.

Inman, K. and Rudin, N., *Principles and Practice of Criminalistics: The Profession of Forensic Science*, CRC Press, Boca Raton, FL, 2000.

Kirk, P. L., The ontogeny of criminalistics, *J. Criminal Law Criminol. Police Sci.*, 54, 235–238, 1963.

Kirk, P., *Crime Investigation*, 2nd ed., John Wiley & Sons, New York, 1974, 15.

Locard, E., Dust and its analysis, *Police J.*, 1, 177, 1928.

Locard, E., The analysis of dust traces. Part I–III, *Am. J. Police Sci.*, 1, 276, 401, 496, 1930.

Osterburg, J.W., *The Crime Laboratory; Case Studies of Scientific Criminal Investigation*, Indiana University Press, Bloomington, 1968.

Robertson, B. and Vignaux, G.A., *Interpreting Evidence*, John Wiley & Sons, Chichester, 1995.

Saferstein, R., *Criminalistics: An Introduction to Forensic Science*, 7th ed., Prentice-Hall, Englewood Cliffs, NJ, 2001.

Sensabaugh, G.F., Biochemical markers of individuality, in *Forensic Science Handbook*, Saferstein, R., Ed., Prentice-Hall, Englewood Cliffs, NJ, 1982, 338–415.

Stoney, D.A., Evaluating associative evidence: choosing the relevant question, *J. Forensic Sci. Soc.*, 24, 473, 1984.

Stoney, D.A., What made us ever think we could individualize using statistics? Proceedings of the 12th IAFS Meeting, Adelaide, Australia, *J. Forensic Sci. Soc.,* 31, 197, 1990.

Thornton, J., The snowflake paradigm, letter to the editor, *J. Forensic Sci.,* 31, 399, 1986.

Tuthill, H., *Individualization: Principles and Procedures in Criminalistics.* Lightening Powder Company, Salem, OR, 1994.

Wilson, T., Automated fingerprint identification systems, *Law Enforcement Technol.,* 45–48, 1986.

The Collection and Preservation of Physical Evidence

Before an item of evidence can be examined, it must be taken to the laboratory. This is not as trivial as it sounds. The conditions in which biological molecules exist in the body are carefully controlled and very specific. From the moment biological material leaves the body, it is in a foreign environment and changes begin to take place. DNA is packed very tightly in the chromosomes of a cell; stretched out to its full length, each chromosome might be meters long. Outside their natural protected environment, these long thin molecules can be very fragile. DNA is subject to degradation (breaking into smaller fragments), and that degradation can have an effect on the ability to obtain a useful result from DNA typing. The more severe the degradation, the smaller the fragments become. As the DNA fragments degrade, their average size may become smaller than the fragment length at a particular locus. If the average size of DNA fragments in a degraded sample is smaller than any particular region of interest, weak or no results will be obtained. One of the advantages of the newer STR systems is that very small regions are targeted, so that even substantially degraded DNA may still produce a profile.

Factors leading to the degradation of DNA include time, temperature, humidity (leading to the growth of microorgansims), light (both sunlight and UV light), and exposure to various chemical substances. Combinations of these conditions are often found together in the environment. Numerous studies have been conducted to determine the effects of these conditions, which, with a few exceptions, tend to degrade the samples into smaller fragments. An important outcome of these studies is the finding that these environmental factors will not change DNA from one type into another; in other words, an HLA DQA1 type 1.1 will not change into a 1.2, nor will an STR type change from a 5,9 to a 6,8. Rather, the degradation changes the DNA from a sample that can be typed into a sample that gives no type at all. This is an important part of the validation of any genetic typing system because it means that the biological component of the system will not produce false positive results. In other words, because one profile cannot be changed into another, there is no danger that environmental degradation will produce a complete DNA pattern that would include someone who is not the donor of the sample. Degradation can limit the usefulness of DNA typing, but does not invalidate it.

Further, these studies have also shown that DNA is much more stable than the conventional genetic markers used in forensic examinations. While many of the conventional protein and enzyme markers degrade beyond typability in a 2- to 3-month period (antigenic systems such as ABO are an exception), DNA under normal environmental conditions remains stable and typable for years. This is especially true of PCR-based systems, which can tolerate significant degradation and still yield readable types.

A special cause for concern might be the appearance of only one allele at a particular locus in an individual instead of the more commonly seen two alleles. Is the sample from a true homozygote, or is one of two distinct alleles missing for a different reason? There might be several explanations for this phenomenon (see Chapter 7); one that must be considered is obviously degradation of the larger allele, but not the smaller one. This is where an assessment of the quality of a sample is key to correctly interpreting the results (see below, Appendix C).

An important goal in collecting and preserving biological evidence is to halt any degradative process already in progress and limit any future deterioration. In general, biological processes are slowed by removing moisture and lowering the temperature. Thus, the goal of the crime scene investigator is to dry a sample and freeze it as soon as practical.

I.   Extraneous Substances

Just as important as preserving the biological integrity of the sample is the consideration of any extraneous substances that might interfere in the analysis. Various of these substances have different effects on typing. Nonbiological substances (e.g., dyes, soaps, and other chemicals) can affect the sample by interfering in the analytical procedures (see Chapter 6). This type of interference typically produces an inconclusive result or no type.

Non-human biological material includes physiological substances or DNA from other organisms. Although cross-typing is occasionally seen in some systems, it generally does not interfere with interpretation of the final result. A particular concern is the growth of microorganisms. Crime scene samples such as blood and semen provide a fertile environment for the growth of bacteria and fungi. As they grow, these microorganisms secrete biochemicals that degrade the human DNA in the sample. Even so, the DNA type will simply go away, as opposed to being magically converted into someone else's type. Partially degraded DNA must be interpreted carefully by an experienced analyst.

So, what of the "C" word, contamination? We define **contamination** as the inadvertent addition of an individual's physiological material or DNA during or after collection of the sample as evidence. It is important to differentiate between a "mixed sample" and a "contaminated sample." A mixed sample is one that contains DNA from more than one individual and in which the mixing occurred before or during the commission of the crime. A contaminated sample is one in which the material was deposited during collection, preservation, handling, or analysis.

Among the considerations in determining whether a second DNA type would even be detected is the method of testing involved. For example, PCR-based testing, where the DNA in the sample is copied millions of times over, is an inherently more sensitive technique than RFLP. This also makes a PCR test more likely to detect traces of a second type, whatever the source. Other factors include the total amount of DNA in the sample and the ratio of the components.

With proper attention to sample collection, preservation, and handling, contamination can be greatly minimized. Proper procedures during evidence collection would include the wearing and intelligent changing of gloves, the use of fresh or cleaned implements, and proper packaging. Once the sample is in the laboratory where it can be dried and chilled, the potential for contamination is mostly from other samples undergoing processing at the same time. This is where the training and qualifications of the analyst and quality control of the laboratory come into play. Safeguards are set up not only to guard against contamination from other laboratory samples, but just as importantly, to detect contaminated samples should they occur. Precautions include processing evidence and reference samples separately in space or time, restricting PCR product to an isolated room, and using controls to detect contamination in any batch of samples. The greatest danger is a sample switch by the analyst because this would actually result in an incorrect DNA type, as opposed to no type.

II. Collection of Evidence

Two main methods exist to collect a sample for subsequent analysis in the laboratory. These are: (1) collecting the stained item directly, or (2) removing the stain onto a more suitable or easier to handle substrate. The first method is preferred because it does not risk loss by manipulation. Simply, one picks up the item, packages it in some suitable manner, and transports it to the laboratory for proper preservation until analysis. This is most appropriate for items such as clothing, or any other item that might fit into a box or bag. The removal is left to the analyst, who is in a much better position to evaluate and correctly process the sample. The second method is to remove the biological material to a better substrate (e.g., transferring a stain on asphalt to a cotton swatch) by rehydrating the stain with distilled (preferably sterile) water and soaking it onto a clean cotton cloth substrate (see Figure 2.1). Rehydrating and soaking onto a cloth substrate tends to minimize loss and makes the stain easier to work with in the laboratory. However, it does introduce moisture, which must be removed as soon as possible. The moisture is removed by drying the stain, usually by placing it into a container such as an open test tube, that allows the cloth to dry quickly. If the sample is allowed to remain wet for any length of

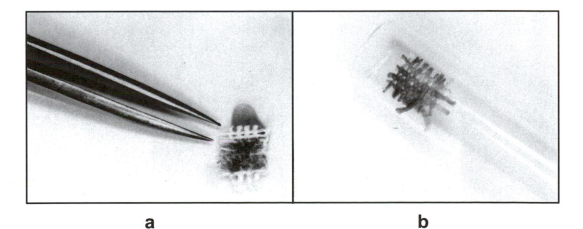

a   **b**

Figure 2.1 Evidence collection. One way to collect a dried bloodstain on a hard substrate, such as a window or floor, is to wick up the stain onto a small piece of cotton fabric moistened with sterile distilled water. The swatch (a), now containing the evidentiary material, is transported to the laboratory in a clean test tube (b).

time, then the degradative processes discussed above may start to take effect. Alternatively, the sample can be scraped from a substrate using a clean (preferably sterile) scalpel. Scraping does not rehydrate the sample, and thus does not introduce moisture and contribute to degradation. However, it does risk loss of sample by failing to remove all of the material, or by inadvertent loss during the scraping process. All of these methods have their uses, and the choice of any particular method is a matter of judgment and experience on the part of the crime scene investigator, whether it is a detective, technician, or forensic scientist. All work well when performed properly.

A good practice when collecting evidence is to collect one or more unstained samples from an area adjacent to the obvious stain or physiological fluid. The purpose of this exercise is to determine what was on the substrate (the object or surface upon which evidence is found) before the evidence was ever deposited. This sample serves as a control for biological material already present on substrates such as bed sheets and panty crotches and may allow for the subtraction of extraneous genetic types from the final profile (see Chapter 7). Additionally, it functions as a control for evidence collection and handling procedures. If sloppy technique is used, for example, not changing gloves when appropriate, and contamination is incurred that later shows up as a type after analysis, the substrate sample may show this same type.

III.   Preservation of Evidence

Once a sample has been collected, it must be dried (or remain dry). It should also be stored frozen, although for DNA this is less important than for the conventional protein and enzyme systems. The sample should not be subjected to fluctuations in either temperature or humidity. Most laboratories will have dedicated freezers for evidence storage.

IV.   Evaluation of Evidence

Before an evidence item is analyzed for DNA type, presumptive tests are performed to establish the type of biological material that is present. It would be wasteful to run a full spectrum of DNA tests only to find no result because ketchup or shoe polish was analyzed. Presumptive color tests for various fluids such as blood, semen, or saliva may be performed at the scene before a sample is collected, or in the laboratory. However, it is crucial to understand that the point of performing presumptive tests is simply to determine whether it is worth proceeding to more definitive testing. Rarely should conclusions be drawn from the presumptive tests themselves. In the event that confirmatory testing is either not performed or proves unsuccessful, any statements about the results of a presumptive test must carefully explicate the capabilities and limitations of the test. Sometimes, the analyst is unable to establish the identity of the physiological fluid tested. DNA typing may neverthless be successful, but its value is reduced in the context of the case.

Once the identification of a sample as a particular biological substance is established, either by testing or history, preliminary tests are conducted to establish the "**state of the DNA**" contained in the sample. It is possible to run tests that reveal the quality of the DNA (how much degradation is present) in an item of evidence, how much total DNA is present, and how much of the total DNA is human. A yield gel (Appendix C2) will tell how much total DNA is present, and will also show how much degradation has occurred. The quantitation of the human component of the total DNA present can be achieved via a method known as a slot blot (Appendix C1). At one time, an evaluation of the "state of the DNA" was crucial in making decisions about what might be accomplished with any particular sample, for example, whether RFLP was possible or whether a PCR method was more suitable. Because the current STR systems are relatively tolerant of poor-quality DNA, and a larger amount of DNA is needed to run a yield gel than to simply type it, most laboratories no longer routinely run yield gels. However, establishing the amount of human DNA is still critical because the best STR results are achieved within a relatively narrow window of input DNA.

A. RFLP

RFLP testing requires a minimum amount of DNA of relatively **high molecular weight (HMW)**. HMW DNA means DNA with an average fragment size of about 20,000 to 25,000 bp (20 to 25 kilobase pairs, kb). In other words, degradation cannot have fragmented the DNA to an average size much smaller than this. Thus, when reference is made to HMW DNA, it is with regard to how much degradation has taken place and whether this would permit or preclude an RFLP analysis. If DNA that has been severely degraded is typed using RFLP, the danger exists that HMW bands for any one locus might be missed. For example, a two-banded pattern might erroneously be typed as a one-banded pattern, or larger bands from a second contributor to the sample might be missed. Absent knowledge of the amount of degradation in a sample, this might lead to a false exclusion.

In addition, a minimum amount of DNA is needed to successfully perform an RFLP analysis. This minimum amount is somewhat lab dependent, and also varies with the probe labeling method (radioactive or chemiluminescent) but tends to be in the 10- to 50-ng range. That is, there must be 10 to 50 nanograms (ng) of HMW human DNA to reasonably expect an RFLP result, although this does not categorically preclude a typable result with less. The yield gel and slot blot results assist in determining whether an extracted DNA sample meets these criteria.

B. PCR

Most PCR-based systems require much smaller stretches of intact (nondegraded) DNA than RFLP. Fragments as small as a few hundred base pairs may yield a successful PCR result in many cases. The main advantage of PCR-based systems, however, is their sensitivity. Often, samples containing as little as 0.3 to 0.5 ng of DNA (on the order of 100 times less material than needed for RFLP) can be successfully typed. A few hundred sperm (out of the hundreds of millions in a normal ejaculate) or a blood droplet the size of a large pinhead can easily provide this amount of DNA. (See Figure 5.16.)

In addition to the amount of human DNA and its quality, the presence of extraneous substances also enters into the evaluation of the evidence. Everything from the material on which a stain is deposited (e.g., leaves, soil, blue jeans, glass) to chemicals added before, during, or after the deposition of the stain (e.g., oils, spermicides, bleach, soap, soda) can affect the ability to extract or otherwise analyze the sample. There are usually several different methods that can be employed to optimize the yield and quality of the DNA extracted; knowing the history of the sample will help in deciding which path to follow. For example, blue denim is known to contain dyes that combine with DNA and inhibit both restriction digestion in an RFLP analysis and amplification in the PCR. A method has been developed that will remove much of this dye and allow for full analysis. Thus, an analyst presented with stains on blue jean material will consider the need to perform this clean-up procedure. Another example is soil, which contains many microorganisms. Evidence collected from this substrate will become severely degraded and replete with non-human DNA in a short period of time. An analyst faced with evidence of this type will want to know how much human and non-human DNA is present, as well as how much degradation has occurred to the human DNA. In most cases, regardless of how large the stain is, the analyst will be forced to use a PCR method because the DNA will be too degraded to permit an RFLP analysis.

The collection and preservation of evidence plays an important role in determining the success of DNA analysis. Careless handling that does not halt normal biological processes of degradation may compromise the analyst's ability to perform certain tests. Drying samples and placing them into cold storage as soon as possible after collection is the best way to ensure that no further harm is done to a sample than has already occurred as a result of being shed during a crime.

Further References

Akane, A., Matsubara, K., Nakamura, H., Takahashi, S., and Kimura, K., Identification of the heme compound copurified with deoxyribonucleic acid (DNA) from bloodstains, a major inhibitor of polymerase chain reaction (PCR) amplification, *J. Forensic Sci.*, 39(2), 362–372, 1994.

Baechtel, F.S., Presley, K.W., and Smerick, J.B., D1S80 typing of DNA from simulated forensic specimens, *J. Forensic Sci.*, 40(4), 536–545, 1995.

Barnett, P.D., Blake, E.T., Super-Mihalovich, J., Harmor, G., Rawlinson, L., and Wraxall, B., Discussion of "Effects of presumptive test reagents on the ability to obtain restriction fragment length polymorphism (RFLP) patterns from human blood and semen stains," *J. Forensic Sci.*, 37(2), 69–70, 1992.

Comey, C.T., Budowle, B., Adams, D.E., Baumstark, A.L., Lindsey, J.A., and Presley, L.A., PCR amplification and typing of the HLA DQ alpha gene in forensic samples, *J. Forensic Sci.*, 38(2), 239–249, 1993.

Cosso, S. and Reynolds, R., Validation of the AmpliFLP D1S80 PCR Amplification Kit for forensic casework analysis according to TWGDAM guidelines, *J. Forensic Sci.*, 40(3), 424–434, 1995.

Cotton, R.W., Forman, L., and Word, C.J., Research on DNA typing validated in the literature, *Am. J. Human Genetics*, 49(4), 898–903, 1991.

Crouse, C.A. and Schumm, J., Investigation of species specificity using nine PCR-based human STR systems, *J. Forensic Sci.*, 40(6), 952–956, 1995.

Culliford, B.J., *The Examination and Typing of Blood Stains in the Crime Laboratory*, U.S. Government Printing Office, Washington, D.C., 1971.

Duewer, D.L., Currie, L. A., Reeder, D.J., Leigh, S.D., Liu, H.K., and Mudd, J.L., Interlaboratory comparison of autoradiographic DNA profiling measurements. 2. Measurement uncertainty and its propagation, *Anal. Chem.*, 67(7), 1220–1231, 1995.

Fildes, N. and Reynolds, R., Consistency and reproducibility of AmpliType PM results between seven laboratories: field trial results, *J. Forensic Sci.*, 40(2), 279–286, 1995.

Hochmeister, M.N., Budowle, B., Borer, U.V., and Dirnhofer, R., Effects of nonoxinol-9 on the ability to obtain DNA profiles from postcoital vaginal swabs, *J. Forensic Sci.*, 38(2), 442–447, 1993.

Kimpton, C. et al., Report on the second EDNAP collaborative STR exercise, European DNA Profiling Group, *Forensic Sci. Int.*, 71(2), 137–152, 1995.

Laber, T.L., Giese, S.A., Iverson, J.T., and Liberty, J.A., Validation studies on the forensic analysis of restriction fragment length polymorphism (RFLP) on LE agarose gels without ethidium bromide: effects of contaminants, sunlight, and the electrophoresis of varying quantities of deoxyribonucleic acid (DNA), *J. Forensic Sci.*, 39(3), 707–730, 1994.

McNally, L. et al., The effects of environment and substrata on deoxyribonucleic acid (DNA) isolated from human bloodstains exposed to ultraviolet light, heat, humidity, and soil contamination, *J. Forensic Sci.*, 32(5), 1070–1077, 1989.

Presley, L.A., Baumstark, A.L., and Dixon A., The effects of specific latent fingerprint and questioned document examinations on the amplification and typing of the HLA DQ alpha gene region in forensic casework, *J. Forensic Sci.*, 38(5), 1028–1036, 1993.

Roy, R. and Reynolds, R., AmpliType PM and HLA DQ alpha typing from pap smear, semen smear, and postcoital slides, *J. Forensic Sci.*, 40(2), 266–269, 1995.

Schneider, P.M.B. et al., Report of a European collaborative exercise comparing DNA typing results using a single locus VNTR probe, *Forensic Sci. Int.*, 49(1), 1–15, 1991.

Schwartz, T.R., Schwartz, E.A., Mieszerski, L., McNally, L., and Kobilinsky, L., Characterization of deoxyribonucleic acid (DNA) obtained from teeth subjected to various environmental conditions, *J. Forensic Sci.*, 36(4), 979–990, 1991.

Shipp, E., Roelofs, R., Togneri, E., Wright, R., Atkinson, D., and Henry B., Effects of argon laser light, alternate source light, and cyanoacrylate fuming on DNA typing of human bloodstains, *J. Forensic Sci.*, 38(1), 184–191, 1993.

Walsh, D.J., Corey, A.C., Cotton, R.W., Forman, L., Herrin, G.L. Jr., Word, C.J., and Garner, D.D., Isolation of deoxyribonucleic acid (DNA) from saliva and forensic science samples containing saliva, *J. Forensic Sci.*, 37(2), 387–395, 1992.

Waye, J.S. and Fourney, R.M., Agarose gel electrophoresis of linear genomic DNA in the presence of ethidium bromide: band shifting and implications for forensic identity testing, *Appl. Theoret. Electrophoresis*, 1(4), 193–196, 1990.

Waye, J.S., Michaud D., Bowen J.H., and Fourney R.M., Sensitive and specific quantification of human genomic deoxyribonucleic acid (DNA) in forensic science specimens: casework examples, *J. Forensic Sci.*, 36(4), 1198–1203, 1991.

Webb, M.B., Williams, N.J., and Sutton, M.D., Microbial DNA challenge studies of variable number tandem repeat (VNTR) probes used for DNA profiling analysis, *J. Forensic Sci.*, 38(5), 1172–1175, 1993.

Wilson, R.B., Ferrara, J.L., Baum, H.J., and Shaler, R.C., Guidelines for internal validation of the HLA DQ alpha DNA typing system, *Forensic Sci. Int.*, 66(1), 9–22, 1994.

A Short History of DNA Typing

3

 In 1944, Oswald Avery defined the role of the cellular component known as **DNA** (**deoxyribonucleic acid**) as the vehicle of generational transference of heritable traits. In 1953, James Watson and Francis Crick elucidated the structure of the DNA molecule as a **double helix**. In science, as in art, form follows function; the very nature of the molecule provided an explanation for its unique properties, including the ability to propagate itself faithfully from generation to generation.[1] In 1980, David Botstein and co-workers were the first to exploit the small variations found between people at the genetic level as landmarks to construct a human gene map. The particular type of variation they used is called **restriction fragment length polymorphism** or **RFLP**.

In 1984, while searching for disease markers in DNA, Alec Jeffreys discovered a unique application of RFLP technology to the science of personal identification. His method, which he termed "**DNA fingerprinting**," was modified to detect loci sequentially rather than concomitantly, and was adopted by crime laboratories for general use in the United States. Scientists generally agree that a more descriptive and inclusive term for the process, as it was eventually applied, is **DNA typing** or **DNA profiling**. In 1986, the **polymerase chain reaction** (PCR) was invented by Kary Mullis, who received a portion of the Nobel Prize in Chemistry for his discovery. PCR, more than any other scientific advance since perhaps the elucidation of the structure of DNA, has changed the face of molecular biology. Most crime laboratories today employ PCR-based DNA typing systems.

It should be noted that DNA analysis, in general, has a much broader usage and longer history than just identification of crime scene samples. As mentioned, an initial and ongoing application is the search for genes implicated in disease. With the completion of the **human genome project**, virtually the entire human genome (minus a few recalcitrant regions) has been sequenced and ordered. The ongoing effort has already led to the identification of genes involved in diseases such as Huntington's chorea, cystic fibrosis, muscular dystrophy, and various genetically influenced cancers. The information will now be used in a major drug discovery effort that will include personalizing therapies for genetically based diseases using individual DNA configurations. A specific application already in place is in monitoring bone marrow transplants in leukemia patients. In this application, DNA typing is more rapid and less error-prone than other blood typing methods; when the blood of the patient shows the donor's pattern, the transplant has

---

[1] Interestingly, the dimensions of a DNA helix, as measured across the width of the helix and between each turn, assume the proportions of the golden mean, a classic proportion found throughout nature and widely exploited in art.

succeeded. In addition to improved diagnosis and drug therapies, actual gene replacement is already in clinical trials for some of these diseases.

Immigration and paternity disputes were among the first legal arenas in which DNA typing was used. Families have been reunited, both in the United States and abroad, when DNA tests proved the identity of a child or sibling. Paternity determinations are now exclusively DNA based. Singer Michael Jackson was cleared in a paternity case when DNA typing showed another man to be the father. Questions about paternity cross all boundaries — ethnic, racial, socio-economic, and even historical. Recently, a technique that involves typing only the paternally transmitted Y chromosome (Y-STRs) was used to show that Thomas Jefferson likely fathered children with his slave Sally Hemmings.

Knowledge of the way DNA is inherited in a family can give valuable clues about the identity of missing persons. Biological remains, for example, can be identified by typing potential parents or siblings and determining the probability of a close genetic relationship between them and the deceased. Similarly, a child abducted at a very young age might be reunited with his or her biological parents based on the outcome of comparative DNA testing.

Through DNA testing methods, the Armed Forces DNA Identification Laboratory (AFDIL) has identified the remains of numerous Vietnam War veterans two decades after they died in combat. A program exists in which samples from all members of the armed forces are collected and stored, much in the same way that fingerprints have been collected for decades. The application of DNA typing to recovered remains has provided long-overdue closure to many families and effectively eliminates any need for the "tomb of the unknown soldier." DNA typing systems are invaluable in the identification of bodies and body parts from mass disasters. After the Waco disaster in Texas, which involved badly charred remains, numerous bodies were identified and linked as families by the use of PCR DNA typing methods. The DNA in this situation was minimal and badly degraded; this is a good example of the value of PCR in examining otherwise intractable samples. DNA typing is now a standard tool used in the identification of body parts recovered from airline disasters and also those recovered from mass graves resulting from war crimes, such as in Bosnia. One of the more creative uses of PCR DNA typing was in the conviction of one defendant in the World Trade Center bombing. Minute amounts of DNA in the saliva used to lick an envelope showed the same type as the defendant.

Because of its relative stability as compared to other biological molecules, DNA — and in particular a certain type of DNA, mitochondrial DNA (mtDNA) — has become an important tool in the study of anthropology and ancient history. At the University of Minnesota–Duluth, researchers performed DNA tests on lung tissue from an 1100-year-old mummified Chiribaya Indian and found a match with the DNA of the tuberculosis bacterium. This exonerates Christopher Columbus of the charge of introducing the deadly tuberculosis strain to the New World. The study of Egyptian mummies and other ancient remains by DNA typing has already revealed much about historical migration patterns and contributed to our still-limited understanding of human evolution. One body of work helped resolve several questions about the Russian royal family, including positive identification of the burial remains of Czar Nicholas II and the elimination of an "Anastasia" impostor (see Sidebar 5). Y-chromosome markers, together with information gleaned from matrillinealy inherited mitochondrial DNA, have provided anthropologists with a tool to investigate mass migrations and ancestral origins. Although it is not possible for an individual to determine her exact genetic makeup, interesting information about African tribal origins and Jewish heritage has already been discovered. And, of course, the fictional dinosaur park on a remote island off the coast of Costa Rica has long since been completed.

Animal geneticists are typing DNA in endangered species, such as cheetahs and whales, to track migration and breeding patterns. This information can be used in captive breeding programs to increase genetic diversity in anticipation of reintroducing the animals into the wild. Another interesting application was the use of DNA testing in solving the 1994 killing of a jogger by a mountain lion in California (Sidebar 1). Inroads have also been

---

Sidebar 1

To Catch a Cougar
(or, written in blood)

On December 10, 1994, a nude female body was discovered at Cuyamaca Rancho State Park in San Diego County, California. The head had been scalped and the body bore numerous puncture wounds. Because of the nude condition of the body, and the apparent violence of the attack, the incident was initially treated as a homicide. However, scalping is also consistent with a mountain lion attack. Along the path created by a set of drag marks were strewn various items of bloody clothing. At the end was the body, exhibiting wounds clearly indicative of feline claws and teeth.

Because cougars generally return to the site of a kill to collect their bounty at a later time, the body was removed as soon as the on-site investigation was completed and replaced with a fresh deer carcass tagged with a radio transmitter. Within the hour, the deer had been moved. Tracking hounds were used to tree an adult male mountain lion, which was subsequently shot in the chest (so as not to disturb potential evidence around the mouth or in the stomach) and killed. The head and all four paws were bagged.

The victim was immediately identified; however, it was still necessary to confirm that the correct cat had been destroyed. The carcass was autopsied at the California Department of Fish and Game Wildlife Forensic Laboratory, and various items of evidence were submitted to the California Department of Justice Forensic DNA Laboratory for human DNA testing. The items included bloody fur from the front paw, a claw from the left rear paw, fur from the lip area, and a portion of the stomach contents containing what appeared to be a large piece of human scalp tissue with hair still attached. A reference blood sample from the victim was also submitted for comparison.

A section of the scalp, as well as the bloody front paw fur, were extracted using the organic method (see Chapter 6). When checked on a yield gel (Chapter 6; Appendix C2), the paw fur sample (lane 9) appeared to contain a huge amount of DNA, and the scalp (lane 11) none.

The samples on the extreme right are the victim's reference (lane 13) and a positive control (lane 14). In an innovative move by the analyst, the yield gel was subjected to a small-scale Southern blotting, and probed with the same human-specific probe usually used for slot blot quantitation (see Chapter 6; Appendix C1). As expected, no signal was evident for the scalp tissue, but neither was there any evidence of human DNA on the bloody paw fur. This suggested that the DNA recovered was either bacterial, or the cat's own blood.

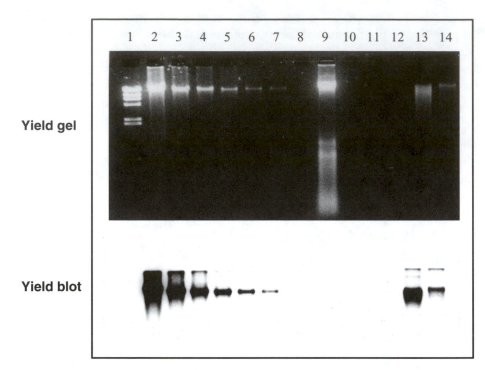

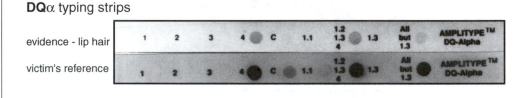

The other two samples, the claw and lip hair, had been judged to contain probably DNA only of sufficient quality and quantity for PCR DQαtyping, so were extracted using the Chelex method (see Chapter 6). The samples were amplified and a small portion was run on a product gel (Chapter 6; Appendix C4) to check for successful amplification. Only the lip hair sample showed any PCR amplification product and even that was quite faint. It was, however, enough to show a type of 4,4 on a strip, the same type as the victim.

made into poaching when carcasses and steaks have been matched to biological evidence found at the original location of an animal. The ability to extract and type DNA from bone means that illegal ivory can be tracked, as well as other horns and tusks prized by some cultures. DNA profiling is also slowly beginning to be used in plant identification cases, for example, to answer questions about timber harvesting and wildland fire origins.

The first forensic use of DNA took place in England and made use of Alec Jeffrey's original method of "DNA fingerprinting." In conjunction with police investigation, the Home Office was able to identify Colin Pitchfork as the one responsible for the murders of two young girls in the English Midlands. Significantly, an innocent suspect was the first accused murderer to be freed based on DNA evidence. One of the novelties of this case was that every male between the ages of 13 and 34 (almost 4000 men) residing in three nearby villages was required to donate a blood sample for analysis. The details of this case are chronicled in the book *The Blooding* by Joseph Wambaugh.

In the United States, private companies were the first to analyze DNA samples for forensic use. Both federal (FBI) and state forensic laboratories were close on their heels.

Sidebar 2

The Kevin Green Story
(or, murder isn't always a family affair)

When DNA's power of discrimination is combined with its innate stability over time, innocent people are freed and guilty culprits are identified. Kevin Green was 22 when he was sent to prison on the testimony of his wife, who swore he was the one who beat her nearly to death in an attack that caused her to lose her memory and her baby.

On September 30, 1979, Dianna Green was 2 weeks overdue with the couple's first child, and in no mood (or condition) for sex. Her husband, Kevin, feeling the normal anxiety and frustration of an almost-father, argued with his wife and finally left for a bite to eat. While he was gone, an intruder entered the room and bludgeoned and raped Dianna as she lay in bed. Kevin later told police that he found her unconscious and bleeding from a fractured skull when he returned from his meal. For a month after the attack, she lay in a coma. Her full-term fetus, a baby girl she named Chantal, was stillborn due to lack of oxygen. Dianna finally healed and awoke, but was left with memory lapses from the blows to her head.

Orange County, California, police initially suspected that the crime was the handiwork of the "Bedroom Basher," an as-yet unidentified assailant who spread terror throughout Orange County in the 1970s. However, when Dianna reported to the police that her newly returned memory had vividly revealed to her that Kevin, her husband, was her assailant, they charged Green instead. He denied the allegation and maintained his innocence. At his trial, a worker at a fast-food restaurant testified that Kevin was there at the time of the attack. Neighbors said he was not home and that his car was gone about the same time. And his lawyers insisted that Dianna Green's memories could not be trusted. Nevertheless, Kevin Green was convicted of the murder of his own unborn child, largely on the strength of his wife's testimony.

Kevin Green spent 16 years in prison, during which time DNA and the databank became a tool in the forensic science laboratory. In the mid-1990s, Orange County, California, criminalists used DNA technology to link the "Bedroom Basher" cases dating from the late 1970s. But a suspect who matched the DNA profile obtained from the victims remained elusive. While doing a routine search of the California Convicted Offender database, state analysts found a match between one of the Orange County rapes and Gerald Parker. Parker, already a convicted rapist, was then serving a sentence in one of California's state prisons, but was due for release. When Parker was questioned about the additional crimes, he readily confessed. He told authorities that he stalked his victims, waited until they were alone, broke into their homes, and bashed their heads with a bat, board, or mallet. He raped his victims while they were unconscious, and at least one may have been raped while dead. Parker also offered that he had committed the rape and murder of Dianna Green. Investigators were puzzled because this was a solved case, but they nonetheless submitted evidence from Dianna Green to the Orange County Crime Laboratory. Results showed that the DNA profile from semen found on the rape kit of Dianna Green matched Gerald Parker, not Kevin Green.

Green was not only freed, but the judge made a finding that he was completely innocent. During the release of Kevin Green, Judge Robert Fitzgerald told him, "You are about to wake up after a nightmare. You may exit the building through any door you like."

Most states, as well as many counties and cities, now boast their own forensic DNA laboratories. DNA testing for identification is, in fact, now ubiquitous around the world. International forensic DNA conferences are held regularly and provide a forum for scientific exchange. Due in part to the increased scrutiny of DNA laboboriess, forensic labs in general have implemented a process of peer review, self-regulation, and accreditation.

Since DNA testing was first introduced in the United States in 1986, it has been used in tens of thousands of cases. Of interest are FBI reports that fully one third of all suspects in rape cases are excluded by DNA evidence. Although this number is exaggerated due to the routine submission and testing of unlikely suspects (such as the standard testing of consenting partners), it is still indicative of the power of DNA analysis to free innocent men accused of a crime (see Sidebar 2). As we discuss further in Chapter 8, the exclusion of a suspect by DNA is absolute; there is no question of a statistical probability. Numerous wrongly convicted men continue to be freed from prison after old evidence is retested using the newer DNA techniques. The Innocence Project at Yeshiva University, run by Barry Sheck and Peter Neufeld (members of O.J. Simpson's defense team), has been key to this effort. As of this writing, DNA testing has freed more than 80 convicts, some of them death-row inmates. At least one man has been exonerated by DNA after he died of natural causes while awaiting execution.

Further References

Science and Medicine:

Arnheim, N. and Erlich, H., Polymerase chain reaction strategy, *Annu. Rev. Biochem.*, 61, 131–156, 1992.

Avery, O.T., MacLeod, C.M., and McCarty, M., Studies on the chemical nature of the substance inducing transformation of Pneumococcal types. *J. Exp. Med.*, 79, 137–158, 1944.

Botstein, D., White, R.L., Skolnick, M., et al., Construction of a genetic linkage map in man using restriction fragment length polymorphisms, *Am. J. Human Genetics*, 32, 314–331, 1980.

Davies, K. and Williamson, B., Gene therapy begins (editorial), *Br. Med. J.*, 306(6893), 1625, 1993.

Erlich, H.A. and Arnheim, N., Genetic analysis using the polymerase chain reaction, *Annu. Rev. Genetics*, 26, 479–506, 1992.

Erlich, H.A., Gelfand, D., and Sninsky, J.J., Recent advances in the polymerase chain reaction, *Science*, 252(5013), 1643–1651, 1991.

Gill, P., Jeffreys, A.J., and Werrett, D.J., Forensic application of DNA fingerprints, *Nature*, 318, 577–579, 1985.

Jeffreys, A.J. et al., Individual specific "fingerprints" of human DNA, *Nature*, 316, 76–79, 1985.

Lenstra, J.A., The applications of the polymerase chain reaction in the life sciences, *Cellular Molec. Biol.*, 41(5), 603–614, 1995.

Mullis, K.B, Faloona, F., Scharf, S. J., Saiki, R.K., Horn, G.T., and Erlich, H.A., Specific enzymatic amplification of DNA *in vitro*: the polymerase chain reaction, *Cold Spring Harbor Symp. Quant. Biol.*, 51, 263–273, 1986.

Rich, D.P. et al., Development and analysis of recombinant adenoviruses for gene therapy of cystic fibrosis, *Human Gene Therapy*, 4, 461, 1993.

Watson, J.D. and Crick, F.H.C., A structure for deoxyribose nucleic acid, *Nature*, 171, 737–738, 1952.

Science News and Reports:

Bishop, J.E., The gene hunters; muscular dystrophy yields up secrets to genetic probes; teams of scientists raced to find a major cause, can now hope for a cure; next, replacing dystrophin, *Wall Street Journal*, 1988.

Chase, M., DNA injection in gene therapy is called success, (University of California at San Francisco scientists report success with direct injection of DNA in the treatment of cystic fibrosis), *Wall Street Journal*, July 9, 1993.

Moore, A.H., Genetics: The money rush is on, *Fortune*, May 30, 1994.

U.S. Congress, Office of Technology Assessment. *Mapping Our Genes — Genome Projects: How Big, How Fast?*, OTA-BA-373, Washington, D.C., 1988.

Scientific Forensic Articles:

Alford, R.L. and Caskey, C.T., DNA analysis in forensics, disease and animal/plant identification, *Curr. Opin. Biotechnol.*, 5(1), 29–33, 1994.

Allard, J.E., Murder in south London: a novel use of DNA profiling. *J. Forensic Sci. Soc.*, Jan–Mar, 32(1), 49–58, 1992.

Boles, T.C., Snow, C.C., and Stover, E., Forensic DNA testing on skeletal remains from mass graves: a pilot project in Guatemala. *J. Forensic Sci.*, 3, 349–355, 1995.

Blackett, R.S. and Keim, P., Big game species identification by deoxyribonucleic acid (DNA) probes, *J. Forensic Sci.*, 37(2), 590–596, 1992.

Brauner P. and Gallili, N., A condom — the critical link in a rape, *J. Forensic Sci.*, 5, 1233–1236, 1993.

Brinkmann, B., Rand, S., and Bajanowski, T., Forensic identification of urine samples, *Int. J. Legal Med.*, 105(1), 59–61, 1992.

Brown, T.A. and Brown, K.A., Ancient DNA: using molecular biology to explore the past, *Bioessays*, 16(10), 719–726, 1994.

Clayton, T.M., Whitaker, J.P., and Maguire, C.N., Identification of bodies from the scene of a mass disaster using DNA amplification of short tandem repeat (STR) loci, *Forensic Sci. Int.*, 76(1), 7–15, 1995.

Corach, D., Sala, A., Penacino, G., and Sotelo, A., Mass disasters: rapid molecular screening of human remains by means of short tandem repeats typing, *Electrophoresis*, 9, 1617–1623, 1995.

Costello, J. and Zugibe, F.T., Identification of a homicide victim by a Casio data bank watch, *J. Forensic Sci.*, 39(4), 1117–1119, 1994.

Debenham, P.G., DNA typing. Heteroplasmy and the Tsar, *Nature*, 380(6574), 484–485, 1996.

Fisher, D.L., Holland, M.M., Mitchell, L., Sledzik, P.S., Wilcox, A.W., Wadhams, M., and Weedn, V.W., Extraction, evaluation, and amplification of DNA from decalcified and undecalcified United States Civil War bone, *J. Forensic Sci.*, 38(1), 60–68, 1993.

Gill, P., Kimpton, C., Aliston-Greiner R., Sullivan, K., Stoneking, M., Melton, T., Nott, J., Barritt, S., Roby, R., Holland, M., et al., Establishing the identity of Anna Anderson Manahan, *Nature Genetics*, 9(1), 9–10, 1995.

Gill, P., Ivanov, P.L., Kimpton, C., Piercy, R., Benson, N., Tully, G., Evett, I., Hagelberg, E., and Sullivan K., Identification of the remains of the Romanov family by DNA analysis, *Nature Genetics*, 6(2), 130, 1994.

Guglich, E.A., Wilson, P.J., and White, B.N., Forensic application of repetitive DNA markers to the species identification of animal tissues, *J. Forensic Sci.*, 39(2), 353–361, 1994.

Hagelberg, E., Gray, I.C., and Jeffreys, A.J., Identification of the skeletal remains of a murder victim by DNA analysis, *Nature*, 352(6334), 427–429, 1991.

Haglund, W.D., Reay, D.T., and Tepper, S.L., Identification of decomposed human remains by deoxyribonucleic acid (DNA) profiling, *J. Forensic Sci.*, 3, 724–729, 1990.

Hochmeister, M.N., Budowle, B., Borer, U.V., Rudin, O., Bohnert, M., and Dirnhofer, R., Confirmation of the identity of human skeletal remains using multiplex PCR amplification and typing kits, *J. Forensic Sci.*, 40(4), 701–705, 1995.

Jeffreys, A.J., Allen, M. J., Hagelberg, E., and Sonnberg, A., Identification of the skeletal remains of Josef Mengele by DNA analysis, *Forensic Sci. Int.*, 56(1), 65–76, 1992.

Jeffreys, A.J., Brookfield, J.F.Y., and Semeonoff, R., Positive identification of an immigration test case using human DNA fingerprints, *Nature*, 317, 818–819, 1986.

Lee, H.C., Ruano, G., Pagliaro, E.M., Berka, K.M., and Gaensslen, R.E., DNA analysis in human bone and other specimens of forensic interest: PCR typing and testing, *J. Forensic Sci. Soc.*, 2, 213–216, 1991.

Morton, N.E., DNA forensic science 1995, *Eur. J. Human Genet.*, 3(2), 139–144, 1995.

Murray, B.W., McClymont, R.A., and Strobeck, C., Forensic identification of ungulate species using restriction digests of PCR-amplified mitochondrial DNA, *J. Forensic Sci.*, 40(6), 943–951, 1995.

Sajantila, A., Strom, M., Budowle, B., Karhunen, P.J., and Peltonen, L., The polymerase chain reaction and post-mortem forensic identity testing: application of amplified D1S80 and HLA DQ alpha loci to the identification of fire victims, *Forensic Sci. Int.*, 51(1), 23–34, 1991.

Sensabaugh, G.F., Forensic application of the polymerase chain reaction, *J. Forensic Sci. Soc.*, 31(2), 201–204, 1991.

Sullivan, K.M., Forensic applications of DNA fingerprinting, *Molec. Biotechnol.*, 1(1), 13–27, 1994.

Sweet, D.J. and Sweet, C.H., DNA analysis of dental pulp to link incinerated remains of homicide victim to crime scene, *J. Forensic Sci.*, 40(2), 310–314, 1995.

Weedn, V.W. and Roby, R.K., Forensic DNA testing, *Arch. Pathol. Lab. Med.*, 117(5), 486–491, 1993.

Wegel, J.G. Jr. and Herrin, G. Jr., Deduction of the order of sexual assaults by DNA analysis of two condoms, *J. Forensic Sci.*, 39(3), 844–846, 1994.

Whitaker, J.P., Clayton, T.M., Urquhart, A.J., Millican, E.S., Downes, T.J., Kimpton, C.P., and Gill, P., Short tandem repeat typing of bodies from a mass disaster: high success rate and characteristic amplification patterns in highly degraded samples, *Biotechniques*, 18(4), 670–677, 1995.

Zhang, Y.P. and Ryder, O.A., Phylogenetic relationships of bears (the Ursidae) inferred from mitochondrial DNA sequences, *Molec. Phylogenetics Evolution*, 3(4), 351–359, 1994.

Forensic News Articles:

Abbey, D.M., The Thomas Jefferson paternity case, *Nature*, 397(6714), 32, 1999.

Baker, P., Death-row inmate gets clemency (Virginia Governor L. Douglas Wilder pardons mentally retarded Earl Washington, Jr. whose guilt was questioned by new DNA evidence), *Washington Post*, v117, 1994.

Beardsley, T., DNA fingerprinting reconsidered (again), *Sci. Am.*, 267(1), 26, 1992.

Biederman, P.W., In the genes; sabertooth a relative of modern-day big cats, DNA tests show (findings in article by George T. Jefferson, Dennis A. Gilbert), *Los Angeles Times*, 111, Oct. 29, 1992.

Bishop, J.E., DNA testing emerges from courtroom to detect whales killed unlawfully, *Wall Street Journal*, Sept. 9, 1994.

Bishop, J.E., Strands of time; a geneticist's work on DNA bears fruit for anthropologists; variations in fragments hint some American natives may hail from Polynesia; the controversy over Eve, *Wall Street Journal*, Nov. 10, 1993.

Broune, M.W., DNA experts expect to identify massacre victims (Drs. Michael M. Baden and Dragan Primorac will examine bodies found in mass grave in Bosnia and Herzegovina by Croatian officials), *New York Times*, v143, 1994.

Brown, D., Anthropology: looking at DNA to date migration (researching genetic interrelatedness of tribes through DNA variations), *Washington Post*, v117, 1994.

Clue in DNA and isotopes help identify ivory origin (An effort to help regulate the trade in elephant ivory), *New York Times*, v139, 1990.

Dean, C., DNA tests may help solve whale mystery; scientists investigate the failure of a species to reproduce, *New York Times*, v138, 1988.

DNA clears Floriday death row inmate 11 months after he dies of cancer, December 15, 2000, http://www.cnn.com/2000/LAW/12/14/death.row.dna.ap.

DNA identifies murder victim buried 8 years, *Los Angeles Times*, v110, August 5, 1991.

DNA test shows Virginia woman wasn't Anastasia, *Reuter*, Oct. 4, 1994.

Erickson, D., Do DNA fingerprints protect the innocent? *Sci. Am.*, 265(2), 18, 1991.

Fleishman, J., Haunted by massacre, Bosnian families look to DNA tests, *Philadelphia Inquirer*, http://inq.philly.com/content/inquirer/2000/11/05/front_page/MASSACRE0.5.htm.

Foster, E.A. et al., Reply to "The Thomas Jefferson paternity case," *Nature*, 397(6714), 32, 1999.

Franklin-Barbajosa, C. and Menzel, P., The new science of identity, *National Geographic*, 115, 1992.

Hunt, L., DNA used to identify murder victim (DNA fingerprinting identifies British girl), *Washington Post*, v114, 1991.

King, P.H., Killing of jogger Barbara Schoener by mountain lion shocks residents of cool California, *Los Angeles Times*, v113, 1994.

Kolata, G., Call it the DNA bug (DNA extracted from 120 million-year-old weevil preserved in amber), *New York Times*, v142, 1993.

Leary, W.E., Genetic record to be kept on members of military (DNA samples to be obtained from all American service members for purpose of identifying future casualties of war), *New York Times*, v141, 1992.

Monroe, L.R., Day of the condor? Genetic 'fingerprinting' may help save endangered birds, *Los Angeles Times*, v107, 1988.

Okie, S., Gene hunters set sights on evolution; tracking Kenya's big game for their DNA (scientists Pieter W. Kat and Peter Arctander collect tissue samples from living specimens to construct genetic portraits), *Washington Post*, v116, 1993.

Okie, S., Genetics: clues to birds' behavior, *Washington Post*, v112, 1989.

Pyle, A. and Colvin, R.L., DNA test links couple, dead baby (Patty Chavez case alleging that her baby was switched in the hospital), *Los Angeles Times*, v110, 1991.

Rensberger, B., 8,000-year-old genetic link found; Florida bog may reveal Indians' kinship to vanished people, *Washington Post*, v111, 1988.

Rensberger, B., A mummy's revelation: TB came to new world before Columbus (University of Minnesota research may have found DNA from tuberculosis bacterium in mummified woman who died 1,040 years ago, exonerating Christopher Columbus), *Washington Post*, v117, 1994.

Rivera, C., Laura Bradbury death shown by DNA evidence (3-year-old who disappeared in 1984), *Los Angeles Times*, v110, 1990.

Robinson, E., Tzar Nicholas's bones identified: two Romanovs still unaccounted for (DNA analysis proves bones found buried in Russian forest are those of Tzar Nicholas II, his wife and three of their four daughters), *Washington Post*, v116, 1993.

Schefter, J., DNA Fingerprints on trial, *Popular Science*, 60, 1994.

Schmeck, H.M., Jr., DNA from mummy is almost intact, *New York Times*, v134, 1985.

Schmeck, H.M., Jr., Intact genetic material extracted from ancient Egyptian mummy; feat is latest in series using DNA to examine evolution, *New York Times*, v134, 1985.

Schwartz, J., Paleontology: film takes its cue from DNA clue (*Jurassic Park* motion picture's plot premise rapidly becoming fact; DNA from ancient weevil found intact), *Washington Post*, v116, 1993.

Skorechki, K. et al., Y Chromosomes of the Jewish Priests, *Nature*, 385(32), 1997.

Specter, M., Microbiology reunites families: long-lost children's genes match parents', *Washington Post*, v112, 1989.

Squires, S., Tracking telltale genes in America's ancient mystery (original migration to North America), *Washington Post*, v113, 1990.

Sullivan, W., Archeologists find intact brains 7,000 years old still containing DNA, *New York Times*, v134, 1984.

Tests confirm that bones were last Russian czar's (DNA tests completed on bones of Czar Nicholas II, executed in 1918 with other members of his family), *New York Times*, v144, 1995.

The International Human Genome Mapping Consortium, Initial sequencing and analysis of the human genome, *Nature*, 409, 860–921, 2001.

Thomas, M.G. et al., Origins of Old Testament priests, *Nature*, 394(6689), 138–140, 1998.

Thompson, L., Analyzing the genes of unknown soldiers; military plans program to identify remains through stored DNA samples, *Washington Post*, v114 , 1991.

Venter, J.C., The Sequence of the Human Genome, *Science*, 291(5507), 1304–1351, 2001.

Wambaugh, J., *The Blooding*, William Morrow & Co., Inc., New York, 1989.

Yoon, C.K., Forensic science. Botanical witness for the prosecution, *Science*, 260, 894–895, 1993.

Anastasia claimant a fraud, *Reuter*, Oct. 5, 1994.

Tests clear Jackson in paternity suit, *Reuter*, Oct. 5, 1994.

Jefferson fathered slave's last child, *Nature*, 396(6706), 27–28, 1998.

Rensberger, B., Mummy's DNA preserves a link to ancient life; 2,400-year-old tissue shows researchers new paths for deciphering the past, *Washington Post*, v108, 1985.

Overturned Convictions:

6 years later, conviction is overturned (Leonard Callace rape case conviction overturned because DNA test was negative), *New York Times*, v142, 1992.

DNA clears man convicted of rape (Ronald Junior Cotton), *New York Times*, v144, 1995.

DNA testing frees man jailed in rape; calling data crucial, Virginia Governor pardons a man who served 6 1/2 years (Walter T. Snyder Jr. is pardoned by L. Douglas Wilder), *New York Times*, v142, 1993.

DNA tests clear man imprisoned for 4 years (Glen Dale Woodall, in prison for abduction and rape of two women, West Virginia), *New York Times*, v141, 1992.

DNA tests free man held 10 years for rape (Frederick Rene Daye), *New York Times*, v144, 1994.

DNA tests free man in jail for decade (Edward W. Honaker receives pardon after tests prove that he could not have been the rapist in 1985 case), *New York Times*, v144, 1994.

Farnsworth, C.H., A man guilty only of being a misfit (Guy Paul Morin, cleared of murder by DNA evidence for murder of Christine Jessup, Queensville, Ontario), *New York Times*, v144, 1995.

Foderaro, L.W., DNA frees convicted rapist after 9 years behind bars (Charles Dabbs), *New York Times*, v140, 1991.

Gellman, B., DNA test clears man convicted of SE rape (Washington, D.C.), *Washington Post*, v113, 1990.

Genetic testing fails to prove a rape case (Gary Dotson case), *New York Times*, v137, 1988.

Glaberson, W., Rematch for DNA in a rape case; beneficiary is now likely to challenge test's reliability (The case of Kerry Kotler in Suffolk County, New York), *New York Times*, v145, 1996.

Hua, T., Reza, H.G., and Romney, L., New suspect charged as man held 17 years is freed; crime: DNA test points investigators to an ex-Marine already in custody. Police link him to six slayings (Kevin Lee Gree freed; Gerald Parker charged), *Los Angeles Times,* v115, 1996.

Kennedy, J.M., DNA test clears man convicted of rape (Mark Bravo of Norwalk, California), *Los Angeles Times,* v113, 1994.

Kolata, G., DNA tests are unlocking prison cell doors (DNA testing used to investigate cases of people who say they have been wrongly convicted; Innocence Project), *New York Times*, v143, 1994.

Kunkel, T., Reasonable doubt? Witnesses say Ed Honaker's a rapist. His genes say he's not. A forensic whodunit (DNA test shows it extremely unlikely convicted rapist was guilty, he is likely to be released after 9 1/2 years in prison), *Washington Post*, v117, 1994.

Montgomery, D., Prisoners play the DNA card for high stakes (prisoners using DNA testing to prove they were wrongly convicted of crimes), *Washington Post*, v116, 1993.

Prosecutor says DNA tests may free man in rape case (James M. Catterson) (New York Pages), *New York Times*, v142, 1992.

Rabinovitz, J., Rape conviction overturned on DNA tests; the reversal comes after the man had served 11 years in prison (Kerry Kotler), *New York Times*, v142, 1992.

Stolberg, S., DNA tests clear man charged in rapes (Richard Lee Nichols spent four months in Los Angeles County Jail), *Los Angeles Times*, v111, 1992.

Sullivan, R., Semen wasn't defendants', F.B.I. expert testifies at jogger trial (Federal Bureau of Investigation testimony that DNA analysis of semen found in Central Park jogger), *New York Times*, v139, 1990.

Valentine, P.W., Jailed for murder, freed by DNA (Kirk Bloodsworth cleared of killing Dawn Hamilton after being proven innocent by PCR DNA amplification procedure; includes related information), *Washington Post*, v116, 1993.

The Scientific Basis
of DNA Typing

4

I.   Why DNA?

Forensic DNA analysis involves the intersection of several scientific disciplines, including molecular biology, genetics, and statistical analysis. To understand the usefulness as well as the limitations of DNA in the analysis of physical evidence, it is important to be familiar with some of the basic principles underlying these diverse disciplines. In the next two sections, we summarize some of the main ideas and concepts of molecular biology and genetics. Here is the disclaimer: volumes have been written about each of these subjects. We have purposefully simplified, streamlined, boiled-down, and in some cases ignored information to illustrate basic principles. By definition, information presented in this way is somewhat less accurate than would be a full academic treatment. Our hope is to provide a context in which to interpret a result from a forensic laboratory.

What is the scientific basis for the use of DNA evidence in criminal investigation? It is an accepted fact that, with the exception of identical twins, each individual's DNA is unique. It is, after all, the genetic material that contains all the information necessary for any organism to develop and function. Approximately 99.5% of the DNA code is the same for all people. This is what makes us human beings rather than turnips or porcupines. It is only the other 0.5% (one-half percent) that is of interest to forensic scientists. This portion varies greatly between individuals and manifests itself in individual traits such as eye color, hair color, and blood type. More often, the differences in DNA sequence do not show themselves in physical appearance, but must be investigated using special laboratory techniques.

II.   An Introduction to Human Genetics

Genetics is the study of heredity and variation in biological organisms. It can be considered either on an individual basis, such as the inheritance of particular traits from parent to child, or on a more global basis, such as tracking the movement of genetic markers in a population. Both concepts are integral to the use of DNA in forensic analysis.

A. The Physical Basis of Heredity

Let us consider first the mechanism for transmitting genetic information from one generation to the next. All living things are composed of **cells**, the smallest units of life (Figure 4.1). One cell is about one tenth the diameter of a hair, and about three trillion cells are contained in the human body. Most body cells (the major exception being red blood cells) contain a smaller entity, called the **nucleus**, which is the organization center for the cell. Genetic information resides in the nucleus of the cell and is organized into physical structures called **chromosomes**. Chromosomes are generally transmitted as intact units from parent to child. Thus, markers residing close together on the same chromosome are inherited together[1]; they exhibit **genetic linkage**. In contrast, markers on different chromosomes are generally inherited independently of one another. This principle is called **random assortment**. Markers that exhibit random assortment are not inherited together, or associated with each other in a given population, more often than might be expected by chance. Traits that show random assortment are said to be in **linkage equilibrium**. Conversely, markers that show genetic linkage, such as those close together on the same chromosome, are said to be in **linkage disequilibrium**; in a population, they are associated together more often than chance would predict.

B. Alleles: Variations on a Theme

Human cells contain 23 pairs of chromosomes. Each person has two copies of each chromosome; one comes from Dad and one from Mom (Plate 1). Thus, you inherit half of Dad's genetic blueprint and half of Mom's, which together provide you with a full complement. As mentioned previously, small variations in an individual's DNA allow for differentiation between people. Different forms of the same gene or marker are called **alleles**. The simplest example of different alleles was observed in 1866 by Gregor Mendel, the father of modern genetics. He noticed that, for example, peas could be either green *or* yellow, wrinkled *or* round, and that he could follow these traits through many generations. Green and yellow are alternate forms (**alleles**) of the same gene; wrinkled and round are different alleles of another gene. ABO blood types are an example of different alleles of the same gene in humans. If the alleles at a particular location (**locus**) in the genome are the same on both chromosomes of a pair, the situation is called **homozygous**. If, on the other hand, a small difference is present at the specified locus, so that different alleles are present on each chromosome, the situation is called **heterozygous**. Differences may or may not be physically manifest. When **gametes** (eggs and sperm) are formed, each receives, at random, half the genetic complement of each parent (Plate 1) The chromosomes are distributed so that each gamete contains exactly one copy of each chromosome, for a total of 23. This means that if a parent is heterozygous for a particular marker, only one of the two possible alleles will be distributed to each gamete. Thus, alleles of the same gene segregate away from each other. This means that you will inherit two chromosomes 6, one from each parent, and two chromosomes 7, one from each parent; you should never get both chromosomes 6 or both chromosomes 7 from the same parent (Plate 1). This principle

---

[1] This is an extreme simplification. Due to a genetic phenomenon called **crossing-over**, an exchange of material between homologous chromosomes (recombination) can occur quite frequently. This is particularly true for markers located far apart from each other on the same chromosome. In fact some markers that have been physically mapped to the same chromosome show no genetic linkage whatsoever. For a more in-depth discussion of this phenomenon, please refer to the references.

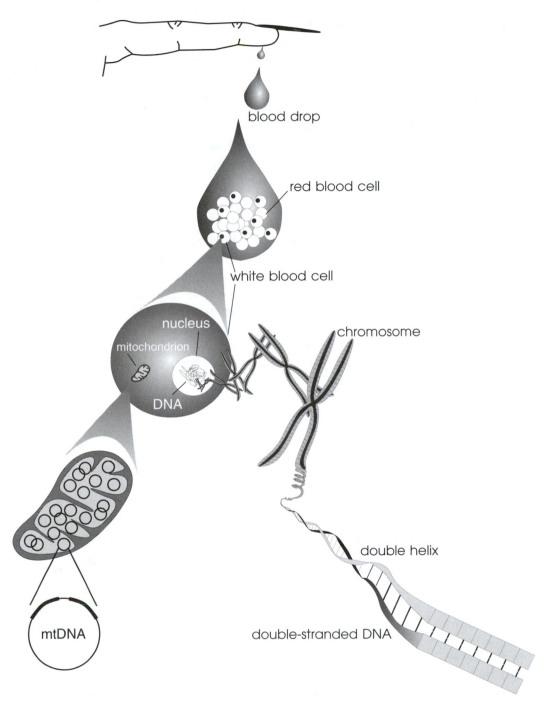

Figure 4.1 From blood to DNA.

is called **independent segregation**. It is a mechanism for assuring that the progeny ends up with the proper number (two) of each of the 23 chromosomes. Both independent segregation and random assortment contribute to the continuing diversification and genetic hardiness of a species.

One pair of the 23 chromosomes contains the information that determines gender. These chromosomes are given letters, rather than numbers, and are designated **X** and **Y**; males have one **X** and one **Y** chromosome (**XY**), and females have two **X** chromosomes (**XX**). Female eggs can contain only **X** chromosomes, while male sperm can contribute either an **X** or a **Y** chromosome. Therefore, gender is determined by the paternal component. The information contained in the sex chromosomes is so different that they even look different visually. Gender can be determined by DNA testing, and is sometimes a useful piece of information in case investigation.

C. Population Genetics

All genetic markers are found in the population with particular frequencies. For example, it is well-known that ABO blood groups exhibit different frequencies; in the Caucasian population, for example, the B blood type is found in approximately 10% of the people. Each allele of the markers used in DNA analysis also exhibits a particular population frequency. It is important to determine the frequency with which markers occur to attach a measure of strength to any particular genetic type. If a type is found in 50% of the population, the fact that a crime scene sample and a suspect share the type is not particularly impressive. If, however, that genetic type is found in only one out of a million people, the fact that both the sample and the suspect have that type carries much greater weight.

In forensic analyses, it is common to test many different markers. The most powerful way to express the overall strength of **genetic concordance** is to multiply the individual frequencies of the different markers. With each added marker, the strength of a genetic concordance increases. This calculation is only legitimate, however, if the markers in question pass certain genetic and statistical tests. The first is that the population in question approaches **Hardy-Weinberg equilibrium (H-W)**.[2] This basically means that the alleles at one locus show no *a priori* correlation with each other. If they did, it could artificially increase the strength of the genetic concordance. These conditions are approached in large, random mating populations; and in the absence of large changes due to migration, natural selection or gene mutation. Second, genotypes at different genetic loci must lack correlations with each other in the population. This is known as **linkage equilibrium** (LE). One of the ways a population can deviate from Hardy-Weinberg equilibrium and/or linkage equilibrium is if a large degree of **substructure** is present due to distinct, but undetected **subpopulations**. This might occur if small groups within a larger mixed population tend to mate mostly with each other, thus creating a relatively isolated reproductive group. Within the general population of New York City, for example, some ethnic groups show a high rate of intra-ethnic marriage. Frequencies of alleles in such groups could deviate from those obtained by a sampling of the larger, mixed population. The chance of any two people within a subpopulation sharing genetic markers might then be different from that

---

[2] This is another extreme simplification. The statistical determination of whether a real population is in Hardy-Weinberg equilibrium, the significance of the factors considered, and the implications of the conclusion are more fully discussed elsewhere. For a full discussion of population genetics, please refer to the references.

predicted using allele frequencies obtained from a general population survey. If the profile in question is found at a higher frequency in the subpopulation than in the general population, the strength of similar genetic patterns might be overestimated. Population surveys of many different ethnic groups around the world have provided an estimate of the level of genetic difference between them. This data has allowed scientists to understand the potential effect of population substructure on a statistical estimate of a profile frequency. It has also allowed the derivation of statistical adjustments that take the known level of substructure into account and produce a very conservative estimate of the rareness of any particular profile frequency. The general conclusion is that, with the inclusion of several statistical safeguards and over many variable loci, we can be confident that, for random unrelated individuals, the profile frequency in question will be overestimated (more common than it actually is). In any event, it is most crucial to understand that any frequency estimate is just that — an estimate — and is only intended to be used as a tool to understand the strength or weight of the evidence, in this case a profile "match." We discuss the mechanics of frequency estimation in Chapter 8.

III.   An Introduction to the Molecular Biology of DNA

DNA is sometimes referred to as the blueprint of life. The information for the blueprint is encoded in the four chemical building blocks of DNA: **Adenine (A)**, **Thymine (T)**, **Guanine (G)**, and **Cytosine (C)** (Plate 2). These units, called **bases**, are strung together in a linear fashion, like beads on a string. The specific sequence of the bases determines all the genetic attributes of a person. The properties of the DNA molecule are directly related to its physical structure.

DNA in nature takes the form of a double helix (Plate 2). Two ribbon-like entities are entwined around each other and are held together by crossbars, like rungs of a ladder. Each rung is composed of two bases that have strong affinities for each other; collectively, these forces hold the DNA molecule together. Each rung of two bases is called a **base pair**. Only specific pairings between the four bases will match up and stick together. **A** always pairs with **T**, and **G** with **C**. This obligatory pairing, called **complementary base pairing**, is exploited in all DNA typing systems. When the double helix is intact, the DNA is called **double-stranded**; when the two halves of the helix come apart, either in nature or in the test tube (*in vitro*), the DNA is called **single-stranded**.

In nature, complementary base pairing is responsible for the ability to accurately replicate the DNA molecule, with its genetic information, and pass it on to the next generation. The double helix is unzipped by special enzymes, and new building blocks (**nucleotides**) are brought in. Each nucleotide contains one base attached to a piece of the backbone ribbon. Using each half of the original helix as a template, a second half is created, resulting in two molecules identical to the original. The order of bases in the new strands is specified by the existing strands. Each original base captures a complementary replacement to complete the base pair. This process can be recreated *in vitro* to a limited extent, and is the basis of the **polymerase chain reaction (PCR)** (Plates 5 and 6), which will be discussed in more detail in Chapters 5 and 6.

Short segments of complementary single-stranded DNA also show a specific affinity for each other *in vitro*, defined again by the specific base sequence. Under appropriate conditions, complementary DNA fragments will find each other and stick together. Technically, this is referred to as **reannealing** or **hybridization**. In the laboratory, it is crucial that the chemical conditions for hybridization be exact. These conditions, which are determined by scientific experimentation, are called **stringency** conditions. If the stringency is too high, no hybridization will occur; if the stringency is too low, reannealing will be less than exact and some DNA fragments might stick together even if they are not a perfect complementary match. If the sequence at a particular location in the genome is of interest, single-stranded fragments can be artificially synthesized to target that location. These single-stranded fragments of known sequence are variously called DNA **probes**[3] or DNA **primers**, depending on their intended use. Complementary base-pairing is essential to the detection of the genetic variations described in the next chapter section.

IV.   Two Kinds of Variation

Through scientific investigation, mostly as a by-product of disease research, standard locations in the genome have been established where the sequence varies more than usual between people. A molecular location is called a **locus (one locus, two or more loci)**. The existence of multiple alleles of a marker at a single locus is called **polymorphism**. When such loci exhibit extreme numbers of variants (as many as hundreds), they are called **hypervariable**. Variations, or polymorphisms, can occur either in the sequence of bases at a particular locus or in the length of a DNA fragment between two defined end-points. **Sequence polymorphisms** are like different spellings for the same word in British English and American English. When you see *analyze* spelled as *analyse*, the word and meaning are still recognizable. For example, the two double-stranded DNA fragments:

```
A G C T C A A T C G              A G A T C A A T C G
: : : : : : : : : :    and    : : : : : : : : : :
T C G A G T T A G C              T C T A G T T A G C
```

exhibit sequence polymorphism at the third base pair from the left; the fragments are recognizable as similar, with a small variation. **Length polymorphisms** (Plates 3 and 8) are most easily analogized to a train that can accommodate different numbers of boxcars. The engine and caboose define the ends of the train; the total length may vary according to the number of cars attached between them at any one time. Each boxcar contains the same small DNA sequence; the following is an example of three boxcars, or consecutive repeated DNA sequences.

```
A G C T C A A T C G – A G C T C A A T C G – A G C T C A A T C G
: : : : : : : : : :   : : : : : : : : : :   : : : : : : : : : :
T C G A G T T A G C – T C G A G T T A G C – T C G A G T T A G C
```

In genetic terminology, the boxcars are termed **tandem repeats**. A locus that shows variation in the number of tandem repeats is called a **variable number tandem repeat** (**VNTR**) locus. A particular number of tandem repeats (e.g., 35) defines a VNTR allele at that locus. Different laboratory techniques are used to investigate the two kinds of variations.

---

[3] DNA probes were first created by isolating, or cloning, small pieces of genomic DNA, and replicating them using microorganisms. Today, DNA fragments of known sequence are often artificially synthesized in a laboratory.

V.   Enzymes: The Workhorses of the Biological World

It is impossible to discuss any biochemical reaction, in nature or *in vitro*, without referring to **enzymes**. Enzymes are the biochemical workers that get the job done. They are protein based and able to catalyze the formation or breakdown of other biological components many times over. Various enzymes in the laboratory are used for everything from breaking cells open to synthesizing DNA. Modern molecular biology (or any biology for that matter) would not exist as such without enzymes. When enzymes are isolated from nature and asked to perform their function in a test tube, it is crucial to recreate their natural environment as closely as possible; otherwise they may not perform as expected.

Enzymes that catalyze the addition of components are called **polymerases**. An example of this is *Taq* **polymerase**, an enzyme that directs the addition of nucleotides in the replication of DNA. This is the enzyme that makes PCR possible. *Taq* polymerase possesses the unusual quality of maintaining its activity even after exposure to heat. As we discuss later, this attribute is critical to the PCR reaction.

Restriction enzymes belong to a class of enzymes that break DNA into smaller pieces. Restriction enzymes were originally conceived by nature to protect bacteria from viral invaders. They do this by recognizing specific small DNA sequences that occur in the virus, and cutting viral DNA at all the places that sequence occurs. The bacterium's own DNA is protected from being chopped to pieces by another biochemical mechanism. Molecular biologists have isolated these enzymes (there are at least hundreds) and co-opted them for their own uses. Restriction enzymes also cut human DNA with the same sequence specificity as the original intended viral DNA.

Most important, any restriction enzyme under the proper conditions always cuts DNA at places where a specific base sequence occurs, and no other. For example, the restriction enzyme *Hae*III cuts a double-stranded DNA molecule at any site where the sequence **CCGG** occurs, and it always cuts between the **C** and the **G** (Plate 3). This means that any particular genome can reproducibly be cut into pieces of the same number and size. The number and size of DNA fragments will vary between the genomes of different people when polymorphisms occur.) The enzyme most often used for forensic RFLP analysis in the United States is called *Hae*III. In Europe, most labs use an enzyme called *Hinf*I.

Further References

Alberts, B., *Molecular Biology of the Cell*, 3rd ed., Garland Publishing, New York, 1999.

Federal Bureau of Investigation, *VNTR Population Data: A Worldwide Study*, Volumes I-IV, FBI Academy, Quantico, VA, 1993.

Griffiths, A.J.F., Miller, J.H., Suzuki, D.T., Lewontin, R.C., and Gelbart, W.M., *An Introduction to Genetic Analysis*, 5th ed., W.H. Freeman and Co., New York, 1993.

Hartl, D.L. and Clark, A.G., *Principles of Population Genetics*, 3rd ed., Sinauer Associates, Sunderland, MA, 1997.

Lander, E.S. and Budowle B., DNA fingerprinting dispute laid to rest, *Nature*, 371, 735–738, 1994.

Lewin, B., *Genes ViI*, Oxford University Press, New York, 1999.

Lodish, H., *Molecular Cell Biology*, W.H. Freeman, New York, 1999.

Stryer, L., *Biochemistry*, 4th ed. W.H. Freeman, New York, 1995.

Watson, J.D., Hopkins, N.H., Roberts, J.W., Steitz, J.A., and Weiner, A.M., *Molecular Biology of the Gene*, 4th ed., Benjamin/Cummings, 1987.

An Overview of Forensic DNA Typing Systems

5

Most laboratories today employ one of the commercially available automated **short tandem repeat** (**STR**) multiplex systems for forensic DNA typing of new case material. However, several other systems have been used since the inception of forensic DNA analysis more than a decade ago, and some laboratories retain the capability to analyze samples using various different marker systems and detection platforms. Each of these systems has its own capabilities and limitations, and it is useful to understand the current technology in the greater historical context. Additionally, it is helpful to have a working knowledge of previous systems when reviewing or reanalyzing old cases where they have been used. In this chapter, we present an overview of DNA typing systems in approximate chronological order.

I.   RFLP Analysis

The first technique that was adapted for forensic DNA analysis was **RFLP** (**restriction fragment length polymorphism**). This kind of analysis determines variation in the length of a defined DNA fragment (Plate 3). When complete, an RFLP pattern looks like a very simple supermarket bar code (Figures 5.1 and 5.2). In looking at two samples, the pattern of bars on the **autoradiograph** is compared to determine if they could have originated from the same source. Although it has been usurped by newer technology for reasons we discuss later in this chapter, RFLP retains the highest degree of discrimination per locus. This is because the RFLP loci that were chosen for forensic use may show as many as hundreds of variations at each locus. Consequently, if two samples originate from different sources, RFLP can differentiate them using fewer loci than other systems. Additionally, RFLP can more readily determine whether a single sample contains DNA from more than one person, and it is more likely to differentiate the contributors. This attribute is inherent in the genetics of the system and is independent of advances in technology. The huge **power of discrimination** (P_d) associated with RFLP analysis is due both to the hypervariability at each locus and the ability to look at many loci. Laboratories that performed RFLP could choose to analyze as many as 15 different loci. Unfortunately, the RFLP technique requires a greater amount of better quality DNA than the newer PCR-based techniques. Because forensic evidence is often old, degraded and of limited quantity, RFLP analysis is sometimes not possible. The technique is also laborious and difficult to

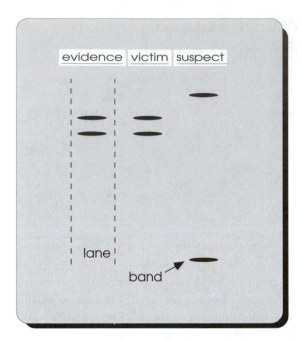

Figure 5.1 Representation of an RFLP autorad. Each sample is run in a lane, which is viewed vertically by convention. Each of the dark bars is called a band. All the bands in a lane come from one sample. The autorad is read by comparing the pattern of bands between different lanes.

automate, limiting its utility for building and using large DNA databases. Although a few laboratories still maintain RFLP capability, the method is likely to entirely disappear from active use in the near future.

II.   PCR Amplification

PCR (**polymerase chain reaction**) is a general technique for increasing the amount of a specific section of DNA in a sample. This is called DNA amplification. The procedure was so innovative that its inventor was awarded the Nobel Prize in 1993. PCR is often referred to as molecular Xeroxing™ (Figure 5.3). It is generally designed so that only a small segment of the DNA of interest is copied, and this is accomplished with extremely high fidelity to the original. In this way, information can be gained from samples that might otherwise be refractory to analysis because of limited or degraded starting material.

The DNA samples prepared using PCR can be analyzed in a variety of different ways. In general, the PCR-based genetic systems show less variation per locus than RFLP loci. Therefore, results may be obtained for a sample of limited quantity and quality, but the P_d is lower for the same number of loci. However, the power of PCR-based systems lies in the ability to analyze many loci simultaneously, and to automate much of the process. Over the past several years, PCR megaplexes containing as many as 16 loci have been developed, greatly increasing the nominal P_d of these systems for single-source samples. However, because of the low to moderate variation present at each individual locus, current PCR-based systems remain limited in their ability to resolve mixtures.

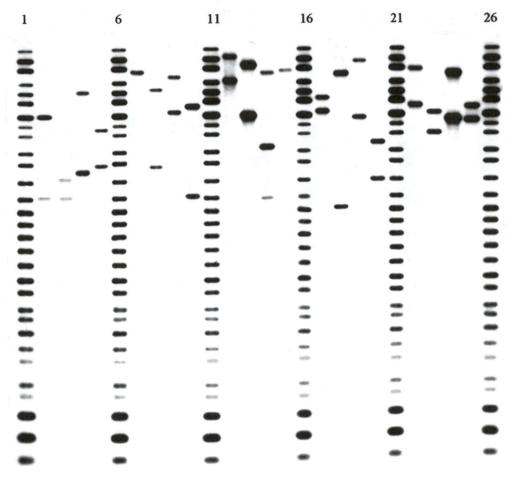

Figure 5.2 A population autorad. Lanes 1, 6, 11, 16, 21, and 26 contain the molecular ladder. The other lanes each contain a DNA sample from a different individual. The locus probed is D4S139.

A. HLA DQα/HLA DQA1

The first system to become available for forensic analysis of PCR-amplified DNA was called **HLA DQα**. This is the historical name of the locus that is analyzed and is still used to refer to the original typing format for this system. The kind of variation present at this locus resides in the DNA sequence. Some of the bases in this 242-bp region vary between people. This variation is detected using specially designed molecular probes, synthetic fragments of DNA designed to be complementary to, and thus target, particular subregions within this locus. The original probe set detected six common DQα alleles that, in combination, determined 21 possible genotypes. Because only one locus with limited variability was analyzed in this system, the P_d was much lower than for RFLP or other PCR-based systems that were subsequently developed. The chief advantages of HLA DQα were the novel ability to investigate very small samples and the rapidity of analysis. The final results are seen as a series of blue dots on a paper-like strip (Figure 5.4). A comparison of the pattern of the dots between typing strips indicates whether two samples may have originated from the same source.

Sidebar 3

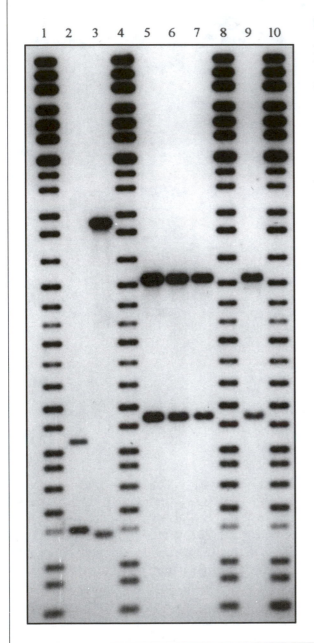

The Bungled Burglary (or, the burglar that couldn't)

Once in a criminalist's lifetime there may occur a truly simple, straightforward case; what appears obvious is actually true. Of course, it helps if the suspect confesses to a crime that was never completed. In 1992, an aspiring burglar hurled a rock through a plate glass window in a Bank of America in northern California. He removed the pieces of broken glass, entered the bank through the broken window, and unsuccessfully attempted to open the locked teller drawers. Having failed to complete his task, he fled, leaving a telltale trail of blood — straight to the Sheriff's department to "turn himself in for the burglary of the Bank of America." Three blood swabs were collected from the scene and submitted with a sample collected from the self-indicted suspect.

SB3. One RFLP probing of the autorad from this case. Lanes 1, 4, 8, 10 contain molecular ladders. Lane 2 contains a control sample that is used by all U.S. labs performing forensic RFLP analysis, and lane 3 contains an intralaboratory control for which the results are known, but not to the analyst. Lanes 5, 6, and 7 contain the three samples collected from the crime scene, and lane 9 contains the suspect's blood sample. (Portions of the molecular ladder have been cropped from this photo.)

Due to a reorganization and renaming of the DQ gene cluster by the genetics community, the DQα locus is now referred to as **DQA1**. DQA1 also designated an improved forensic typing system for this locus, in which subtypes of the 4 allele as well as the 1 allele were detected (Figures 5.4 and 5.5). This resulted in a total of 28 detectable types, increasing the P_d slightly. DQα now refers only to the original typing system in which the 4 alleles

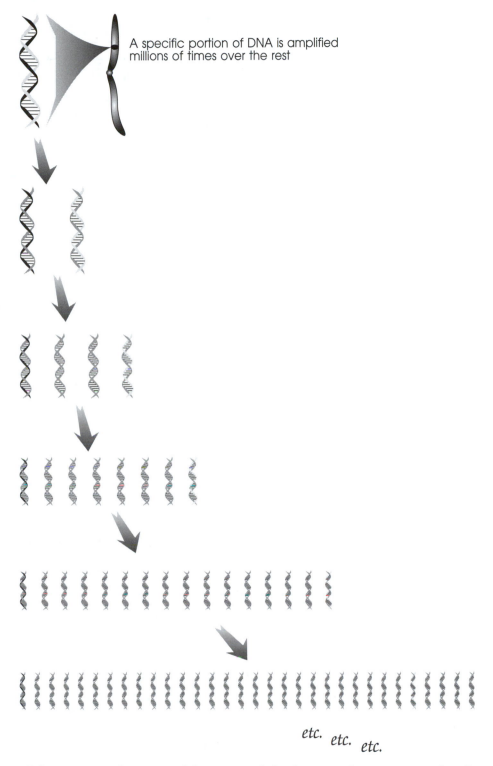

A specific portion of DNA is amplified millions of times over the rest

etc. etc. etc.

Figure 5.3 Overview of PCR amplification. A defined region of DNA is copied millions of times. With each round of amplification, the number of copies doubles, resulting in a theoretical geometric increase in the number of copies of that fragment over the rest.

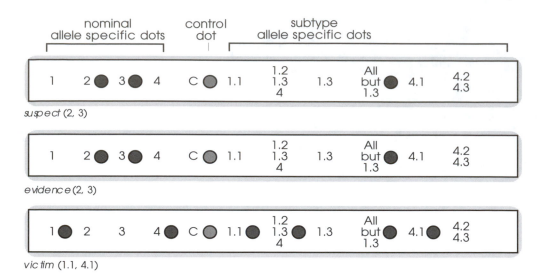

Figure 5.4 Representation of a DQA1 reverse dot blot. A total of 11 probes are present on each strip. In this case, the suspect and evidence samples show an identical pattern of dots, while the victim sample shows a different pattern. The "C" dot is a control probe that shows up regardless of DQA1 type. The dots to the left of "C" (1, 2, 3, and 4) give the nominal allele designations; the dots to the right of "C" are used to determine some of the subtypes into which the 1 and 4 alleles can be subdivided. The DQA1 system is able to distinguish the 4.1 subtype from the nominal 4 allele, an improvement over the DQα system. Interpretation of DQA1 results is discussed further in Chapter 7.

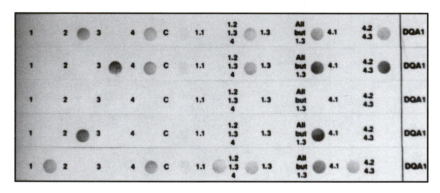

Figure 5.5 A DQA1 reverse dot blot. Above are five typing strips, each representing a different individual.

were not subtyped. DQA1 properly refers to the locus itself and the subsequent typing system which added subtyping of the 4 allele. Throughout this book, when we use the term DQα, we are referring to the original kit developed by Cetus. When the designation DQA1 is used, we refer to the second iteration of the test developed by Roche Molecular Systems (RMS)[1] and manufactured by (then) Perkin-Elmer, that included the subtyping of the 4 allele and was offered only in concert with the AmpliType® PM+DQA1 kit.

_____

[1] In 1991, Roche Diagnostics purchased all PCR rights from Cetus and formed a new division, Roche Molecular Systems (RMS).

Sidebar 4

Quintanilla
(or, invention is a mother of a necessity)

In the spring and summer of 1987, two women from the San Francisco Bay Area were abducted and brutally sexually assaulted. Because both the descriptions and MOs appeared quite similar, the police suspected that these assaults might be related. A separate police artist sketch was prepared according to the description of the assailant given by each victim (see sketch). Both victims described a young Hispanic male, thin and approximately 5'6" to 5'8" tall.

(A)

| suspect 1 | police sketch 1 | police sketch 2 | A. Quintanilla |

One victim (victim 1) identified an individual from a photo lineup as her attacker. She subsequently identified him both in a live lineup and at a preliminary hearing. A photo of this suspect is shown on the far left of the police sketches above. Conventional serological typing of the sexual assault evidence was uninformative with respect to the semen donor's types. The defendant was eager to have the recently developed forensic DNA testing performed on this evidence. With approval from the prosecution, Dr. Edward Blake was retained by the defense to perform the work. Dr. Blake had been working closely with Cetus Corporation in the development of the DQα marker system using the polymerase chain reaction (PCR).

Dr. Blake performed the analysis using an early version of this typing system (see figure below). The typing process at that time consisted of fixing the amplified product to strips and then hybridizing the strips with sequence specific oligonucleotide (SSO) probes. The color reaction initially used a dye that turned red, so red dots (reproduced here in B/W) indicated a positive reaction. Subtypes were determined from separate reactions using radioactively labeled probes (not shown).

(B)

Nominal DQα Typing – original dot blot
(old nomenclature)

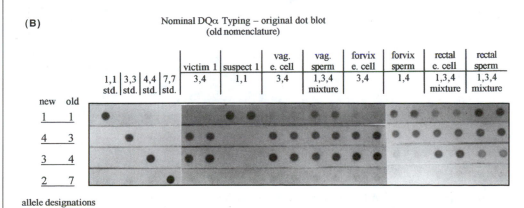

allele designations

The semen donor associated with victim 1 was reported as a 1.1,3 in the nomenclature in use at that time. This type is equivalent to a 1.1,4 in current nomenclature. A sample from the defendant was analyzed using the same system and found to be either a type 1.2,1.3, or a type 1.3,1.3 (it was not possible to distinguish between the two at the time). In either case, the defendant identified by the victim was eliminated as the donor of the semen sample. In an act of courage and conviction, the district attorney did not challenge this new test, but dismissed charges against this suspect.

Dr. Blake subsequently also typed evidence from victim 2 (see figure below). By this time, the DQα typing system had progressed to the reverse dot blot format. In a reverse dot blot, the probes are fixed to a single strip and amplified product is hybridized to them. Current nomenclature had been established, but the red dye was still in use. The semen evidence from victim 2 also showed a type 1.1,4, thus linking the two sexual assaults.

(C)   **Reverse Dot Blot**

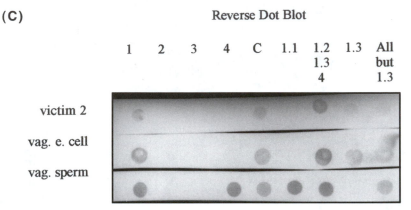

Two years after the first attack, Armando Quintanilla was arrested for an attempted assault at virtually the same location in Mountain View as the first victim had reported. A photograph of Quintanilla is shown on the right of the police sketches above. Detectives felt that the similar MO, the close locations of all three attacks, and the resemblance of Quintanilla to the physical descriptions from the first assaults warranted further investigation. They submitted a reference sample from Quintanilla to Dr. Blake for testing. Quintanilla was typed as a 1.1,4 (see figure below) and therefore included as a possible donor of the semen samples in all three cases. RFLP analysis was also attempted on some of the sexual assault evidence, but the results were inconclusive.

(D)

Quintanilla

Finally, a second item of evidence from victim 1 was analyzed using the present-day reverse dot blot format with preprinted strips (see below). By this time, the dye had been changed to a blue color (reproduced here in B/W). This item was also from a type 1.1,4 individual. A DQα type 1.1,4 occurs in less than 10% of the population. Based on the totality of the evidence, a jury convicted Armando Quintanilla of numerous felonies. He was sentenced to 99 years plus life.

(E)   **Final form of Manufacturer's Reverse Dot Blot DQα Typing Strips**

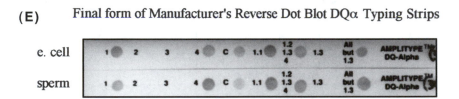

B. AmpliType® PM+DQA1

The **AmpliType® PM+DQA1** system, commonly known as **polymarker,** was just an expansion of the technique used in HLA DQA1 analysis. The trick was to increase the P_d while retaining all the advantages of PCR. A system was developed in which several markers at

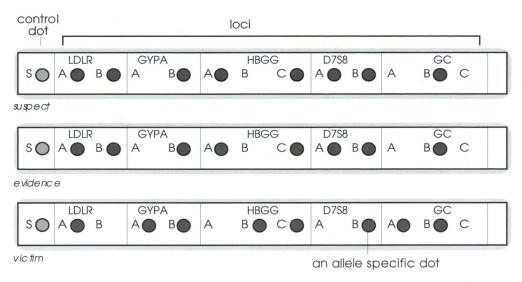

Figure 5.6 Representation of a polymarker reverse dot blot. A total of 13 probes are present on each strip. In this case, the suspect and evidence samples show an identical pattern of dots, while the victim shows a different pattern. The "S" dot is a control probe that shows up regardless of polymarker type; it is equivalent to the "C" dot in the DQA1 system. The five typing loci each have either two or three possible alleles. Interpretation of polymarker strips is discussed more fully in Chapter 7.

different loci were analyzed at the same time, a procedure now commonly known as **multiplexing**. Although each of the five additional markers (Figures 5.6 and 5.7) contained less individual variation (only two or three alleles at each locus) than DQA1, the combined result, along with that from DQA1, increased the power of the test considerably. The combined P_d for the five polymarker loci is on the order of 1 in 200. So theoretically, for every 200 comparisons between two people chosen at random, about 199 pairs would have different PM types and one pair would have the same type. Together with DQA1, the power of discrimination increased to about 1 in 2000. A disadvantage of the PM loci in particular is that it is often more difficult to interpret the results from samples containing DNA from more than one contributor because of the low P_d *per locus*. As in HLA DQ/A1 analysis, the final results are seen as a series of blue dots, and a comparison of the pattern of the dots between typing strips indicates whether two samples might have originated from the same source. Although many laboratories adopted the AmpliType® PM+DQA1 system, and it was in common usage for almost a decade, it too is being phased out in favor of the third generation PCR-based **short tandem repeat** (STR) systems that we discuss later in this chapter.

C.   D1S80

An interim PCR system that was used briefly by some forensic DNA laboratories until the late 1990s was called **D1S80** (see Figure 5.8). D1S80 refers to the DNA locus that is typed. Like RFLP, the variation present at this locus resides in the length of a defined DNA fragment as determined by the number of tandem repeats (a VNTR). However, because of its relatively smaller size, this fragment was amenable to amplification by PCR. In the forensic science literature, systems of this nature are called **amplified fragment length**

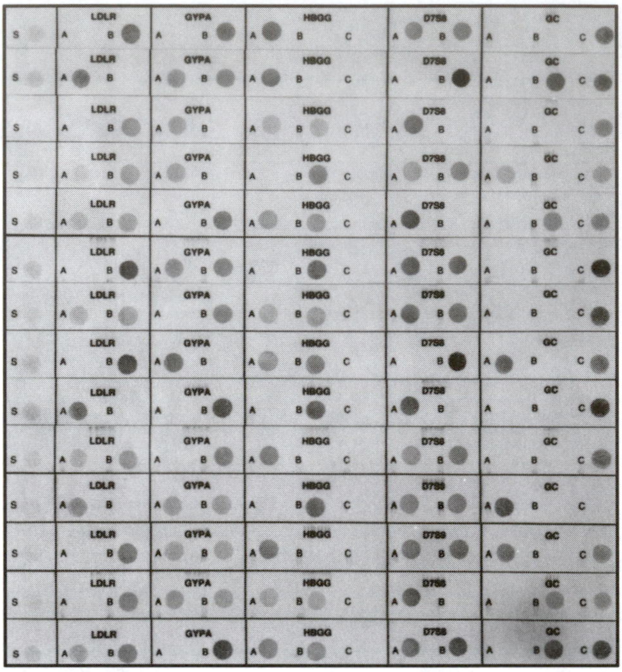

Figure 5.7 A polymarker reverse dot blot. Fourteen PM typing strips, each representing a different individual.

polymorphisms (**AMP-FLPs, AFLPs,** or **AMFLPs**). In the D1S80 system, fragments in the range of hundreds of base pairs are amplified, about an order of magnitude smaller than the fragments normally analyzed in RFLP typing. Thus, D1S80 analysis combined the advantages inherent in any PCR system (specifically the ability to analyze samples of limited quantity and quality) with the greater variation generally seen in length-based systems. Like DQA1, because only one locus was analyzed in this system, the P_d was not as high as RFLP or the subsequently developed multi-locus STR systems. Also, the D1S80 locus in particular contains two alleles that are common among many people in some racial groups. If one of these two alleles is present in the samples being analyzed, the strength of the test result is reduced. In contrast to RFLP analysis, where all of the DNA is processed and the regions of interest are detected with molecular probes, in D1S80 analysis, the regions defined by the PCR amplification are effectively purified before the DNA is analyzed. D1S80 loci are detected as **discrete alleles** and thus can be compared directly to a standard ruler made up of most alleles found in the population (**allelic ladder**) which is run on the same gel. This was a significant improvement that was also employed in subsequent STR systems. In D1S80, the amplified DNA fragments were commonly detected using a silver stain, the final result of which looks much like the simplified supermarket bar code often used to describe RFLP. D1S80 analysis has generally been abandoned in favor of STR systems.

D.   STRs

Short tandem repeats (**STRs**) are similar to the D1S80 system described above, except that the repeat units are shorter. The loci chosen for forensic use generally have a tandem repeat unit of 2 to 5 bp and may be repeated from a few to dozens of times. The number of alleles

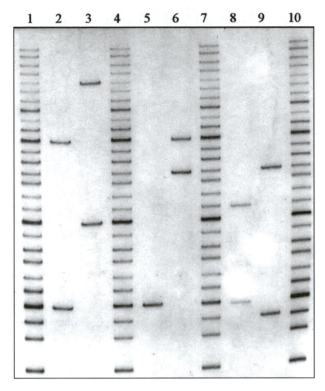

Figure 5.8 A D1S80 silver-stained gel. Lanes 1, 4, 7, and 10 contain the allelic ladder to which all questioned samples are compared. Lanes 2, 3, 5, 6, 8, and 9 each contain a sample from a single individual. All except lane 5 are heterozygotes, so the variant alleles present on the two chromosomes each produce a band. The sample in lane 5 is a homozygote; the alleles on the two chromosomes are the same size and are represented by a single band. (Courtesy of Roche Molecular Systems.)

present in the population varies from about 5 to 20, depending on the locus. STR loci are detected as discrete alleles and thus can be compared directly to an allelic ladder run on the same gel, simplifying comparison and analysis. The size of the DNA fragments produced by amplification of STR loci is in the range of about 200 to 500 base pairs. This makes STRs an ideal choice for degraded DNA. Although each locus is only moderately polymorphic, many such loci exist and are used simultaneously. Further, PCR amplification of many different loci is commonly performed simultaneously in the same tube (**multiplexing**), producing savings of time, materials, and most important, sample. The STR loci chosen for forensic use have alleles that are reasonably well distributed in any given population.

STR loci may be detected and analyzed manually using a silver stain (Figure 5.9; Plate 8). Alternatively, several systems have been developed where fluorescence is used to detect the bands, either during or after the separation (Figures 5.10, 5.11, and 5.12; Plate 8). Fluorescence is amenable to automated detection, increasing throughput and greatly facilitating subsequent analysis and storage of data (Plates 10 to 15). There are also several technical advantages to the use of fluorescent detection of STR loci. The main disadvantage is expense, as sophisticated equipment is necessary for the process. Both manual and automated systems have been used to analyze STRs, but most laboratories have moved to one of several commercially available automated platforms.

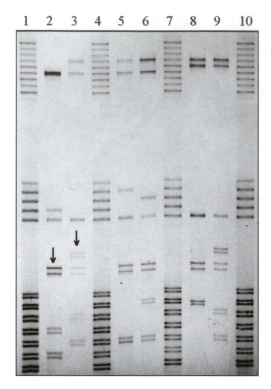

Figure 5.9 An STR silver-stained gel. Lanes 1, 4, 7, and 10 each contain a mix of the allelic ladders to which all questioned samples are compared. In this case, three loci have been analyzed simultaneously; thus, three distinct sets of non-overlapping bands are present in each vertical ladder lane. Lanes 2, 3, 5, 6, 8, and 9 each contain samples from a single individual. Each band is compared directly to one in the ladder lane, thus establishing the allele present in the sample. Note that all bands appear as doublets in the lower part of the gel; the reason for this is discussed in Chapter 7. In addition to the three multiplexed STR loci, the gender identification locus has been added to this system. In each sample lane (but not in the ladder lanes), either one or two doublets (see arrows) are present in the vertical space between the middle and bottom sets of STR allelic ladder bands. One doublet indicates a female (lane 2); a pair of doublets indicates a male (lane 3).

E. Gender Identification

It is often useful to know if male or female components are present in a forensic sample. The **amelogenin** locus, which is coincidentally the gene for tooth pulp, shows a length variation between the sexes (Figure 5.13). One region of the female form of the gene contains a small deletion (6 bp) in nonessential DNA and produces a shorter product when amplified by PCR. When this region is analyzed, a female with two X chromosomes will show one band. A male with both an X and a Y chromosome will show two bands, one the same size as the female and one slightly larger. An advantage of this system over previous loci used for gender differentiation is that both the male and female forms of the gene are detected and can be compared. Analysis of this locus is often appended to another PCR system such as a multiplex STR system. In this way, no additional sample need be expended for gender determination, which in and of itself might eliminate only 50% of the population.

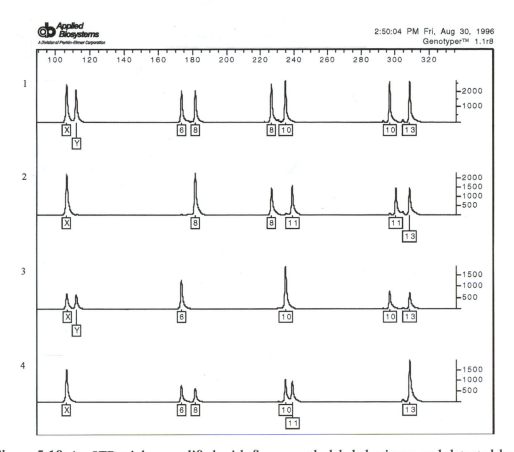

Figure 5.10 An STR triplex amplified with fluorescently labeled primers and detected by a dynamic detection automated sequencer. In this case, none of the three STR loci amplified have overlapping alleles, so the same green fluorescent primer was used to label all of them. The data is reproduced here in black and white. The final results of the electrophoretic run are viewed as a computer-generated histogram. Each peak is derived directly from one allele (that corresponds to one band). Each corresponding vertical gel lane (see, e.g., Plates 9 and 10b) is represented as a horizontal panel; the top of the gel (larger fragments) is on the right, and the bottom (smaller fragments) is on the left (see Plate 9). The location of the peak is directly proportional to the migration distance, and the area under the peak is directly proportional to the intensity of the signal. The computer software compares the bands (peaks) in a sample to a molecular ladder, run in the same lane, to determine their sizes in base pairs. The fragment size is then directly compared to an allelic ladder run in another lane and the alleles are automatically called by the software. The samples in this study are from a father (lane 3), mother (lane 2), son (lane 1), and daughter (lane 4). Note that each child shows a different combination of the parental alleles. Both males show both an X band and a Y band at the gender identification locus (far left), and both females, only an X band of double intensity. The data are from the AmpF*l*STR® Green™ I PCR amplification kit detected on an ABI PRISM® 310 Genetic Analyzer.

F.   Y-STRs

STRs are also found on the human Y chromosome. Like autosomal (non-sex chromosome) STR markers, Y-STRs are amenable to typing small or degraded samples of DNA and can be analyzed on the same instrumental platforms. Because the Y chromosome is specific to males, Y-STRs can be useful in extracting male-specific information from a sample. This

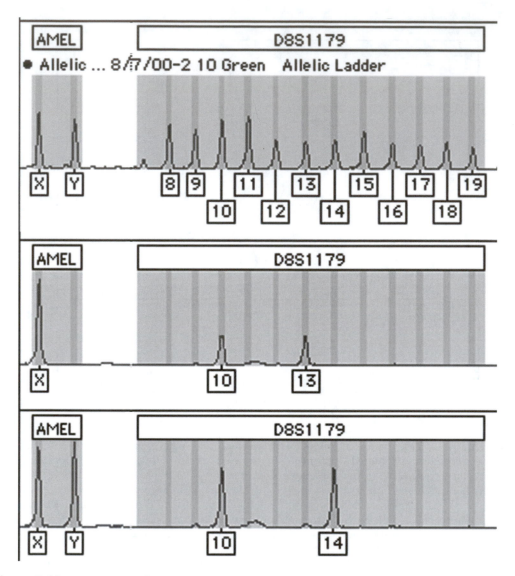

Figure 5.11 Genotyping of two loci analyzed with fluorescently tagged primers. Two loci are used to illustrate the final typing step, accomplished with the assistance of a computer. The top panel contains the allelic ladder, a sample containing most of the possible alleles at a locus. The types are labeled below each peak. The bottom two panels contain different samples to be typed using the allelic ladder. Each sample is compared by the computer to the allelic ladder. Where an evidence peak lines up with an allelic ladder peak, the computer places the type below the evidence peak. The left-most locus is amelogenin, the gender identification locus. The first sample is labeled X, representing a female; while the second sample (bottom panel) is labeled X,Y, representing a male. For the locus D8S1179, the first sample shows peaks corresponding to alleles 10 and 13 in the ladder, while the second sample shows peaks corresponding to alleles 10 and 14 in the ladder. This comparison and allele calling is performed for all loci analyzed by this method. The data are from the AmpF*ℓ*STR® Profiler Plus™ PCR amplification kit detected on an ABI PRISM® 310 Genetic Analyzer.

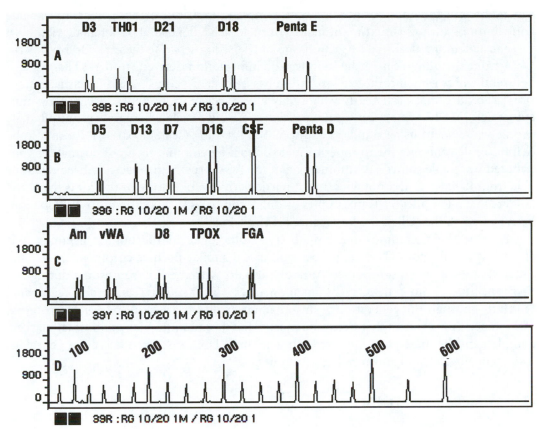

Figure 5.12 An STR 16-plex amplified with fluorescently tagged primers. This sample is analyzed at loci with overlapping alleles, so three colors are required to separate them. The data are reproduced here in black and white. The figure represents the typing of one person. The basic orientation of the computer-generated histogram is similar to that in Figure 5.10. Panel A shows five non-overlapping loci, panel B shows six non-overlapping loci, and panel C shows another five loci. Panel D shows the in-lane molecular ladder used to correct for sample-to-sample electrophoretic variation. The typing of 16 loci in one amplification step confers immense powers of discrimination to the system. It is unreasonable to think that any random unrelated person would have this same DNA profile. (Courtesy of Promega Corporation.)

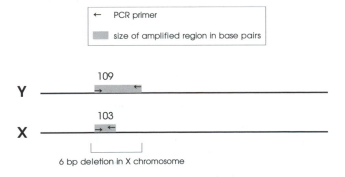

Figure 5.13 Structure of the amelogenin locus. One region of the amelogenin locus contains a 6-bp deletion in females, making it useful for gender identification. A pair of primers situated outside this region produces different size fragments in males and females. This locus, which is not an STR, is analyzed in conjunction with multiplex STR systems.

can be helpful for non-sperm containing samples comprised of both male and female contributions such as a mixture of bloods or male saliva deposited on a female victim. In these instances, a differential extraction cannot be used to separate the male-derived sperm DNA from the other cells in the sample. The information derived from Y-STRs can also be useful where only incomplete separation has been achieved using a differential extraction procedure, and particularly where only a few sperm are present among many non-sperm cells. Y-STR typing can sometimes detect a male profile where only a single female profile was evident using standard autosomal STR typing (see Sidebar 10). It can also be helpful in determining the number of male donors by eliminating any information contributed by female sources. A commercial kit for Y-STR typing has recently become available from ReliaGene Technologies, Inc. A particularly useful feature of this kit is the allelic ladders that allow allele calls in samples by direct comparison. Six different Y-STR loci can be typed using the ReliaGene kit (Figure 5.14).

Because the Y chromosome has no true homologue in the human genome, it is effectively **hemizygous**. That is, it does not have a similar partner chromosome like the other 22 autosomal chromosomes. Although it pairs with the X chromosome during cell division, little or no genetic recombination takes place, and it is inherited reasonably faithfully through the generations. This attribute makes it a useful marker for paternal inheritance. Any changes that occur are mostly due to mutation. Y-chromosomal markers complement the maternally inherited mitochondrial DNA discussed below for genealogical, archeological, and anthropological studies.

G.   Mitochondrial DNA

The vast majority of the genetic material in the human genome resides in the nucleus of each cell, and all of the genetic typing systems and procedures described so far make use of loci found in **nuclear DNA**. Some additional bits of genetic material exist, however, and are contained in other small subcellular compartments called **cell organelles**. One of these is the **mitochondrion** (pl., **mitochondria**), in which some of the processes of cellular respiration take place.

Mitochondria in human cells contain an autonomous circle of DNA that codes for some proteins that control these functions. The mitochondrial genome is about 16.5 kb and, of interest to forensic scientists, contains a noncoding hypervariable control region. In particular, two segments exist within this 1100-bp control region (Figure 5.15), also called the **D-loop**, that tend to mutate with an extremely high frequency, about 10 times that of nuclear DNA. This high mutation rate makes the region attractive for use in individual identification. It has been estimated that **mitochondrial DNA** (**mtDNA**) may vary about 1% to 2% between unrelated individuals; that is, on average, about one or two nucleotides out of every hundred is different. Empirical experience verifies that any two individuals differ by an average of eight nucleotides in the approximately 800-bp region commonly sequenced by forensic laboratories. In other words, mtDNA sequences are highly variable between unrelated individuals. The complete 16,569 nucleotide sequence of human mtDNA has been established for a reference individual. All comparisons are made to this reference, called the Anderson sequence.

Another unique quality of mitochondrial DNA is its inheritance pattern. As discussed in Chapter 4, nuclear DNA is inherited in equal parts from both parents. Due to the

Y-PLEX™6 Ladder

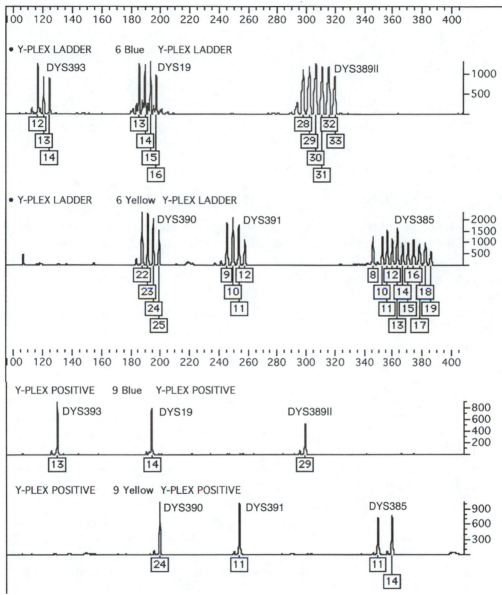

Figure 5.14 A Y-STR allelic ladder and sample. The Y chromosome of males contains STR loci that can be analyzed in the same fashion as STR loci on the autosomal chromosomes. Because the Y chromosome has no homologue, these loci show only one peak per male sample. The Reliagene Y-PLEX™ 6 kit types six different Y-STR loci. The top two panels contain the allelic ladders, similar to those explained in Figure 5.11. The bottom two panels contain a sample from one person. (Courtesy of Reliagene Technologies, Inc.)

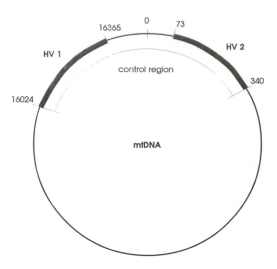

Figure 5.15 Locations of the two hypervariable regions on the mitochondrial DNA circle.

technicalities of fertilization,[2] genetic material from mitochondria is inherited only from the egg cell of the mother; thus, mtDNA is said to exhibit **maternal inheritance**.[3] Therefore, the mtDNA type of an individual cannot be heterozygous, or exhibit two different types, because no homologous contribution is received from the father. Because the mtDNA circle is a genetic element that lacks a homologous counterpart in the genome and it can be described as **hemizygous**, mtDNA is also sometimes referred to as haploid or **monoclonal**. As described for the Y chromosome, this quality is useful in tracking families and populations because the genetic element survives more or less intact throughout many generations and does not acquire new variation by genetic recombination.[4] However, new variations are gained by mutation.

Theoretically, all copies of the mtDNA sequences within an individual and between maternal relatives should be identical. Perhaps in part because of the high mutation rate, mtDNA sometimes exhibits a condition that is only rarely observed in nuclear DNA — a single individual may show a mixture of types. This is called **heteroplasmy**. In further contrast to nuclear DNA, which shows the same single type throughout the body, various body tissues can exhibit heteroplasmy of mtDNA to varying degrees. It is now thought that all individuals are heteroplasmic to some degree, although the heteroplasmy is not always detected using mtDNA typing systems. In Chapter 7 we describe some of the interpretational ramifications of these unusual attributes of the mtDNA typing system.

Last but not least, up to thousands of copies of the mtDNA genome may be present in a single cell. Because of its abundance and its relatively small size in comparison to

---

[2] In most higher organisms, the egg cell is much larger that than sperm cell that fertilizes it. Consequently, the new individual acquires all cell organelles from the female parent. Sperm mtDNA enters the egg and is preferentially destroyed.

[3] As detection has been improved, some experiments in other animals have shown that about 1 in 10,000 times, some mtDNA from the father may make it into the offspring. "Paternal leakage" does not appear to occur at a detectable frequency in humans.

[4] Chromosomal recombination in the nuclear genome takes place during meiosis, the process by which gametes (eggs and sperm) are formed. During this process, genetic alleles that originally came from either parent are mixed up and rearranged (shaken, not stirred). Because mtDNA is inherited only from the mother, this has no possibility of happening, and, barring mutation, mtDNA is inherited faithfully.

nuclear chromosomes, mtDNA is often the last typable DNA present in a small, old, or badly degraded sample. If no results are obtained with any other system, often the mtDNA can be typed. MtDNA is commonly used to type the dead cells in hair shafts, bones, and teeth. However, because mtDNA constitutes only a single locus, and presents some technical and interpretational challenges, mtDNA in criminal investigations is best reserved for cases where nuclear DNA analysis has failed due to minimal quality or quantity. At present, only a few forensic DNA laboratories in the country have mtDNA analysis capabilities.

Sidebar 5

The Czar's Bones
(or, what difference a base pair?)

Whose bones are buried in a multiple grave in Yekaterinburg, Russia? In 1991, the Soviet government ordered the excavation of a shallow pit that was rumored to hold the remains of the Romanovs, the Russian Imperial family executed in 1918 by the Bolsheviks. Six months after the shooting, a Russian investigator, Nicholas Sokolov, recovered some scraps of physical evidence from the probable grave site, including several fingers and bottles of congealed fat, but apparently no bodies; he concluded that they had been burnt to ashes. In April 1989, Russian filmmaker Geli Ryabov announced that he knew where the Romanovs were buried. Working from photographs and the Kremlin report of Yakov Yurovsky, the executioners' leader, he and geologist Alexander Avdonin had located the grave 10 years earlier, 5 miles from the site investigated by Sokolov. They had opened the grave and exhumed three skulls, only to return them to the ground the following year. Skeletal reconstruction, dental records, and computer projection and superimposition of their facial images were consistent with the remains being those of Czar Nicholas II, his wife Alexandra, and three of their children, along with three servants and the family doctor. There was some disagreement between the Russian scientists and an American team led by William Maples as to the identity of the two missing bodies. Although both agreed that the Czarevich Alexei accounted for one, the Russians thought that the missing female was grand duchess Marie, while Maples insisted that it was Anastasia.

In September 1992, Pavel Ivanov carried samples to England to have them tested by Peter Gill and Kevin Sullivan at the British Forensic Science Service Laboratory. Genetic typing of several STR loci confirmed the relationship among the five family members and determined the sex of each individual. MtDNA typing was then employed to confirm that the family was indeed the Romanovs. DNA from the bones was compared to samples obtained from known living relatives in the direct matrilineal line of descent. Mitochondrial D-loop sequences from Czarina Alexandra and her three daughters were identical to that of Prince Philip, husband of England's Queen Elizabeth II. His maternal grandmother was Czarina Alexandra's sister, so all inherited their mtDNA from the mother of both Alexandra and her sister.

The results concerning the Czar himself were highly convincing. When mtDNA from his purported bones was analyzed, a rare anamoly, now called heteroplasmy surfaced. This means that at one base position two different bases were found; the sequencing consistently showed both a C and at T at that point, indicating the presence of two variant populations of mtDNA in the same person. Because the mitochondrial genome is inherited only from one parent, the mother, it was assumed that only one type should be present in a person, making this situation highly unusual. Two of the Czar's maternally linked living relatives, including Countess Xenia Cheremetiff-Sfiri, the great-granddaughter of the Czar's sister, and the Duke of Fife, showed only a T at that point in the sequence. (The Czar's nephew, Tikhon Kulikovsky, refused to cooperate.) Researchers were "98.5%" sure that the bones belonged to the Czar, but the evidence was not completely convincing. The experiments were repeated by Erika Hagelberg of Cambridge University and Mary-Claire King of the University of California at Berkeley, providing independent confirmation that the heteroplasmy was not due to contamination or experimental error. Finally, the Russian authorities authorized the exhumation of Czar Nicholas II's brother, the Grand Duke of Russia, Georgij Romanov, who died of tuberculosis in 1899. Ivanov took these samples to Victor Weedn at the Armed Forces DNA Identification Laboratory (AFDIL). Weedn's group not only confirmed the heteroplasmy in Nicholas, but found a mixture of C and T at position 16169 of the mitochondrial genome of Georgij Romanov. The Grand Duke showed exactly the same heteroplasmy as his brother, confirming the identity of the remains as Czar Nicholas II, as well as solving a scientific riddle. Both brothers must have inherited their unusual mtDNA sequences from their mutual mother, and the rareness of this variation leaves virtually no doubt as to the identity of the Czar's bones. (See Chapters 5 and 7 for more discussion of mtDNA.)

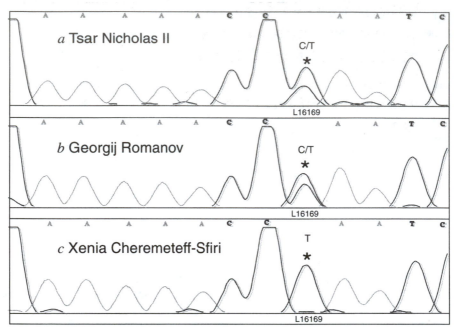

Fig. 2 Automated sequence chromatographs comparing mtDNA sequences at position 16169. *a*, Sequence from bones of putative Tsar Nicholas II, showing heteroplasmy with cytosine predominating thymine; *b*, sequence from bones of Grand Duke Georgij Romanov, showing heteroplasmy with thymine predominating cytosine; *c*, sequence from Countess Xenia Cheremeteff-Sfiri, homoplasmic for thymine.

The original four-color data printout has been reproduced here in black and white. (Courtesy of Armed Forces DNA Identification Laboratory (previously published in *Nature Genetics*, 12, 417.))

A mystery still remains, however, regarding the fate of the two younger Romanov children whose bodies were not found with the others in the grave. There have been numerous contestants for the titles of Grand Duchess Anastasia and Czarevich Alexei. Alexei was a known hemophiliac, unlikely to have survived the violent attack on his family. The most infamous claimant to the identity of Anastasia was the late Anna Anderson, who died in Charlottesville, Virginia, in 1984. Using hair samples saved by her husband and stored in books, scientists showed that her mtDNA sequences failed to match those of her purported mother, the Czarina Alexandra. They showed instead that she was maternally related to a German man called Carl Maucher; Maucher's great-aunt, Franzisca Schanzkowska, disappeared in Berlin at about the same time as Anderson surfaced there. The mystery of Anastasia, youngest daughter of Czar Nicholas II, will no doubt continue to perplex researchers and inspire books and movies for decades to come.

References

Anastasia claimant a fraud, *Reuter*, Oct. 5, 1994.

Debenham, P.G., DNA typing. heteroplasmy and the tsar, *Nature*, 380, 484–4, 1996.

DNA test shows Virginia woman wasn't Anastasia, *Reuter*, Oct. 4, 1994.

Editorial, Romanovs find closure in DNA, *Nature Genetics*, 12, 417–420, 1996.

Gill, P. et al., Identification of the remains of the Romanov Family by DNA analysis, *Nature Genetics*, 6(2), 130–135, 1994.

Gill, P. et al., Establishing the identity of Anna Anderson Manahan, *Nature Genetics*, 9(1), 9–10, 1995.

Glausiusz, J., Royal D-loops, *Discover*, Jan., 1994.

Ivanov, P.L. et al., Mitochondrial DNA sequence heteroplasmy in the Grand Duke of Russia Georgij Romanov establishes the authenticity of the remains of Tsar Nicholas II, *Nature Genetics*, 12, 417–420, 1996.

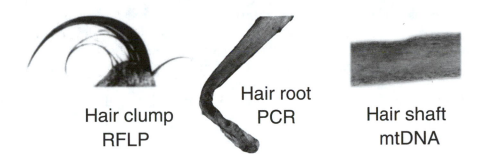

Hair clump
RFLP

Hair root
PCR

Hair shaft
mtDNA

Figure 5.16 How much do you need? A clump of pulled hair (left) typically contains enough material for successful RFLP typing. A single hair root (center) provides enough nuclear DNA for PCR STR typing, but not enough for RFLP. A hair shaft (right) contains sufficient mitochondria for successful mtDNA typing, but is inadequate for PCR STR or RFLP typing. (Hair shaft courtesy of the San Diego Sheriff's Department Crime Laboratory.)

III. What Kinds of Samples Can Be Analyzed?

The DNA in a cell is contained in a small region called the nucleus. Almost all body fluids and organs contain cells with nuclei. Common examples include blood, semen, saliva, and hair roots. Although the red cells in blood do not contain nuclei, white cells do, so blood is easily typed for nuclear DNA. The cells in the outside layer of skin contain few or no nuclei; however, nucleated cells may be transferred from the skin surface through sweat and sebaceous (oil) secretions. Because of this, it is sometimes possible, using the more sensitive PCR-based techniques, to obtain a DNA type deposited on an item through casual contact. In addition to perspiration and oil, urine (when concentrated) and feces also frequently contain enough nucleated cells to type using PCR-based systems. Most internal organs can also be analyzed for nuclear DNA, as can bone in certain circumstances. To type hair for nuclear DNA markers, it is generally necessary to obtain samples which include a root. Old bones, hair shafts, and nail clippings are usually refractory to nuclear DNA typing, but can be typed using mtDNA (Figure 5.16).

IV. How Much Sample Do You Need?

The amount of sample needed to obtain a conclusive result in any particular typing system varies greatly on a case-by-case basis. Environmental and historical factors, which are discussed at great length in Chapter 2, influence to a large extent the quality and quantity of DNA present in a forensic sample. For example, a bloodstain the size of a quarter that has been sitting on a rock in the Sahara Desert for 10 years will yield significantly less tractable DNA than the same-size stain which has, yesterday, been deposited on a cotton swatch in a laboratory and immediately dried and frozen. However, some generalizations can be made, assuming that the sample is relatively fresh and unadulterated. RFLP techniques require more DNA of better quality than PCR-based techniques because only the amount of DNA originally extracted from the sample can be tested. Because the PCR technique amplifies the DNA over the amount originally obtained, less is needed to start with. A fresh, dime-size bloodstain will generally yield sufficient DNA for a strong RFLP result; in contrast, only 1/10 to 1/100 of this stain might be needed to obtain a conclusive result from a PCR-based system (Figure 5.16). This is one of the major reasons for the migration to PCR-based systems. All other things being equal, less semen or saliva than blood is needed to obtain an equivalent type. This is because the concentration of sperm cells in semen, or epithelial cells in saliva, is higher than the concentration of white blood cells in blood. Other types of samples may vary accordingly, depending on the density of nucleated cells per sample.

Further References

Akane, A., Seki, S., Shiono, H., Nakamura, H., Hasegawa, M., Kagawa, M., Matsubara, K., Nakahori, Y., Nagafuchi, S., and Nakagome, Y., Sex determination of forensic samples by dual PCR amplification of an X-Y homologous gene, *Forensic Sci. Int.*, 52(2), 143–148, 1992.

Anderson, S., Bankier, A.T., Barrell, B.G., Debrujin, M.H., Coulson, A.R., Drouin, J., Eperon, I.C., Nierlich, D.P., Roe, B.A., Sanger, F., Schreir, P.H., Smith, A.J., Staden, R., and Young, I.G., Sequence and organization of the human mitochondrial genome, *Nature*, 290, 457–465, 1981.

Baasner A., Schafer C., Junge A., and Madea B., Polymorphic sites in human mitochondrial DNA control region sequences: population data and maternal inheritance, *Forensic Sci. Int.*, 98(3), 169–178, 1998.

Bar, W., Brinkmann, B., Budowle, B., Carracedo, A., Gill, P., Holland, M., Lincoln, P.J., Mayr, W., Morling, G., Olaisen, B., Schneider, P., Tully, G., and Wilson, M., DNA Commission of the International Society for Forensic Genetics: Guidelines for mitochondrial DNA typing, *Int. J. Legal Med.*, 113(2), 193–196, 2000.

Blake, E., Mihalovic, J., Higuchi, R., Walsh, P.S., and Erlich, H., Polymerase chain reaction (PCR) amplification and human leukocyte antigen (HLA)-DQ alpha oligonucleotide typing on biological evidence samples: casework experience, *J. Forensic Sci.*, 37(3), 700–726, 1992.

Budowle, B. and Sprecher, C.J., Concordance study on population database samples using the PowerPlex™ 16 kit and AmpFℓSTR® Profiler Plus™ kit and AmpFℓSTR® COfiler™ kit, *J. Forensic Sci.*, 46(3), 637–641, 2001.

Culliford, B.J., *The Examination and Typing of Blood Stains in the Crime Laboratory*, U.S. Government Printing Office, Washington, D.C., 1971.

Erlich, H.A., Ed., *PCR Technology: Principles and Applications for DNA Amplification*, Stockton Press, New York, NY, 1989.

Erlich, H.A., Gelfland, D., and Sninsky, J.J., Recent advances in the polymerase chain reaction, *Science*, 252, 643–651, 1991.

Fregeau, C.J. and Fourney, R. M., DNA typing with fluorescently tagged short tandem repeats: a sensitive and accurate approach to human identification, *Biotechniques*, 15(1), 100–119, 1993.

Gill, P., Kimpton, C.P., Urquhart, A., Oldroyd, N., Millican, E.S., Watson, S.K., and Downes, T.J., Automated short tandem repeat (STR) analysis in forensic casework — a strategy for the future, *Electrophoresis*, 16(9), 1543–1552, 1995.

Hammond, H.A., Jin, L., Zhong, Y., Caskey, C.T., and Chakraborty, R., Evaluation of 13 short tandem repeat loci for use in personal identification applications, *Am. J. Human Genet.*, 55(1), 175–189, 1994.

Holland, M.M., Fisher, D.L., Lee, D.A., Bryson, C.K., and Weedn, V.W., Short tandem repeat loci: application to forensic and human remains identification, *Exs*, 67, 267–274, 1993.

Jeffreys, A.J. et al., Applications of multilocus and single-locus minisatellite DNA probes in forensic medicine, in *DNA Technology and Forensic Science*, J. Ballantyne, G. Sensabaugh, and J. Witkowski, Eds., Cold Spring Harbor Laboratory Press, Cold Spring Harbor, NY, 1989.

Jeffreys, A.J., Wilson, V., and Thein, S.L., Individual specific "fingerprints" of human DNA, *Nature*, 316, 76–79, 1985.

Kasai, K., Nakamura, Y., and White, R., Amplification of a variable number of tandem repeats (VNTR) Locus (pMCT118) by the polymerase chain reaction (PCR) and its application to forensic science, *J. Forensic Sci.*, 35, 1196–1200, 1990.

Kawasaki, E., Saiki, R., and Erlich, H., Genetic analysis using polymerase chain reaction-amplified DNA and immobilized oligonucleotide probes: reverse dot-blot typing, *Meth. Enzymol.*, 218, 369–381, 1993.

Kimpton, C., Fisher D., Watson, S., Adams, M., Urquhart, A., Lygo, J., and Gill, P., Evaluation of an automated DNA profiling system employing multiplex amplification of four tetrameric STR loci, *Int. J. Legal Med.*, 106(6), 302–311, 1994.

Kloosterman, A.D., Budowle, B., and Daselaar P., PCR-amplification and detection of the human D1S80 VNTR locus, amplification conditions, population genetics and application in forensic analysis, *Int. J. Legal Med.*, 105(5), 257–564, 1993.

Linch, C.A., Whiting, D.A., and Holland, M.M., Human hair histogenesis for the motochondrial DNA forensic scientist, *J. Forensic Sci.*, 46(4), 844–853, 2001.

Mullis, K.B. and Faloona F., Specific synthesis of DNA *in vitro* via a polymerase catalyzed chain reaction, *Meth. Enzymol.*, 155, 335–350, 1987.

Mullis, K.B., Faloona, F., Scharf, S.J., Saiki, R.K., Horn, G.T., and Erlich, H.A., Specific enzymatic amplification of DNA *in vitro*: the polymerase chain reaction, *Cold Spring Harbor Symp. Quant. Biol.*, 51, 263–273, 1986.

Naito, E., Dewa, K., Yamanouchi, H., and Kominami, R., Sex typing of forensic DNA samples using male- and female-specific probes, *J. Forensic Sci.*, 39(4), 1009–1017, 1994.

Nakamura, Y. et al., Variable number of tandem repeat (VNTR) markers for human gene mapping, *Science*, 237, 1616–1622, 1987.

National Research Council, *DNA Technology in Forensic Science*, National Academy Press, Washington, D.C., 1992.

Prinz, M., Boll, K., Baum, H., and Haler, B., Multiplexing of Y chromosome specific STRs and performance for mixed samples, *Forensic Sci. Int.*, 85(3), 209–218, 1997.

Redd, A.J., Clifford, S.L., and Stoneking, M., Multiplex DNA typing of short tandem repeat loci an the Y-chromosome, *Biol. Chem.*, 378(8), 923–927, 1997.

Reynolds, R., Sensabaugh, G., and Blake, E., Analysis of genetic markers in forensic DNA samples using the polymerase chain reaction, *Anal. Chem.*, 63(1), 2–15, 1991.

Sullivan, K. M., Hopgood, R., and Gill, P., Identification of human remains by amplification and automated sequencing of mitochondrial DNA, *Int. J. Legal Med.*, 105(2), 83–86, 1992.

Urquhart, A., Kimpton, C.P., Downes, T. J., and Gill, P., Variation in short tandem repeat sequences — a survey of twelve microsatellite loci for use as forensic identification markers, *Int. J. Legal Med.*, 107(1), 13–20, 1994.

Urquhart, A., Oldroyd, N.J., Kimpton, C.P., and Gill, P., Highly discriminating heptaplex short tandem repeat PCR system for forensic identification, *Biotechniques*, 18(1), 116–118, 120–121, 1995.

U.S. Congress, Office of Technology Assessment, Genetic Witness: Forensic Uses of DNA Tests, OTA-BA-438, Washington, D.C., 1990.

Procedures for Forensic DNA Analysis

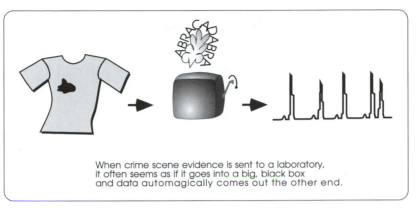

When crime scene evidence is sent to a laboratory,
it often seems as if it goes into a big, black box
and data automagically comes out the other end.

I.   Isolation of DNA

Before any type of testing can be performed, DNA must be isolated from the
rest of the cellular components, as well as from any nonbiological material
that might be present (see Figures 6.1, 6.2, and Plate 4). This operation must
be performed carefully and thoroughly; any residual material may hamper
subsequent analysis in two ways. First, the different enzymes that act on the
DNA during the test procedure require specific environments to work efficiently and properly; the material that Nature designed them to work on is
DNA, and they work best when no foreign material is present. Second, some extraneous
substances cause DNA to degrade, or fall apart. This may continue to happen, even during
analysis, until the substance is removed. It is always preferable to clean the DNA from any
possible harmful materials as expeditiously and as thoroughly as possible.

The isolation or extraction procedure varies somewhat according to the type of biological evidence present (e.g., blood, semen, saliva, or hair); the amount of evidence (which
influences the type of test that is subsequently performed); and the kinds of cells present.
These determinations are made by visual inspection, microscopic examination, and the
presumptive tests discussed previously.

A.   Chelex Extraction

Sometimes, if only the most minute sample is present (e.g., a speck of barely visible blood),
a method called **Chelex extraction** is employed. This consists of boiling the sample in a
solution containing minute beads of a chemical called Chelex. The boiling breaks open
the cells, releasing the DNA, and the Chelex binds up most other extraneous materials that
might interfere in subsequent analysis. The Chelex beads are removed, along with most

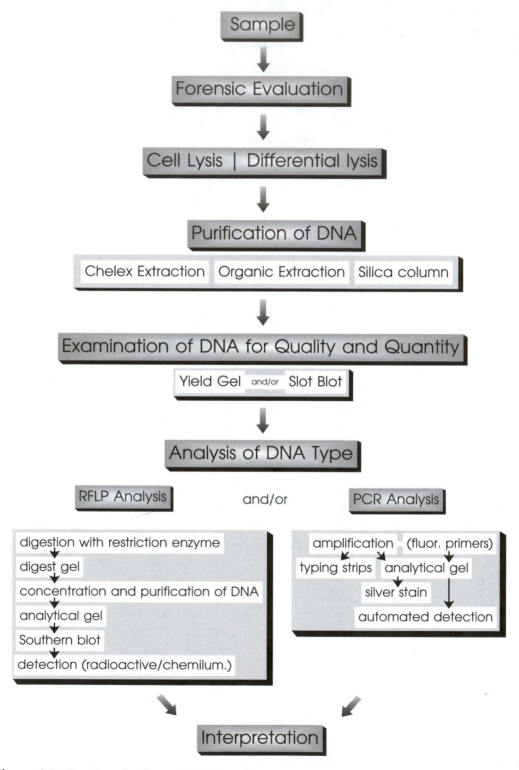

Figure 6.1 Flowchart for forensic DNA typing.

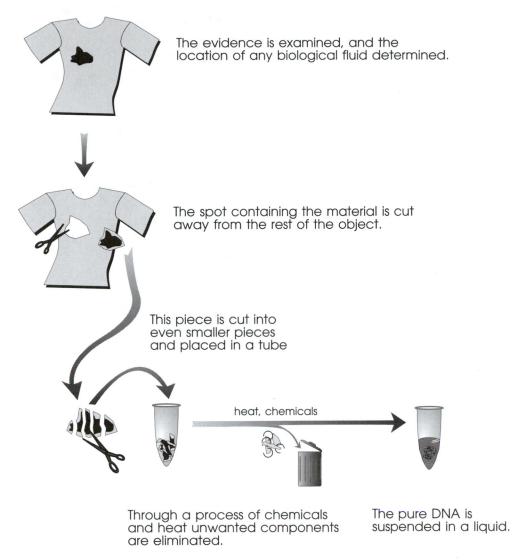

The evidence is examined, and the location of any biological fluid determined.

The spot containing the material is cut away from the rest of the object.

This piece is cut into even smaller pieces and placed in a tube

heat, chemicals

Through a process of chemicals and heat unwanted components are eliminated.

The pure DNA is suspended in a liquid.

Figure 6.2 Flowchart for organic extraction of DNA.

other non-DNA components, leaving the DNA behind. Because this extraction technique breaks apart the two strands of the DNA double helix, it has generally been reserved for very small samples where only PCR-based analysis was anticipated. DNA must be double-stranded in order to perform RFLP analysis, but PCR can be performed on either single-stranded or double-stranded DNA. Although this extraction method was popularized and worked well for samples intended for reverse dot blot analyses, it is not the extraction method of choice for samples that will be analyzed using STRs. Although STRs are a PCR-based system, so single-stranded DNA is not a problem, STR analysis seems to work better with DNA extracted by one of the following methods than with Chelex-extracted DNA.

B.   QiaAmp Extraction

Although not commonly employed at the time of this writing, a silica column-based method is used by some laboratories to remove the DNA from other cellular components after the cells are broken open (lysed). The DNA extract is passed over a small column containing miniscule beads composed of a substance to which DNA adheres under certain chemical conditions; all other materials are washed off the column. The chemical conditions are then changed to release (elute) the cleaned DNA, and it is collected from the bottom end of the column in a drop of liquid. DNA isolated in this way is of high quality and double-stranded, and can be used for a wide variety of applications.

C.   Organic Extraction

In most other situations, a general method called **organic extraction** (Figure 6.2) is usually employed. The organic extraction method is more likely to maintain the DNA in large pieces, and cleans the DNA more thoroughly than does Chelex extraction. The presence or absence of sperm, either alone or along with other types of cells, directs which variation of the organic extraction procedure might be performed. Sperm cells are more difficult to break open than, for example, blood, saliva, or vaginal cells, and require extra chemicals. As will be discussed later, this fact is put to good use when mixed samples, such as a vaginal swab from a rape case, are analyzed.

If no sperm cells are either noted microscopically or suspected from the nature of the case, a simple organic extraction is performed. In this procedure (Figure 6.2), the sample (a piece of fabric, for example) is cut into small pieces and soaked in a warm solution to gently release cells from the substrate on which they are deposited. Using another chemical mix and mild heat, the cells are broken open, releasing the DNA. The DNA is then isolated from any other components using various organic solvents. It is from this step that the name "organic extraction" is derived. The DNA is further purified and concentrated using special filters or by precipitation, producing an extract suitable for use in either RFLP or PCR-based analysis.

D.   Differential Extraction

A special situation involves samples in which sperm are present along with other types of cells, often of vaginal origin. Many cells found in forensic evidence can be lumped into a category called **non-sperm cells** (sometimes less correctly called e**pithelial cells** or **e. cells**). This category includes saliva, skin, buccal, and vaginal cells, as well as those found in urine and feces. The different properties of sperm cells from all other cells are exploited in order to separate them from each other before any DNA is isolated. This simplifies the final interpretation because, in many cases, the victim's and suspect's types may be analyzed and compared separately.

The type of procedure used to isolate DNA from a mixed sample of sperm and non-sperm cells is called **differential extraction** (Plate 4); it is a variation of the organic extraction procedure. The cells (including both non-sperm and sperm cells) are first removed from the substrate by soaking in a gentle solution. The sample is incubated in one set of chemicals that specifically break open only the non-sperm cells. The liquid containing them (called the **non-sperm fraction**) is then removed to a separate tube. The DNA from the non-sperm fraction is extracted using the normal organic extraction procedure. The sperm cells are treated with some extra chemicals to help remove them from the substrate and also break them open; this is called the **sperm fraction**. Once DNA is released from the sperm cells, it goes through the same organic extraction procedure as all other samples. The result of a differential extraction is two tubes, one containing DNA

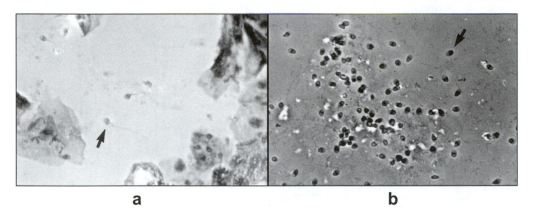

a   b

Figure 6.3 Photomicrographs of a differential extraction. Panel A shows a sexual assault sample before differential extraction. The very large, irregular objects are epithelial cells (e. cells) from the female and the minuscule round objects are sperm, some with tails still attached. In panel B, the e. cells have been lysed, leaving a concentrated sample of sperm heads. The arrows point to sperm cells. The photographs were taken using phase contrast at 400X magnification. The photograph was enlarged an additional 5X.

all or mostly from sperm and the other containing DNA all or mostly from non-sperm cells (Figure 6.3).

Due to the nature of the sample, separation of the non-sperm cell DNA from sperm cell DNA may not always be complete. For example, if the sample is in poor condition, some sperm cells may have already popped open, releasing their DNA prematurely. Because the method of separation depends on initially intact sperm cells, some of this free sperm DNA may show up in the final non-sperm cell fraction. Alternatively, in a mix of many non-sperm cells and just a few sperm, some non-sperm cell DNA may persist among the sperm and may be detected in the final sperm fraction. The interpretation of such results is discussed in Chapter 7.

II.   Determining the Quality and Quantity of DNA

Before any analysis proceeds, it is imperative to determine how much DNA — in particular, how much human DNA — is present. Sometimes, it is also important to determine the quality of the DNA, specifically how degraded it is. Specific tests are performed to assess these parameters before proceeding with any analysis. Depending on the particulars of a case and what specific information the analyst deems useful, any of these methods might be employed.

A.   Determination of Quantity

Forensic samples frequently contain DNA co-extracted from microbial organisms such as yeast and bacteria. This DNA does not interfere with the interpretation of the sample because it is generally not detected, but must be taken into account for decisions made during the analysis. For RFLP analysis, it was necessary to consider both the total DNA content and the proportion of human DNA; quantitative information about total DNA was used to calculate how much restriction enzyme to add to each reaction. The proportion of human DNA determined how much sample to load on the analytical gel. For RFLP, in

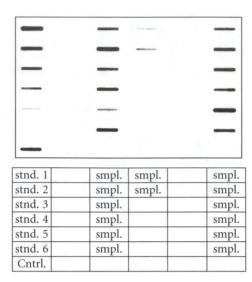

stnd. 1		smpl.	smpl.		smpl.
stnd. 2		smpl.	smpl.		smpl.
stnd. 3		smpl.			smpl.
stnd. 4		smpl.			smpl.
stnd. 5		smpl.			smpl.
stnd. 6		smpl.			smpl.
Cntrl.					

Figure 6.4 A slot blot. The first column contains the quantitation standards in decreasing concentration from top to bottom. The lowermost slot contains a positive control for which the quantity of DNA is known. The other lanes contain the evidence and reference samples, as well as controls for other parts of the procedure, such as extraction and handling. The concentration of an unknown sample is obtained by comparing it to the standards. *stnd.*, quantitation standard; *cntrl.*, positive control sample; *smpl.*, sample.

particular, the quality of the final analytical result depended, in part, on using the same amount of human DNA for each sample. This was referred to as "balancing the samples." It was also important for reverse dot blot PCR tests, but is less critical for current STR systems. For PCR-based reactions in general, the amount of total DNA is less important than the amount of human DNA present in the sample. In particular, the addition of too much sample to an amplification reaction is as undesirable as too little sample.

The method of this assessment is currently determined mostly by the typing system to be used. For PCR-based analyses, the size of the DNA is less important than how much human DNA is present. For most laboratories, a **slot blot** has been the method of choice to determine the amount of human DNA. A small portion of the sample is removed and tested, leaving the majority of the sample untouched. The amount of human DNA in extracted samples is visually compared to known standards and the quantity estimated (Figure 6.4; Appendix C1). Most forensic laboratories use a kit manufactured by Applied Biosystems, called Quantiblot®, for this procedure. A new method, called AluQuant™, has just been introduced in kit form by Promega Corporation. This method is similar to a slot blot in that it depends on the specificity of human-specific DNA probes, but the mechanism of light production and the detection technology differ. In contrast to a film with visible bands, light produced by samples quantitated using the AluQuant™ system are read by a luminometer (an instrument that quantifies light output) and the results appear as figures in a table. It remains to be seen whether this method will indeed live up to its claims of increased accuracy, and whether it will be adopted by the forensic community.

B.   Determination of Quality

For RFLP analysis in particular, it was important to know how degraded the DNA was and also something about the total DNA in the sample. DNA remaining in relatively large

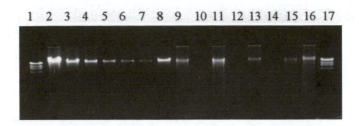

Figure 6.5 A yield gel. Lanes 1 and 17 contain a molecular ladder used to judge how far the gel has run. Lanes 2 through 7 contain HMW quantitation standards in decreasing concentration from left to right. Lane 8 contains the same control sample used in the slot blot (see Figure 6.4). The samples to be quantitated appear in lanes 9, 11, 13, 15, and 16.

pieces is said to be of high molecular weight. HMW DNA was critical to obtaining an RFLP result. Typically, a **yield gel** has been used for determining the state of the DNA and also for quantitating the total amount of DNA present (Figure 6.5; Appendix C2). A yield gel requires double-stranded DNA in relatively high quantity for a result to be obtained. For this reason, it is typically not used by many laboratories performing only PCR-based analyses. If can, however, provide information regarding the average size of DNA fragments, which can sometimes assist in interpreting STR results from highly degraded samples. Occassionally, a **Southern blot** (see Chapter 6.III) might be performed on the yield gel, and the membrane probed with the same human-specific probe used for the slot blot (see Appendix C1); this method also provides an assessment of the proportion of human DNA in a sample.

III. RFLP Analysis

As described previously, RFLP analysis measures the size of the DNA fragments produced by restriction enzymes. The decision to proceed with RFLP analysis is made only after it is determined that the sample contains sufficient HMW human DNA for this type of analysis to be successful. The amounts of DNA, restriction enzyme, and other components are carefully calculated, and then combined in a small tube that is incubated in a warm bath overnight (Figure 6.6a, step 1). It is important that all specified sites are cut, so that no artificially large pieces remain. When some sites are left uncut, the sample is said to be partially digested. This is determined by removing a small portion of the sample and comparing it to uncut (undigested) and completely digested standard samples of DNA on a digest gel (Figure 6.7; Appendix C3). If digestion is not complete, certain steps of the extraction procedure can be repeated in an attempt to purify the sample of any inhibitors that might prevent the restriction enzyme from working properly. The sample is then subjected to another dose of enzyme. When it is determined that the reaction is in fact complete, and no detecable "partials" remain, the analyst proceeds to the next step of separating the pieces according to size. At this point, all that is visible is a colorless liquid in a colorless tube.

A blue dye is added to the solution containing the cut (digested) DNA, and each sample is loaded into its own preformed indentation in a slab of gel-like material called **agarose** (Figure 6.6a, step 2). An electric field is then applied to the agarose gel (Figure 6.6a, step 3). Because DNA carries an overall negative (−) charge, all of the DNA fragments will start to

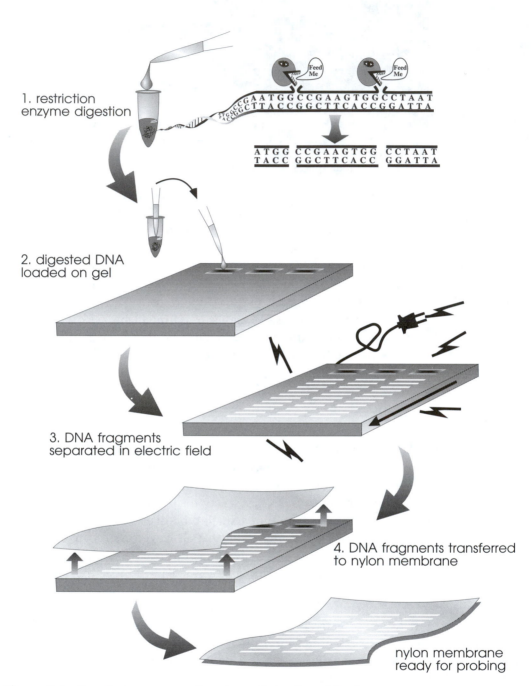

Figure 6.6a Restriction enzyme digestion and Southern blotting.

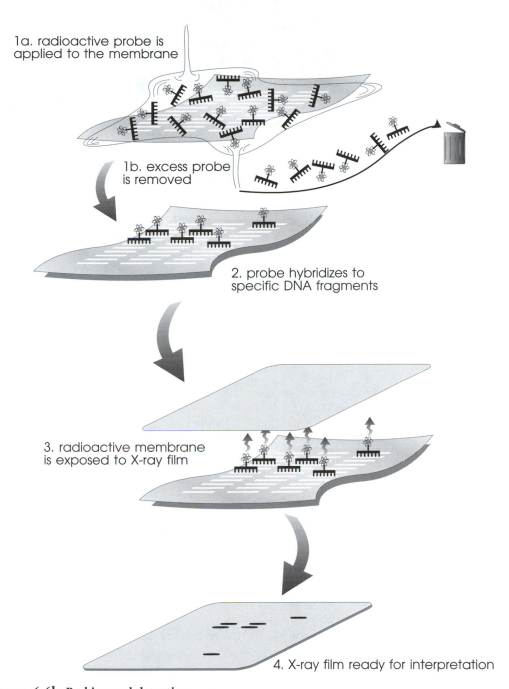

Figure 6.6b Probing and detection.

Figure 6.7 A digest gel. Lanes 1 and 10 contain a molecular ladder, lane 2 contains a known undigested sample, and lane 3 contains a known digested sample. The remaining lanes contain completely digested samples.

migrate toward the positive (+) pole. The setup is conveniently arranged so that the positive (+) end of the electric field is at the opposite end of the gel from where the DNA is loaded.

An essential element of the process is that the gel material used to make up the slab is full of microscopic holes through which the DNA fragments pass on their way to the other end (Figure 6.6a; Plate 3). Because it is easier for the smaller fragments to fit through these pores, they migrate faster and are the first to reach the bottom of the gel; the larger fragments migrate more slowly and lag toward the origin. At the end of the overnight run, the DNA sample originally loaded into each well has formed an array of fragments from largest to smallest in a lane leading to the end of the gel.

At this point, the DNA is still invisible to the naked eye. Sometimes, the gel is soaked in a dye, called **ethidium bromide**, that binds to DNA and makes it temporarily visible under ultraviolet light (Figure 6.8). Under these conditions, the DNA fragments appear as a smear because the dye exposes all of the DNA fragments and cannot distinguish between them. This confirms that the samples were loaded in the gel and that the gel has run as expected.

To detect the specific polymorphic fragments of interest, the DNA must be transferred to a solid support. The gel is soaked in a chemical that causes the two strands of the DNA double helix to separate into single strands. A piece of nylon membrane is laid on top of the gel and a layer of absorbent material on top of that. The absorbent material draws up liquid from the gel and the DNA fragments along with it. This is the same idea as using a sponge to soak up a wet stain. When the single-stranded DNA fragments hit the nylon membrane, they adhere and are permanently transferred to it. This procedure is called **Southern blotting** (Figure 6.6a, step 4).

To detect DNA originating from designated locations in the genome, short fragments of DNA (called probes) are labeled with a radioactive or chemiluminescent tag. These probes are designed to match the places in the genome that are well-characterized and highly polymorphic. Under the correct conditions, DNA strands that match will unite into a double-stranded form. Any probe fragments that have not bound specifically are washed away so as not to interfere with the signal. This process is called **hybridization** (Figure 6.6b, step 1). The labeled fragments signal where they have hybridized and this signal is recorded on a sheet of X-ray film (Figure 6.6b, step 3). The pattern recorded on the X-ray film is the image that has been likened to a simplified supermarket bar code (Figure 6.9). Each piece of exposed film is called an **autorad**, short for autoradiogram or autoradiograph. Although this terminology is inaccurate for the newer chemiluminescent probes, it has been grandfathered into the system because the result looks identical. Some refer to chemiluminescent results as lumigraphs, or simply films. Generally, two bands are detected

Figure 6.8 A stained analytical gel. Samples on an agarose gel after electrophoresis and staining with ethidium bromide. The genomic DNA samples in lanes 2, 3, 5, 6, 7, and 9 show as streaks because ethidium bromide stains all DNA and the entire genome's worth is visualized.

in each sample lane (Figure 6.6b, step 4). This is because a different allele is usually inherited from each parent (heterozygous).

In the loci chosen for forensic use, different numbers of repeat units are often present between the two cuts of the restriction enzyme, producing DNA fragments of different sizes (Plate 3). If a person is homozygous for a particular locus (i.e., he has inherited the same length allele from both parents), only one band will be detected on the autorad. What we have described here is the detection of one locus, or location, in the genome. In forensic DNA analysis, as many as five or six loci are commonly analyzed, so ten to twelve bands are ultimately detected, one or two bands at a time, in each lane. Each probe detects a different locus.

Once the information from the first probe is recorded, it is removed (**stripped**) and the nylon membrane is exposed to the next probe in the series. After the second probe has been detected and recorded, the process is repeated for every additional probe. The exposed films (or autorads) from each particular probe provide a permanent record of the results of the analysis. The band locations are compared from lane to lane to identify any similar patterns. Samples that look visually similar are then subjected to computer imaging and analysis. To aid in this analysis, an artificially constructed molecular ruler is run on each gel; the computer then has an objective internal standard from which to calculate band (fragment) sizes. A sample for which the results are known is also run on each gel to

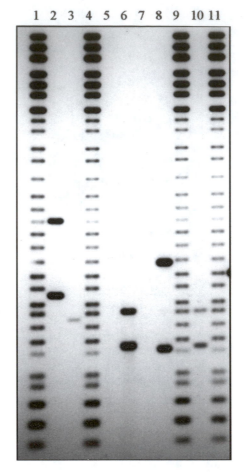

Figure 6.9 An RFLP autorad. The locus probed is D2S44. Lanes 1, 4, 9, and 11 contain molecular ladders. Lanes 5 and 7 contain no sample. The pattern of bands in lanes 6 and 10 appear indistinguishable. All other samples show different patterns, both from these two and from each other.

monitor whether the system is working as expected. In the United States, this standard sample is taken from an immortal cell line and is known as **K562**. If two samples are suspected to have originated from the same source, a calculation is also performed to estimate how often the type occurs in the population. This subject is discussed more fully in Chapter 8.

IV. PCR Amplification

PCR amplification is often performed on samples that are deemed too minuscule or highly degraded to give a reliable RFLP result. This process faithfully replicates a defined segment of DNA millions of times and is dependent on the *Taq* polymerase enzyme. In contrast to the restriction enzymes discussed previously, this enzyme does not cut DNA into pieces, but rather replicates it. An essential feature of this particular enzyme is that it can survive high temperatures and still keep working. As will be seen, this is key to the "chain reaction" used to replicate the DNA.

Three main steps make up any amplification procedure, and are repeated dozens of times (Plate 5).

1. **Denaturation.** The first step is to separate the two strands of the DNA double helix (denaturation) so that each stand can be used as a template for the synthesis of a new strand. As discussed previously (Chapters 5 and 6), the sequence of bases added to make a single strand of DNA into a double strand is determined entirely by the previously existing strand. Denaturation is accomplished by subjecting the DNA to fairly high heat, necessitating the heat-stable *Taq* enzyme.

2. **Annealing.** The second step involves the annealing of **DNA primers**. Primers, like the probes used in RFLP, are short synthetic pieces of DNA that match defined locations by complementary base pairing. In this case, they are called **primers** because they mark the starting location of the synthesis of new DNA and prime the reaction. Two different primers define the end-point of a particular segment that is to be amplified, one at each end.

3. **Extension**. In the third step, the raw materials of DNA (single bases) are hooked together by *Taq* polymerase to create new DNA strands. The chemical form in which a base is added to DNA is called a **nucleotide**. The location and order are exactly defined by the original strands of DNA and the primers. If the next base on a beginning template of DNA is an **A**, it will only pair with a **T**, so the enzyme pulls a free **T** from the raw materials and adds it to the growing end of the new strand. In this way, the new strand is manufactured, base by base, with a sequence complementary to the beginning template. At the end of the first cycle of PCR, the segment of interest has been duplicated.

The three steps are repeated over and over again (Plate 6), each time doubling the number of copies of DNA and ultimately resulting in millions of copies identical to the original. This is why the process is often called molecular Xeroxing™. At this point, the sample is a colorless liquid in a colorless tube.

Sometimes, a **product gel** (Appendix C4) is run using a small portion of the sample to check that the PCR reaction has been successful. This procedure is more commonly employed if a nonelectrophoretic method, such as a reverse dot blot, will be used to analyze the sample; it is not particularly useful if the sample will be analyzed using STRs because it simply reproduces the analysis in a less discriminating form. If the *Taq* polymerase enzyme has been inhibited for any reason, no amplification will occur. This would be evidenced by the failure to detect bands on a product gel. This situation would most often preclude obtaining a final typing result. If no PCR product is detected, certain steps of the extraction procedure can be repeated in an attempt to purify the samples of any inhibitors that might prevent the enzyme from working properly. Alternatively, other techniques can be used to overcome the inhibition without further purification of the sample. Another amplification run can then be attempted.

V.   Analysis of PCR Product

Depending on the type of polymorphism being investigated, the product of PCR reactions, henceforth called PCR product, is analyzed in one of two ways. Sequence polymorphisms

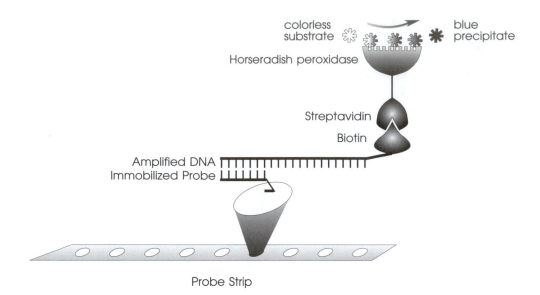

Figure 6.10 Detection of PCR product on a reverse dot blot.

are detected using a hybridization procedure or, sometimes, by direct sequence analysis. Length polymorphisms are most commonly detected using various electrohoretic procedures similar to the gel used in RFLP analysis. A variation of this technique uses a very thin capillary column to contain the separation medium.

A.   Sequence Polymorphisms

1.   AmpliType®PM+DQA1

We have mentioned the phenomenon of complementary base pairing. Under the appropriate conditions, only those single strands that match *exactly* will hybridize. If only one or a few bases are different, the two strands will fail to attach to each other. This is the scientific basis for the detection of sequence polymorphisms. A nylon strip, to which DNA probes have been attached, is challenged with the PCR product (Figure 6.10). These strips are commercially available and contain specific DNA sequences originating from the same locus in the genome as the DNA that has been amplified by PCR. When the probes are attached to the typing strip, the format is known as a **reverse dot blot**. Each probe is a specific sequence of DNA that defines an allele (Figure 6.11). These types of probes are known as **sequence-specific oligonucleotides** (**SSO**). They are sometimes also referred to in the forensic science literature as **allele-specific probes** (**ASO**), although this is technically incorrect. The SSO probes on the strip define a finite number of variations (types) seen in that particular region. The type of the sample is revealed by hybridization of the amplified DNA to a specific immobilized probe on the strip.

At this point, the strip is still white with invisible dots of attached probe. When DNA segments are amplified for subsequent analysis of sequence polymorphisms, the primers used in the reaction are labeled with a biological tag called **biotin.** After all the PCR product has bound to the probe strip, any excess unbound PCR product is removed, and a **streptavidin/horseradish peroxidase conjugate** is applied and binds tightly to the biotin (Figure 6.10). The biotin molecule has a very strong affinity for the protein **streptavidin** and the

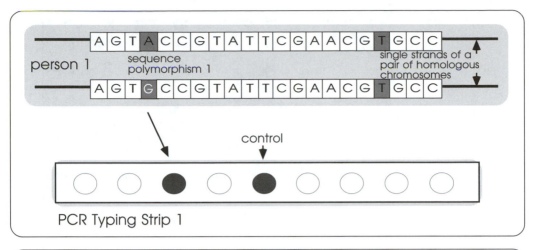

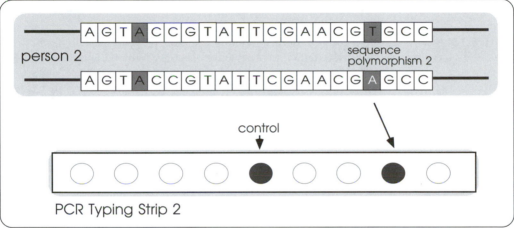

Figure 6.11 Typing sequence polymorphisms using a reverse dot blot format. For each person, a pair of homologous chromosomes is represented; only one strand of the original double-stranded molecule is depicted. The reverse dot blot typing procedure is designed to detect differences on only one of the two DNA strands.

streptavidin is chemically linked to the enzyme **horseradish peroxidase** (**HRP**). Upon the addition of a colorless substrate (tetramethylbenzidine (TMB)), the HRP releases a blue color in the presence of hydrogen peroxide. Dots to which DNA has adhered, via the rest of the long chain of reagents, turn blue (Figure 6.11). The pattern of dots corresponds to the alleles present in the sample (Figure 6.10); these are the infamous "blue dots." Both the HLA DQA1 locus and the polymarker loci are analyzed in this fashion (Figures 6.11, 6.12, and 6.13). The results are recorded and saved using standard photographic techniques. The strips themselves are normally discarded because the blue color is unstable when exposed to light.

2. *Mitochondrial DNA (mtDNA)*

The variations exhibited in the two hypervariable regions of the mtDNA circular chromosome are generally point mutations, although small deletions and insertions can also occur. Currently, direct DNA sequencing is used by the few laboratories that have implemented

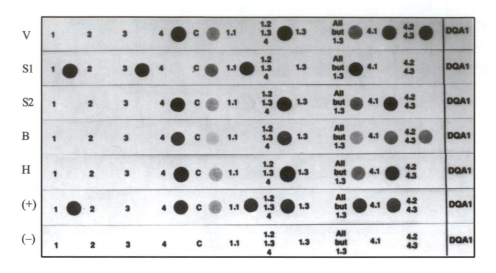

Figure 6.12 A DQA1 reverse dot blot. In this previously adjudicated case used in development of the DQA1 typing system, a victim (V), two evidence samples of blood and hair (B and H), and two suspects (S1 and S2) were typed. The blood shows the same pattern of dots as the victim, and the hair as suspect 2. Suspect 1 is excluded from contributing any of the evidence. The bottom two strips are a positive typing control (+) and a negative typing control (–), respectively. These DQA1 strips demonstrate the value of adding the 4.1 and 4.2/4.3 probes. Without these subtyping probes, samples V, S2, B, and H cannot be distinguished. For more about reading the numeric types from DQA1 strips, see Chapter 7. (Courtesy of Roche Molecular Systems.)

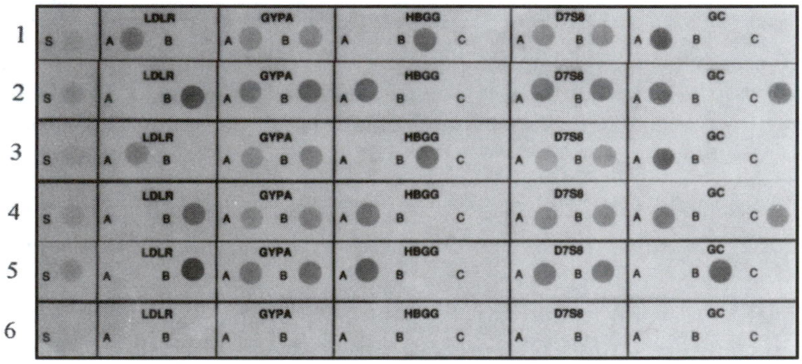

Figure 6.13 A polymarker reverse dot blot. Strips 1 and 3 show the same composite type, as do strips 2 and 4. Strips 5 and 6 are positive and negative typing controls, respectively.

mtDNA typing. Another method that should soon be released in kit form relies on the same sequence-specific hybridization technology as the AmpliType® PM+DQA1 system. We first address mtDNA sequencing.

The most basic and comprehensive method of comparing DNA fragments is to obtain the complete nucleotide sequence of each. This method is not practical for use on most genomic samples, especially at loci selected for high variability. Because most people are heterozygous at the nuclear DNA loci chosen for forensic analysis, two variant alleles may be present at the locus in question, and there is no way to sort out the two different sequences that would be obtained from this scenario. At this point in time, DNA sequencing is also time-consuming, cumbersome, and technically challenging. The disadvantages usually outweigh the advantages, and it is not, at present, the method of choice for use on the nuclear loci used in forensic analysis. The mtDNA locus is currently the only marker system in the forensic venue to be analyzed by direct DNA sequencing. This is nominally possible because the region is small; only a single locus is analyzed, and, by Nature, only a single allele is normally present in an individual.

Most DNA sequencing is now performed using one of the automated platforms, either gel based or capillary based. The reactions and analysis steps performed up to that point are essentially the same for any of the automated detection methods — or for that matter for purely manual sequencing. They are a variation on the traditional Sanger sequencing method that has been commonly used in molecular biology for two decades.

The Sanger method is predicated on the use of **base analogues** — nucleotides that look enough like the real thing to be incorporated into a growing strand of DNA *in vitro*, but which, once incorporated, terminate the synthesis. These analogues are called **dideoxynucleotides**. The regular nucleotides that make up DNA are, more specifically, **deoxynucleotides** and we use the terms interchangeably here. Like PCR, a specific oligonucleotide primer is annealed to a predetermined site on the DNA strand to be sequenced; unlike PCR, the segments to be copied are only defined by a primer on the starting end. In the presence of DNA polymerase and added nucleotides, the primer is extended, using the existing strand as a template for synthesis of a complementary DNA strand.

The dideoxynucleotides are used as follows (Figure 6.14). Four different tubes of reactions are prepared for each segment of DNA to be sequenced, each containing a different one of the four possible dideoxynucleotides. For example, in one reaction, a portion of the normal adenine (**A**) deoxynucleotide complement is replaced by the equivalent **A** dideoxynucleotide. Every so often, and in a random fashion, an **A** dideoxynucleotide will be incorporated instead of an **A** deoxynucleotide, terminating the growing chain and marking the position of an **A**. By the end of the reaction, the tube will contain a mixture of fragments, all terminated at **A**s and marking the position of all the **A**s in that sequence. The remaining three tubes will contain finished reactions marking the position of the **G**s, **T**s, and **C**s, respectively. In a variation using PCR technology called **cycle sequencing**, the reactions are repeated many times, greatly increasing the amount of product and therefore the sensitivity and ease of detection. It is also common to preamplify a defined region using standard PCR procedures before attempting any sequencing reactions.

In the original manual sequencing method, one of the normal deoxynucleotides is radioactively or chemiluminescently labeled so that all fragments can be visualized. The fragments are separated by electrophoresis through a polyacrylamide gel, and each of the reactions is run in a different lane. This results in four, side-by-side ladders from which the sequence can be read simply by following them sequentially up the gel (Figure 6.14).

Automated sequencing exploits fluorescent-based detection of the sequencing products. Fluorescent tags in four different colors, one for each reaction, are incorporated into the sequencing reactions, and the sequencing products are loaded into a gel or capillary column that is contained within a special detection instrument. Real-time laser detection of the color-specific fragments allows the reactions to be combined into one gel lane or

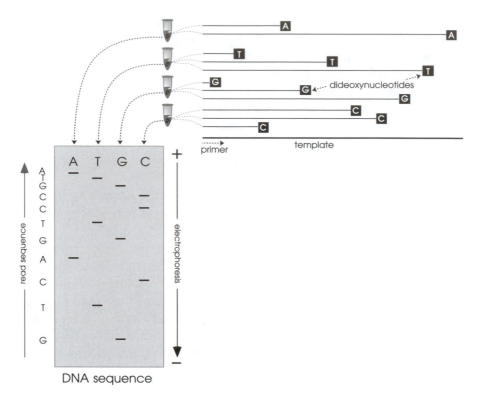

Figure 6.14 Manual sequencing using the Sanger method. The radioactively or chemilumines-cently labeled sequencing products from each of four separate tubes are loaded on a polyacry-lamide gel and separated by electrophoresis. The gel is exposed to X-ray film to visualize the bands. The sequence is read from the smallest fragment at the bottom of the gel, upward through progressively larger sequence products. Each fragment is longer by exactly one nucleotide.

capillary column, thereby saving time and materials. Because each fragment is detected as it passes a preset location in the gel or capillary column during the electrophoresis, the resolving power is increased over the manual method and longer stretches of sequence can be read from a single run. The data from each sequencing run is routed to a computer file for analysis, storage, and eventual comparison. The final output is usually shown as a series of overlapping colored peaks (Plate 7), each of which is correlated to a termination point that marks the location of a specific base. Fluorescence-based automated detection technology is also used with STRs.

The regions of the mitochondrial genome to be sequenced have yet to be standardized between labs. This may also not be necessary, as the sequences to be compared can simply be designated for each case.

A completely different approach to the analysis of the mtDNA hypervariable regions involves the identification of mutational hot spots and the creation of a set of defined probes for these sites (Figure 6.15; Plate 15). This type of test, based on the same technology as the Amplitype®PM+DQA1 tests described earlier, has been developed by Roche Molecular Systems, and it is hoped that it will soon be available as a commercial kit. MtDNA probe strips contain a total of 31 immobilized probes that distinguish variants in 10 segments that span **hypervariable region I** (**HVI**) and **hypervariable region II** (**HVII**), resulting in hundreds of possible types. Defined regions of HVI and HVII are amplified

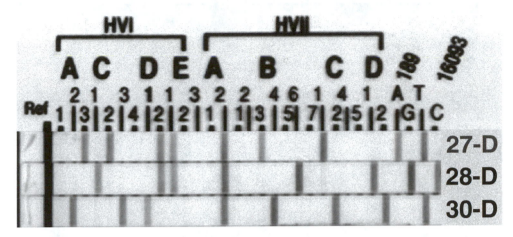

Figure 6.15 Detection of sequence variation in mtDNA. Results obtained using linear arrays of sequence-specific oligonucleotide (SSO) probes are shown. Three unrelated individuals were typed using a panel of 31 SSO probes immobilized in a linear array on strips of nylon membrane. This panel of SSO probes detects sequence variation in ten segments that span the HVI and HVII hypervariable regions of the mtDNA circle. An individual's "mitotype" is determined by examining the pattern of positive signals on the linear array. For example, the mitotype for individual 27-D is 32212310AT. See Plate 15 for a more in-depth explanation of this typing system. (Courtesy of Roche Molecular Systems.)

and allowed to interact with the strip. Where a particular sequence complementary to the immobilized probe occurs, hybridization takes place, and the area (now a line rather than a dot) turns blue. An individual type is read by noting the presence and location of blue lines in each region of the strip that correspond to the defined alleles in each section of HVI or HVII. Because it is presented in a digital format, this setup is ideal for computerized detection, analysis, storage, and comparison. Although less total information is obtained than with direct sequencing, the ease of use and lack of necessity to purchase additional expensive equipment are large advantages. We address interpretational issues in Chapter 7.

B.   Length Polymorphisms (D1S80, STRs, Gender ID)

PCR can be used to amplify some relatively short length polymorphisms. This is a much simpler process than RFLP analysis because the DNA of interest has already been amplified many times over the rest and for all practical purposes is the only DNA present. Amplified STRs have now become the system of choice for forensic DNA testing. The procedures for all three detection systems discussed are similar. The PCR product is either loaded into a gel, similar to that used for RFLP, but made out of a different substance called **polyacrylamide**, or introduced into a capillary column containing a liquid form of the same substance. This gel material is more appropriate for analyzing the smaller size PCR products than the agarose used for RFLP. In the manual method, the gel is run in a similar fashion to that described previously, and the PCR fragments are separated by length (Plate 8). The bands can be stained directly; and because no extraneous DNA is present, the secondary detection method of probing and hybridization used in RFLP is no longer needed to detect the amplified fragments. A silver stain is used to visualize the separated DNA bands (see Sidebar 6) and the gel is then dried to be kept as a permanent record.

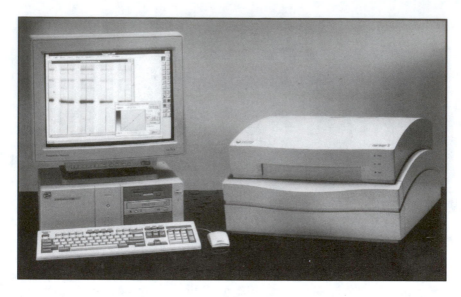

Figure 6.16 The Molecular Dynamics FluorImager®. In forensic science, this instrument is used for fluorescent detection of length polymorphisms such as STRs. It detects fragments in a static mode after the gel run has been completed. (Courtesy of Molecular Dynamics.)

The pattern of bands obtained by this method is visually compared between samples, as well as to an allelic ladder consisting of examples of most or all alleles known to exist at each locus. Just as in RFLP analysis, each locus will produce one or two bands representing the alleles present. STRs, in particular, show a higher incidence of homozygotes (one-banded patterns) because the system is less polymorphic. If several loci are amplified in the same tube, they are consequently run in the same lane. A lane containing the products from three loci may contain from three to six bands, depending on whether the person is homozygous (one band) or heterozygous (two bands) at each locus. This assumes that the original sample came from only one person; otherwise, more bands are possible. Each locus has its own allelic ladder for comparison, and a multiplex system intended for manual analysis is ideally constructed so that the alleles from each locus do not overlap. The gender locus, having only two possible alleles (one male and one female), is often appended to an STR multiplex system.

STRs are now most commonly analyzed using fluorescent detection and automated analysis. Several variations on this theme may be encountered. In the first method, the acrylamide gel is run as for manual analysis, but the gel is read by a computerized laser detection system (Figure 6.16; Plate 10a) instead of directly by eye. The information is stored in the computer, and a printout can also be obtained. The results (Figure 6.17) look similar to the pattern obtained using silver staining. In the second system, a laser beam detects the fluorescent bands as they are running through the gel (Figure 6.18; Plate 10b) or capillary column (Figure 6.19; Plate 11). Data is stored and analyzed in much the same way. The results, called electropherograms, are usually presented as a series of peaks (Figure 6.20; Plates 12, 13, and 14). Both systems are currently in use and each has gained a large population of advocates. All of these automated systems rely on a fluorescent tag that is incorporated into the PCR product during amplification. Plate 9 shows the relationship of the bands obtained using the gel systems to the peaks obtained from electronic detection systems.

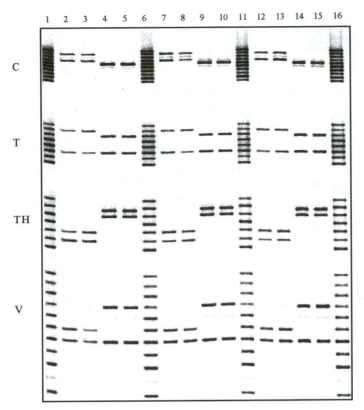

Figure 6.17 STRs and amelogenin typed using a static detection system. An STR quadraplex (CSF1PO, TPOX, THO1, and vWA) detected using a Hitachi FMBIO® 100 fluorescent scanner. One PCR primer of each pair was labeled with a fluorescent primer. The gel was run on a bench apparatus, dried, and then imaged using a computer detection system. The allelic ladders are located in lanes 1, 6, 11, and 16. The samples in lanes 2, 3, 7, 8, 12, and 13 are all from one individual. The samples in lanes 4, 5, 9, 10, 14, and 15 are all from another individual.

Figure 6.18 The ABI PRISM® 377 DNA Sequencer. In forensic science, this instrument is used for the automated analysis of length polymorphisms, primarily STRs, and for mtDNA sequence analysis. A polyacrylamide slab gel is used to separate fluorescently labeled fragments that are detected with a laser as they run past a predetermined point. The computer software then assists with data analysis and allelic typing. (Courtesy of Perkin-Elmer/Applied Biosystems Division.)

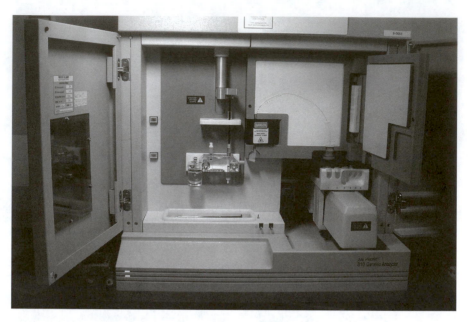

Figure 6.19 ABI PRISM® 310 Genetic Analyzer. In forensic science, this instrument is used for the automated analysis of length polymorphisms, primarily STRs, and for mitochondrial DNA sequence analysis. A capillary column filled with liquid acrylamide polymer is used to separate fluorescently labeled fragments that are detected with a laser as they run past a predetermined point. The computer software then assists with data analysis and allelic typing. (Courtesy of Serological Research Institute.)

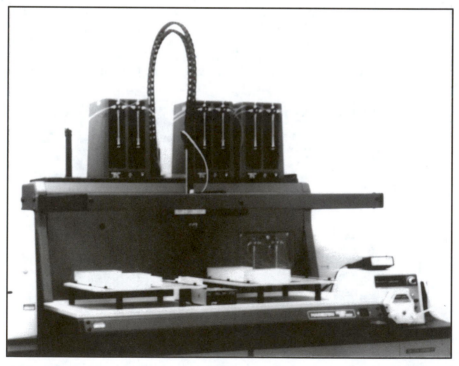

Figure 6.20 The extraction robot. In forensic science, this instrument is used in the automated extraction of DNA from database samples.

One major advantage of fluorescent detection is that only one of the two denatured strands from each DNA duplex is visualized. Because the resolution power of the gel system is so high, each strand of complementary DNA may run slightly differently because of its complementary nucleotide sequences. For fluorescent detection, only the primer complementary to one strand is tagged, thus eliminating any confusion resulting from reading doublets at each allele. Additionally, the use of multiple colored fluorescent tags allows the combination of STR loci in which the lengths of some alleles overlap. These systems can be run in the same gel lane and still be clearly distinguished by color. In the case of automated detection, special sizing standards of yet a different color are run in the same lane as each sample. In-lane sizing standards mean that the computer will calculate the size of a particular band against a ruler that has been subjected to exactly the same electrophoretic micro-environment as the sample, rendering extremely precise results. Sample bands are still compared to an allelic ladder generated for each locus for the purpose of calling a type.

Although D1S80 analysis is still used by some laboratories, it has largely been supplanted by powerful STR multiplexes, in which 8 to 15 loci, in addition to the gender identification locus, are amplified simultaneously in the same tube. Because local, state, and national databases have been standardized on STRs, this technology is likely to remain prevalent for some time.

VI. Automated Analysis Systems

The word "robot" was invented in 1920 by the Czech playwright Karel Capek to describe the slave-type creatures in his play *R.U.R.* Since that time, the word has come to be applied to any manufactured device, usually envisaged as humanoid in shape (although it does not have to be) and made of metal (although again, it does not have to be), that is capable of doing work ordinarily done by human beings. The word "robotics" was coined by Isaac Azimov in his book *I Robot*, a book that inspired the first invention of a working robot by George C. Devol, Jr., in 1954.

Automation of DNA typing is a goal for those laboratories that desire a greater throughput of case material, or that have large numbers of samples that require the same repetitive handling procedures. Instruments exist that can perform many of these tasks, and efforts have successfully used the capabilities of various kinds of instrumental robots.

The typing process can be understood as a series of independent steps. These steps may include extraction of DNA, digestion with a restriction enzyme, electrophoresis, PCR setup and amplification, detection, and typing. Each has different requirements for handling, setup, and quality control. Examples of automation include automated detection of bands during electrophoresis using fluorescence technology (Figures 6.16, 6.18, and 6.19), extraction, restriction digestion, and amplification of DNA (Figure 6.20), and determination of band sizes and genotypes using computer-assisted imaging techniques. The thermal cycler itself is an automated system for controlling the time and temperature cycles necessary for PCR amplification of DNA.

Technologies currently under development in other areas of molecular biology include DNA-on-a-chip (similar to computer chips, with hundreds of DNA sequences on a small wafer); small-scale PCR, in which microscopic drops of DNA are amplified and typed in minutes rather than hours; sequencing by hybridization, a variation of the DNA on a chip

Sidebar 6

A Case of Victim's Evidence (or, one bled and the other pled)

The year was 1995, the location an otherwise nondescript furniture moving company in Palm Beach County, Florida. That morning, the owner of the establishment noticed that one of his usually punctual employees failed to arrive for work at the usual hour. The owner contacted the man's sister, and when she offered no explanation for her brother's absence, immediately reported his absence to the authorities. A police search was initiated, and a few days later the mystery was solved in a most unfortunate way. The employee's body was found stuffed into the trunk of a van that had been abandoned in a local hotel parking lot. As soon as foul play was suspected, an investigation was launched to uncover a suspect. Almost concurrently with the discovery of the body, a suspect was uncovered. As is common in brutal murders, the assailant was an acquaintance of the victim; in this case, he had apparently already threatened the deceased regarding an overdue loan.

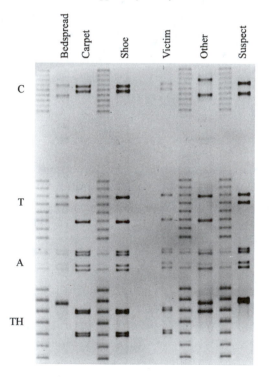

(Courtesy of Palm Beach County Sheriff's Office Crime Laboratory.)

A search of the suspect's apartment revealed bloodstains on his bedspread, carpet, and a tennis shoe. The evidence was collected for DNA analysis, and blood samples were also obtained from the suspect and his roommate for comparison. The reference samples from the victim, suspect, and the suspect's roommate, as well as the bloodstains found in the apartment, were analyzed in ten PCR-based marker systems. Specifically, they included the polymarker loci (LDLR, GYPA, HBGG, D7S8, GC) along with DQA1, and an STR triplex (CSF1PO, TPOX, THO1) along with the gender identification locus, amelogenin (see Chapters 5 and 6). The evidentiary stains from the carpet and the tennis shoe produced clear DNA profiles that were the same. They were also indistinguishable from that of the victim. Both the suspect and the roommate were excluded from having contributed those bloodstains. No evidence was found, either physical or otherwise, to link the roommate to the crime. The suspect pled guilty to first degree murder.

technology; and automated differential extractions, in which the separation of sperm from non-sperm cells in rape cases is accomplished with little human manipulation.

A. Automated DNA Extraction and Amplification

Perhaps the most useful applications of robotic handling in the forensic DNA laboratory are the extraction of DNA from liquid and dried blood samples, and the subsequent preparation of the DNA for further analysis. The following describes a typical robotic setup that performs these functions.

1. Liquid Blood Transfer

Bar codes are placed onto the blood tubes, speeding the process of entering samples into the computer that controls the robot. The liquid blood-handling robot has a single probe head that uses disposable tips to aliquot blood samples. The robot processes 88 samples together on a metal rack and, depending on the program used, will also prepare bloodstains for long-term storage of each sample. The robot places an aliquot of the liquid blood into a specific location on a 96-well plate, and then places another aliquot of blood onto a stain card. Blanks, quality control samples, and quantitation standards are also placed onto the plate to fill the remaining wells. Once all bloods have been sampled and stains prepared, the stains are allowed to dry, and the 96-well plate is sent to the next step in the DNA extraction process.

2. DNA Extraction

A robot with a multi-probe head (MPH) is used for DNA extraction. The robot extracts DNA from liquid blood samples using an adsorption technique. The liquid blood in each well is passed through a column containing a DNA-adsorbing material. After non-DNA material is washed away, the DNA is eluted from the column using a combination of heat and chemicals. Depending on the program used, the robot can process two or four 96-well plates in approximately 4.5 hours.

3. Quantitation

The extracted DNA is now quantitated. An aliquot of each DNA sample is transferred from each extracted DNA plate to a special plate and diluted. Picogreen is then added to each sample. Picogreen is a dye that intercalates into the DNA double helix, and allows the concentration of DNA to be measured using a spectrofluorometer. The data for each sample is stored in a computer that calculates the concentration of each sample based on the quantitation standards present on each plate.

   The computer uses the quantitation data for each plate to make PCR daughter plates normalized to a specific volume and concentration of DNA. The robot makes two PCR daughter plates for each extracted DNA plate. The first plate is archived (for amplification at a later time), and the second PCR plate is used for amplification.

4. Amplification

The amplification robot uses a multi-probe head (MPH). First, the robot creates a dilution plate from the PCR plate and then adds each sample to an optical plate along with a PCR "master mix." The automated system then prepares quarter-volume reactions for each sample. The plate is then placed into a thermal cycler designed to accommodate the 96-

well plate. The amplified samples can then be run on any instrument or gel designed for such a purpose, as previously outlined in this chapter.

5.   *Robot Issues*

Although many more samples are analyzed by this process than could be accomplished using manual methods, it is not hands-free. As with all mechanical devices and computers, errors can occur during the processing of samples. The following quality control steps are examples of measures taken to ensure the integrity of the samples and their analysis.

a. Well-to-well carryover.   When handling many samples in close proximity to each other, contamination can occur. The laboratory performs validation studies that detect sample spillover from one well to the next. The robot protocol is designed to minimize potential contamination. It also specifies where to place reagent blanks to detect contamination if it occurs.

b. Bar code reader.   The bar code reader has a small error rate when scanning numbers. To address this challenge, a witness is assigned the task of checking the number that appears on-screen as bar codes are entered. As the robot operator scans the bar code of each blood tube into the computer, she will read aloud the bar code number from the blood tube. The witness looks at the screen to confirm correct entry of the bar code number. The witness also checks that the position of the blood tube on the rack corresponds to the position on the computer screen.

c. Transfer errors.   Problems occasionally occur in the transfer of a sample from one step of the process to another. These include clots in the blood, low blood volume in the tube, or bubbles in the blood. Typically, an alarm sounds when the robot encounters one of these problems, indicating that human intervention is required.

B.   Summary of Automated Procedures

The trend toward automation carries a danger. As robots and computers take over the mundane tasks of DNA typing, it is tempting to allow the reproducibility of the non-human aspect to usurp the importance of trained judgment in the evaluation of results and rendering of opinions. Regardless of the evermore technical evolution of the field, there will always be the need for a person to sit in front of a jury and say in plain English what was done and what the results mean in that particular case.

Sidebar 7

Minisatellite Variable Repeat Analysis (MVR)

In 1990, yet another tool for the analysis of polymorphisms in DNA was unveiled by Alec Jeffreys (who developed the original RFLP typing system). This system combines the advantages afforded by PCR amplification of sequence-variant alleles with the detection of discrete lengths of DNA. Each locus is a VNTR (variable number tandem repeat), consisting of hundreds of tandem repeats; however, the primary polymorphism lies in the sequence of each repeat. The first locus to be developed, D1S8 (MS32) was first analyzed by RFLP. Within the 19-bp sequence of each repeat, one base pair in particular shows hypervariability. As it so happens, this results in the presence or absence of a *Hae*III restriction enzyme cut site. Because each of the hundreds of repeats may show either variant, the sequence of which is completely independent of that on the homologous chromosome, the number of possible alleles in the population is huge. It is in fact much higher than any other single-locus system. Additionally, the information so far suggests that the alleles are relatively evenly distributed in the population.

Analysis of the D1S8 variation was easily transferred to PCR technology by designing primers specific to the two alternate sequence variants. A third primer, the same for each pair, is designed to bind just outside the repeat region in invariant flanking DNA. The presence of a specific sequence in any particular repeat is then evidenced as fragments of DNA corresponding to the length between the flanking primer and the location of the repeat within the array. In the PCR reaction, the repeat sequence-spe-

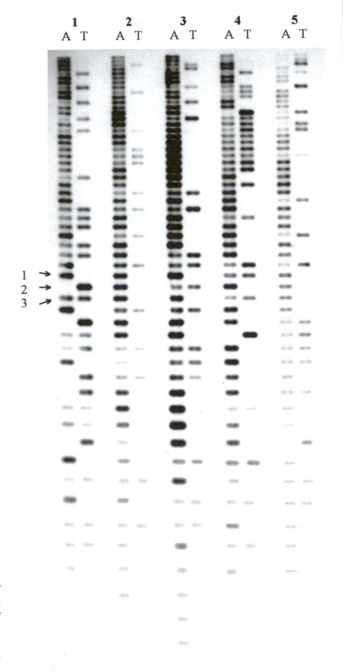

An MVR autorad. Each pair of lanes represents one individual and is read together as a type. The five samples on this gel each show a different MVR type.

cific primers will bind to all of their complementary repeat units; thus, their locations will be represented as an array of sequentially sized PCR product fragments. The fragments are separated by electrophoresis on an agarose gel and detected by Southern blotting and hybridization to chemiluminescent probes. An important point is that the reaction for each of the two sequence-specific primers is carried out in a separate tube, and they are loaded in adjacent lanes. Some work has also been done toward labeling the variant primers with different colored fluorescent tags, and using an automated laser detection system, thus negating the need for separate reactions and gel lanes.

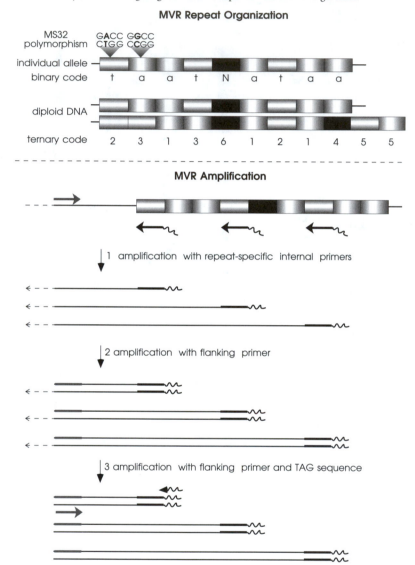

MVR analysis — amplification. In the first round of PCR (step 1), sequence-specific primers, which are present in low concentration, bind to a small number of repeats per molecule. In the second round of PCR (step 2), these molecules are truncated by amplification from the invariant flanking primer, producing a representative set of fragments. In subsequent rounds (step 3), the existing set of PCR-defined fragments is amplified equally, and to a large degree, using high concentrations of the invariant flanking primer, along with a fourth primer that binds to a non-repeat-specific TAG introduced on the end of each sequence-specific primer.

The allele on each chromosome is read as a binary code marking the repeats in sequence as to the presence or absence of one of the two designated primer binding sites. Occasionally, neither primer binds, giving a null allele. Null alleles are also produced at the 5′ end of the gene, where one allele typically runs out of repeats before the other. In a diploid genome, such as in humans, the full code is a compilation of the binary code read for each chromosome, resulting in a ternary code with six possible variations labeled 1 through 6. The system stands to become even more powerful as more

MVR-type loci are developed. Because the results produce a digital code, MVR analysis is a natural for computerized detection, analysis, storage, and comparison. Additionally, this confers immunity to electrophoretic distortions such as band shifts and negates any requirement for gel system standardization. Because the alleles are discrete sequence polymorphisms, they can be determined precisely, eliminating any imprecision associated with band sizing. MVR has been grossly underutilized in forensic analysis, in part because it was introduced relatively late in the decision-making process of choosing standard systems, and also because although scientifically elegant, it is intellectually challenging.

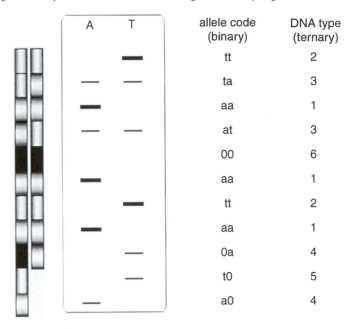

allele code (binary)	DNA type (ternary)
tt	2
ta	3
aa	1
at	3
00	6
aa	1
tt	2
aa	1
0a	4
t0	5
a0	4

MVR detection and analysis. At each repeat position, six different states are possible: (1) two As, (2) two Ts, (3) one A and one T, (4) one A and one null, (5) one T and one null, and (6) two nulls. Two of the same repeat variants are seen as a double-intensity band.

References

Hopkins, B., Williams, N.J., Webb, M.B., Debenham, P.G., and Jeffreys, A. J., The use of minisatellite variant repeat-polymerase chain reaction (MVR-PCR) to determine the source of saliva on a used postage stamp, *J. Forensic Sci.*, 39(2), 526–331, 1994.

Jeffreys, A.J., MacLeod, A., Tamaki, K., Neil, D.L., and Monckton, D.G., Minisatellite repeat coding as a digital approach to DNA typing, *Nature*, 354(6350), 204–209, 1991.

Jeffreys, A.J., Monckton, D.G., Tamaki, K., Neil, D.L., Armour, J.A., MacLeod, A., Collick, A., Allen, M., and Jobling, M., Minisatellite variant repeat mapping: application to DNA typing and mutation analysis, *Exs*, 67, 125–139, 1993.

Monckton, D.G., Tamaki, K., MacLeod, A., Neil, D.L., and Jeffreys, A.J., Allele-specific MVR-PCR analysis at minisatellite D1S8, *Human Molec. Genet.*, 2(5), 513–519, 1993.

Neil, D.L. and Jeffreys, A.J., Digital DNA typing at a second hypervariable locus by minisatellite variant repeat mapping, *Human Molec. Genet.*, 2(8), 1129–1135, 1993.

Tamaki, K., Huang, X.L., Yamamoto, T., Uchihi, R., Nozawa, H., and Katsumata, Y., Applications of minisatellite variant repeat (MVR) mapping for maternal identification from remains of an infant and placenta, *J. Forensic Sci.*, 40(4), 695–700, 1995.

Tamaki, K., Monckton, D.G., MacLeod, A., Allen, M., and Jeffreys, A.J., Four-state MVR-PCR: increased discrimination of digital DNA typing by simultaneous analysis of two polymorphic sites within minisatellite variant repeats at D1S8, *Human Molec. Genet.*, 2(10), 1629–1632, 1993.

Yamamoto, T., Tamaki, K., Kojima, T., Uchihi, R., Katsumata, Y., and Jeffrey, A.J., DNA typing of the D1S8 (MS32) locus by rapid detection minisatellite variant repeat (MVR) mapping using polymerase chain reaction (PCR) assay, *Forensic Sci. Int.*, 66(1), 69–75, 1994 .

Yamamoto, T., Tamaki, K., Kojima, T., Uchihi, R., and Katsumata Y., Potential forensic applications of minisatellite variant repeat (MVR) mapping using the polymerase chain reaction (PCR) at D1S8, *J. Forensic Sci.*, 39(3), 743–750, 1994.

Further References

Akane, A., Seki, S., Shiono, H., Nakamura, H., Hasegawa, M., Kagawa, M., Matsubara, K., Nakahori, Y., Nagafuchi, S., and Nakagome, Y., Sex determination of forensic samples by dual PCR amplification of an X-Y homologous gene, *Forensic Sci. Int.*, 52(2), 143–148, 1992.

Applied Biosystems AmpFLSTR® COfiler™ PCR Amplification Kit User's Manual.

Applied Biosystems AmpFLSTR® Profiler Plus™ PCR Amplification Kit User's Manual.

Asimov, I., *Asimov's Chronology of Science and Discovery*, Harper Collins, 1994.

Budowle, B., Baechtel F.S., Comey, C.T., Giusti, A.M., and Klevan, L., Simple protocols for typing forensic biological evidence: chemiluminescent detection for human DNA quantitation and restriction fragment length polymorphism (RFLP) analyses and manual typing of polymerase chain reaction (PCR) amplified polymorphisms, *Electrophoresis*, 16(9), 1559–1567, 1995.

Budowle, B. et al., Analysis of the VNTR locus (D1S80) by the PCR followed by high-resolution PAGE, *Am. J. Human Genet.*, 48, 137–144, 1991.

Budowle, B., Waye, J.S., Shutler, G.G., and Baechtel, F.S., *Hae* III — a suitable restriction endonuclease for restriction fragment length polymorphism analysis of biological evidence samples, *J. Forensic Sci.*, 35(3), 530–536, 1990.

Caskey, C.T. and Hammond, H., DNA-based identification: disease and criminals, in *DNA Technology and Forensic Science*, J. Ballantyne, G. Sensabaugh, and J. Witkoski, Eds., Cold Spring Harbor Laboratory Press, Cold Spring Harbor, NY, 1989.

Cetus Corporation, AmpliType User Guide for the HLA DQα Forensic DNA Amplification and Typing Kit, 1990, Section — Interpretation, Cetus Corporation, Emeryville, CA.

Edwards, A., Hammond, H.A., Jin, L., Caskey, C.T., and Chakraborty, R., Genetic variation at five trimeric and tetrameric tandem repeat loci in four human population groups, *Genomics*, 12(2), 241–453, 1992.

Erlich, H.A., Ed., *PCR Technology: Principles and Applications for DNA Amplification*, Stockton Press, New York, 1989.

Erlich, H.A., Gelfland, D., and Sninsky, J.J., Recent advances in the polymerase chain reaction, *Science*, 252, 643–651, 1991.

Erlich, H.A., HLA DQ alpha typing of forensic specimens, *Forensic Sci. Int.*, 53(2), 227–228, 1992.

Fisher, D.L., Holland, M.M., Mitchell, L., Sledzik, P.S., Wilcox, A.W., Wadhams, M., and Weedn, V.W., Extraction, evaluation, and amplification of DNA from decalcified and undecalcified United States Civil War bone, *J. Forensic Sci.*, 38(1), 60–68, 1993.

Fregeau, C.J. and Fourney, R.M., DNA typing with fluorescently tagged short tandem repeats: a sensitive and accurate approach to human identification, *Biotechniques*, 15(1), 100–119, 1993.

Ginther, C., Issel-Tarver, L., and King, M.C., Identifying individuals by sequencing mitochondrial DNA from teeth, *Nature Genetics*, 2(2), 135–138, 1992.

Gusmao, L., Gonzalez-Neira, A., Pestoni, C., Brion, M., Lareu, M.V., and Carracedo, A., Robustness of the Y STRs DYS19, DYS389 I and II, DYS390 and DYS393: optimization of a PCR pentaplex, *Forensic Sci. Int.*, 106(3), 163–172, 1999.

Kasai, K., Nakamura, Y., and White, R., Amplification of a variable number of tandem repeats (VNTR) Locus (pMCT118) by the polymerase chain reaction (PCR) and its application to forensic science, *J. Forensic Sci.*, 35, 1196–1200, 1990.

Kawasaki, E., Saiki, R., and Erlich, H., Genetic analysis using polymerase chain reaction-amplified DNA and immobilized oligonucleotide probes: reverse dot-blot typing, *Meth. Enzymol.*, 218, 369–381, 1993.

Klevan, L., Horton, L., Carlson, D.P., and Eisenberg, A.J., Chemiluminescent detection of DNA probes in forensic analysis, *Electrophoresis*, 16(9), 1553–1558, 1995.

Mullis, K.B. and Faloona F., Specific synthesis of DNA *in vitro* via a polymerase catalyzed chain reaction, *Meth. Enzymol.*, 155, 335–350, 1987.

Mullis, K.B., Faloona, F., Scharf, S.J., Saiki, R.K., Horn, G.T., and Erlich, H.A., Specific enzymatic amplification of DNA *in vitro*: the polymerase chain reaction, *Cold Spring Harbor Symp. Quant. Biol.*, 51, 263–273, 1986.

Naito, E., Dewa, K., and Yamanouchi, H., Kominami, R., Sex typing of forensic DNA samples using male- and female-specific probes, *J. Forensic Sci.*, 39(4), 1009–1017, 1994.

Perkin-Elmer AmpliType™ User Guide, Version 2, 1990.

QiaAmp™ minikit and QiaAmp DNA blood minikit, Qiagen, 1999.

Reynolds, R., Walker, K., Varlaro, J., Allen, M., Clark, E., Alavaren, M., and Erlich, H., Detection of sequence variation in the HVII region of the human mitochondrial genome in 689 individuals using immobilized sequence-specific oligonucleotide probes, *J. Forensic Sci.*, 45(6), 1210–1231, 2000.

Robertson, J.M., Sgueglia, J.B., Badger, C.A., Juston, A.C., and Ballantyne, J., Forensic applications of a rapid, sensitive, and precise multiplex analysis of the four short tandem repeat loci HUMVWF31/A, HUMTH01, HUMF13A1, and HUMFES/FPS, *Electrophoresis*, 16(9), 1568–1576, 1995.

Sanger, F.S., Nilken, S., and Coulson, A.R., DNA Sequencing with chain-terminating inhibitors, *Proc. Nat. Acad. Sci. U.S.A.*, 74, 5463–5467, 1977.

Scherczinger, C.A., Bourke, M.T., Ladd, C., and Lee, H.C., DNA extraction from liquid blood using QIAamp, *J. Forensic Sci.*, 42(5), 893–896, 1997.

Sinclair, K. and McKechnie, V.M., DNA extraction from stamps and envelope flaps using QIAamp and QIAshredder, *J. Forensic Sci.*, 45(1), 229–230, 2000.

Southern, E.M., Detection of specific sequences among DNA fragments separated by gel electrophoresis, *J. Molec. Biol.*, 98, 503–527, 1975.

Walsh, D.J., Corey, A.C., Cotton, R.W., Forman, L., Herrin, G.L., Jr., Word, C.J., and Garner, D.D., Isolation of deoxyribonucleic acid (DNA) from saliva and forensic science samples containing saliva, *J. Forensic Sci.*, 37(2), 387–395, 1992.

Walsh, P.S., Metzger, D.A., and Higuchi, R., Chelex 100 as a medium for simple extraction of DNA for PCR-based typing from forensic material, *Biotechniques*, 10(4), 506–513, 1991.

Waye, J.S., Michaud, D., Bowen, J.H., and Fourney, R.M., Sensitive and specific quantification of human genomic deoxyribonucleic acid (DNA) in forensic science specimens: casework examples, *J. Forensic Sci.*, 36(4), 1198–1203, 1991.

Interpretation of DNA Typing Results

7

 In this chapter, we address many of the sample-specific and system-specific issues that must be considered when drawing an inference of common source based on DNA testing. The material discussed in this chapter is most definitely aimed at the intermediate user. We originally included it in response to requests from our readers and because interpreting the results from a scientific test is the most crucial part of a criminalist's job. We have continued to expand the discussion in this iteration, although the line between an introductory and advanced volume begins to blur. This is a natural consequence of a rapidly advancing technology and an increasingly sophisticated audience. A review of Chapters 4, 5, and 6 may be helpful to the novice reader.

I. Complicating Factors

Several factors can influence the straightforward interpretation of any DNA typing result. These are enumerated below, along with a brief explanation of their potential effects on evaluating the meaning of the evidence. Specific interpretational issues related to each system are then discussed in detail.

A. Multiple Contributors

When more than one human individual has contributed biological material to an evidentiary sample, multiple DNA profiles may be detected. Depending on the particular sample and how it was analyzed, it may or may not be possible to resolve the contributors to the mixture. Factors contributing to the ability to resolve a mixture include whether the sample contains sperm, how many contributors are present, the relative contributions of the donors, and which system is used to analyze the evidence. Each case is different and must be approached with thought and intelligence from the very start, beginning with sample collection.

Mixtures can be classified as sperm-containing or non-sperm-containing. The reason for this is that potentially sperm-containing samples are processed in a special way so as to attempt to physically separate the sperm from the rest of the sample, hence simplifying the mixture before the DNA is analyzed. This process is called a differential extraction and the procedure is discussed in detail in Chapter 6, Plate 4, and below. In samples where it is not possible to separate the contributors before DNA analysis, the interpretation is more complex. We also discuss different approaches to interpreting non-sexual-assault evidence.

1. Sexual Assault Evidence

A special case exists when multiple donors are individually represented by **sperm cells** and **non-sperm cells**. Typically, non-sperm cells in sexual assault evidence originate from the vaginal epithelium of a female victim, so this material has historically been termed the **epithelial cell** (**e. cell**) fraction or the female fraction. However, these non-sperm cells could also originate from the urethral lining or external genital surfaces of a male, either the perpetrator or a victim; they could also be white blood cells present in all body fluids. Because the differential extraction procedure is designed to separate sperm cells from everything else, it is operationally more correct to refer to everything other than a sperm cell as a non-sperm cell. Additionally, this distinction helps avoid misinterpretation of evidentiary results arising from assumptions about who might have contributed to the **sperm fraction** or **non-sperm fraction** resulting from a differential extraction.

Sperm-containing sexual assault evidence may come in the form of a swab from an orifice, for example, vaginal, oral, or rectal, from a "site of accumulation" such as panty crotches or bed sheets, or from just about any other surface, including the bodies of the perpetrator or victim. If the differential extraction procedure is completely successful, and only two individuals have contributed to the sample, the sperm and non-sperm fraction can usually be interpreted as single source samples and mixture interpretation is avoided. However, separation is not always entirely successful, and some non-sperm DNA may leak into the sperm fraction or some sperm DNA may end up in the non-sperm fraction. (Figure 7.1) This leads to patterns with more than two alleles per locus. Frequently, however, the carry-over results in only a minor contribution representing the other contributor, and the major profile can still be called essentially as a single source. This is especially true because the victim's profile is usually known and can be used to determine which carry-over alleles originate from her. Even in situations where the differential extraction is unsuccessful, such as when the sample contains very few sperm in relation to other types of cells, the victim's known profile may be subtracted from the mixture, allowing the determination of a "sperm donor profile" from the alleles foreign to her.

Y-STRs (see Chapters 5 and 6) are also proving to be useful in resolving sexual assault mixtures that for one reason or another have been recalcitrant to standard autosomal analysis (see Figure 5.14 and Sidebar 10). Because Y-STRs only detect male DNA, they can sometimes detect a male profile where an autosomal analysis detects only a female profile. In the case of multiple male contributors, the use of Y-STRs can also assist by at least excluding the detection of any female contributors.

A critical step in the examination of sexual assault evidence is thorough documentation of the sample and its analysis. This includes a gross visual examination of the evidence as well as a microscopic examination of any cellular material recovered. This assists in choosing a useful analytical scheme, in making decisions during the testing process, and in interpreting the results.

2. Non-sexual Assault Mixtures

Mixtures of body fluids that do not contain semen as one of the components pose additional interpretational challenges. This is because no way exists to physically separate any

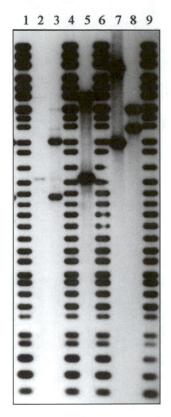

Figure 7.1 An RFLP autorad from a sexual assault case. Lanes 1, 4, 6, and 9 contain molecular ladders. Lane 2 contains the non-sperm fraction, and lane 3 contains the sperm cell fraction from the sexual assault sample. Lane 5 contains the victim's reference blood sample, lane 7 contains the suspect's blood sample, and lane 8 contains a sample from the boyfriend. As expected, the non-sperm fraction contains the same two bands as the victim's reference. Note the evidence of carryover from the non-sperm fraction into the sperm fraction, particularly for the bottom band. Also evident in the sperm fraction are bands in the same place as those in the boyfriend's sample. The suspect is excluded from having contributed to the sexual assault sample.

of the components. A typical situation resulting in a difficult mixture might be a crime scene where multiple people are bleeding. This could include any combination of victims and assailants. Because each person contributing biological material will donate, on average, two alleles per locus to the sample, multiple alleles (be they bands, dots, or peaks) may be detected.

Using current STR megaplex systems, it is usually obvious that a mixture is present; it may be less obvious how many individuals contributed or which alleles belong to which contributors. Ironically, RFLP analysis, despite its other shortcomings, remains the standard for resolving mixtures. This is because so many alleles exist in the population at each locus that individuals rarely share alleles. Therefore, all or most of the alleles in a mixture are actually detected; rarely are overlapping or hidden alleles a problem. In the early PCR-based systems (specifically, AmpliType® PM+DQA1), the loci exhibited so few variations in the population (for the polymarker loci, only two or three), that unless one contributor was obviously present as a major component, resolution of individual profiles was fre-

Sidebar 8

The Simpson Saga
The Blood in the Bronco

On June 12, 1994, Nicole Brown (NB) and Ronald Goldman (RG) were brutally murdered. O.J. Simpson (OS) was charged with the commission of the crime, and among the evidentiary items confiscated was his white Ford Bronco. A bloody smear on the passenger side of the center console was initially noted and sampled on June 14, 1994. At least three relevant forensic questions can be asked about this evidence.

1. How was the stain deposited?
2. When was the stain deposited?
3. Who may have contributed to this stain?

   For the purposes of this exercise we will not attempt to address how and when the stain was deposited. We will concentrate on what the evidence can tell us about who contributed to the stain.

   DNA testing was used to investigate the source(s) of the stain. Both DQα and D1S80 tests were performed on the two evidence samples collected in June 1994. From the results, it was concluded that one stain included Simpson as a donor, while excluding NB and RG. The other showed a mixture consistent with OS and RG. A larger sample was collected on September 1, 1994. It should be noted that in the intervening time period, the Bronco was burglarized. Although the items taken were themselves of no evidentiary value, the integrity of the bloodstain evidence could no longer be guaranteed. Three separate swatches were collected that more nearly covered the large area of the smear. These samples were also analyzed for DQα and D1S80. Let's examine the data from two of these swatches in detail.

EVIDENCE 1	1●	2	3	4●	C●	1.1●	1.2 1.3● 4	1.3	All but 1.3 ●	AMPLITY DQ-Alph
substrate control	1	2	3	4	C	1.1	1.2 1.3 4	1.3	All but 1.3	AMPLITY DQ-Alph
EVIDENCE 2	1●	2	3	4●	C●	1.1●	1.2 1.3● 4	1.3	All but 1.3 ●	AMPLITY DQ-Alph
substrate control	1	2	3	4	C	1.1	1.2 1.3 4	1.3	All but 1.3	AMPLITYF DQ-Alph

Above is a set of DQα strips showing the results from two of the later samplings, along with their substrate samples. (A substrate sample is collected from an apparently clean area near an evidentiary stain. It is a way of assessing which, if any, genetic types might be present in the background.) One of the ways an analyst avoids even an unconscious bias is to analyze the evidence before comparing it with the reference samples. In this case, both evidence strips show the same pattern of dots, and even the intensities are similar. In both samples, all the dots, with the exception of 2 and 3, are positive, so we can safely eliminate anyone with a 2 or 3 allele from having contributed to this sample. The next step is to note that more than two alleles are manifest. Because any normal individual has, at most, two alleles at any one genetic locus, this is a clear indication of multiple contributors.

From an examination of the nominal dots to the left of "C," we note the presence a 4 allele and a 1 allele. The 1.1 and 1.3 dots are both positive and, although the 1.3 dot is substantially lighter, both are stronger than the "C" dot. The 1.1 and 1.3 subtype, at least, are represented. Is the 1.2 allele also present? Consider the more difficult "trio" and "all but 1.3" dots, both of which are positive and greater than "C." The "trio" dot may be positive due to the presence of the 1.2 allele, the 1.3 allele or the 4 allele individually, or any combination of them. Because we can confirm the presence of both the 4 allele and the 1.3 allele, the "trio" would be positive regardless of the presence of a 1.2 allele, and thus cannot be used to determine its presence. This consequently makes the "all but 1.3" dot useless in determining, along with the "trio," the presence of a 1.2 allele. In short, from the pattern of dots on these strips, it is impossible to tell if a 1.2 allele is present in the sample or not.

At this point in the interpretation, the analyst would normally draw up a chart of alleles excluded (2, 3), those positively present (1.1, 1.3, 4), and those about which there is insufficient information to determine presence or absence (1.2). He would also list possible pairwise associations of the alleles into genotypes of the possible contributors (we will spare you this exercise). Enumeration of the types in the DQα system depends in part on compound dots that together determine a type. Because of this, the analysis of mixtures becomes a bit complex. In addition, a mixture of bloodstains is often more difficult to interpret than a sexual assault mixture, in which at least one of the contributing types (the victim's) is often known.

Now let's take a look at the DQα types of the three principals in this crime. OS is a 1.1,1.2, NB a 1.1,1.1, and RG a 1.3,4. Because none of them possess a 2 or 3 allele, none are excluded on that basis from having contributed to the samples.

Both of these samples were also analyzed using the D1S80 system. The advantage of D1S80 is that the interpretation of alleles present is straightforward — there are no hidden alleles. The disadvantage is that two D1S80 alleles, 18 and 24, are quite common in the population. The D1S80 results from both console swatches showed bands at 18, 24, and 25. (One of them is shown below as CS). This is, again, clearly indicative of a mixture. Can genotypes be assigned? It depends on what can be assumed. If it can be assumed that there are only two donors, then clearly the 24 and 25 alleles are present as a genotype based on the similar intensities of the bands as compared to the 18 band. If two or more donors are assumed, then the alleles cannot be paired into genotypes with confidence. No information is gleaned from either the DQα or D1S80 results that supports one assumption over the other.

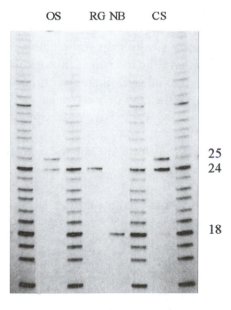

The final interpretation might be summarized as follows:

1. More than one individual contributed to the blood samples collected from the console of the Bronco.
2. All individuals carrying the 2 and 3 DQα alleles are eliminated as contributors to the detected DNA. All others are included as possible donors.
3. Individuals included in the evaluation in Step 2 are eliminated if they do not have some combination of the D1S80 18, 24, or 25 alleles. The remainder are included as possible donors.

The genotypes of the three reference samples each contain some combination of the DQα 1.1, 1.2, 1.3, or 4 alleles. Each also contains at least one of D1S80 18, 24, or 25 alleles. Thus, none of the three principles are eliminated as possible contributors to this sample.

Another way of evaluating the results would be to examine combinations of types from the reference samples to see if any combination could produce the pattern seen in the evidence stain. The Bronco console stain(s) cannot be just a mix of NB and OS; they both lack the DQα 1.3 and 4 alleles. All other combinations are possible (NB/RG; OS/RG; NB/OS/RG). Similarly, the stain(s) cannot be a mix of only OS and RG; neither carry the D1S80 18 allele. The stain(s) also cannot be a mix of only NB and RG; neither has the D1S80 25 allele. Other combinations cannot be eliminated (NB/OS; NB/OS/RG).

Thus, all pairwise combinations of the reference genotypes are eliminated by the results from either one or the other marker system. Only a mixture of all three could account for the evidentiary pattern. Therefore, the stain was either contributed by a mixture of all three principles, or by two or more unknown individuals. Likelihood ratios would assist in determining which of these hypotheses was a more likely cause of the evidence.

(Courtesy of Dr. Ed Blake, Forensic Science Associates.)

quently hopeless. Most STR loci exhibit moderate amounts of variation in the population. Therefore, it is not uncommon for individuals to share alleles. This makes it more difficult to determine individual profiles from evidence samples where the components are present in approximately equal amounts. However, an obviously major component can often be resolved and treated like a single-source sample for frequency calculations.

Another aid to the interpretation of mixtures is the reasonable assumption of the presence of one of the contributors, such as the habitual wearer of a garment. For example, if a mixture is detected in what otherwise looks like a single-source bloodstain on the shirt of a suspect, it is useful to determine a reference profile for the suspect, and whether his profile is detected on an apparently unstained portion of the shirt. Similar to the victim's profile in the sexual assault evidence discussed above, the suspect's profile here can be subtracted from the mix of alleles to generate a "foreign donor profile," in this case perhaps the victim. The regular collection and analysis of substrate samples in this type of situation can greatly assist in the interpretation of such a mixture. What must be rigorously avoided, however, is the indiscriminate pairing of two alleles in a questioned sample simply because they are associated in a reference sample. This could potentially be misleading because those two alleles may have been contributed independently in the evidence sample.

Y-STR testing has already proved helpful in resolving some non-sexual assault mixtures containing both male and female contributors (see Sidebar 10). However, at this writing, most laboratories are not yet performing Y-STR testing, and it is useful only in certain types of cases. Also, because of the genetic nature of the Y-STR loci (they must be considered genetically linked, and thus count as essentially one locus for the purposes of calculating profile frequencies), they cannot provide the kind of statistics typically resulting from the analysis of autosomal loci.

Because each case is different, there is no set rule that can cover every instance. Thoughtful interpretation of mixtures relies on the analyst's understanding of the capabilities and limitations of the analytical system, validation studies performed by the community and each laboratory, the nature of the evidence, and the question being asked.

B. Degradation

When DNA is subjected to any environment outside the body, it is not as stable as when it is inside the body. If the environmental conditions become extreme, the physico-chemical properties of the DNA may change. The environmental conditions that lead to these changes include time, temperature, humidity, light, and chemicals (see Chapter 2). Normally, these conditions degrade the DNA. Fragmentation of the DNA can be mild or severe, depending on the particular circumstances. Degraded DNA may or may not affect the analysis, depending on its extent and the DNA typing system employed. For example, RFLP analysis detects DNA fragments between approximately 0.6 and 20 kb in length. If the average size of DNA fragments in a highly degraded evidence sample (e.g., a bloodstain that was on an asphalt road in the sun for 2 or 3 days) is in the 2- to 4-kb range, then it is unlikely that any fragments larger than this would be detected, although any fragments smaller than this range would be. This circumstance immediately suggests the possibility of a single-banded RFLP pattern that does not reflect the true profile of the donor at that locus, potentially leading to a false exclusion or, theoretically, a false inclusion[1]. Degradation of a DNA sample can be assessed by a yield gel, a test that provides information about the average fragment size. This information can be used to predict whether RFLP analysis would likely produce a band pattern that could be interpreted with confidence, or whether another marker system that tests smaller regions of DNA would have a better chance of success.

The PCR-based tests are generally better suited for the analysis of smaller DNA fragment sizes than RFLP. The evidence example above, in which the DNA was degraded to fragment sizes of 2 to 4 kb, would be perfectly suited to any of the suite of PCR tests currently available to forensic workers. This, of course, was a main impetus in the move to PCR-based systems, in particular STRs. The regions chosen for STR analysis are not only very small (less than 500 bp), but are very close to each other in size; in particular, the alleles within each locus occupy a very limited size range. Because of this, it is not only more likely that a sample subjected to extreme conditions of heat, humidity, or chemical exposure will yield a result, but the possibility of losing an allele at a heterozygous locus because of degradation is practically eliminated.

In general, the longest fragments of DNA required are less than 1 kb, and in some cases they are as small as 103 bp (gender identification). This means that degraded DNA has a high likelihood of being successfully typed by these methods.

C. Extraneous Substances

As discussed in Chapter 2, we reserve the word "contamination" for the introduction of extraneous substances into an evidence sample after recognition by responsible personnel. Anything that might have been present in the sample or on the substrate before the crime event occurred, or that happened to the sample before its recognition as evidence, falls into the "dirty world syndrome." It may confound our ability to analyze or interpret the evidence, but it is an integral part of the sample and should not be construed as somehow automatically detracting from the reliability of the sample as useful evidence. Whether extraneous substances are inherent in a DNA-containing sample or result from negligence,

---

[1] This would be almost inconceivable if multiple loci were examined because the pattern of degradation would have to be such that it exactly mimicked a particular reference profile. It also assumes that the analyst is unaware or has blatantly disregarded the degraded state of the sample.

the effect on the sample is much the same: inhibition of restriction or amplification enzymes, degradation of human DNA by bacterial enzymes, or worst-case, the introduction of extraneous human DNA producing an erroneous result that points to a wrong donor or multiple contributors.

1.   Chemical Inhibition of Enzymes

Because both the RFLP and PCR tests rely on enzymes (restriction enzymes and *Taq* polymerase, respectively; see Chapters 4 and 6) to perform properly, any agent that interferes with enzymatic function will potentially inhibit their ability to act on DNA. This includes a variety of commonly encountered substances, such as dyes used in clothing (particularly denim dyes) and some biological substances (in particular, the red-colored heme in blood). A first attempt is made to eliminate these substances during the extraction/purification phase of analysis. Depending on the system, inhibition might be diagnosed at various points of the analysis by evaluative tests (product gel, digest gel; see Chapter 6, and Appendices C3 and C4) or at the end of the analysis. Several common solutions are applied to overcome inhibition of enzymatic activity. These include repurifying the sample, adding more *Taq* polymerase, reducing the amount of input DNA (effectively diluting the inhibitor), or adding the chemically inert protein bovine serum albumin (BSA). Each of these methods has proven effective under various conditions; the analyst is required to use judgment and experience in deciding which may be preferred in a particular situation. BSA protein seems to bind and disable inhibitors and is now commonly included in commercial reaction mixes. This is a standard molecular biological technique for optimizing enzyme reactions. More extreme measures include the use of special beads that bind dyes present in a substrate, and that can then physically be removed before any further enzymatic reaction is attempted.

2.   Non-human DNA

By definition, all organisms contain DNA. Given that the world is a dirty place, it is not unusual to find evidence samples that contain non-human DNA. Examples include microorganisms (bacteria, fungi) such as would normally be found in physiological fluids and soil, as well as DNA from plants and non-human animals. Non-human DNA is not troublesome, *per se*, because the DNA tests used for forensic purposes are designed to be human (or at least higher primate) specific; that is, they do not cross-react with other animal species, or at least any reaction with other species occurs outside the region where human results are expected to occur[2]. However, the presence of microorganisms that produce DNA-destroying enzymes contributes to the degradation of human DNA. This can severely affect the results by rendering an evidence sample untypable. Further, all tests rely on an accurate estimate of the amount of human DNA present in a sample to work optimally. This means that the analyst must calculate the amount of total DNA, as well as the amount of human DNA, present in a sample, both to intelligently choose a marker system(s) to use and also to optimize the outcome of the analysis. The slot blot quantitation test (Appendix C1) is designed to help the analyst do just that.

---

[2] In one of the systems (D1S80) that was used briefly for forensic analyses, a research study uncovered a bacterial species that produced bands within the same region within which human results were expected. This was one of several factors that eventually led to the abandonment of this system in favor of STRs.

II.   System-Specific Interpretational Issues

The factors discussed in the previous chapter section may all interact with each other to affect the DNA and consequently the resulting analysis and interpretation. Forensic DNA typing protocols have been tested, optimized, and validated using samples that have purposely been subjected to most conceivable environmental insults and complicating factors. The effects have been categorized, and usually a diagnostic test or flag has been devised to detect their occurrence. These clues alert the analyst and assist him in choosing the most informative analytical path to follow and to intelligently interpret the results of the test. The following two chapter subsections (A and B) discuss some topics relating to reading and interpreting the results from specific systems, including consequences of the more common environmental conditions encountered in forensic casework.

A.   RFLP

Because the RFLP loci used in forensic DNA testing are so highly variable, most individuals inherit a different allele from each parent, producing a characteristic profile of two bands at each locus. Deviation from this expected norm might be due to normal genetic variation, or it might result from artifacts either inherent in the samples or generated by analytical conditions. In the following chapter subsections (1, 2, and 3), we delineate some common variations and discuss their etiology and interpretational consequences.

1.   Multi-(more than two) banded Patterns

When more than two bands are seen in an RFLP profile, the key question is whether more than one individual has contributed to the profile (a mixture), or whether the profile represents a single individual and the extra bands are artifacts. The following outlines the circumstances whereby extra bands may be observed in the absence of multiple donors.

a. Three-banded patterns.   In certain rare genetic circumstances, an individual may consistently show three bands at a particular locus (Figures 7.2 and 7.3). This seems contradictory to our knowledge of chromosomes existing as pairs. One explanation for three-banded patterns might be that a point mutation occurs inside a VNTR sequence, that creates a novel restriction enzyme site. Thus, a VNTR that normally would show a band size of 8 kb would be split into two smaller bands (e.g., 2 kb and 6 kb). These infrequent mutations do show Mendelian inheritance (passed faithfully to offspring), indicating a

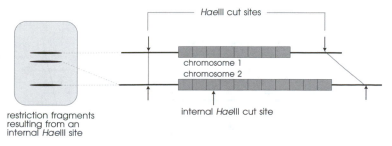

Figure 7.2 Diagram of the molecular basis of a three-banded RFLP pattern.

3-banded pattern
↓

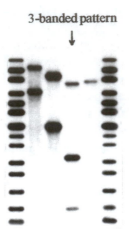

Figure 7.3 **RFLP autorad of a three-banded pattern.** *Hae*III sites internal to a VNTR produce three-banded patterns. They are found relatively frequently at locus D4S139. This is an example of one such pattern.

true genetic origin as opposed to a temporary biological or technical artifact. When verified as authentic, three-banded patterns contribute to the rareness of a particular profile.

b. Partial digestion by the restriction enzyme (partials).   When the restriction sites along a strand of DNA are chemically blocked, or when the enzyme is hindered from functioning at full capacity or is present in insufficient quantity for the amount of DNA present, some proportion of the restriction sites in the genome may remain uncut (Figures 7.4, 7.5, and 7.6). This means that some DNA strands will be longer than would be expected after a complete digestion. The extra length of the fragment is predictable to some extent because the restriction sites are found at fixed positions relative to the repeat sequence of interest. Thus, partial digestion results in some fragments of correct size and some slightly larger. The distance (in base pairs) from the sites immediately bracketing the VNTR to the next sites out in the flanking regions can be measured empirically. Partial digestion results in the presence of the normal bands expected for a particular sample, as well as the appearance of larger DNA fragments, usually fainter in intensity than the primary (real) bands. The size of these larger fragments can be measured and compared to the predicted

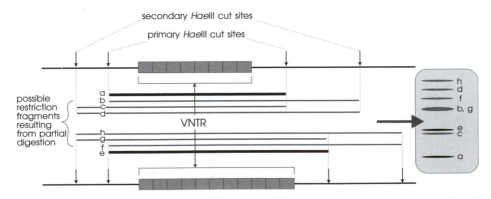

Figure 7.4 Diagram of the molecular basis of partial digestion in RFLP analysis.

Figure 7.5 A digest gel demonstrating incompletely digested samples. Lane 1 contains a molecular ladder, and lane 2 is blank. Lane 3 contains a known completely digested control sample. Lanes 4 and 5 contain samples that are completely digested by the restriction enzyme, as evidenced by the faintly visible, low-molecular-weight smears. Lanes 6 and 7 contain duplicate samples that show evidence of a substantial amount of HMW DNA, indicating incomplete digestion. Lanes 8 and 9 contain duplicate samples that both show sharp bands migrating even slightly higher than those in lanes 6 and 7. These samples are, most likely, completely uncut.

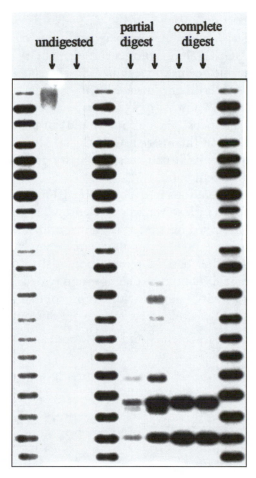

Figure 7.6 An RFLP autorad demonstrating incomplete digestion. Lanes 2 and 3 contain the undigested samples from lanes 6 and 7 in Figure 7.5. One consequence of this may be that only a faint smudge is visible at the top of the autorad, or sometimes no signal at all. A more classical presentation of partially digested samples is found in lanes 5 and 6 (the samples from lanes 8 and 9 in Figure 7.5): a number of fainter bands are seen *above* the primary bands. The samples in lanes 7 and 8 (from lanes 4 and 5 in Figure 7.5) are completely digested.

sizes based on the known pattern of sites progressing outward from the primary fragment. The consistent appearance of these predictable larger fragments over two or three loci is convincing evidence of partial digestion as opposed to the presence of another contributor.

Partial digestion occurs in a sufficient number of forensic samples that a diagnostic test has been devised for use partway through the analysis. This is known as a "test gel," or a "restriction digest gel" (see Chapter 6; Appendix C3). It is adequate to detect gross failures to digest by a restriction enzyme. In the event of partial digestion, the analyst may subject the sample to additional clean-up procedures or adjust the reaction conditions to obtain complete digestion. It must be emphasized here that truly complete digestion almost never occurs, and that with long exposures faint partial digestion bands may often be detected.

c. Star activity.   Every enzyme requires highly specific biochemical conditions for optimal performance. "Star activity" is the technical molecular biology term that refers to relaxation of the specificity of a restriction enzyme for the particular base sequence that defines its cut site. For example, *Hae*III under the proper conditions cleaves DNA only when it encounters the sequence **GGCC** (along with its complementary sequence **CCGG**). Under certain conditions, the enzyme begins to recognize closely related sequences, for example, **GGGC**. The result of this decreased enzyme specificity is the appearance of bands smaller than the true allele (Figures 7.7 and 7.8). To illustrate, assume the presence of a **GGGC** sequence internal to a VNTR locus. The enzyme would cut the normal **GGCC** sequences and additionally cut the DNA at the internal **GGGC** site. This would result in two bands rather than one for each allele. Each pair of star activity-generated fragments would be smaller than their primary parent band.

One of the original considerations in choosing *Hae*III for forensic work is its remarkable ability to resist star activity. However, as experience with the enzyme has grown, star activity has, in fact, been observed under certain non-optimal analytical conditions. Star bands are sometimes even more intense than the primary bands in a profile. This may not only lead to false exclusions, but has the remote potential to produce false positives as well[3]. Fortunately, this problem is simple to diagnose and remedy. The choice of an enzyme (*Hae*III) refractory to star activity, coupled with a protocol that avoids conditions leading to it and a diagnostic test for detecting it, serve to avoid this unwelcome prospect.

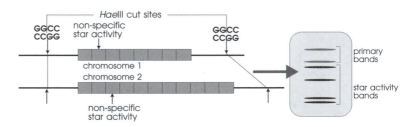

Figure 7.7 Diagram of the molecular basis of star activity.

---

[3] Like the situation with degradation discussed above, this would be almost inconceivable if multiple loci were examined, because the pattern of star activity would have to be such that it exactly mimicked a particular reference profile. It also assumes that the analyst has accepted the results at face value without considering an alternative explanation.

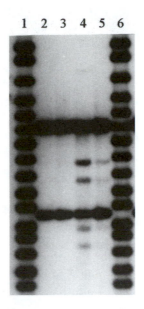

Figure 7.8 RFLP autorad demonstrating star activity. The samples in lanes 2 and 3 are properly digested; no evidence of extra bands is seen. The samples in lanes 4 and 5 were purposely subjected to conditions (in this case, resuspending a dried DNA sample in distilled water) known to promote star activity. Extra fainter bands are seen *below* the primary bands.

d. Incomplete stripping of probe from a previous probing.   RFLP patterns are detected by reaction with a locus-specific probe that is labeled either chemiluminescently or radio-actively. At the end of the detection period, the probe is removed before the next one is applied (see Chapter 6). Sometimes, when the subsequent probing is developed, faint bands are detected that are clearly in the same positions as those from the previous probe. This tends to be more evident with radioactive labeling. Incomplete stripping is easily diagnosed by a comparison of consecutive autorads, determining both visually and by sizing that the weak secondary bands are in the same location as those from the previous exposure.

e. Summary of multi-banded patterns in RFLP.   Multi-banded patterns may be caused by the presence of multiple donors, genetic mutation (three-banded patterns), incomplete stripping of probe from a prior hybridization, partial digestion by the restriction enzyme, or relaxed specificity of the restriction enzyme (star activity). When an analyst is attempting to differentiate between these possibilities, several tests will assist with this task. Incomplete stripping is proven by visual and sizing comparison of the current and previous autorads. Partial digestion results in bands that are of a known increment larger than the primary bands in a profile. The persistent finding, over several loci, of bands that are predictably larger than the primary bands is sufficient to conclude that partial digestion has occurred. Fortunately, this is also easily rectified by redigestion of the sample. Star activity results in bands smaller than the primary profile bands. The reduction in intensity of a monomor-phic (invariant) band (e.g., D7Z17), with the concomitant increase in intensity of the lower bands, are a clear indication that star activity has occurred. True genetic three-banded patterns show no evidence of partial digestion (the sizes are not consistent with partials for that locus and extra bands are not seen at other loci) and show no evidence of star activity (the monomorph has adequate intensity and there are no extra bands at other loci). This kind of rare mutation actually lends weight to a conclusion that two samples share a common source.

2.   *Single-Banded Patterns*

Because the RFLP loci used in forensic DNA testing are so highly variable, most individuals inherit a different allele from each parent, producing a characteristic profile of two bands at each locus. There are occasions, of course, when by chance the same allele is inherited from both parents. This offspring will show a single band on an RFLP autorad at this locus, and is described as homozygous. There are other conditions, however, that may lead to the appearance of a single band on an RFLP autorad when, in fact, the individual is heterozygous. These conditions are enumerated below.

a. Closely spaced bands.   There is a practical limit to the ability of the RFLP analytical gel to resolve two restriction fragments that differ by only one or a few repeat units. For example, the D1S7 locus has a repeat sequence that is only 9 bp in length, yet the fragment sizes are usually in the 4- to 12-kb range. The analytical gel is simply not capable of discriminating between a fragment 6200 and 6209 bp in length. These two bands appear as a single band, giving the gross visual impression that the individual is homozygous at this locus, when, in fact, at the molecular level the person is heterozygous. Due to the physical nature of the gel, this limitation becomes more pronounced toward the top, as fragment sizes become larger and thus less well separated. This inability to detect all of the alleles in a system has given rise to the term "continuous allele system" because the boundaries between adjacent alleles are not discrete; just where one allele stops and another starts is ambiguous in the detection system. As discussed in Chapter 8, RFLP alleles are identified as falling into a size class defined by externally imposed boundaries, rather than as individual alleles. It is important to emphasize that this is a property of the separation and detection technologies, and is not a characteristic of the genetics of the organism.

b. Bands running off the bottom of the gel.   One of the criteria for selecting RFLP loci for forensic work is that the range of possible band sizes correspond to those retained by the gel during electrophoresis. The loci commonly used produce bands primarily between about 0.6 and 20 kb in length, but some alleles fall outside these extremes. The larger bands generally present no problems because they can still be seen even if their sizes cannot be measured accurately (see Chapter 8). The smaller bands, however, are much more difficult to detect. This is because they are more diffuse at the lower end of the gel, and because the smallest ones may literally (although rarely) run off the end of the gel during electrophoresis. Thus, it is possible to have a profile with a detected band and an undetected band; this produces a single-banded pattern. Again, this looks like the profile of a homozygous individual when, in fact, the sample donor is heterozygous at that particular locus. Failure to detect very small alleles is also a property of the separation and detection technologies.

c. Degradation.   As outlined in Chapter 2, it is possible for DNA to be degraded to a point where an insufficient amount of DNA remains above a certain fragment length to produce an RFLP profile with bands in that region (Figures 7.9, 7.10, and 7.11). Imagine breaking a pane of glass with a hammer. The number and size of glass fragments produced depend on the number of blows and their intensity. One or a few blows produce a few

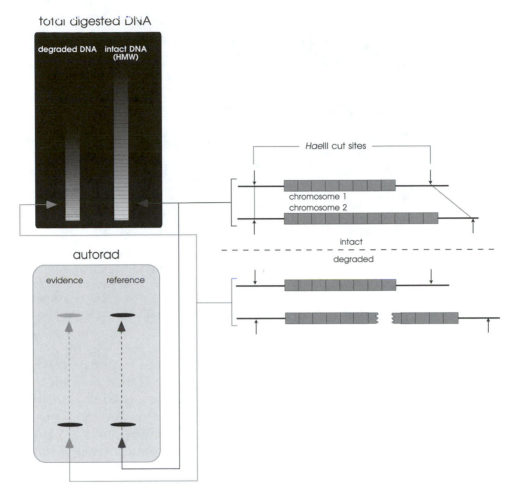

Figure 7.9 Diagram of the molecular basis of degradation.

larger shards of approximately similar size (all of which are smaller than the original pane), whereas many repeated or very hard strikes create microscopic pieces of glass, leaving no larger pieces. Degradation of DNA (the glass pane) occurs as a result of chemical or physical damage (the hammer). The greater the damage, the smaller the average size of the DNA becomes. When the average size becomes so small that one or both degraded ends of some of the molecules are internal to the termini defined by the restriction enzyme, the smaller fragments will be detected while the larger ones will be lost as distinct entities.

Degradation (as manifest by average fragment size) can be detected via a yield gel (Appendix C2). This is a miniaturized version of the RFLP analytical gel where the total DNA present in an extracted sample is viewed (not just DNA from a specific locus). The average size of the DNA can be estimated by comparison to a reference ladder of molecular size standards run on the same gel. In this way, an analyst can determine whether the DNA is of sufficient quality to allow a successful analysis by RFLP. If the DNA sample appears highly degraded or even somewhat degraded, the analyst might elect to run a PCR system (which does not require HMW DNA), or temper his interpretation of RFLP results with the knowledge that some information may be missing. In particular, he would be wise not to include or exclude based on any band above the average size of the DNA. Take a situation

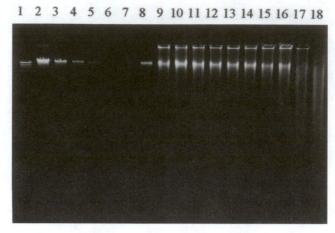

Figure 7.10 A yield gel demonstrating degradation. The first lane contains the molecular ladder and lanes 2 through 8, the standards and control. Lanes 9 through 18 contain DNA from DNA semen samples that have been held at 65°C for varying lengths of time before extraction. The duplicate samples in lanes 17 and 18 were heated for 1 month, and are the only samples on the gel that show any evidence of degradation. The resulting autorads are shown in Figure 7.11.

in which, due to environmental factors, the average DNA size is about 7 kb. For a heterozygous individual with an intact pattern of bands at 10 and 4 kb, the 10-kb band will not be detected because there are no (really too few) fragments of that size, while the 4-kb band will be detected. For this one locus, this results in a single-banded pattern from a heterozygous individual. Other loci in this profile might be affected differently or not at all.

Degradation leading to single-banded patterns is normally, but not always, an issue for evidence rather than reference samples; the analyst has no control over the degradation of evidence samples prior to collection. Reference samples, however, are normally collected specifically for genetic typing purposes, and steps should have been taken to preserve the sample by curtailing degradative processes (see Chapter 2). Thus, a typical situation is exemplified in a profile comparison where the reference sample shows two bands, while an evidence sample shows a single band that "matches" the lower band of the reference. Exceptions to this general expectation might include reference samples taken from homicide victims where the body was not found immediately or that have not been collected and preserved properly by, for instance, the medical examiner. In this sort of instance, a dried evidence stain found on a suspect's shirt, for example, might be better preserved than the reference sample from a deteriorating corpse, and the evidence would show two bands while the reference might show a single ("matching") lower band.

d. Summary of single-banded patterns.   Four possible causes may contribute to the appearance of single-banded patterns at any RFLP locus: true homozygosity, closely spaced bands, nondetection of one extremely small band, or degradation that destroys the larger of two alleles at a locus. In the latter three situations, a profile from a heterozygous individual appears as homozygous. The analyst in possession of this knowledge interprets the results of an analysis with the appropriate caution and scientific conservatism. The implications of single-banded patterns extend to the statistical estimation of a profile frequency, in particular the assumption of independent inheritance of the alleles. This issue is discussed in detail in Chapter 8.

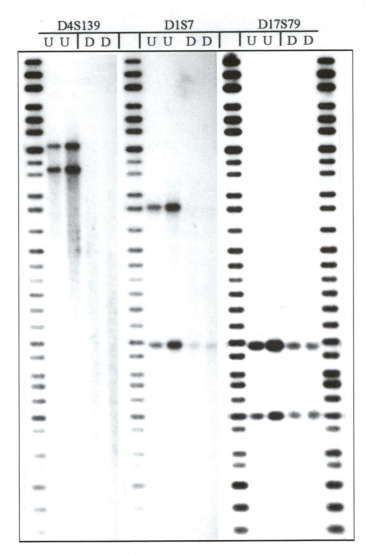

Figure 7.11 RFLP autorads demonstrating degradation. The same two duplicate samples were run together on a gel and the resulting membrane probed with three different probes. Each of the three probes generally produces band sizes in different regions of the autorad. Within each set of four, the duplicate samples on the left (from lanes 15 and 16 in Figure 7.10) were mostly undegraded, and the duplicate samples on the right (from lanes 17 and 18 in Figure 7.10) were highly degraded. At locus D4S139, the only remaining evidence of the degraded samples is a low-molecular-weight smear. At locus D1S7, the top band in the degraded samples is completely gone, leaving an apparent single-banded pattern. At locus D17S79, the remaining DNA fragments in the degraded samples are still of sufficient length to produce two clear bands. U, undegraded; D, degraded.

3.   *Summary of RFLP Interpretational Issues*

The immense diversity (the great capacity to discriminate between individuals) of these hypervariable loci that makes them so attractive for forensic work also presents analytical challenges and renders them susceptible to environmentally induced alterations. Much work has been performed to determine whether these artifacts constitute fatal flaws, or merely complications that can be factored into the conclusions drawn from analytical

Figure 7.12 The "ON-OFF" signal by which reverse dot blots are interpreted.

results on a case-by-case basis. The enormous amount of validation and proficiency testing performed using RFLP systems has led to the consensus among crime laboratories and academic experts that the difficulties can be adequately addressed and accounted for in most cases, and that the advantages conferred by the discrimination power of the RFLP loci can be used properly and conservatively. These analytical challenges emphasize the need for education, training, and experience. The forensic scientist applies her best judgment to the analysis and interpretation of these special types of samples, and is required to understand the capabilities and limitations of each test and employ that knowledge to differentiate an artifactual profile from a true profile.

B.   PCR Systems

Throughout the short history of forensic DNA analysis, several methods have already been used for the detection and analysis of PCR products at specific loci. The first methods were based on the detection of allele-specific sequence differences and were constructed so as to indicate that a particular sequence was either present (signal on) or absent (signal off) (Figure 7.12). This detection system took the form of a dot blot, where each dot represented one allele. Initially, only one locus (DQA1) was amplified; eventually, DQA1 was co-amplified (multiplexing) along with the five polymarker loci. This expanded the utility of PCR because the same amount of DNA could be used to analyze as many as six loci simultaneously. In subsequently developed length-based systems, PCR products are run on a gel or through a capillary. They are visualized either as bands, similar to RFLP, or as peaks if the detection and analysis is carried out using automated equipment. In the most recent systems, as many as 16 loci are co-amplified and the products separated using laser detection of fluorescent tags. In addition to the myriad of nuclear DNA systems that take advantage of PCR, mitochondrial DNA analysis also exploits DNA amplification. Regardless of the individual differences between systems, certain issues are different from RFLP typing and common to all PCR reactions. We detail them in the following section.

1.   Nuclear DNA Systems

a. Mixed samples.   Because of the increased sensitivity of any PCR-based system, mixtures may be detected where RFLP might have only detected the major component of the sample. The detection of a mixture is based on the presence of more than two alleles at more than one locus[4] or significant differences in the intensity of the alleles within loci[5].

---

[4] Occasionally, an authentic three-banded (or three-peaked) pattern is observed at an STR locus. This is likely due to a genetic duplication of all or part of the locus at another location. When verified, this kind of rare mutation can contribute to the rareness of a profile.

[5] Occasionally, a mutation in the primer binding site of an STR locus may lead to low or no amplification of that allele. Thus, the same locus amplified using different sets of primers might look heterozygous in one system and homozygous in another system. However, this does not compromise our ability to link evidence and reference samples, as both should exhibit the same mutation if they indeed originate from a common source. In fact, it contributes to the rarity of a profile.

However, the amplification process itself creates its own concerns specific to samples containing multiple contributors. Especially in multiplexed systems, the possibility exists that all alleles initially present may not be equivalently amplified, and consequently that dot or band intensities will not reflect the ratios of the components they represent in the original evidence. This would be of particular concern within a locus because it might lead to inappropriate pairing of alleles.

Studies with many different marker systems have repeatedly shown that samples mixed in certain ratios will produce relatively predictable allele intensities. For example, samples mixed in a 1:1 ratio show relatively equivalent allele intensities (whether detected by dot blot or electrophoretic systems). Samples in which the types from two different sources are present in more disparate ratios (e.g., 1:2 to about 1:10) manifest the alleles from one person as greater in amount than the alleles from the other person. When the difference reaches a sufficiently divergent level (more than the normal variation in intensity expected with any particular system), experienced analysts may elect to call major and minor types. We also know that when the ratio of major to minor types reaches sufficient disparity, the minor type is not amplified to detectable levels. As a practical matter, when sample ratios become greater than about 1:10, the minor type is rarely detectable and the sample does not appear as a mixture.

Because of the low to moderate heterozygosity inherent in the markers amenable to PCR-based analysis, it is rarely possible to determine the complete profile of a minor contributor, or of contributors in a relatively equal mixture, independently from the evidence. This leads to ambiguity about potential contributors that must be properly expressed both in the conclusion and frequency statements of a report. Given sufficient disparity, it is often possible to determine the complete profile of the major contributor to a mixture.

i. Sequence-based systems. Because only seven alleles are detected by the DQA1 marker system, mixed samples often involve individuals with common alleles. Additionally, not all alleles are detected by autonomous probes, thereby complicating the analysis. If the ratio between the amounts of the major and minor contributors is relatively large, the genotype of the major contributor can usually be identified. Specifically, mixture ratios greater than 1:5 show at least moderate differences in intensity between the major and minor contributors. The more widely disparate the ratio of the contributors, the easier it is to determine major and minor types. When it appears that more than one contributor is represented in a sample, and it is suspected that they share one or more alleles, the analyst will exercise appropriate caution in assigning genotypes. Particularly for the minor contributor, the analyst may outline the possible genotypes that could be present to produce the observed result.

Because of the many primer sets and probes involved in the polymarker system, amplification and typing conditions (especially temperatures) are crucial in obtaining consistent results. For example, if the temperature of the water bath used to type the samples varies even by less than a degree, the dot intensities within a locus begin to change relative to each other. The LDLR (low-density lipoprotein receptor) locus is particularly sensitive to temperature variation. This makes the interpretation of major and minor types in mixtures even more difficult than with a single-locus sequence variant system, such as DQA1. Additionally, because each of the five additional loci in polymarker is only biallelic or triallelic, the likelihood of allele sharing between two individuals is concomitantly higher.

Sidebar 9

The Case of the Disappearing Sperm (or, whose type is it anyway?)

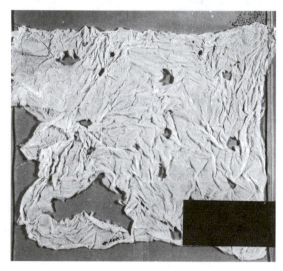

Sometime in 1992, a young woman was accosted by a man as she was getting into her car in a mall parking lot. She was sexually molested, but vaginal penetration was not even attempted. Instead, her assailant forced her to perform oral sex and ejaculated in her mouth. The victim spit the ejaculate into a piece of facial tissue, which was subsequently recovered as evidence. The suspect quickly got out of the car and disappeared. To date, no suspects have been apprehended.

A microscopic analysis of the tissue sample revealed surprisingly few sperm. A few epithelial (non-sperm) cells were noted, presumably from the inside of the victim's mouth. The samples were typed using the DQα marker system, the only PCR test validated for forensic use at that time. Unfortunately, the victim's reference (not shown), the non-sperm fraction (strip 1), and the sperm cell fraction (strip 3) all showed the same type, a 1.2,3 (see below). Was the assailant's type actually 1.2,3 or was the type in the sperm fraction due to carry-over of non-sperm cells into the sperm fraction? For low-discrimination systems, this interpretational challenge is always a possibility in instances of low sperm levels, particularly when a relatively large number of non-sperm cells are present. In this case, the apparent large number of non-sperm cells were not seen when examined microscopically, but were inferred from the initial α-amylase assay. The non-sperm cells might have been missed visually because their cell membranes had already burst, leaving no visible cells but plenty of DNA. Sperm are much more hardy and tend to survive even harsh conditions intact. Although the sperm fraction is well-washed during separation, trace amounts of a large initial proportion of non-sperm cell DNA might still remain. With very little sperm DNA present, one must consider both the possibility that the 1.2,3 DQα type represents the sperm contribution, or alternatively, that it is solely due to carry-over from the victim's non-sperm cells.

	1	2	3	4	C	1.1	1.2 1.3 4	1.3	All but 1.3	AMPLITYPE™ DQ-Alpha
e. cell fraction	1	2	3	4	C	1.1	•	1.3	•	AMPLITYPE™ DQ-Alpha
negative control	1.	2	3	4	C	1.1		1.3		AMPLITYPE™ DQ-Alpha
sperm fraction	1	2	3	4	C	1.1		1.3	•	AMPLITYPE™ DQ-Alpha

In this case, it was decided that no conclusion could be drawn from the test results.

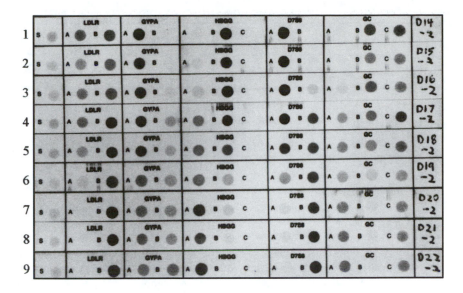

Figure 7.13 Polymarker strips from a mixture study. Two individual samples were typed separately (strips 1 and 9) and mixed in increasingly similar proportions, as shown in the figure, until a 50:50 mixture was reached (strip 5). These types of experiments help to establish at what proportion of a sample a minor type will become detectable, and when the two components are too close in relative contribution to call a major type.

All of these reasons contribute to a more challenging interpretation of mixtures in samples typed with the AmpliType® PM+DQA1 system (Figure 7.13). There is some discrepancy in the field as to the willingness of different analysts to call genotypes rather than single alleles from a polymarker typing that shows evidence of multiple contributors. As in DQA1, an influential factor is the perceived ratios of the two putative donor profiles; the more disparate, the more confidence an analyst can have in assigning alleles to a genotype.

ii. Length-based systems. Due to the increased power of discrimination of the length-based PCR systems (D1S80 and STRs), the presence of multiple donors is more easily detected than for the sequence-based markers. This is manifest by the presence of more than two alleles at more than one locus. Given the medium heterozygosities of these systems, it is common to find mixtures in which the two (or more) donors share alleles. This limits the ability to pair alleles into the genotypes of the donors, which in turn restricts our ability to narrow the pool of possible contributors. As with all PCR-based markers, validation studies show that a minor DNA contributor present at ratios less than about 1:10 of the major contributor is unlikely to be detected. Studies have also shown that when small amounts of DNA are amplified, the observed band or peak intensities do not always represent the ratio of the contributors. This phenomenon further restricts the ability to pair alleles into genotypes in low-level mixtures.

b. Degradation. DNA derived from case material may be degraded for a variety of reasons. Degradation results in a decrease in the average size of the DNA fragments in the sample. The consequences for sequence-based PCR systems are different than for length-based PCR based systems.

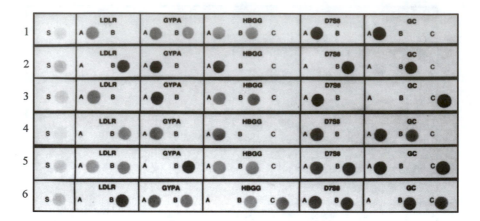

Figure 7.14 Polymarker analysis of degraded samples. Six typing strips, each from a different individual. The samples are from a previously adjudicated case. All the DNA samples in this demonstration run were moderately degraded. The homozygote dots are generally darker than the heterozygote dots. There is also a general trend, within each strip, of increasing intensity from left to right when comparing only homozygotes or only heterozygotes. (Courtesy of Roche Molecular Systems.)

i. Sequence-based PCR systems. Because the DQA1 alleles are all the same length, differing only at specific locations within the DQA1 locus, degraded DNA will have the same effect on all alleles; no allele is preferentially affected. The amplified polymarker regions do have different lengths, however, and loci may be lost in order from the largest to the smallest in samples with degraded DNA (Figure 7.14).

ii. Length-based PCR systems. One consequence of the wide range of D1S80 allele sizes is the potential for misinterpretation of typing results from degraded DNA. As in RFLP, degradation might result in the loss of a larger allele while leaving a smaller one intact. Consequently, a heterozygote might appear to be a homozygote. Allele sizes are so similar within any of the STR loci used in forensic analysis that rarely is one allele of a heterozygous pair preferentially lost because of degradation. Preferential allele loss occurs only when the quantity of DNA is limited, resulting in peaks or bands that are at or near the threshold detection limit. Highly degraded DNA may, however, still result in differential amplification between loci (discussed below).

c. Contamination. We devoted a previous section to the general issue of contamination (see Chapter 2). For laboratories performing nuclear DNA testing, the detection of contamination is uncommon. Most laboratories take appropriate precautions to separate PCR product (amplified DNA), the main source of possible laboratory contamination, from unamplified samples. Negative controls also serve to detect contamination, should it occur in a particular analysis. The interpretation of questioned samples in a case where "unexpected" results — read suspected contamination — have occurred vary by laboratory.

d. Amplification. The components of a PCR reaction are critical. Each must be added at a concentration within predetermined limits, and at the correct time, for the amplification to proceed optimally. Further, the specific amplification conditions (denaturation, annealing, and extension temperatures; the length of time the reaction is held at these temperatures; and the number of amplification cycles) must be thoroughly tested during development and validation to minimize the occurrence of the artifacts outlined below.

i. Stochastic fluctuation. Stochastic fluctuation is frequently confused with preferential amplification (see below). True stochastic fluctuation results from sampling errors at very dilute concentrations of DNA. Such an error may occur when only a portion of a DNA extract is removed to another tube for amplification. If the DNA from very few cells is represented in the total sample, the chromosome pairs may not be equally represented in the sample taken for amplification. For example, if only two cells were initially present, there would be two copies of each of the chromosomes of pair number 1. It might be possible that, during sampling, two copies of chromosome 1a (containing allele X) would be removed to the amplification tube, and zero copies of chromosome 1b (containing allele Y). Because chromosome 1b never made it into the amplification tube, it obviously would not be amplified and would not be represented in the final results. The profile would appear as a homozygote of allele X from chromosome 1a. In other words, the end result could be detection of only one of the two alleles, leading to the erroneous conclusion that the sample comes from a homozygote rather than a heterozygote. The solution to this problem is to establish, through experimentation, a minimum amount of input DNA that reproducibly amplifies all of the alleles in a known sample under specific amplification conditions. Many laboratories set a lower limit below which they will not amplify a sample at about 250 to 300 picograms. Others will amplify a sample even if no human DNA can be detected and interpret the results with the caveat that a complete profile might not be expected.

ii. Preferential amplification. Preferential amplification refers to the amplification of one allele to a much greater degree than another one in the same reaction. This would result in a heterozygote appearing to be a homozygote. The phenomenon has also been dubbed "allelic dropout." The causes of preferential amplification are different between sequence-based and length-based PCR systems.

Preferential amplification originally became an issue with the original DQα system using the early thermal cyclers that showed some variation in the temperatures measured between positions in the heat block. This resulted in incomplete denaturation of some samples prior to annealing and extension, that in turn led to the observation of preferential amplification. The nature of the chemical bonds that hold the DNA base pairs together determines that **G:C** base pairs are stronger than **A:T** base pairs, and thus require a slightly higher temperature to melt (denature) them. If one allele (of two or more present in a PCR reaction) contains more **G:C** base pairs than average, then it may not fully denature if the denaturation temperature is a bit low. Because the amplification primers must bind to single-stranded DNA, incomplete denaturation inhibits the primers from annealing in subsequent rounds, causing amplification of the GC-rich allele to lag. This results in some heterozygote samples that erroneously type as homozygotes (Figure 7.15). In the early *TC* version of the thermal cycler from Perkin Elmer, some of the positions at the outer edges of the unit did not always reach the same temperature as the inner positions during the denaturing cycle. The solution to this problem was twofold; the thermal cycler was redesigned to distribute the heat more evenly between all of the wells, and a protocol was developed for the calibration and testing of each instrument. Since these early occurrences, no problems have been reported with preferential amplification due to unequal block

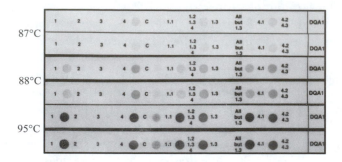

Figure 7.15 Preferential amplification of DQA1. The DQA1 genotype of all the samples shown is known to be a 1.1,4.1. When the denaturation step during amplification is performed at 95°C, as specified in the manufacturer's protocol, all dots are of equal intensity. At 88°C, every dot is somewhat less intense because all the DNA is incompletely denatured. The 1.1 allele (which has a higher **GC** content) is affected to a greater degree relative to the 4.1 allele. At 87°C, all dots are yet lighter and the 1.1 allele has completely disappeared, giving the false impression that the type is a 4.1 homozygote. (Courtesy of Roche Molecular Systems.)

temperatures. In a laboratory that uses properly calibrated thermal cyclers, preferential amplification is a non-issue.

An additional solution that entirely obviates this problem is the careful screening and adoption of marker systems that are relatively insensitive to temperature variation. The criteria include the selection of regions exhibiting an average **GC** content, and in multiplexed systems, markers in which the base pair composition is similar between both the alternate alleles and different loci in the reaction. The polymarker loci developed for forensic use were selected to minimize the problem of preferential amplification.

The *Taq* polymerase has a processivity limitation that results in shorter stretches of DNA being amplified more efficiently than longer sequences. This is of little consequence for markers based on sequence polymorphisms, such as DQA1 and the polymarker loci; but for PCR systems based on disparate length polymorphisms, this phenomenon must be addressed. The wide variation in allele sizes made D1S80 particularly susceptible to preferential amplification. The consequence of this processivity limitation on length polymorphisms is that under certain circumstances the longer alleles may not be consistently extended to their full length. This may result in a dearth of complete copies of the larger allele, reducing the intensity of the discrete band. The resulting discrepancy in the comparative intensities of the bands might lead to an interpretation of the presence of a mixture or, if the band is absent altogether, reading the type as a homozygote rather than a heterozygote.

The STR loci used in forensic analysis are sufficiently short, and of similar length, that rarely does the processivity of the *Taq* enzyme become an issue. Alleles within loci are amplified with approximately the same efficiency, and preferential amplification is seldom seen with the current protocols.

iii. Heteroduplex formation. Heteroduplex formation is the annealing of two strands of DNA that have a similar, but not exactly the same, nucleotide sequence (two perfectly complementary strands of DNA are termed homologous and form a homoduplex). For most PCR reactions, the conditions of annealing are so stringent that this does not occur. For some very closely related sequences, however, this phenomenon can occur with some demonstrable effect on the results of the testing. Heteroduplex formation can occur when sequence polymorphisms are closely related (as in the 1.3 and 3 alleles in the DQA1 system) and may inhibit the amplification of a specific allele relative to another under certain conditions. In PCR-amplified fragment length polymorphisms, single strands from the different alleles present in the amplification mix may mispair, giving rise to novel bands on the gel. Although this phenomenon was observed with D1S80 on silver-stained gels, it has largely been eliminated for STR systems analyzed using automated platforms.

iv. Enzyme inhibition.   The PCR reaction relies on an enzyme (*Taq* polymerase, or one of its derivatives or cousins) to replicate the DNA. As with any enzyme, *Taq* is susceptible to difficulties in function if conditions are not optimal. Certain substances inhibit the *Taq* enzyme. The solutions to this problems have been described earlier in this section.

e. Threshold limits.

i. Sequence-based systems.   It is important to have some predetermined limit to distinguish between what is a signal that actually represents a DNA allele and what is noise. This takes different forms, depending on the marker system and detection platform. Determination of threshold limits is discussed separately for each system below.

The DQA1 typing system includes a built-in threshold control called the "C" dot. This is a probe recognized by all of the alleles, but its concentration is such that it is the weakest-reacting probe on the typing strip. The purpose of this control is to help the analyst determine what dots represent true alleles, and which, if any, faint or weak signals are artifactual and therefore should not be considered in interpreting the result. If the typing dots are all of greater or equal intensity to "C," the analyst can have confidence that they are genuine alleles from a contributor to the sample. The "C" dot is also helpful as a guide in interpreting mixtures. If some dots are less than "C," as might occur in, for example, a highly disparate mixture, then there is some chance that an allele from a minor contributor has not been detected because it was present at such a low starting level that it never amplified properly. If a sample is so weak that the "C" dot is not present, then it is possible that some alleles present in the sample may not have been detected on the typing strip. The alleles that are detected may still be called with confidence, but may not represent the full complement of the sample, whether from a single source or from multiple contributors.

The polymarker equivalent to the DQA1 "C" dot is the "S" dot. This is a threshold control designed to signal that enough input DNA was amplified to reliably detect all the alleles present in a single-source sample. Because the "S" dot is actually the DQA1 sequence, which is larger than any of the five polymarker loci, it may preferentially disappear in a highly degraded sample. Thus, it is not the same kind of threshold control as the DQA1 "C" dot. Dot intensities greater than the "S" dot may be called with confidence; for dots that fall below the "S" dot, which would only occur in a mixed sample, the full genotype of all minor contributors may not be represented; those below are considered inconclusive for calling full genotypes. If the "S" dot is not present, full genotypes may not be represented; however, because of the greater length of the region required to produce an "S" dot, some thought and intelligence are required to interpret such a sample. The results of a product gel can be helpful in determining the cause of a missing "S" dot.

Because the length-based systems (D1S80 and STRs) lack an internal detection threshold control similar to the AmpliType® PM+DQA1 system, each individual laboratory must establish its own threshold limits based on validation studies using known samples. For STRs, this is expressed as the relative fluorescent units (RFUs) below which a laboratory will not interpret a sample. Often, interpretation guidelines allow for some analyst discretion based on the particular attributes of the sample or case circumstances.

f. System-specific considerations.   Some phenomena occur only in specific DNA typing systems. We consider these issues below.

i. Sequence-based PCR marker systems.   Virtually all laboratories that performed forensic DNA analysis in the 1990s employed the commercial kits developed originally by Cetus Corporation (now Roche Molecular Systems (RMS)) to type several sequence-specific loci. These markers included some of the earliest developed for forensic use, in particular DQA1 and the polymarker loci that were eventually combined into the AmpliType® PM+DQA1 kit. These systems were all presented in a reverse dot blot format (see Chapter 6), and contained all of the critical materials and reagents for both the amplification and typing of samples. The types are read as a combination of "on" or "off" signals (blue dots) for each system. For the five polymarker loci, this is relatively straightforward; but for the DQA1 system, some alleles cannot be read directly. It is important to understand both the rules followed to read genetic types from the strips and some of the limitations inherent in the technology.

DQA1. This discussion focuses on reading the DQA1 typing strips. The original DQα strips were read in a similar fashion without the additional subtyping of the 4 allele. There are seven alleles in the DQA1 system: 1.1, 1.2, 1.3, 2, 3, 4.1, and the 4.2/4.3 alleles that are not distinguished. All the different pairwise combinations of these seven detectable alleles yield a total of 28 different genotypes. Examples of heterozygous DQA1 types would be 1.3,2 or 3,4.1. Homozygotes are designated 3,3 or 1.2,1.2, for example.

One of the complicating factors inherent in this typing system is that the 1.2 allele does not have a specific probe; instead, its presence is deduced by reading a combination of probes that react with more than one subtype. Specifically, a probe exists for the 1.1 allele, as well as a probe that reacts with the 1.3 allele. These alleles can be typed based exclusively on a positive reaction (blue dot) in the position of each of their specific probes on the strip. One of the probes has been designed to react simultaneously with the 1.2, 1.3, and 4 alleles and is labeled as such. If a sample reacts with this "trio" but not with the individual 1.1 or 1.3 probes, the 1.2 allele must then, by elimination, be present. The last difficulty to overcome is differentiating a 1.2,1.3 heterozygote from a 1.3,1.3 homozygote. This is solved by one last probe, the "all but 1.3," that reacts with every allele *except* the 1.3. Thus, in a 1.2,1.3 individual, the "all but 1.3" probe is positive, while in a 1.3 homozygote this dot is negative.

Let's take two illustrative examples:

1.   A strip showing blue dots at the nominal 1 and 4 positions must represent a sample containing a subtype of the 1 allele and a subtype of the 4 allele (Figure 7.16a). In this example, the 1.1 and 4.1 dots also light up, as do the "trio" and the "all but 1.3" dots. The positive 1.1 signal indicates which 1 subtype is present, as does the positive 4.1 dot. The other two dots light up superfluously due to the presence of, respectively, the nominal 4 allele (the "trio") and both the 1.1 and nominal 4 alleles (the "all but 1.3"). These dots are not needed to interpret this particular type. The DQA1 type of this sample is 1.1,4.1.

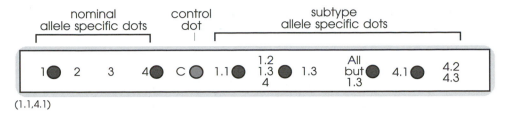

(1.1,4.1)

Figure 7.16a A DQA1 strip showing a type of 1.1,4.1.

2. A strip showing blue dots at the nominal 1 and 3 positions must represent a sample containing some subtype of 1 and a 3 allele (Figure 7.16b). In this example, the "trio" and the "all but 1.3" dots also light up. Because no nominal 4 dot is present, we know that this is not the source of the "trio" dot; the absence of a dot at the 1.3 probe indicates that the 1.3 allele is also not the source of the positive "trio" signal. Therefore, by the process of elimination, we are left with the 1.2 allele as the source of the "trio" dot. The DQA1 type of this individual is then 1.2,3.

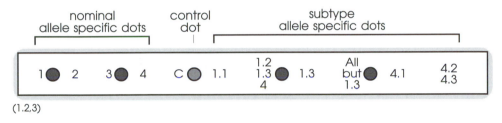

(1.2,3)

Figure 7.16b A DQA1 strip showing a type of 1.2,3.

An occasional occurrence noted with the DQA1 typing system is the appearance of weak positive signals in the 1 subtyping dots with single-source samples such as reference bloods. These are usually so much less intense than the "C" dot that they are barely visible. The 1 subtypes are so close in sequence that sometimes cross-reaction occurs between, for example, amplified 1.2 product and the 1.3 typing probe on the strip. In this case, the "trio" dot is strongly positive, while the 1.3 dot shows only a slight blue color. This is minimized (although not always completely eliminated) by calibrating the water bath used to develop the typing strips and maintaining it at the recommended temperature for typing. The weak nature of these artifactual dots and their predictable appearance with certain 1 subtypes make this an annoying but rarely substantive problem in typing evidence samples.

g. Length-based marker systems.
i. Doublets.   To achieve the high resolution necessary for the separation of STR alleles, it is required to both separate (denature) the single DNA strands in the sample and employ a denaturing gel system that prevents them from reannealing during electrophoresis. Because the complementary strands of each fragment have different nucleotide compositions, they migrate slightly differently on the high-resolution gels employed in this system. Consequently, the smaller alleles are reproducibly resolved as doublets (Figure 7.17). When the gel is stained to detect the bands *after* electrophoresis (with silver or a fluorescent dye), both doublet strands of a single allele are stained equally. Because this phenomenon is completely understood, reproducible, and applies equally to samples and allelic ladders, it does not constitute an interpretational issue.

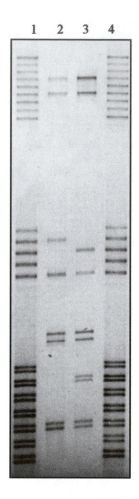

Figure 7.17 An STR silver-stained gel demonstrating doublets. The alleles falling in the bottom third of the gel are resolved as doublets. The sample and ladders can be directly compared.

However, an advantage inherent in the automated detection systems using fluorescent PCR primers is that only one of the two DNA strands is labeled, and thus the other, although present, is invisible. Although primarily an aesthetic consideration, the presence of only one band per allele is easier for non-scientists (such as the jury) to comprehend.

ii. Non-template-directed nucleotide addition. Split peaks seen in STR electropherograms result from a phenomenon known as non-template-directed nucleotide addition. The *Taq* enzyme places a single nucleotide, usually an **A**, at the end of each amplification region when extension has been completed. This makes the strand one base pair larger than the original sequence of interest. Because this trait of the enzyme is not easily curbed, most PCR reactions will have a final extension period that allows the enzyme to add the final **A** to every strand. If the final addition step is incomplete, two poorly resolved bands or peaks appear in the final result. See Plate 16a for an example.

iii. Stutter. Stutter refers to the consistent observation of a minor band one repeat unit smaller, or occasionally larger, than the primary STR band (Figure 7.18). In D1S80 analyzed

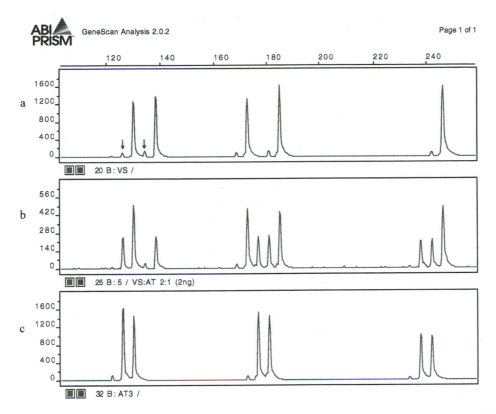

Figure 7.18 An STR printout of peaks demonstrating a mixture and stutter. Each panel represents a DNA sample that has been amplified at three different loci (multiplexed) and run and detected on the ABI PRISM® 377 DNA Sequencer. Panels (a) and (c) each represent one individual, and panel (b) contains a 2a:1c mix of the two. Notice that even in the lanes containing DNA from one individual, small peaks are present just before each main allele peak (arrows). This is an example of stutter. Even in the mixed sample, however, the stutter does not interfere with discerning the types present in the sample. The peaks representing true alleles are clearly distinguishable. The peak heights representing the alleles belonging to each individual are proportional to their concentration in the mixture.

on silver-stained polyacrylamide gels, stutter bands were observed as "shadow bands" just underneath the darker main band. The occurrence of stutter is much reduced for shorter repeat units such as found in STRs. However, some STR loci are more prone to this occurrence than others (this appears to be sequence related), and there tends to be a higher percentage of stutter in alleles with a greater number of repeats (i.e., a ten-repeat allele shows more stutter than a three-repeat allele at the same locus). A conclusive mechanism for this phenomenon has not yet been determined.

Stutter becomes an issue, particularly in putative mixed samples, when a decision must be made as to whether a band is due to stutter (and is therefore an artifact) or if it is a true allele from another DNA source. The threshold for stutter in forensic systems is generally about 5 to 15% of the primary band. For example, at a locus where the maximum stutter has been determined to be about 15% of the main allele, any band or peak immediately adjacent to a primary allele that is less than 15% is interpreted as stutter; any band or peak comprising more than 15% of the primary allele may be interpreted as a true allele. The experienced analyst makes this judgment based on the attributes of the sample and the specifics of the case. Actual stutter values vary slightly between users and many laboratories determine their own stutter values during validation. Others choose to use the conservative values provided by the manufacturer.

iv. Primer binding site mutations.   Recall that the PCR process begins when a primer is annealed to denatured DNA strands. Primers are designed with specific traits in mind, including their location relative to the sequence of interest. Most of the population have the same sequence in the area where the primer binds. In some cases, a small percentage of people have a mutation in the primer binding site. If the primer is complementary to one sequence, it may not anneal efficiently to the alternate sequence containing the mutation. This failure to bind results in the concomitant failure to amplify the STR of interest.

If one chromosome in a heterozygous person has the normal primer sequence while the homologous chromosome has the mutation, it is possible that the person will type as a homozygote rather than as a true heterozygote. One solution to this dilemma is to include primers to both sequences in the PCR reaction so that both will amplify. Another solution is to ensure that all samples compared to each other are typed using the same manufacturer's kit. In such a situation, two samples from the source will show the same type, regardless of any sequence differences at the primer binding site.

One consequence of this phenomenon is that searching a database with a profile developed using one manufacturer's primer pairs may not "match" a profile from the same source if that sample is typed using a different manufacturer's primer set. See Chapter 9 for a further discussion of search strategies that overcome this challenge.

v. Differential amplification.   Differential amplification has come to refer to differences between loci amplified in the same reaction. Differential amplification might occur either because of different optimum amplification requirements needed for locus-specific primer pairs or because of large variations in size between loci. Empirical developmental studies performed before a kit is released for use determine the optimum conditions for amplification of all loci in a reaction. That a kit performs as expected should be validated by each individual laboratory using known samples. Although the amplified regions of loci within each PCR-based system are both relatively small and close in size, differential amplification of the smaller loci over the larger ones may still be seen under difficult conditions, for example, if an amplification inhibitor is present. If the DNA in a sample is degraded to an average size that is close to the size of the amplified region, a relatively greater number of smaller size fragments will remain intact and capable of being amplified. In STR multiplex reactions, this means that the smaller loci may be preferentially amplified and typed relative to the larger loci.

vi. Detection.   Each DNA typing system is detected in a slightly different way, and some interpretation issues arise as a specific consequence of the detection method. For the automated systems using fluorescently tagged primers (Plates 10 to 14), for example, the ABI PRISM® 310 or 377 Genetic Analyzer or the Hitachi FMBIO instrument, electronics, software, and hardware embody both the savior and the devil. Two common artifacts resulting from these system components are detailed below.

The four fluorescent dyes used in detecting DNA fragments exhibit spectral overlap. In both the 310 and 377 instruments, special computer software compensates for the spectral overlap of four or five fluorescent dyes. The computer applies an algorithm to remove this overlap and normalize the baseline of each color (Plate 12). Occasionally, the computer fails to properly compensate for spectral overlap This results in the appearance of artifactual peaks at the same location in different colors. This phenomenon is known as "pull-up," so-called because one color seems to "pull up" peaks in other colors (Plate 16b). Minor amounts of pull-up do not interfere with the interpretation of a sample. Large amounts of pull-up mean that the computer has miscalculated the amount of spectral overlap. In this case, the software can be recalibrated and the electronic data reanalyzed. This problem can be easily rectified without consuming additional sample.

The laser detector and CCD camera in both instruments automate data collection. However, because of the sensitivity of the capillary column in the 310 instrument, any fluctuation in the current results in electronic noise that manifests as artifacts in the data. Electrical spikes generate extraneous peaks in the electropherogram. Such peaks are easily distinguished from authentic DNA peaks by their abrupt beginning and ending, and narrow peak width. Plates 16c and 16d show two different kinds of spikes; an experienced analyst would never mistake either of these artifacts for a DNA allele. If it is not clear whether a peak represents an electrical artifact or an authentic allele, another aliquot of the same amplified sample may be re-run on the instrument. A DNA peak will be reproducible; a spike will not.

vii. Sequence variation in length-based marker systems. Undetected sequence-based subtypes can certainly be present in a length-based marker system due to the degeneracy of the repeat units. A frequent question is: how do you know that there is no difference in the sequence between two samples that share the same length-based profile? This is best understood as a conditional probability; given the rarity of the profile already obtained, what is the probability that two samples would be distinguished with any kind of further testing? This further testing could encompass additional length-based loci or sequence-based analysis, either within the length-based loci already tested or, for that matter, anywhere else in the genome. The answer to the conditional question depends both on the rarity of the profile already obtained and on the probability of seeing a difference at some locus chosen for further testing. If the frequency of the profile is already very rare (e.g., 1 in billions or trillions), then regardless of where or how one looks, it is unlikely that a difference will be found. Furthermore, sequence polymorphisms are, by nature, less discriminating than length-based polymorphisms — biology and genetics limit the number of sequence variants possible. This means that two samples that are different are much more likely to be distinguished by a multitude of length-based markers than by one more sequence-based marker, especially one that is not particularly polymorphic.

2. *Mitochondrial DNA*

While sequence-based systems for nuclear DNA typing are being phased out, mtDNA typing is becoming more prevalent. The relatively few laboratories that currently offer mtDNA testing services use standard DNA sequencing techniques. A strip-based system for typing mitochondrial DNA markers has also been developed and should soon be available as a commercial kit for general use (Plate 15). Although issues involving the detection platform are similar to the AmpliType® PM+DQA1 system, interpretational guidelines specific to mtDNA are quite different from those for nuclear DNA markers.

a. Detection threshold. Like STR testing, a lower detection threshold and a lower interpretation limit for mtDNA typing must be established by each individual laboratory doing the testing. This is essential regardless of whether direct sequencing or SSO detection is employed. Again, this should be based on validation studies using known samples of various concentrations.

For a number of different reasons, both practical and technical, it was also decided to omit a minimum DNA threshold control probe from the mtDNA typing strips. From research and validation studies, it has been established that if no signal is detected for any of the alleles within a designated mtDNA typing location, this means that the sequence present is not one of those detected by the marker system — essentially, it is a null allele. From the work performed to date, it appears that alleles do not preferentially disappear when insufficient amounts of DNA are amplified; simply no type is obtained for the sample. In any case, it is still rarely possible to say anything definitive about a minor component.

b. Multiple donors. As with other systems, multiple contributors to a sample analyzed for mtDNA may complicate interpretation of the results. In particular, because of the complex nature of the reactions and their dependence on the actual DNA sequence, the relative amounts of two components might not reliably be determined by direct sequencing. Because the SSO probe system does not depend on sequencing reactions, the detected relative contributions of two components appear, from initial studies, to accurately reflect the actual ratio in known mixture samples. Similar to other PCR-based systems, a minor contributor can be detected down to a ratio of at least 1:10. When the two components are present in relatively disparate proportions, the type of the major contributor can usually be called reliably, but determination of a full profile for the minor contributor might not be possible. Alleles from the minor contributor could either be masked by the major contributor or may not be detected. Like any genetic typing system, when the two components are present in relatively equal amounts, many combinations of the two sequences are possible; the independent determination of individual profiles is not feasible, regardless of which mtDNA typing system is used. The existence of multiple donors can generally be distinguished from heteroplasmy because more than one base position will show more than one type. The absence of either sequence from simultaneously processed negative controls supports its integral presence in the original sample.

c. Contamination. Because mtDNA typing is, by its very nature, exquisitely sensitive, laboratory contamination takes on a new meaning. The DNA Commission of the International Society for Forensic Genetics (ISFG) proposes some appropriately extreme guidelines to restrict the entry of exogenous DNA into samples in the laboratory. In addition to the standard practices in any PCR laboratory, the guidelines suggest physical separation of laboratory spaces for processing of evidence and reference samples, duplicate analyses whenever possible, and an increased emphasis on the analysis of substrate samples. Because many copies of mtDNA exist relative to nuclear DNA, it is not uncommon, even in the most rigorously maintained mtDNA laboratory, to occasionally see typing results in negative control samples. The guidelines suggest that if the type obtained from the blank is the same as that from an evidence sample, the analysis must be repeated; otherwise, it may be interpreted in light of all the results in the case, including other positive and negative controls and results from duplicate analyses.

d. Heteroplasmy.   The difference with the greatest implication for interpretation between mtDNA typing systems and nuclear DNA typing systems is the existence of heteroplasmy. We have described this phenomenon previously in Chapter 5. Briefly, it means that a mixture of types can coexist in the same sample from a single source. Heteroplasmy is thought to originate either by mutation during the formation of egg cells in the female ovaries (germ line mutation) or by mutation during the division of any cell in an individual's body (somatic mutation). It is likely due to the high mutation rates seen in the control region of mtDNA. The existence, frequency, and distribution of heteroplasmy in humans has become well-documented. It can vary between different body tissues, with blood showing the lowest incidence in the population (generally less than 2%) and hair typically exhibiting the greatest incidence, appearing in at least one third of all individuals. These frequencies may well be underestimates because none of the typing systems detect all locations in the mtDNA molecule that might show heteroplasmy, nor do they detect minor components of less than about 1 in 10. In fact, it is now generally accepted that most individuals are heteroplasmic to at least some degree, even if not detectable by a particular typing system. Additionally, preliminary evidence suggests that the state of heteroplasmy in an individual may change over time, increasing with age. This is in contrast to nuclear DNA, in which we depend on a profile to remain stable over the life of an individual.

Why should we care about this aspect of mtDNA biology for the purposes of forensic typing? In most cases, none of the samples being compared exhibit heteroplasmy; therefore, it does not constitute an interpretational challenge. However, if one of the samples does exhibit heteroplasmy, the interpretation is less straightforward. The most obvious issue is that if two different tissues are compared, or if the same individual is compared many years apart, the samples may not show the same pattern of heteroplasmy. This occurs most frequently when evidence hairs (or sometimes a single hair) are compared to a blood or saliva reference standard (Figure 7.19). Because hair shafts cannot be typed for nuclear DNA, this is exactly the type of evidence for which mtDNA typing is often attempted. And, unfortunately, this is the tissue in which heteroplasmy is highest. Experiments have shown that any one hair might have a different dominant sequence than a blood reference from the same person, or could even show a complete switch in sequence at a particular location. Some workers suggest that, particularly in the case of hairs, a more appropriate reference sample would come from the same tissue (e.g., a group of pooled hairs). Other workers disagree that this is even a reasonable or relevant proposition. Regardless, it has yet to be established how many hairs would provide a reliable reference sample, and how the number and heteroplasmic distribution of evidence hairs might affect the weight of the evidence. For example, how is one to judge whether two evidence hairs exhibiting sequences that differ at one base pair result from one heteroplasmic individual or two different individuals? There is no simple solution to this challenge of choosing an appropriate reference sample and basis of comparison.

Although guidelines have been issued by the ISFG for the interpretation of mtDNA evidence, they are complex, based on evolving data, and not always very helpful (Table 7.1). In particular, the forensic DNA community is still struggling with an appropriate way to convey the weight of this kind of evidence. If an evidence hair exhibits heteroplasmy not seen in a blood sample, the donor of the blood sample might or might not be the source of the hair. The hair could originate from an individual whose blood showed either one of the sequences seen in the hair, or any heteroplasmic state in between. Proponents argue that the current practice of adding the frequencies of all possible single-state

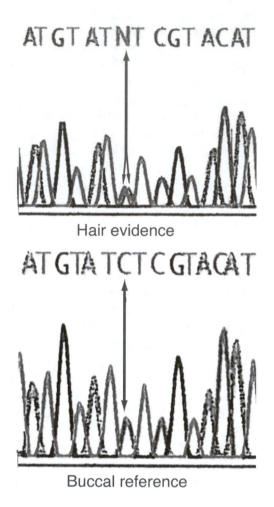

Figure 7.19 Heteroplasmy in mtDNA. In this case example, a single hair collected from the crime scene (top sequence) displayed a C/T heteroplasmy at position 16093, a known mutational hot spot. The nucleotide present is designated as "N," and the split arrows point to the two different bases present at the same position. The reference sample, a buccal swab (bottom sequence) collected from the suspect, showed only a C at that position. (Courtesy of MitoTyping and Technologies, Inc.)

sequences that could theoretically give rise to the evidence profile, and presenting the data as a count rather than a frequency, justifies the simplified conclusion of "not excluded." They submit that the strength of hundreds of matching bases is so great that it outweighs the chance that the true perpetrator differs from the suspect by one base pair. While this might ultimately prove to be correct, only limited data exist as yet on which to base this opinion. Others suggest that simply adding the frequencies of all possible donor types is a rather crude estimate of the strength of the evidence. It fails to take into account many aspects of the biology of mtDNA, such as mutation rates, relative heteroplasmy rates, inheritance patterns, sampling error, and population substructure. The ISFG has suggested that the data be interpreted in light of these considerations and that likelihood ratios could be an appropriate vehicle with which to communicate the relative weight of various hypotheses. But these recommendations have yet to be generally adopted by laboratories

Table 7.1 Guidelines for Mitochondrial DNA Typing (DNA Commission of the International Society for Forensic Genetics)

Relationship of Reference to Evidence	Conclusion
Unequivocally different	Excluded as originating from the same source
The same, no heteroplasmy	Cannot be excluded as originating from the same source
The same, including any heteroplasmy	Cannot be excluded as originating from the same source
Heteroplasmy in one sample, but not the other	Common maternal lineage cannot be excluded
Differ by a single nucleotide, no heteroplasmy	Could be inconclusive, but may be exclusionary
Differ by more than one nucleotide	Careful analysis indicated

From Bar et al., 2000.

issuing case reports based on mtDNA typing. Certainly, the common forensic DNA report conclusion of "can't be excluded" means something very different for an mtDNA case where heteroplasmy is involved, than where 13 STR markers show exactly the same profile in evidence and reference samples.

3. Summary of PCR Interpretational Issues

The application of PCR to forensic evidence increases the analyst's ability to type samples that are both smaller and in poorer condition than was previously possible. While the first PCR systems lacked the ability to differentiate between many people in a population, subsequent research expanded the number and kind of DNA loci that could be analyzed by PCR. Increasing the power of discrimination was achieved by the addition of many moderately heterozygous loci, rather than by searching for a few hypervariable regions such as exist for RFLP systems. Current PCR systems now rival the discriminating power of RFLP.

As more useful PCR systems were developed, novel strategies emerged for increasing the speed and efficiency of the analytical process. The creation of multiplex systems and the invention of electronic detection strategies increase both the types of samples that can be analyzed as well as the speed of analysis. But each advance also creates the opportunity for artifacts related to the analysis; results extrinsic to the sample may appear in the intermediate or final data.

We have detailed some of these artifacts in the previous section, but there is much that was not covered. It is neither surprising nor disturbing that complex systems yield complex results. The lesson to be learned is that apparently simple results (e.g., a DNA profile consisting of 13 pairs of numbers) arise from complicated biological reactions and sophisticated electronic and computer assistance, and must be evaluated with knowledge of the capabilities and limitations of the system. We find it unfortunate that we need to make this point both to lay individuals and experts alike. We have seen far too many analysts defend their results simply because they pushed the button on the machine and results "automagically" emerged. The new systems require more education, training, and skill than the previous ones, not less.

III. Summary of DNA Interpretation Issues

The emphasis on additional education, training, and skill inevitably drives a field to specialization, and that trend is easily seen in the discipline of DNA analysis. But it is

Sidebar 10

Separating the Men from the Sample (or, Y we do STRs)

The utility of Y-STR testing is demonstrated in these two case examples. In neither case was any convincing evidence of a contributor foreign to the female victim detected using the standard complement of STR markers. However, in both cases, a foreign male profile was readily detected using Y-STRs. The outcome for the suspect in each case was very different.

Case 1

In this case, the victim claimed to have been orally copulated. She reported no penetration and no semen was detected on any of the tested items. The vaginal swab was positive for the presence of amylase, suggesting the presence of saliva. Autosomal typing yielded only the victim's DNA. In the electropherogram below, note the high peak height and the absence of any foreign alleles. The allelic typing results are listed in the table. The autosomal testing was repeated by a second laboratory using the Applied Biosystems, Profiler Plus and COfiler system but still failed to detect any alleles foreign to the victim.

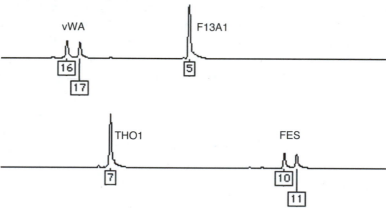

The Y-STR profile, as seen in the electropherogram below, matched the suspect's DNA. The allelic typing results are listed in the table.

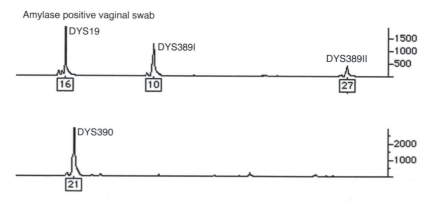

Autosomal and Y STR Typing Results for the Amylase-Positive Vaginal Swab

Loci Samples	VWA	F13A1	THO1	FES	DYS19	DYS389I	DYS389II	DYS390
Victim	16, 17	5	7	10, 11	n/a	n/a	n/a	n/a
Vag swab	16, 17	5	7	10, 11	16	10	27	21
Suspect	16, 18	7, 15	6, 7	10, 11	16	10	27	21

Note: n/a = not applicable.

Estimated Frequencies for the Y Haplotypes

African American	Caucasians	Hispanics	Asians
1 in 20	1 in 130	1 in 147	1 in 116

The Y-STR results were introduced during the trial and the jury found the suspect guilty.

Case 2

In this case, the suspect had previously been convicted of rape based on other evidence. DNA testing had not been available at the time. Post-conviction testing was requested. STR testing in 1998 had been performed by another laboratory using the Promega CTTA system. Material from a slide made from the victim's vaginal swab was analyzed at three autosomal loci and the gender identification locus, amelogenin. The same extract was retested using the Y-STR approach. The results are shown in the table below.

Autosomal and Y STR Typing Results for the Vaginal Swab Slide

Loci Samples	CSF1PO	TPOX	THO1	Amel	DYS19	DYS389I	DYS389II	DYS390
Victim	10,11	9,11	8,9	X	n/a	n/a	n/a	n/a
Vag. smear SF	10,11**	9,11	8,9	XY	14	10	**26**	**25**
Suspect	10,11	6,8	7,8	XY	14	10	25	23

[a] Indicates that additional results were obtained that were too weak to be conclusively identified as DNA alleles. The bands could not be distinguished from background.

The autosomal DNA type that was obtained matched the victim. The only DNA foreign to the victim was the Y allele at amelogenin, indicating that the DNA extract contained a mixture and that male DNA was present. Note that if the [**] really represent additional alleles at the locus CSF1PO, this would exclude the suspect because he has the same type as the victim.

The same extract was used for subsequent Y-STR typing. Despite low peak intensity, it was possible to generate a complete four-locus haplotype. The electropherogram is shown below. This haplotype differs from the suspect's haplotype at two loci. Exclusions are highlighted in bold in the table. The exclusion was accepted by the court system and the suspect was released from prison.

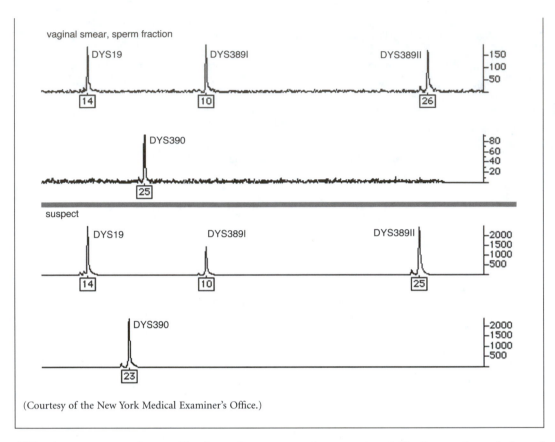

(Courtesy of the New York Medical Examiner's Office.)

difficult to separate the application of competent interpretive skills from a knowledge of the problem in front of you. Too many analysts see the problem as a blood or semen stain examination, rather than the general criminalistics problem of the question of source or contact. The framing of intelligent questions is inimical to the analysis of physical evidence in a specific case. The interpretation of PCR results must follow both from an understanding of the physical evidence in a case as well as from a deep knowledge of the specific systems used to analyze the evidence.

Further References

Akane, A., Matsubara, K., Nakamura, H., Takahashi, S., and Kimura, K., Identification of the heme compound copurified with deoxyribonucleic acid (DNA) from bloodstains, a major inhibitor of polymerase chain reaction (PCR) amplification, *J. Forensic Sci.*, 39(2), 362–372, 1994.

Akane, A., Seki, S., Shiono, H., Nakamura, H., Hasegawa, M., Kagawa, M., Matsubara, K., Nakahori, Y., Nagafuchi, S., and Nakagome, Y., Sex determination of forensic samples by dual PCR amplification of an X-Y homologous gene, *Forensic Sci. Int.*, 52(2), 143–148, 1992.

Baasner, A., Schafer, C., Junge, A., and Madea, B., Polymorphic sites in human mitochondrial DNA control region sequences: population data and maternal inheritance, *Forensic Sci. Int.*, 98(3), 169–178, 1998.

Baechtel, F.S., Presley, K.W., and Smerick, J.B., D1S80 typing of DNA from simulated forensic specimens, *J. Forensic Sci.*, 40(4), 536–545, 1995.

Benzinger, E.A., Emerek, E.A., Grigsby, N.L., Lovekamp, M., Deadman, H.A., Thompson, J.L., Sallee, P.J., and Riech, A.K., Products of partial digestion with Hae III. 1. Characterization, casework experience and confirmation of the theory of three, four, and five banded RFLP pattern origins using partial digestion, *J. Forensic Sci.*, 42(5), 850–863, 1997.

Benzinger, E.A. and Duewer, D.L., Products of partial digestion with Hae III. 2. Quantification, *J. Forensic Sci.*, 42(5), 864–872, 1997.

Bar, W., Brinkmann, B., Budowle, B., Carracedo, A., Gill, P., Holland, M., Lincoln, P.J., Mayr, W., Morling, G., Olaisen, B., Schneider, P., Tully, G., and Wilson, M., DNA Commission of the International Society for Forensic Genetics: Guidelines for mitochondrial DNA typing, *Int. J. Legal Med.*, 113(2), 193–196, 2000.

Barnett, P.D., Blake, E.T., Super-Mihalovich, J., Harmor, G., Rawlinson, L., and Wraxall, B., Discussion of "Effects of presumptive test reagents on the ability to obtain restriction fragment length polymorphism (RFLP) patterns from human blood and semen stains," *J. Forensic Sci.*, 37(2), 69–70, 1992.

Budowle, B. and Sprecher, C.J., Concordance study on population database samples using the PowerPlex™ 16 kit and AmpF*l*STR® Profiler Plus™ kit and AmpF*l*STR® COfiler™ kit, *J. Forensic Sci.*, 46(3), 637–641, 2001.

Calloway, C.D., Reynolds, R.L., Herrin, G.L., and Wyatt, W.A., The frequency of heteroplasmy in the HVII region of mtDNA differs across tissue types and increases with age, *Am. J. Hum. Genet.*, 66, 1384–1397, 2000.

Carracedo, A., D'Aloja, E., Dupuy, B., Jangblad, A., Karjalainen, M., Lambert, C., Parson, W., Pfeiffer, H., Pfitzinger, H., Sabatier, M., et al., Reproducibility of mtDNA analysis between laboratories: a report of the European DNA Profiling Group (EDNAP), *Forensic Sci. Int.*, 97(2–3), 165–170, 1998.

Comey, C.T., Budowle, B., Adams, D.E., Baumstark, A.L., Lindsey, J.A., and Presley, L.A., PCR amplification and typing of the HLA DQ alpha gene in forensic samples, *J. Forensic Sci.*, 38(2), 239–249, 1993.

Cosso, S. and Reynolds, R., Validation of the AmpliFLP D1S80 PCR Amplification Kit for forensic casework analysis according to TWGDAM guidelines, *J. Forensic Sci.*, 40(3), 424–434, 1995.

Cotton, R.W., Forman, L., and Word, C.J., Research on DNA typing validated in the literature, *Am. J. Hum. Genet.*, 49(4), 898–903, 1991.

Crouse, C.A., Vincek, V., and Caraballo, B.K., Analysis and interpretation of the HLA DQ alpha "1.1 weak-signal" observed during the PCR-based typing method, *J. Forensic Sci.*, 39(1), 41–51, 1994.

Crouse, C.A. and Schumm, J., Investigation of species specificity using nine PCR-based human STR systems, *J. Forensic Sci.*, 40(6), 952–956, 1995.

Duewer, D.L., Currie, L.A., Reeder, D.J., Leigh, S.D., Liu, H.K., and Mudd, J.L., Interlaboratory comparison of autoradiographic DNA profiling measurements. 2. Measurement uncertainty and its propagation, *Anal. Chem.*, 67(7), 1220–1231, 1995.

Erlich, H.A., HLA DQ alpha typing of forensic specimens, *Forensic Sci. Int.*, 53(2), 227–228, 1992.

Fernandez-Rodriguez, A., Alonso, A., Albarran, C., Martin, P., Iturralde, M.J., Montesino, M., and Sancho, M., Microbial DNA challenge studies of PCR-based systems used in forensic genetics, *Adv. Haemogenetics*, 6, 177, 1996.

Fildes, N. and Reynolds, R., Consistency and reproducibility of AmpliType PM results between seven laboratories: field trial results, *J. Forensic Sci.*, 40(2), 279–286, 1995.

Frank, W.E., Llewellyn, B.E., Fish, P.A., Riech, A.K., Marcacci, T.L., Gandor, D.W., Parker, D., Carter, R.R., and Thibault, S.M., Validation of the AmpF*STR™ Profiler Plus PCR Amplification Kit for Use in Forensic Casework, *J. Forensic Sci.*, 46(3), 642–646, 2001.

Fregeau, C.J. and Fourney, R.M., DNA typing with fluorescently tagged short tandem repeats: a sensitive and accurate approach to human identification, *Biotechniques*, 15(1), 100–119, 1993.

Gill, P. et al., DNA Commission of the International Society of Forensic Genetics: Recommendations on Forensic Analysis Using Y-Chromosome STRs, *Int. J. Legal Med.*, 114, 305–309, 2001.

Gusmao, L., Amorim, A., Prata, M.J., Pereira, L., Lareu, M.V., and Carracedo, A., Failed PCR amplifications of MBP-STR alleles due to polymorphism in the primer annealing region, *Int. J. Legal Med.*, 108(6), 313–315, 1996.

Gusmao, L., Gonzalez-Neira, A., Pestoni, C., Brion, M., Lareu, M.V., and Carracedo, A., Robustness of the Y STRs DYS19, DYS389 I and II, DYS390 and DYS393: optimization of a PCR pentaplex, *Forensic Sci. Int.*, 106(3), 163–172, 1999.

Hochmeister, M.N., Budowle, B., Borer, U.V., and Dirnhofer, R., Effects of nonoxinol-9 on the ability to obtain DNA profiles from postcoital vaginal swabs, *J. Forensic Sci.*, 38(2), 442–447, 1993.

Holland, M.M. and Parsons, T.J., Mitochondrial DNA sequence analysis — validation and use for forensic casework, *Forensic Sci. Rev.*, 11(1), 21, 1999.

Kimpton, C., Gill, P., D'Aloja, E., Andersen, J.F., Bar, W., Holgersson, S., Jacobsen, S., Johnsson, V., Kloosterman, A.D., Lareu, M.V., et al., Report on the second EDNAP collaborative STR exercise, European DNA Profiling Group, *Forensic Sci. Int.*, 71(2), 137–152, 1995.

Kline, M.C. and Jenkins, B., Non-amplification of a vWA allele, *J. Forensic Sci.*, 43(1), 250, 1998.

Laber, T.L., Giese, S.A., Iverson, J.T., and Liberty, J.A., Validation studies on the forensic analysis of restriction fragment length polymorphism (RFLP) on LE agarose gels without ethidium bromide: effects of contaminants, sunlight, and the electrophoresis of varying quantities of deoxyribonucleic acid (DNA), *J. Forensic Sci.*, 39(3), 707–730, 1994.

Linch, C.A., Whiting, D.A., and Holland, M.M., Human hair histogenesis for the mitochondrial DNA forensic scientist, *J. Forensic Sci.*, 46(4), 844–853, 2001.

Lygo, J.E., Johnson, P.E., Holdaway, D.J., Woodroffe, S., Whitaker, J.P., Clayton, T.M., Kimpton, C.P., and Gill, P., The validation of short tandem repeat (STR) loci for use in forensic casework, *Int. J. Legal Med.*, 107(2), 77–89, 1994.

McNally, L. et al., The effects of environment and substrata on deoxyribonucleic acid (DNA) isolated from human bloodstains exposed to ultraviolet light, heat, humidity, and soil contamination, *J. Forensic Sci.*, 32(5), 1070–1077, 1989.

Moretti, T.R., Baumstark, A.L., Defenbaugh, D.A., Keys, K.M., Brown, A.L., and Budowle, B., Validation of STR typing by capillary electrophoresis, *J. Forensic Sci.*, 46(3), 661–676, 2001.

Moretti, T.R., Baumstark, A.L., Defenbaugh, D.A., Keys, K.M., Smerick, J.B., and Budowle, B., Validation of short tandem repeats (STRs) for forensic usage: performance testing of fluorescent multiplex STR systems and analysis of authentic and simulated forensic samples, *J. Forensic Sci.*, 46(3), 647–660, 2001.

Parsons, T.J., Muniec, D.S., Sullivan, K., Woodyatt, N., Alliston-Greiner, R., Wilson, M.R., Berry, D.L., Holland, K.A., Weedn, V.W., Gill, P., et al., A high observed substitution rate in the human mitochondrial DNA control region, *Nature Genet.*, 15(4), 363–368, 1997.

Presley, L.A., Baumstark, A.L., and Dixon A., The effects of specific latent fingerprint and questioned document examinations on the amplification and typing of the HLA DQ alpha gene region in forensic casework, *J. Forensic Sci.*, 38(5), 1028–1036, 1993.

Prinz, M., Boll, K., Baum, H., and Haler, B., Multiplexing of Y chromosome specific STRs and performance for mixed samples, *Forensic Sci. Int.*, 85(3), 209–218, 1997.

Reynolds, R., Walker, K., Varlaro, J., Allen, M., Clark, E., Alavaren, M., and Erlich, H., Detection of sequence variation in the HVII region of the human mitochondrial genome in 689 individuals using immobilized sequence-specific oligonucleotide probes, *J. Forensic Sci.*, 45(6), 1210–1231, 2000.

Robertson, J.M., Sgueglia, J.B., Badger, C.A., Juston, A.C., and Ballantyne, J., Forensic applications of a rapid, sensitive, and precise multiplex off lysis of the four short tandem repeat loci HUMVWF31/A, HUMTH01, HUMF13A1, and HUMFES/FPS, *Electrophoresis*, 16(9), 1568–1576, 1995.

Roy, R. and Reynolds, R., AmpliType PM and HLA DQ alpha typing from pap smear, semen smear, and postcoital slides, *J. Forensic Sci.*, 40(2), 266–269, 1995.

Schneider, P.M., Fimmers, R., Woodroffe, S., Werrett, D.J., Bar, W., Brinkmann, B., Eriksen, B., Jones, S., Kloosterman, A.D., Mevag, B., et al., Report of a European collaborative exercise comparing DNA typing results using a single locus VNTR probe, *Forensic Sci. Int.*, 49(1), 1–15, 1991.

Schwartz, T.R., Schwartz, E.A., Mieszerski, L., McNally, L., and Kobilinsky, L., Characterization of deoxyribonucleic acid (DNA) obtained from teeth subjected to various environmental conditions, *J. Forensic Sci.*, 36(4), 979–990, 1991.

Shipp, E., Roelofs, R., Togneri, E., Wright, R., Atkinson, D., and Henry B., Effects of argon laser light, alternate source light, and cyanoacrylate fuming on DNA typing of human bloodstains, *J. Forensic Sci.*, 38(1), 184–191, 1993.

Thompson, W.C., Subjective interpretation, laboratory error and the value of forensic DNA evidence: three case studies, *Genetica*, 96(1–2), 153–168, 1995.

Thompson, W.C. and Ford, S., The meaning of a match: sources of ambiguity in the interpretation of DNA prints, in Farley, M. and Harrington, J., Eds., *Forensic DNA Technology*, Lewis Publishers, Chelsea, MI, 1991.

van Oorschot, R.A.H. and Jones, M.K., DNA fingerprints from fingerprints, *Nature*, 387, 767, 1997.

Walsh, P.S., Erlich, H.A., and Higuchi, R., Preferential PCR amplification of alleles: mechanisms and solutions, *PCR Methods and Applications*, 1(4), 241–250, 1992.

Walsh, P.S., Fildes, N., Louie, A.S., and Higuchi, R., Report of the blind trial of the Cetus AmpliType HLA DQ alpha forensic deoxyribonucleic acid (DNA) amplification and typing kit, *J. Forensic Sci.*, 36(5), 1551–1556, 1991.

Walsh, S., Commentary on Kline, M.C., Jenkins, B., Rogers, S., Non-amplification of a vWA allele, *J. Forensic Sci.*, 43(5), 1103, 1998.

Waye, J.S. and Fourney, R.M., Agarose gel electrophoresis of linear genomic DNA in the presence of ethidium bromide: band shifting and implications for forensic identity testing, *Appl. Theoret. Electrophoresis*, 1(4), 193–196, 1990.

Webb, M.B., Williams, N.J., and Sutton, M.D., Microbial DNA challenge studies of variable number tandem repeat (VNTR) probes used for DNA profiling analysis, *J. Forensic Sci.*, 5, 1172–1175, 1993.

Wilson, M.R., DiZinno, J.A., Polanskey, D., Replogle, J., and Budowle, B., Validation of mitochondrial DNA sequencing for forensic casework analysis, *Int. J. Legal Med.*, 108(2), 68–74, 1995.

Wilson, R.B., Ferrara, J.L., Baum, H.J., and Shaler, R.C., Guidelines for internal validation of the HLA DQ alpha DNA typing system, *Forensic Sci. Int.*, 66(1), 9–22, 1994.

Assessing the Strength of the Evidence

8

Without some expression of the strength of the source determination, the results of an examination are virtually worthless and potentially misleading. This was expressed most emphatically about DNA evidence in the 1992 report of the National Research Council. The ultimate purpose of DNA typing is to test the hypothesis that a particular person is the source of an item of biological evidence. An attempt is made to ascertain whether two samples, frequently evidence and reference, share a common source. The evidence sample (a biological fluid or tissue) and reference (typically a blood sample or buccal swab) are subjected to a battery of DNA tests. Upon completion, the analyst is able to render a determination as to the possible source(s) of the samples. Three conclusions are possible.

1. The profiles are different and therefore must have originated from different sources (**exclusion**). This conclusion is absolute and requires no further analysis or discussion.
2. It is not possible to be sure, based on the results of the test, whether the samples have the same DNA types (**inconclusive**). This might occur for a variety of reasons, including degradation, contamination, or failure of some aspect of the procedure (e.g., inhibition of amplification). One way of thinking about an inconclusive result is that there is no more information after the analysis than before; it is as if the analysis had never been performed.
3. The profiles are the same and could have originated from the same source.

If the profiles are determined to be the same, the question becomes: What is the strength of this result? The remainder of this chapter discusses the basis of some of the concepts used in reaching a conclusion of possible common source, and determining its strength.

I.   Determination of Genetic Concordance

Frequently, the word "match" is used to describe the **genetic concordance** between two samples. Scientists reserve a very narrow meaning for the word "match," and it is quite different than the connotation usually attributed to the word by non-scientists. Scientists are careful to limit the term "match" to mean that no significant differences were observed between two samples in the particular test(s) conducted. It is certainly possible that two samples may be different, but that the test used has failed to reveal those differences. Because DNA tests sample a relatively small percentage of the entire human genome, further analyses might reveal differences that could lead to an exclusion[1]. In contrast, the perception of the general public is that the word "match" connotes an absolute "individualization." A conclusion of genetic concordance merely describes the fact that two samples show the same types. Having said that, however, the strength of DNA typing lies in its immense powers of discrimination. Samples that show genetic concordance over numerous polymorphic DNA loci frequently approach, and in many cases reach, a level that convinces us that they share a unique common source.

In determining whether two samples have the same profile, it is important to know which marker system has been used. For the purposes of determining a profile frequency, it is convenient to divide typing systems into those detecting **continuous alleles** and those detecting **discrete alleles**.

A.   Continuous Allele Systems

RFLP markers are continuous allele systems; discrete individual types (where the exact number of repeat units can be ascertained) are not resolved by the methods used. This is due in large part, to the plethora of alleles possible at one locus and their relative composition. As an example, an allele containing 99 repeats of a 10-bp repeat unit may not be distinguishable from an allele containing 100 repeats of the same 10-bp repeat unit, but may be easily distinguished from an allele of 110 repeats. Therefore, after a visual assessment, a mathematical algorithm is used with the aid of a computer to estimate the fragment sizes.

For RFLP specifically, the first evaluation involves a visual inspection of the profiles. The analyst determines, based on his education, training, and experience, whether the band patterns between profiles show sufficient similarity to proceed to the next step. If the profiles are obviously different, there is no need to determine the size of the fragments to confirm the dissimilarity; the analysis ends at this point with a conclusion that the samples originate from different sources. There may also be situations where the band patterns in the two profiles, while close, do not support a conclusion of possible common source. If, in the analyst's trained judgment, the patterns appear indistinguishable, the profiles are submitted to computer analysis. Figure 8.1 is a computer-generated composite showing profiles in which the patterns appear to be the same.

In this step, a computer is used to measure the fragment length; the measurement is expressed in base pairs. The precision of the experimental measurement is considered in determining whether the band patterns could originate from the same source. The fragment length, as measured by the computer, has some experimental uncertainty associated with it. Research and experience have demonstrated that this is a function of the sample, the specific laboratory methodology, and the computer measurement system. When two profiles are said to "match," it is meant that, while fragments may not be *exactly* the same size, they are the same within the experimental uncertainty of the total method. When fragment lengths are compared between evidence and reference samples from the same source, small differences are seen in the number of base pairs that the computer has calculated for a

---

[1] However, it should also be noted that the probability of finding a difference between two samples decreases with each additional matching locus. The rarer the total profile frequency, the more unlikely it is that a difference between two samples will be uncovered by more testing.

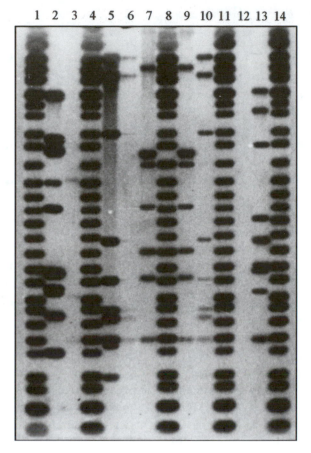

Figure 8.1 A computer-generated composite of the RFLP probings from five loci. It is clear that the pattern of bands is indistinguishable between lanes 5 and 10, and also between lanes 7 and 9.

particular band. These differences are expected from method-induced variation, as well as from sample-to-sample variation. The amount of difference that can occur between two samples from the same source is established through individual laboratory experimentation using known samples. This results in a **match criterion**, usually expressed as a percentage of the band size. It means that measurements of two bands must be within a certain percentage of each other to be considered the same. For example, if the match criteria is ±2.5%, the two samples must have band sizes that are within either +2.5% or −2.5% of their average or they will be excluded as originating from the same source.

B.   Discrete Allele Systems

In the PCR-based systems that have been developed for forensic use, the markers, whether length or sequence polymorphisms, are all detected as discrete alleles; the method clearly differentiates the types. This is facilitated by the existence of fewer alleles at each locus and the relative ease in resolving them. The comparison may be likened to analog (continuous allele) vs. digital (discrete allele) electronics. Genotypes of two samples are either the same or they are not. Ambiguity is present only for situations such as mixtures or weak samples for which a complete genotype cannot be deduced.

II.   Evaluation of Results

Samples may show genetic concordance under three circumstances:

1. **The samples come from a common source.** This means that the evidence sample (e.g., a blood, semen, or saliva sample) comes from the same person who provided the reference sample.
2. **The concordance is a coincidence.** This means that the evidence sample comes from someone other than the person who provided the reference sample. The genetic concordance results from two individuals, the reference donor and the true donor, who coincidentally share the same genetic profile for the particular markers examined.
3. **The concordance is an accident (erroneous).** This means that the evidence sample comes from someone other than the reference donor but that some collection, analytical, or clerical error has occurred such that the evidence and reference samples appear to have the same DNA profile.

Both the analyst and the courts, as well as any interested parties, want to know which of these three alternatives is the true one for the case under consideration. The ultimate strength of the concordance depends on which of these scenarios has produced the same genetic pattern in two samples. If only one or a few individuals have the profile found in the evidence, and the chance of error is small, then concordance between evidence and reference points to a strong inference of common source. If, on the other hand, a large percentage of the population shares the genetic profile detected, then the strength of the genetic concordance is reduced. This situation might occur when analysis of the evidence is limited to systems with relatively low inherent discrimination or when the DNA in the sample is of poor quality or insufficient quantity.

III.   Frequency Estimate Calculations

Once a possible common source has been inferred (by "matching" DNA profiles) between the evidence sample and reference donor, the strength of the inference becomes the next critical question. If many individuals share this profile, then the strength is minimal because some reasonable chance exists that someone else taken at random from the population (e.g., the wrong suspect chosen by the detective) has the same type. If, on the other hand, only a low probability exists that the types found are from someone other than the reference donor, then the inference of common source is strong.

The question then becomes: what is the probability of a "match" if someone *other* than the reference donor is the true donor? (Or, what is the probability of a random match?) The answer has typically been provided in the form of a profile frequency, that is, the number of times that this profile is seen in some reference population. An alternate form of that question is: what is the probability of finding this profile if the reference donor were the true donor compared to the probability of finding this profile if someone other than the reference donor were the true donor? While this seems like a more complicated question, in fact it is a more complete statement of the first question.

In summary, the critical matter in forensic science is to measure the strength of the inference of common source between the biological evidence and the reference donor. A common way of expressing that strength is to incorporate the frequency of the evidence profile in some form.

In simple terms, we want to express how many people might possess the profile seen in the biological evidence. The only way to determine this is by testing a representative number of people from a reference population and counting the number of times each genotype occurs. For genetic marker systems with just a few alleles, it is likely that all of the genotypes will be seen several times in a relatively small sample. For example, the loci that comprise the polymarker system each exhibit only two or three alleles in the population. All the possible combinations of two alleles can produce only three different genotypes; even three alleles can only combine into six different genotypes. With one exception[2], each of these types would be readily observed several times in a population of less than 100 people. This gives us confidence that the observed frequency of any particular type in a sample population represents the frequency in the population at large.

The problem becomes more complex with additional alleles. The DQA1 system contains seven additional alleles that may combine into 28 possible genotypes. A database of 100 people may now not be sufficient to detect all 28 genotypes at their representative frequencies; some might be overrepresented, while others might be underrepresented or missed entirely. We may have to test over 400 people to have confidence that the observed genotype frequencies adequately represent the actual population makeup.

Consider now the hypervariable RFLP loci. Some of these loci have 50 or more alleles, such that each pair can combine into approximately 1275 genotypes. Typing enough people to find how often each of these types occurs would be a daunting task. Further complicate the situation by considering four hypervariable loci, each with 50 alleles. The number of allele combinations at four loci is $(1275) \times (1275) \times (1275) \times (1275)$, or about 2.6 trillion possible genotypes. Testing everyone in order to obtain a fair representation of all these types is clearly impossible. Additionally, because there are only about six billion people alive on Earth at this time, most of these combinations do not even exist.

The solution to this dilemma (how to estimate frequencies when there are a large number of alleles, each at low frequency) is to invoke population genetics theory, particularly two models called **Hardy-Weinberg equilibrium** (**H-W**) and **linkage equilibrium** (**LE**). These models allow for the estimation of genotypes based on individual **allele frequencies**, rather than observed **genotype frequencies**. Because the total number of alleles is much smaller than the possible combinations of those alleles into genotypes, this is clearly a much more practical proposition. The models may be summarized as follows:

The **Hardy-Weinberg** model states that there is a predictable relationship between allele frequencies and genotype frequencies at a single locus. This is a mathematical relationship that allows for the estimation of genotype frequencies in a population even if the genotype has not been seen in an actual population survey.

[2] The HBGG C allele is relatively rare in populations other than African-American. For the purpose of estimating a profile frequency, its frequency is artificially raised to a five-event minimum so that a profile containing this allele was not misrepresented as unduly rare.

Linkage equilibrium is defined as the steady-state condition of a population where the frequency of any multi-locus genotype is the product of each separate locus. This allows for the estimation of a DNA profile frequency over several loci, even if the profile has not been seen in an actual population survey.

IV. Population Substructure

Theoretical application of the H-W model rests on several assumptions[3]. Mating must be random, the mating population large, and migration negligible. However, it can be reasonably argued that mating is not random in most human populations, that some mating populations are not large, and that migration is variable among mating populations throughout the world. In fact, it is well accepted that the U.S. population is a mixture of people of various origins. For example, in New York City, it is well-known that neighborhoods exist of, for instance, Italians, Germans, and Russians. It is also commonly accepted that people tend to mate among those with similar ancestry. This results in matings among people who are more related to each other than to people outside their common ancestry. If a suspect comes from such a group, more people with the same DNA profiles may exist in this particular community than we might estimate from a survey of the general population. The phrases used to express this existence of smaller populations within a larger group include **population subgroups**, **subpopulations**, **population substructure**, and **structured populations**.

Given that the U.S. population is structured to some extent, and the assumptions for H-W cannot strictly be met, how is it possible to use calculations based on these models to arrive at useful frequency estimates? In actual fact, imperfect adherence to H-W and LE does not invalidate the use of these models in estimating frequencies of DNA profiles. This is substantiated by both scientific theory and empirical testing.

Research has shown that the effects of substructuring are predictable. Relative to theoretical H-W proportions, the effect is to increase the occurrence of homozygotes and to reduce the number of heterozygotes at a single locus. The effect on LE is to increase the correlation between some loci, while decreasing the correlation between others. These deviations can be determined and accommodated using statistical correction factors. Once sufficient data has been gathered for a specific population, departures from both H-W and LE can be estimated. This allows for an evaluation of the extent and direction of the error that might occur if frequency estimates are calculated using H-W and LE assumptions.

The concern over the lack of knowledge regarding the effects of population substructure has been addressed by two major studies sponsored by the National Research Council (NRC) of the National Academy of Sciences. The first study, published in 1992, concluded that insufficient knowledge existed to substantiate use of the H-W and LE calculations. Several recommendations were made that resulted in an extremely conservative method of estimating the frequency of a DNA profile (termed the "**ceiling principle**"). In 1996, the second NRC report (known as NRC II) concluded that enough information had been collected since the original study to eliminate the need for the most conservative recommendations

---

[3] Strictly speaking, these assumptions are essential, but not necessarily sufficient for a population to conform to the idealized model, and are particular to human populations.

(including the ceiling principle). This second report (see Further References) is an excellent source for a deeper understanding of the issues and the solutions presented here.

Finally, it is imperative to emphasize that frequencies are estimated for the *evidence profile*, not the *suspect profile*. The race or ethnicity of the suspect is irrelevant when interpreting test results. It is erroneous to assume that the suspect was at the crime scene to determine if the suspect was at the crime scene! It is also not possible to evoke the race or ethnicity of a person by looking at the markers used in forensic DNA testing. Therefore, the choice of a relevant population for determining the frequency of an evidence profile is influenced by external factors and the context of the case, such as eyewitness accounts or the location of the crime. In the absence of such external information, general population frequencies can be employed, and racial or ethnic frequencies are used as comparisons or limits. To put things in perspective, it is useful to remember that in forensic applications of DNA typing, a population frequency estimate is just that — an estimate — and is only used to help us understand the strength of an inference of common source.

A.   Estimating Frequencies

The goal in deriving frequencies for any DNA profile is to provide an estimate that is scientifically conservative; that is, it should not overstate the strength of an inference of common source. Forensic scientists, geneticists, and biostatisticians have devised several methods to accomplish this goal (see Appendix E for an example). We describe here a generic outline of the steps used in estimating profile frequencies.

1.   Continuous Allele Systems (RFLP)

a. Population studies.   Population data is collected for different population groups (commonly Caucasian, African-American, Hispanic, and Asian) and allele sizes at particular loci are measured. Because RFLP is inherently a continuous allele system, it must be transformed into a discrete allele system by a method called **binning**. For any one locus, the length of the autorad is divided into size groups called **bins**. The alleles that fall between any two of these arbitrarily defined boundaries are combined into the same bin[4]. The frequency for all of the alleles in a bin is derived by counting them and dividing by the total number of alleles in the population. A result of this is that very rare alleles that may have been undersampled in the population are assigned artificially high frequencies. Consequently, their rareness is not overstated.

b. Evaluation for H-W and LE.   The frequency of the observed alleles and genotypes within and between loci are tested for departure from H-W and LE. Because some departure always exists, the magnitude is evaluated, and a decision is made to use or reject the frequency data.

c. Calculate genotype frequencies.   The bands from an evidence profile are assigned to the appropriate bin(s) in the population data table. The allele frequencies derived from these bins are used to calculate the genotype frequency at any one locus using the H-W equation. The calculation of homozygote frequencies must be treated differently, however.

---

[4] The binning system provides instructions for very specific contingencies, such as an allele situated on a bin boundary. For more information, see Budowle et al., 1991.

Because, in substructured populations, homozygotes are more prevalent than H-W would predict, a modification is used that ameliorates this effect.

d. Multiplication of loci. The allele frequencies from different loci are multiplied together under the assumption of LE to obtain the frequency of the complete DNA profile. This is usually expressed as "1 in XXX" (e.g., 1 in 3 million), where XXX denotes the number of people who would need to be sampled to see the profile, on average, once.

2. *Discrete Allele Systems (All PCR Systems)*

a. Population studies. Population data is collected for different population groups (commonly Caucasian, African-American, Hispanic, and Asian) and allele frequencies at each locus of interest are calculated.

b. Evaluation for H-W and LE. The frequency of the observed alleles and genotypes within and between loci are tested for departure from H-W and LE. Because some departure always exists, the magnitude is evaluated and a decision is made to use or reject the frequency data.

c. Calculate genotype frequencies. The allele frequencies are used to calculate the frequency of a genotype at any one locus using H-W proportions with, again, one exception. Homozygote frequencies are calculated using a correction factor called *theta* (θ) that accounts for the effect of substructuring. This is different from the method used for continuous allele data. (See Appendix E for an example.)

d. Multiplication of loci. The allele frequencies from different loci are multiplied together under the assumption of LE to obtain the frequency of the complete DNA profile. This is usually expressed as "1 in XXX" (e.g., 1 in 3 million), where XXX denotes the number of people who would need to be sampled to see the profile, on average, once.

3. *Correction Factors*

Different workers have formulated a variety of correction factors and safeguards that ensure conservative frequency estimates. Some of them are discussed in this chapter. NRC II provides further guidance on reasonable corrections that guard against overestimating the strength of the concordance without seriously compromising the power of the tests.

4. *Relatives*

The calculations outlined above are for random, unrelated individuals. A special case exists for related individuals. Siblings, in particular, share more genetic material with each other than anyone else. This is because they inherit their genes from the same two people, Mom and Dad. This idea can be extended to more distant relationships such as children, grandchildren, and cousins. In these relationships, some genetic material is shared; but the more distant the relationship, the fewer genes in common. As a profile frequency becomes so rare that it becomes unreasonable to believe that another random, unrelated person could coincidentally share it, the only realistic possibility for a coincidental match (barring identical twins) is from a sibling. However, it is also true that the more loci tested, the greater the chance to differentiate between siblings. Special calculations are applied to test the hypothesis that a relative of the suspect could be the donor.

5.   *Counting Method*

Others have tried to assess the strength of genetic concordance without using the assumptions of H-W and LE. They simply count the number of times a particular genotype is seen in the database used for the population study. These calculations do not take advantage of population theory and tend to underestimate the strength of the concordance compared to frequency calculations. However, this method is used for assessing the strength of mtDNA results. This is because the mtDNA genome obeys different genetic laws than the chromosomes on which nuclear DNA resides, and the same genetic models cannot be applied to the segregation of mtDNA in the population. In addition, the mtDNA databases are not yet large enough to be confident that an occurrence of a particular type divided by the number of people in the database gives a reasonable estimate of the frequency. Other peculiarities associated with ascertaining the strength of a mtDNA result are addressed in Chapter 7.

6.   *Error Rates*

It has been suggested by some that the estimated profile frequency should be combined in some fashion with an estimate of the "error rate." Although the first National Research Council Committee suggested this practice, the subsequent NRC II Committee recanted this position completely (see Chapter 10). To even have this discussion, we must define what we mean by an error. While scientists understand that different categories of errors exist, and may not differentiate one as more serious than another, forensic scientists must define errors in the context of the law. The law considers a false inclusion (leading to an inference of guilt) as more serious than a false exclusion (leading to an inference of innocence). Therefore, for this purpose, we define an error as a false inclusion or match: two samples are concluded to originate from the same source when, in fact, they do not.

Second, we clarify that a "rate" at which errors are made does not exist as such. To apply a rate suggests that errors occur in some constant way that is predictive. This assumes the rather ridiculous notion that if an analyst or laboratory discovers an error, nothing will be done to prevent that sort of error from happening in the future. It also assumes that a rate determined for a particular analyst, a particular laboratory, or the discipline as a whole, at some point in time, is generally applicable and will remain constant. Finally, it assumes that the risk of error in each case is inherently similar and fails to consider differences due to, at a minimum, the specific circumstances, evidence, and testing procedures. Clearly, none of these assumptions are reasonable. We would suggest that the more useful question is: Did an error occur in this case? In Chapter 10, we mention some safeguards designed to detect and correct such an error, should it occur.

V.   Likelihood Ratios

A.   What Is the Question?

Earlier in this chapter when we first introduced frequency estimates, we suggested that a complete statement about the origin of an evidence profile always involves the comparison of at least two hypotheses, whether explicitly mentioned or not: What is the probability of finding this profile if the reference donor were the true donor, compared to the probability of finding this profile if someone other than the reference donor were the true donor? A more general expression of this thinking was formalized by the Reverend Thomas Bayes in the 18th century. The comparison of two hypotheses is now called a **likelihood ratio (LR)**. The full expression of Bayes' Theorem looks like this:

$$\text{Prior odds} \times \text{LR} = \text{Posterior odds}$$

This may be read: However likely you think a proposition (prior odds), change your judgment (posterior odds) by this additional evidence (LR). Bayes' theorem provides a general model for updating our uncertainty about any proposition. The forensic scientist generally focuses on just the LR portion of the theorem and does not comment on areas outside the realm of physical evidence that affect the prior and posterior odds.

A simple likelihood ratio (LR) is typically written as follows[5]:

$$LR = \frac{P(E \mid H_1)}{P(E \mid H_2)}$$

where:

P = probability

E = evidence of common source.

H = hypothesis (H_1 and H_2 are the two hypotheses under consideration.)

The symbol " $\mid$ " means "given that," or "assuming"; the parentheses are translated as "of." Under the hypothesis proposed above, the numerator of the likelihood ratio is read, "The probability of *evidence of a common source*, assuming that the putative source is the true source." In the same way, the denominator is read, "The probability of *evidence of a common source*, assuming that an alternate source is the true source."

When examining physical evidence, we cannot know the probability of common source given the evidence that we see, but we can calculate the probability of finding this evidence if we assume the proposition to be either true or false. If we assume that the evidence is from the putative source, then the probability of our test showing similar results to the reference is 1 (100%); that is, we are certain that the test results of the evidence and the reference will be concordant. If we assume that the evidence is from some other source, then the probability of seeing concordant results is the chance of encountering this evidence at random. In this situation, a frequency calculation provides a useful approximation of this probability. Thus, in the simplest case of a complete single-source evidence profile, the LR expression reverts to the reciprocal of the profile frequency. For example:

Profile frequency = 1/1,000,000

$$LR = \frac{P(E \mid H_1)}{P(E \mid H_2)} = \frac{1}{1/1,000,000} = \frac{1,000,000}{1} = 1,000,000 \text{ (or 1 million)}$$

---

[5] Formally, a character for "information," I is also included along with each hypothesis [$P(E \mid H_1,I)$]. Because for forensic uses, the information is usually the same for both hypotheses, it cancels out and is rarely articulated.

This could be expressed in words as, "Given the DNA profile found in the evidence, it is 1 million times more likely that it is from the suspect than from another random person with the same profile."

B.   Complex Evidence

From the preceding discussion, it may seem like using an LR to express the strength of the evidence gratuitously complicates the matter while providing no additional useful information. However, where the evidence is more complicated, such as when mixtures, close relatives, or partial profiles are involved, the utility of using an LR to convey the strength of the evidence becomes more evident. For example, an LR is the only way to convey the conditional probability that a sibling of the suspect contributed the evidence or to compare the probability of different numbers of contributors to a mixture. Similarly, the numerator might be less than 1 if it cannot be determined if an allele drop-out occurred in a marginal sample. In Appendix F we provide an example that compares the probabilities of various combinations of a boyfriend, the suspect, and an unknown male as possible multiple contributors to a sexual assault sample. A full treatment of these complicated situations is beyond the scope of this book except to mention their existence and the utility of LRs in interpreting them. We refer both interested readers to Evett and Weir's 1998 volume, *Interpreting DNA Evidence*.

1.   *Mixtures*

One of the most common scenarios in forensic DNA evidence is the presence of an unresolved mixture. This could result from an incomplete differential extraction of a sperm-containing sample, or from a non-sperm-containing sample with multiple contributors. Some practitioners choose not to provide any statistic for a mixture. In our opinion, this is unhelpful, irresponsible, and cowardly. At best, it renders the evidence essentially meaningless and virtually worthless because no weight can be assigned to it. At worst, it is potentially misleading.

a. Probability of Exclusion (P_E).   Of those who agree that some indication of the strength of the evidence must be provided, many choose to provide a **probability of exclusion (P_E)**. This calculation basically adds together the profile frequencies of anyone who could have contributed to the evidence, regardless of logical conditions or obvious differential contributions. While it is often believed to be a conservative statement of the strength of the evidence, in fact much of the time grossly understating it, this cannot always be assumed to be the case.

For example, if four alleles of equal intensity are present at a locus, theoretically between two and four individuals could have contributed the evidence, depending on whether any of them were homozygotes or heterozygotes. However, if one of the putative contributors is a homozygote, then at least two more people must be present to account for all of the alleles; thus, to include that particular homozygote, at least three contributors must be present in the sample. If, from the case circumstances, it is only reasonable to assume two contributors, the person who is homozygous at that locus must be excluded. By definition, a traditional P_E also blatantly ignores differences in allele intensity that might be used to logically pair alleles. Thus, a potential contributor whose allele pair at the locus in question is represented by alleles that would not logically be paired in the evidence would also be falsely included using a P_E calculation. These sorts of assumptions should be stated when providing a P_E so that it is clear that potential contributors might be falsely included.

A modified P_E that allows for separation of obvious major and minor components of a mixture, and where assumptions regarding the number of contributors are stated, can be used to give a lower limit on the strength of the evidence, but rarely provides the best estimate of the strength.

b. LRs.   The use of an LR for mixtures allows for the incorporation of facts about the evidence (e.g., obvious major and minor contributors) and also assumptions (e.g., the number of total contributors). For example, one could compare whether the DNA profile obtained would be more likely under the assumption of two contributors or three contributors. This would lead to inferences about whether particular people would be included or excluded based on the different scenarios. The use of an LR does depend on our ability to state logical, meaningful, and relatively few hypotheses. Sometimes, the evidence is simply too complex for this, and we must default to the modified P_E described above. Occasionally, the evidence is so complex that more alternatives are possible than can reasonably be compared; the evidence is incapable of providing an answer to the relevant question. This is one of the times that an "inconclusive" conclusion can be appropriate. For a further discussion of using LRs to interpret mixtures and other complex results, we again refer the remaining interested reader to the Evett and Weir volume mentioned above.

C.   Articulating the Hypothesis

By convention, LRs used in forensic science have been presented with H_1 as the "prosecution hypothesis" (H_p) and H_2 as the "defense hypothesis" (H_d). This nomenclature has had the unfortunate consequence of alienating many criminalists at first blush. The scientist immediately recoils at the thought of proposing adversarial hypotheses, and some dismiss the utility of LRs without exploring them further. In fact, this nomenclature is completely extraneous to the mathematical reasoning. The scientist may simply use the LR as a tool to compare any number of reasonable hypotheses, without considering which side might advance them. A simple change in nomenclature to $[H_1, H_2, \ldots]$ makes LRs much more palatable to the scientist.

VI.   When Is a DNA Profile Unique?

But what of the ultimate holy grail of forensic science — the ability to declare a DNA profile unique in the world. In some ways that issue is even more contentious than when Alec Jeffreys first gave us multi-locus DNA "fingerprints." Ironically, DNA is actually hobbled by reliable population statistics that allow for the calculation of reasonably accurate profile frequencies. In other disciplines, where numerical estimates are much more difficult, analysts have long provided an opinion of source with little to support it other than training and experience.

The early switch to single-locus RFLP probes made the statistics easier to perform, but ironically reduced the power of the system. When only a few RFLP probes were available, the profile frequencies obtained were clearly not individualizing. We spent so much time protesting that DNA was not akin to the perceived power of dermatoglyphic fingerprints to individualize[6], that it took us a long time to rethink the problem, even when numerous

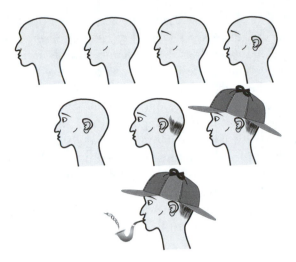

Figure 8.2 The anatomy of a profile. Individual features such as eyes, nose, ears, hair, and accoutrements help us to differentiate one person from the next. With enough features, we can be confident in the identity of any particular person. Genetic markers work in exactly the same way. With enough loci (assuming no laboratory error and disregarding twins), we can become convinced that a sample originates from a particular source.

RFLP probes provided frequencies several thousands of times more rare than the reciprocal of the Earth's population. Part of the reticence was due to the fact that many laboratories never developed the powerful RFLP systems, and instead started with the relatively indiscriminate PCR-based sequence-polymorphic systems at the DQA1 locus and subsequently the five polymarker loci. But STRs have leveled the playing field. Even with only nine STR loci, reciprocal profile frequencies in the millions and trillions are commonly obtained. Using 13 or more loci, the raw reciprocal profile frequencies exceeding quadrillions easily outnumber the total number of people who have ever lived on the face of the Earth[7]. Thus, we are faced once again with the conundrum of whether the DNA analyst can provide an opinion regarding the source of an evidence sample.

In July 2000, the FBI formalized a position they had been suggesting for some time. They used a statistical calculation to determine when, with a large degree of confidence, they would feel comfortable making a "source determination." The FBI suggests that, for crimes committed in the United States, the U.S. population is larger than any relevant suspect population. They are willing to say that if the profile frequency obtained is less than 3.9×10^{-11}, they are 99% certain that no other person in the United States could have contributed the sample (Figure 8.2). They contend that this formula is appropriate even when the suspect population is a genetically isolated subgroup or includes siblings.

On the heels of a decade of controversy, much of it focused on population statistics, many laboratories have been understandably reluctant to make this leap. Opposition has also come from members of the academic statistical genetics community who argue that the FBI "identity calculation" is incorrect and makes unwarranted assumptions, particularly about subpopulations and close relatives. The back-and-forth between these two camps has

---

[6] Ironically, the scientific basis of fingerprint comparison is now being questioned against the quantitative standard that has been set by DNA. For more on this topic, see the references by Cole.
[7] The total number of human births ever has been estimated at about 100 billion (<http://www.prb.org/wf/quickfacts_world.html>).

resulted in a statistics war of sorts, waged on the pages of the FBI's online journal, *Forensic Science Communications* and the AAFS's *Journal of Forensic Sciences*. While the arguments are somewhat enigmatic, it appears that the academic camp is arguing less with the result and more with the process. The debate is unlikely to be resolved before the publication of this book. Regardless of the exact calculations that are used to determine a limit profile frequency, other scientists have suggested that, in the absence of specific case evidence to the contrary, the population of the world might be the more relevant limit on a suspect population. Given the mobility of people in today's society, perhaps one should not assume that the true perpetrator resides on the same continent where the crime was committed.

To put the controversy in perspective, it is useful to remember Dr. David Stoney's now oft-quoted admonition that "individualization cannot be proven; we can only become convinced of it." In any case, we must remember that a declaration of source attribution does not tell us how the sample came to be or whether it is even relevant to the crime event. Whether conveyed by a statistic or an opinion, the relationship of a piece of evidence to a source is only the first step in determining its significance with respect to the crime.

Further References

Balding, D.J., When can a DNA profile be regarded as unique?, *Science & Justice*, 39, 257-260, 1999.

Balding, D.J. and Nichols, R.A., DNA profile match probability calculation: how to allow for population stratification, relatedness, database selection and single bands, *Forensic Sci. Int.*, 64(2–3), 125–40, 1994.

Bellamy, R.J., Inglehearn, C.F., Jalili, I.K., Jeffrey, A.J., and Bhattacharya, S.S., Increased band sharing in DNA fingerprints of an inbred human population, *Human Genet.*, 87(3), 341–347, 1991.

Brookfield, J.F., Statistical issues in DNA evidence, *Electrophoresis*, 16(9), 1665–1669, 1995.

Brookfield, J.F., The effect of relatedness on likelihood ratios and the use of conservative estimates, *Genetica*, 96(1–2), 13–19, 1995.

Budowle, B., Chakraborty, R., Carmody, G., and Monson, K.L., Reply to Weir, *Forensic Sci. Commun.*, 3(1), 2001, <http://www.fbi.gov/hq/lab/fsc/backissu/jan2001/index.htm>.

Budowle, B., Chakraborty, R., Carmody, G., and Monson, K.L., Source attribution of a forensic DNA profile, *Forensic Sci. Commun.*, 2(3), 2000, <http://www.fbi.gov/hq/lab/fsc/back-issu/july2000/index.htm>.

Budowle, B., The effects of inbreeding on DNA profile frequency estimates using PCR-based loci, *Genetica*, 96(1–2), 21–25, 1995.

Budowle, B., Lindsey, J.A., DeCou, J.A., Koons, B.W., Giusti, A.M., and Comey, C.T., Validation and population studies of the loci LDLR, GYPA, HBGG, D7S8, and GC (PM loci), and HLA DQ alpha using a multiplex amplification and typing procedure, *J. Forensic Sci.*, 40(1), 45–54, 1995.

Budowle, B. and Monson, K.L., Greater differences in forensic DNA profile frequencies estimated from racial groups than from ethnic subgroups, *Clin. Chim. Acta*, 228(1), 3–18, 1994.

Budowle, B. and Monson K.L., The forensic significance of various reference population databases for estimating the rarity of variable number of tandem repeat (VNTR) loci profiles, *Exs*, 67, 177–191, 1993.

Budowle, B., Giusti, A.M., Waye, J.S., Baechtel, F.S., Fourney, R.M., Adams, D.E., Presley, L.A., Deadman, H.A., and Monson, K.L., Fixed-bin analysis for statistical evaluation of continuous distributions of allelic data from VNTR loci, for use in forensic comparisons, *Am. J. Hum. Genet.*, 48(5), 841–855, 1991.

Chakraborty, R., De Andrade, M., Daiger, S.P., and Budowle, B., Apparent heterozygote deficiencies observed in DNA typing data and their implications in forensic applications, *Ann. Hum. Genet.*, 56(Pt 1), 45–57, 1992.

Chakraborty, R., Fornage, M., Gueguen, R., and Boerwinkle, E., Population genetics of hypervariable loci: analysis of PCR based VNTR polymorphism within a population, *Exs*, 58, 127–143, 1991.

Chakraborty, R. and Jin, L., Heterozygote deficiency, population substructure and their implications in DNA fingerprinting, *Hum. Genet.*, 88(3), 267–272, 1992.

Chakraborty, R., Jin, L., Zhong, Y., Srinivasan, M.R., and Budowle, B., On allele frequency computation from DNA typing data, *Int. J. Legal Med.*, 106(2), 103, 1993.

Chakraborty, R. and Kidd, K.K., The utility of DNA typing in forensic work, *Science*, 254(5039), 1735–1739, 1991.

Chakraborty, R., Sample size requirements for addressing the population genetic issues of forensic use of DNA typing, *Hum. Biol.*, 642, 141–159, 1992.

Chakraborty, R., Srinivasan, M.R., and Daiger, S.P., Evaluation of standard error and confidence interval of estimated multilocus genotype probabilities, and their implications in DNA forensics, *Am. J. Hum. Genet.*, 52(1), 60, 1993.

Chakraborty, R., Srinivasan, M.R., and de Andrade, M., Intraclass and interclass correlations of allele sizes within and between loci in DNA typing data, *Genetics*, 133(2), 411, 1993.

Chakraborty, R., Zhong, Y., Jin, L., and Budowle, B., Nondetectability of restriction fragments and independence of DNA fragment sizes within and between loci in RFLP typing of DNA, *Am. J. Hum. Genet.*, 55(2), 391, 1994.

Chakraborty, R. and Zhong, Y., Statistical power of an exact test of Hardy-Weinberg proportions of genotypic data at a multiallelic locus, *Hum. Hered.*, 44(1), 1, 1994.

Chakraborty, R. and Li., Z., Correlation of DNA fragment sizes within loci in the presence of non-detectable alleles, *Genetica*, 96(1–2), 27–36, 1995.

Clark, A.G., Hamilton, J.F., and Chambers, G.K., Inference of population subdivision from the VNTR distributions of New Zealanders, *Genetica*, 96(1–2), 7–49, 1995.

Cohen, J.E., The ceiling principle is not always conservative in assigning genotype frequencies for forensic DNA testing, *Am. J. Hum. Genet.*, 51(5), 1165–1168, 1992.

Cohen, J.E., DNA fingerprinting for forensic identification: potential effects on data interpretation of subpopulation heterogeneity and band number variability, *Am. J. Hum. Genet.*, 46(2), 358–368, 1990.

Cole, S., *Suspect Identities: A History of Fingerprinting and Criminal Identification*, Harvard University Press, May 2001.

Cole, S., What counts for identity? The historical origins of the methodology of latent fingerprint identification, *Sci. in Context*, 12(1), 139, 1999.

Cole, S., Witnessing identification: latent fingerprinting evidence and expert knowledge, *Soc. Stud. Sci.*, 28(5–6), 687, 1998.

Collins, A. and Morton, N.E., Likelihood ratios for DNA identification, *Proc. Natl. Acad. Sci. U.S.A.*, 91(13), 6007–6011, 1994.

Deka, R., Shriver, M.D., Yu, L.M., Ferrell, R.E., and Chakraborty, R., Intra- and inter-population diversity at short tandem repeat loci in diverse populations of the world, *Electrophoresis*, 16(9), 659–664, 1995.

D'Eustachio, P., Interpreting DNA fingerprints, *Nature*, 356(6369), 483, 1992.

Devlin, B. and Risch, N., A note on Hardy-Weinberg equilibrium of VNTR data by using the Federal Bureau of Investigation's fixed-bin method, *Am. J. Hum. Genet.*, 51(3), 549–553, 1992.

Devlin, B. and Risch, N., Physical properties of VNTR data, and their impact on a test of allelic independence, *Am. J. Hum. Genet.*, 53(2), 324–329, 1993.

Devlin, B., Risch, N., and Roeder, K., Comments on the statistical aspects of the NRC's report on DNA typing, *J. Forensic Sci.*, 39(1), 28–40, 1994.

Devlin, B., Risch, N., and Roeder, K., No excess of homozygosity at loci used for DNA fingerprinting, *Science*, 249(4975), 1416–1420, 1990.

DNA Advisory Board (DAB), Statistical and population genetics issues affecting the evaluation of the frequency of occurrence of DNA profiles calculated from pertinent population database(s), *Forensic Sci. Commun.*, 2(3), 2000, <http://www.fbi.gov/hq/lab/fsc/back-issu/july2000/index.htm>.

Duncan, G.T., Noppinger, K., Carey, J., and Tracey, M., Comparison of VNTR allele frequencies and inclusion probabilities over six populations, *Genetica*, 88(1), 51–57, 1993.

Edwards, A., Hammond, H.A., Jin, L., Caskey, C.T., and Chakraborty, R., Genetic variation at five trimeric and tetrameric tandem repeat loci in four human population groups, *Genomics*, 12(2), 241–253, 1992.

Evett, I.W., Gill, P.D., Scrange, J.K., and Weir, B.S., Establishing the robustness of short-tandem-repeat statistics for forensic applications, *Am. J. Hum. Genet.*, 58(2), 398–407, 1996.

Evett, I.W., Scranage, J., and Pinchin, R., An illustration of the advantages of efficient statistical methods for RFLP analysis in forensic science, *Am. J. Hum. Genet.*, 52(3), 498–505, 1993.

Evett, I.W., Evaluating DNA profiles in a case where the defence is "it was my brother," *J. Forensic Sci. Soc.*, 32(1), 5–14, 1992.

Evett, I.W., Buffery, C., Willott, G., and Stoney, D., A guide to interpreting single locus profiles of DNA mixtures in forensic cases, *J. Forensic Sci. Soc.*, 31(1), 41–47, 1991.

Evett, I.W. and Gill, P., A discussion of the robustness of methods for assessing the evidential value of DNA single locus profiles in crime investigations, *Electrophoresis*, 12(2), 226–230, 1991.

Herrin, G., Jr., Probability of matching RFLP patterns from unrelated individuals, *Am. J. Hum. Genet.*, 52(3), 491–497, 1993.

Herrin, G., Jr., A comparison of models used for calculation of RFLP pattern frequencies, *J. Forensic Sci.*, 37(6), 1640–1651, 1992.

Jin, L. and Chakraborty, R., Population structure, stepwise mutations, heterozygote deficiency and their implications in DNA forensics, *Heredity*, 74, 274–285, 1995.

Kaye, D.H., The forensic debut of the NRC's DNA report: population structure, ceiling frequencies and the need for numbers, *Genetica*, 96(1–2), 99–105, 1995.

Krane, D.E., Allen, R.W., Sawye, S.A., Petrov, D.A., and Hartl, D.L., Genetic differences at four DNA typing loci in Finnish, Italian, and mixed Caucasian populations, *Proc. Natl. Acad. Sci. U.S.A.*, 89(22), 10583–10587, 1992.

Laber, T.L., Iverson, J.T., Liberty, J.A., and Giese, S.A., The evaluation and implementation of match criteria for forensic analysis of DNA, *J. Forensic Sci.*, 40(6), 1058–1064, 1995.

Lambert, J.A., Scranage, J.K., and Evett, I.W., Large scale database experiments to assess the significance of matching DNA profiles, *Int. J. Legal Med.*, 108(1), 8–13, 1995.

Lange, K., Match probabilities in racially admixed populations, *Am. J. Hum. Genet.*, 52(2), 305–311, 1993.

Lewontin, R.C. and Hartl, D.L., Population genetics in forensic DNA typing, *Science*, 254(5039), 1745–1750, 1991.

Lewontin, R.C., Which population?, *Am. J. Hum. Genet.*, 52(1), 205–206, 1993.

Monson, K.L. and Budowle, B., A comparison of the fixed bin method with the floating bin and direct count methods: effect of VNTR profile frequency estimation and reference population, *J. Forensic Sci.*, 38(5), 1037–1050, 1993.

Morton, N.E., Genetic structure of forensic populations, *Am. J. Hum. Genet.*, 55(3), 587–588, 1994.

Morton, N.E., Genetic structure of forensic populations, *Proc. Natl. Acad. Sci. U.S.A.*, 89(7), 2556–2560, 1992.

Morton, N.E., Collins, A., and Balazs, I., Kinship bioassay on hypervariable loci in blacks and Caucasians, *Proc. Natl. Acad. Sci. U.S.A.*, 90(5), 1892–1896, 1993.

National Research Council, Committee on DNA Technology in Forensic Science, *DNA Technology in Forensic Science*, National Academy Press, Washington, D.C., 1992.

National Research Council, Committee on DNA Technology in Forensic Science, *The Evaluation of Forensic DNA Evidence*, National Academy Press, Washington, D.C., 1996.

Nichols, R.A. and Balding, D.J., Effects of population structure on DNA fingerprint analysis in forensic science, *Heredity (Edinburgh)*, (Pt 2), 297–302, 1991.

Risch, N.J. and Devlin, B., On the probability of matching DNA fingerprints, *Science*, 255(5045), 717–720, 1992.

Sharma, B.R., Thompson, M., Bolding, J.R., Zhong, Y., Jin, L., and Chakraborty, R., A comparative study of genetic variation at five VNTR loci in three ethnic groups of Houston, Texas, *J. Forensic Sci.*, 40(6), 933–942, 1995.

Slimowitz, J.R. and Cohen, J.E., Violations of the ceiling principle: exact conditions and statistical evidence, *Am. J. Hum. Genet.*, 53(2), 314–323, 1993.

Smith, J.C., Anwar, R., Riley, J., Jenner, D., Markham, A.F., and Jeffreys, A.J., Highly polymorphic minisatellite sequences: allele frequencies and mutation rates for five locus-specific probes in a Caucasian population, *J. Forensic Sci. Soc.*, 30(1), 9–32, 1990.

Stoney, D.A., What made us ever think we could individualize using statistics?, *J. Forensic Sci. Soc.*, 3(2), 197–199, 1991.

Stoney, D.A., Reporting of highly individual genetic typing results: a practical approach, *J. Forensic Sci.*, 37(2), 373–386, 1992.

Sudbury, A.W., Marinopoulos, J., and Gunn, P., Assessing the evidential value of DNA profiles matching without using the assumption of independent loci, *J. Forensic Sci. Soc.*, 33(2), 73–82, 1993.

Sullivan, K.M., Gill, P., Lingard, D., and Lygo, J.E., Characterisation of HLA DQ alpha for forensic purposes, Allele and genotype frequencies in British Caucasian, Afro-Caribbean and Asian populations, *Int. J. Legal Med.*, 105(1), 17–20, 1992.

Thompson, W.C., Subjective interpretation, laboratory error and the value of forensic DNA evidence: three case studies, *Genetica*, 96(1–2), 153–168, 1995.

Thompson, W.C. and Ford, S., The meaning of a match: sources of ambiguity in the interpretation of DNA prints, in: Farley, M. and Harrington, J., Eds., *Forensic DNA Technology*, Lewis Publishers, Chelsea, MI, 1991.

Weir, B.S., DNA match and profile probabilities: comment on Budowle et al. (2000) and Fung and Hu (2000), *Forensic Sci. Commun.*, 3(1), 2001, <http://www.fbi.gov/hq/lab/fsc/back-issu/jan2001/index.htm>.

Weir, B.S., Forensic population genetics and the National Research Council (NRC), *Am. J. Hum. Genet.*, 52(2), 437–440, 1993.

Weir, B.S., Population genetics in the forensic DNA debate, *Proc. Natl. Acad. Sci. U.S.A.*, 89(24), 11654–11659, 1992.

Weir, B.S. and Hill, W.G., Population genetics of DNA profiles, *J. Forensic Sci. Soc.*, 33(4), 218–225, 1993.

Population Databases

A partial listing of papers containing information about population databases using RFLP markers, and at the D1S80, DQA1, and "polymarker" loci can be found at the Forensic Education and Consulting Web site, <http://www.forensicdna.com>.

A comprehensive listing of papers containing information about population databases using STR markers, Y-STR markers, and mtDNA can be found at the NIST STRbase WEB site, <http://www.cstl.nist.gov/div831/strbase>.

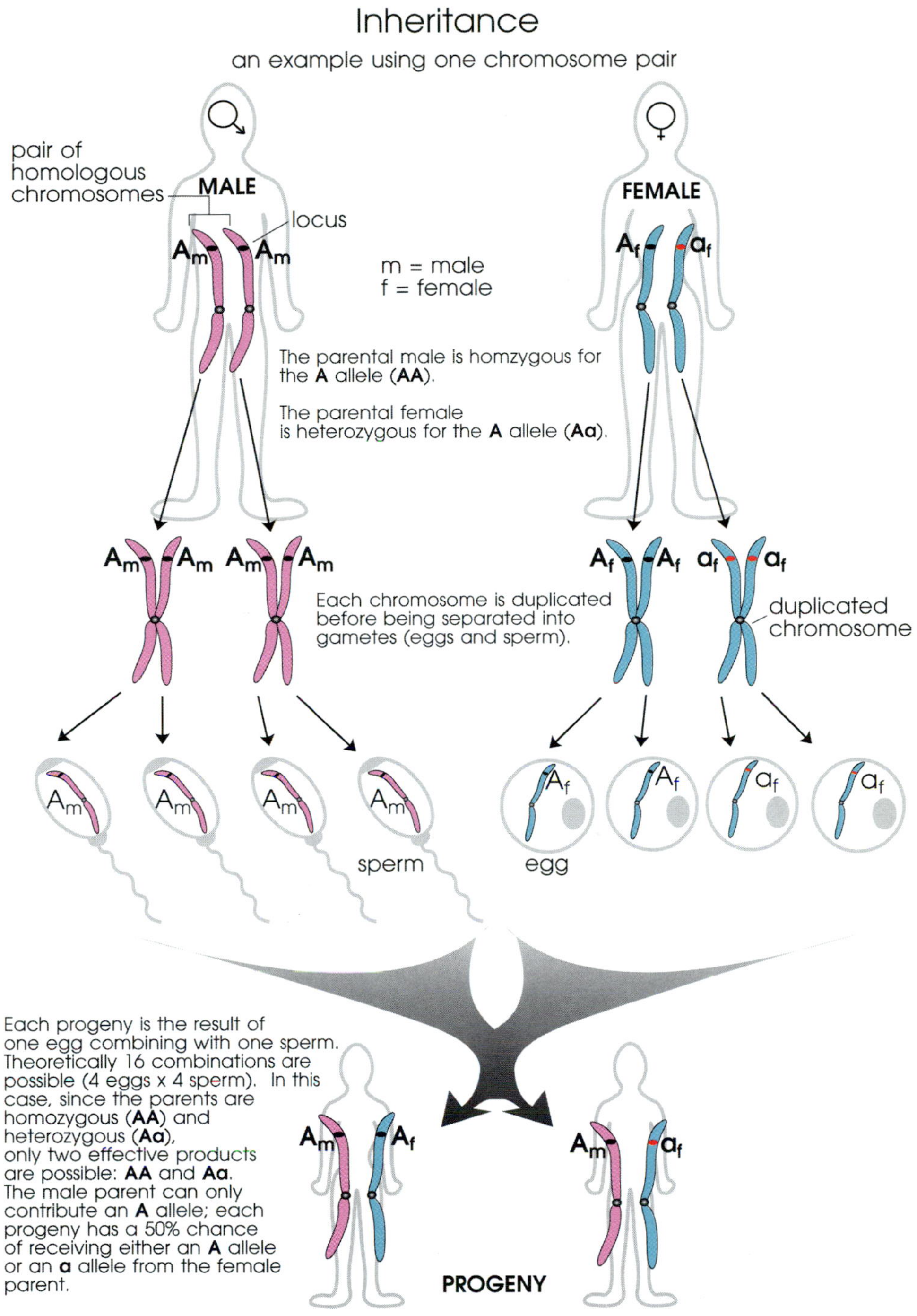

Inheritance

an example using one chromosome pair

pair of homologous chromosomes

MALE

locus

A_m A_m

m = male
f = female

FEMALE

A_f a_f

The parental male is homzygous for the **A** allele (**AA**).

The parental female is heterozygous for the **A** allele (**Aa**).

A_m A_m A_m A_m

Each chromosome is duplicated before being separated into gametes (eggs and sperm).

A_f A_f a_f a_f

duplicated chromosome

A_m A_m A_m A_m

sperm

A_f A_f a_f a_f

egg

Each progeny is the result of one egg combining with one sperm. Theoretically 16 combinations are possible (4 eggs x 4 sperm). In this case, since the parents are homozygous (**AA**) and heterozygous (**Aa**), only two effective products are possible: **AA** and **Aa**. The male parent can only contribute an **A** allele; each progeny has a 50% chance of receiving either an **A** allele or an **a** allele from the female parent.

A_m A_f

A_m a_f

PROGENY

Plate 1   Inheritance.

The DNA Double Helix

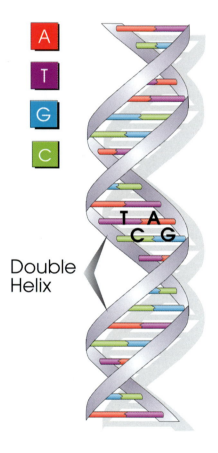

Plate 2   The DNA helix.

Restriction Fragment Length Polymorphism Analysis (RFLP)
of
Variable Number Tandem Repeats (VNTR)

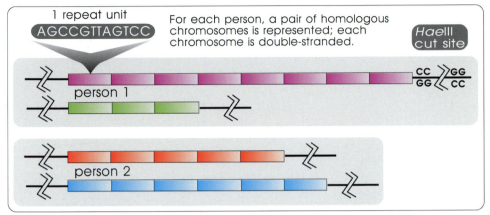

1 repeat unit
AGCCGTTAGTCC

For each person, a pair of homologous chromosomes is represented; each chromosome is double-stranded.

HaeIII cut site

person 1

person 2

The length of the fragment after cutting with HaeIII is determined by the number of repeat units at the locus.

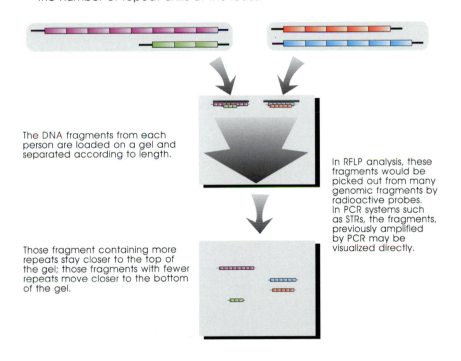

The DNA fragments from each person are loaded on a gel and separated according to length.

In RFLP analysis, these fragments would be picked out from many genomic fragments by radioactive probes. In PCR systems such as STRs, the fragments, previously amplified by PCR may be visualized directly.

Those fragment containing more repeats stay closer to the top of the gel; those fragments with fewer repeats move closer to the bottom of the gel.

Plate 3   **Restriction fragment length polymorphisms (RFLP).**

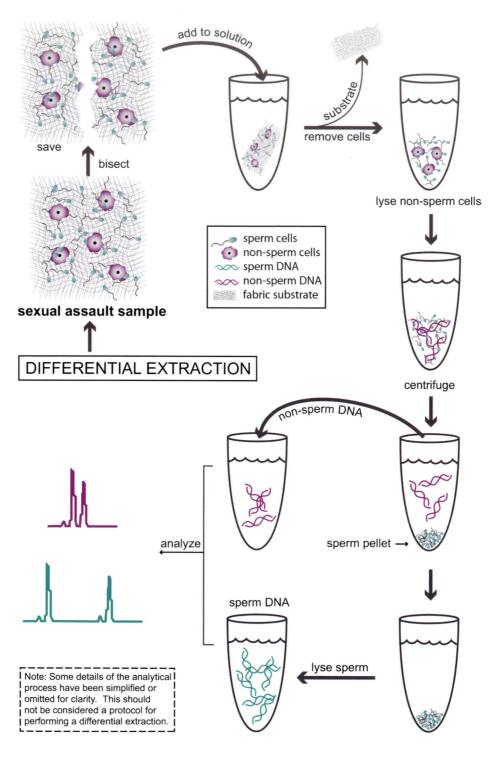

add to solution

substrate
remove cells

save

bisect

lyse non-sperm cells

sperm cells
non-sperm cells
sperm DNA
non-sperm DNA
fabric substrate

sexual assault sample

centrifuge

DIFFERENTIAL EXTRACTION

non-sperm DNA

analyze

sperm pellet →

sperm DNA

lyse sperm

Note: Some details of the analytical
process have been simplified or
omitted for clarity. This should
not be considered a protocol for
performing a differential extraction.

Plate 4   Differential extraction.

PCR Amplification - round 1

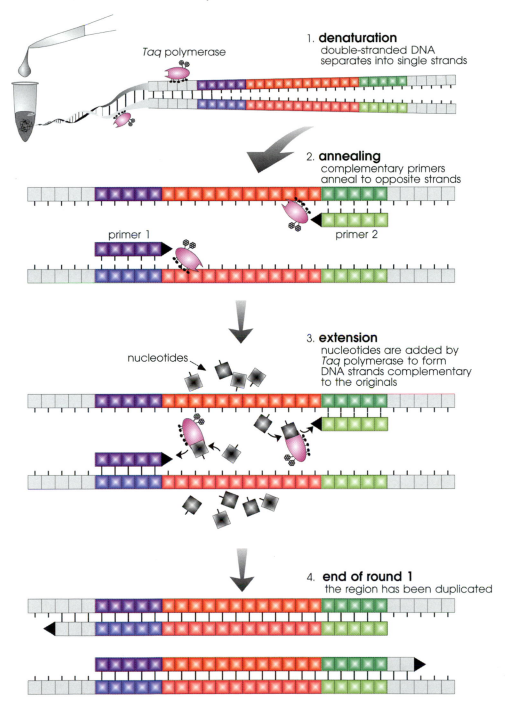

Plate 5   PCR — round 1.

PCR Amplification - round 2

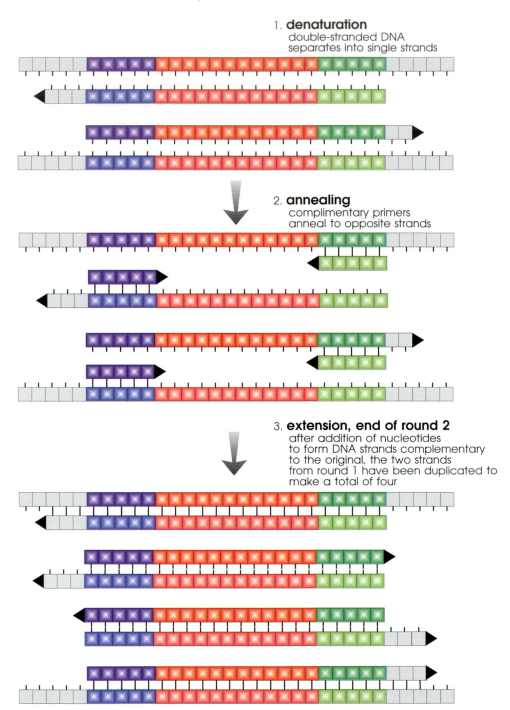

1. **denaturation**
   double-stranded DNA
   separates into single strands

2. **annealing**
   complimentary primers
   anneal to opposite strands

3. **extension, end of round 2**
   after addition of nucleotides
   to form DNA strands complementary
   to the original, the two strands
   from round 1 have been duplicated to
   make a total of four

Plate 6   PCR — round 2.

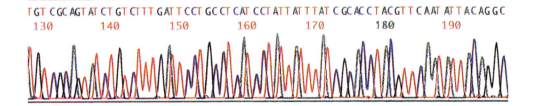

Plate 7 Automated DNA sequencing. An example of DNA sequencing on the ABI PRISM® 310 Genetic Analyzer. Detection of DNA sequencing products occurs during electrophoresis as each fluorescently tagged fragment passes a fixed laser beam. Each of the four DNA bases is represented by a different color. The computer software calls the order of bases and prints each one above the corresponding peak. The DNA sequence is read from left to right. This is the type of result obtained from mitochondrial sequencing. (Courtesy of Mitotyping Technologies, LLC.)

STRs and GENDER ID

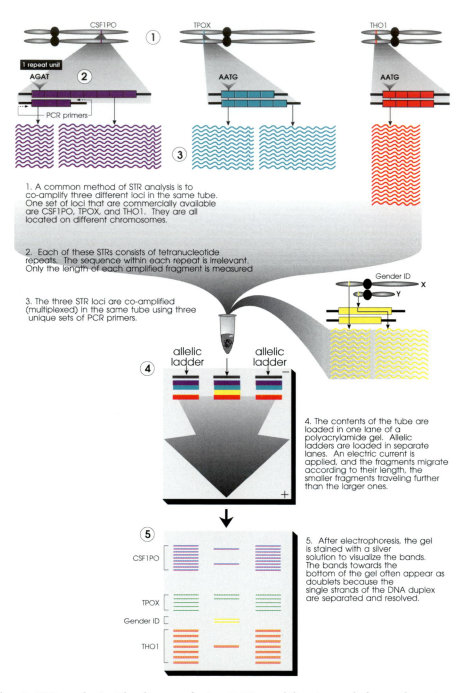

1. A common method of STR analysis is to co-amplify three different loci in the same tube. One set of loci that are commercially available are CSF1PO, TPOX, and THO1. They are all located on different chromosomes.

2. Each of these STRs consists of tetranucleotide repeats. The sequence within each repeat is irrelevant. Only the length of each amplified fragment is measured

3. The three STR loci are co-amplified (multiplexed) in the same tube using three unique sets of PCR primers.

4. The contents of the tube are loaded in one lane of a polyacrylamide gel. Allelic ladders are loaded in separate lanes. An electric current is applied, and the fragments migrate according to their length, the smaller fragments traveling further than the larger ones.

5. After electrophoresis, the gel is stained with a silver solution to visualize the bands. The bands towards the bottom of the gel often appear as doublets because the single strands of the DNA duplex are separated and resolved.

Plate 8 STR analysis. The diagram depicts PCR amplification, gel electrophoresis, and manual detection by silver staining of an STR triplex plus Amelogenin (gender ID). The same general process can be used for any amplified fragment length polymorphism.

The Relationship of Bands to Peaks

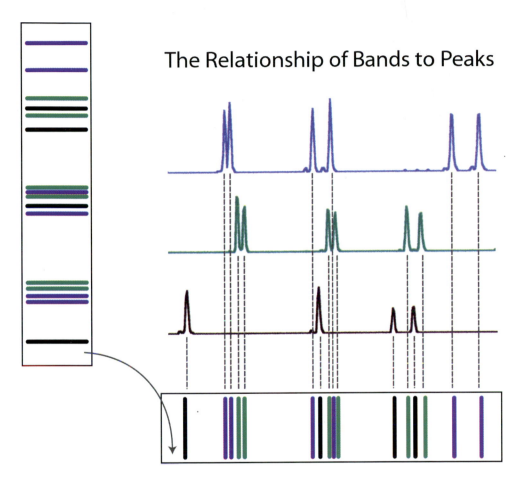

Plate 9 The relationship of bands to peaks. Analysts are most familiar with reading bands on gels after electrophoretic separation of DNA, but STR kits using fluorescently tagged primers require different visualization techniques. Using recent hardware and software innovations, electrophoretically separated DNA fragments are represented as peaks emerging from the instrument over time. Here, a typical band pattern of an electrophoretic separation is represented on the left. Imagine taking the top of this band pattern and rotating it clockwise down to the right corner of the illustration. The band pattern is now horizontal rather than vertical, and each band is represented by a peak above the band. The three colors representing the different fluorescent dye primer tags are each printed on a separated horizontal panel.

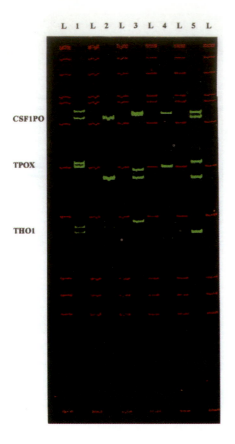

CSF1PO

TPOX

THO1

**Plate 10a STR analysis on the Hitachi FMBIO®
100.** An example of the STR Triplex CTT
(CSF1PO, TPOX, and THO1) analyzed on a
static imager. Each of the five lanes where
green bands are present contains an amplified
sample from a different individual. The lanes
with red bands contain molecular ladders used
to size the amplified fragments. Fluorescently
tagged PCR product fragments are detected
after electrophoresis using a scanning laser,
and the alleles are typed by comparison to an
allelic ladder included in the same run, but in
a different lane (not shown). Typically, the
results are displayed on a black-and-white
printout without showing the internal ladders
(see Figure 6.17).

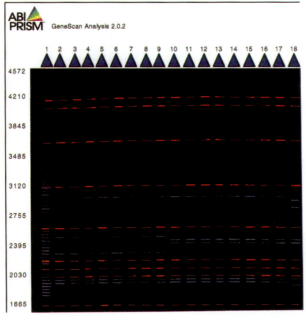

**Plate 10b STR analysis on the
ABI PRISM® 377 DNA Sequencer.** The loci amplified using the
AmpFLSTR® Blue™ PCR kit are
an STR triplex of D3S1358, vWA,
and FGA. Lane 1 contains both
an allelic ladder (blue bands) and
a molecular ladder (red bands).
The remaining lanes contain
amplified samples (blue bands)
and the molecular ladder (red
bands). Detection of PCR product
fragments occurs during electrophoresis as fluorescently tagged
fragments pass a fixed laser
beam. Sizing with an in-lane ladder corrects for any electrophoretic inconsistencies and provides extremely precise estimates
of fragment length. An electropherogram of lanes 5, 12, and 18
are shown in Plate 11.

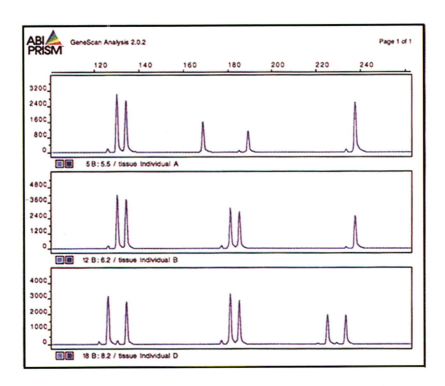

Plate 11 Electropherogram of lanes 5, 12, and 18 from the STR gel in Plate 10b. Each lane of the gel is viewed as a separate panel. The bands appear as peaks along the time axis at the top of the figure. The computer software makes it possible for any of the lanes to be displayed adjacent to any other, even if they are located on opposite sides of the gel or at the beginning and end of a capillary column run. This facilitates a direct visual comparison of any two profiles.

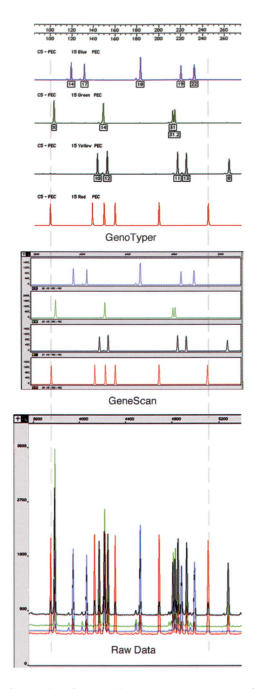

Plate 12 Evolution of STR data from collection to typing. STR data is collected from the ABI PRISM® 377 DNA Sequencer or ABI PRISM® 310 Genetic Analyzer, as "raw data," a complex mix of peaks in overlapping colors (bottom panel). GeneScan® software normalizes the spectral overlap of the fluorescent dyes, sets all of the dyes to the same baseline, and assigns base pair sizes to each fragment (peak) (middle panel). GenoTyper® software assigns allelic types to each peak by comparing each sample peak to the appropriate allelic ladder (top panel). (Courtesy of the San Diego Sheriff's Crime Laboratory.)

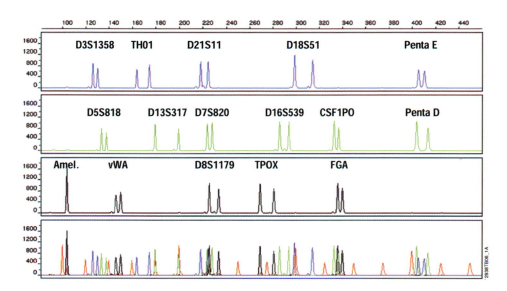

Plate 13 PowerPlex®16. The DNA profile from a single individual at 16 different loci using three fluorescent dyes. The profile is represented in two ways. Each of the top three panels shows alleles for specific loci in the different dye colors; the bottom panel is a composite of the top three panels, as well as the internal lane standard in a fourth color (red). (Courtesy of Promega Corporation.)

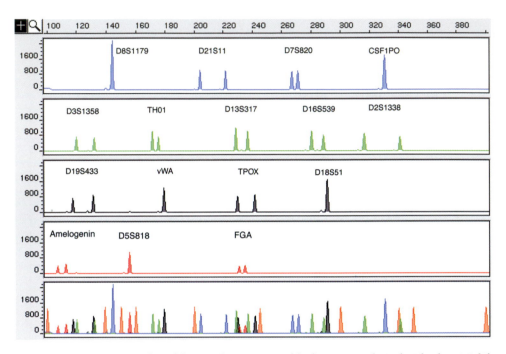

Plate 14 AmpFLSTR® Identifiler™. The DNA profile from a single individual at 16 different loci using four fluorescent dyes. The top four panels show alleles for specific loci in the different dye colors; the bottom panel is a composite of the top four panels, as well as the internal lane standard in a fifth color (orange). (Courtesy of Applied Biosystems.)

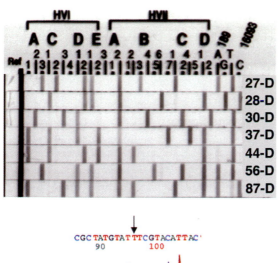

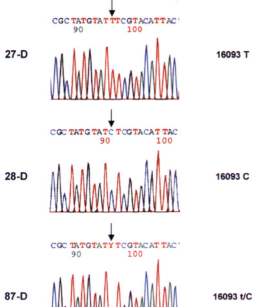

Plate 15 Detection of sequence variation and heteroplasmy in the HVI and HVII regions of mtDNA. Sequence variation and heteroplasmy within the two hypervariable segments of the mitochondrial genome can be detected by a variety of methods. In this figure, results obtained using linear arrays of sequence-specific oligonucleotide (SSO) probes (top) and fluorescent DNA sequence analysis (bottom) are shown. Seven unrelated individuals were typed using a panel of 31 SSO probes immobilized in a linear array on strips of nylon membrane. This panel of SSO probes detects sequence variation in ten segments that span HVI and HVII. Eight of the segments are designated with letters and two are designated by the specific position of the variable nucleotides detected by the probes (189 and 16093). The probes within the eight lettered segments are numbered, and the probes for positions 189 and 16093 are designated with the specific nucleotide distinguished by the probe pairs (e.g., A and G at position 189). An individual's "mitotype" is determined by examining the pattern of positive signals on the linear array. The mitotype for individual 27-D is 32212310AT. The "0" assigned to the HVII D segment indicates that this individual's mitochondrial DNA contains a sequence that cannot bind to either of the HVII D probes. The pattern of probes for individual 28-D contains a weak positive signal at HVII C1. This individual's mitochondrial DNA contains a sequence that is not perfectly complementary to any of the four HVII C probes. Instead, the sequence contains a mismatch that destabilizes the interaction between the PCR product and the HVII C1 probe, leading to a weak signal. An example of heteroplasmy is observed in the probe pattern for individual 87-D. A positive signal is observed at the probe for 16093 C and a weak signal is observed at the probe for 16093 T, indicating the presence of more than one mitochondrial DNA. Contamination and cross-hybridization can be ruled out as explanations for the additional weak signal. Fluorescent DNA sequence analysis of individuals 27-D, 28-D, and 87-D was performed. The region surrounding position 16093 (indicated by arrow) for each of these individuals is shown at the bottom of the figure. Individual 27-D has a "T" at position 16093 and individual 28-D has a "C," as observed on the linear arrays. Individual 87-D has both "T" and "C" at position 16093, as indicated by the two peaks in the sequence. The ratio of "T" to "C" in the sequence is consistent with the ratio of "T" to "C" observed on the linear array for individual 87-D. (Courtesy of Roche Molecular Systems.)

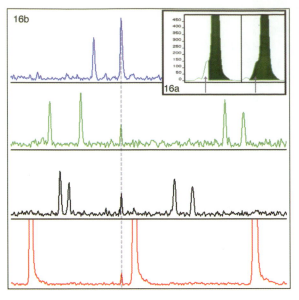

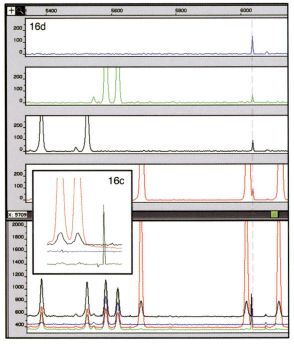

Plate 16a Non-template-directed nucleotide addition. The *Taq* polymerase indiscriminately adds a nucleotide, usually an "A," to the end of amplified fragments. This addition is not always complete; after amplification there may exist a mixed population of molecules, some fragments with the terminal "A" residue, and some without. After electrophoresis, this is manifest by "split peaks." The arrow in the figure points to a shoulder on the left of the main peak representing a population of fragments lacking the terminal "A" nucleotide, while the parent peak represents the dominant population of fragments containing the "A" nucleotide.

Plate 16b Pull-up. When the software fails to compensate adequately for spectral overlap of the fluorescent dyes, peaks that do not represent DNA fragments appear in some colors. In this illustration, a DNA peak detected in the blue dye produces artifactual peaks at the identical locations in the other three colors due to inadequate spectral overlap compensation by the computer. The true blue DNA peak appears to "pull-up" artifactual peaks in the other colors. (Courtesy of the San Diego Sheriff's Crime Laboratory.)

Plate 16c Spike in one color. Non-reproducible peaks that do not represent DNA fragments are occasionally seen in data from the ABI PRISM® 310 Genetic Analyzer. They can often be recognized in the "raw data" by shape. In this example, a single-color spike in green is differentiated from a real DNA peak by its narrow width and the lack of a corresponding peak in the other colors in the raw data. It was confirmed as an artifact by failure to reproduce the peak in a duplicate run of the same sample. (Courtesy of the San Diego Sheriff's Crime Laboratory.)

Plate 16d Spike in four colors. In contrast to Plate 16c, the spike highlighted by the gray dotted line is seen in all four colors in the "raw data" (bottom panel) and in the GeneScan® data (top four panels). In addition to its narrow peak width, this peak was confirmed as an artifact by failure to reproduce the peak in a duplicate run of the same sample.

The DNA Databank

9

I. Premise of a Databank

 If violent criminals would only commit one crime and see the error of their ways, the DNA databank would neither be necessary nor useful. But for whatever sociological reason, there is no such thing as a one-time rapist. Violent offenders will continue to commit crimes until caught (and then usually refine their techniques while in prison). The discipline of criminology studies this phenomenon, and it is not within the scope of this chapter to detail what is known about *recidivism*, the proclivity of an offender to repeat his offenses. Suffice it to say that a large percentage of criminals offend repeatedly throughout their lifetimes.

By definition, violent crimes consist of physical assault against a person. One possible result of such an assault is the shedding of biological evidence by a victim, the assailant, or even a witness. This is commonly blood or semen, but can also be the panoply of other items we have discussed in other chapters, including hair, feces, urine, saliva, tissue, or bone. For rape and other sex crimes in particular, semen from the rapist is a common finding.

Because offenders repeat their violent behaviors until caught, they constantly leave biological traces of themselves at their crime scenes. If a list of repeat offenders existed, detectives could use such a list to start their investigations. Better yet, if a list of offenders including their DNA profiles existed, detectives could compare the DNA from the biological evidence at the scene with the list of DNA profiles, and then get the name of the semen donor from a matching DNA profile on the offender list.

This is the premise of the DNA databank. A collection of DNA profiles from known offenders serves as a list against which unsolved cases can be searched. The value of using DNA as the source material in an investigation of violent crime derives from three factors. The first is the proclivity for violent offenders to continue offending. The second is that violent crimes frequently result in biological evidence being shed as the result of the crime itself. And the third is the power of DNA to discriminate between almost all individuals, leading to the very strong inference that the person matched in the databank to the evidence left at the scene is the donor of the sample.

II. The Difference Between a Databank and a Database

The words *databank* and *database* appear to be used interchangeably, but there is a difference between the two. A databank consists of all of the elements that provide information about offenders and cases. This includes such items as legislation authorizing the databank, the collection of offender samples and casework samples for inclusion in the databank, the analysis of the samples, and the method of transforming the analytical results into a searchable format. A database is merely the computer repository of the minimally required information required to match cases with offenders. Hence, an analyst may use the database to match an offender sample to her unsolved case, and the other elements of the databank to determine the name of the person with the matching profile, whether the offender has committed a qualifying offense, and whether the person is currently in custody. We adhere to these definitions throughout the chapter.

III.   Elements of a Successful Databank

A successful databank will efficiently connect unsolved cases with convicted offenders. The elements required to achieve this success include legislation, collection of samples, the analysis of samples, a database, and a means of communicating between the various labs participating in the effort.

A.   Legislation

Legislation authorizing collection of samples must include those offenses that are committed by violent offenders. Although it may be obvious to include murderers and rapists, less obvious offenses have proven useful in solving violent crimes. For example, a large number of burglars also commit rapes. There seems to be a tendency for career criminals to escalate the types and severity of their crimes as they become older and more successful crooks. Time in "the joint" rarely deters emerging offenders from repeating offenses once they are released from custody. States vary widely in the number and kinds of offenses that qualify an offender for inclusion in the databank. New York, for example, includes all felons, while California allows only those committing one of nine offenses to be incorporated into its databank. At the most extreme, Great Britain takes a blood sample of a suspect upon arrest. This sample is searched against unsolved crimes, and if no hit is obtained, the profile must be removed from the database.

Because individual states are responsible for enacting legislation, no uniformity exists between U.S. states with regard to the number and types of offenses that qualify an offender for inclusion in the databank. Other countries take a more united approach. Canada, Great Britain, South Africa, and Australia all have databank efforts that are controlled by their respective national police forces. The lack of uniformity within the United States naturally brings some inefficiency to the process of solving crimes. Virginia, for example, includes burglary among the eligible offenses. Experts estimate that 50% of the databank hits seen in this state would not be obtained if burglary were eliminated from the statute.

B.   Collection of Samples

1.   *Offenders*

It might at first seem to be a trivial thing to collect blood or buccal swabs from a convicted felon, but several factors make it a logistical nightmare. Although in the past felons went to state prison, in many jurisdictions this is no longer the case. Some felons may serve their

---

Sidebar 11

The Botanical Witness
(or, what the seed pod saw)

Over the past decade, the genomes of humans, as well as many animals, crop plants, and microorganisms, have been well-characterized. Because the DNA sequences, more specifically variable DNA sequences, are known in these cases, it has been possible to develop probes to these loci for the purpose of comparing individuals. However, the majority of organisms have not necessarily been studied in this fashion, and little or no specific information is available about their DNA sequences. RAPD (random amplified polymorphic DNA) analysis uses 10-bp oligonucleotides of randomly generated sequence that have the potential to act as primers in a PCR amplification. Under proper hybridization conditions, some of these primers will bind at many locations in the genomic DNA being tested. Because oligonucleotides complementing both strands are provided, some will anneal in an inverted orientation, forming primer pair combinations spanning a distance amenable to PCR amplification. This is different from a standard PCR amplification in that the size and location of the amplified regions are previously unknown to the investigator (and actually only their size is immediately obvious from the results). On average, about 50 different loci are amplified during a RAPD procedure. The PCR products are then separated by electrophoresis on an agarose gel, and usually visualized as ethidium bromide-stained bands. Depending on the coefficient of inbreeding of the organism, the number of the bands that vary between individuals may be between about 5 and 30. A major caveat to the method is that the intensities of the bands vary both from each other, as well as between runs and laboratories; thus, the interpretation is somewhat subjective and reproducibility of the results can be problematic.

On May 3, 1992, the body of a black female was discovered under a Palo Verde tree in Phoenix, Arizona. In addition to a gouge in the tree and tire tracks and scrape marks in the surrounding dirt, a pager was found at the scene. The pager eventually led sheriff's deputies to Mark Bogen, who immediately became the prime suspect in the murder of Denise Johnson. The suspect admitted to picking up the victim and having sex with her, but denied any involvement in her death. The suspect's truck was searched, and some seed pods from a Palo Verde tree collected. The seed pods from the truck were compared to the Palo Verde tree at the crime scene using RAPD analysis. In this case, the RAPD patterns between the seed pods recovered from the suspect's truck and those from the tree appeared to be an exact match even down to the band intensities. An important point to note is that the comparison had to be made using the seed pods, not the seeds. If the seeds (like human embryos) were a product of cross-pollination, half their genetic material would be from the other parent, and only half their band pattern would correlate with the maternal tree. The seed pods, on the other hand, are entirely derived from the maternal tissue of the tree.

Before the RAPD analysis could be admitted at trial, however, a Frye hearing had to be held; the State of Arizona did not at that time have a Supreme court ruling or statutory legislation upholding the admissibility of DNA evidence. Dr. Tim Helentjaris, then associate professor at the University of Arizona, had performed the work and testified for the prosecution; Dr. Paul Keim, a professor at Northern Arizona University, testified as an expert for the defense. Although, in this case, the patterns of the tree and the pods appeared indistinguishable, Dr. Keim held that the procedure, as a rule, was not reliable and reproducible. He additionally opined that the population database of Palo Verde trees was too small (about 17 trees of the subspecies blue floridium), and the collection methods resulting in a total of 29 Palo Verde trees (i.e., by sheriff's deputies) were flawed. Based on this testimony, Judge Susan Bolton ruled that, for the first time, plant DNA profiles could be admitted as evidence in a criminal trial; however, Dr. Helentjaris was not allowed to present a statistical probability regarding the significance of the pattern match. He testified that the DNA RAPD pattern of the seed pod was indistinguishable from the pattern obtained from the tree at the crime scene, and that it was his opinion that the pod came from the tree.

Based on the DNA profiles and a plethora of other physical evidence, in addition to an incriminating phone conversation and the testimony of the suspect and other court witnesses, Bogen was convicted of the murder of Denise Johnson. He was sentenced to life without the possibility of parole. Although the ruling was upheld by the Arizona State Court of Appeals, a minority opinion argued that the DNA evidence should not have been introduced, but that its inclusion resulted only in "harmless error."

In a similar 1996 case in Santa Clara County, California, a bay leaf was associated with a particular tree using RAPD technology. In this case, however, the DNA evidence was not admitted to trial at all, based on the lack of population data for bay trees.

STR systems and other kinds of DNA analysis systems are beginning to be studied for subjects of the botanical kingdom. Because each species requires development of a specific system, and then a database, this is a much more daunting project than the innovation of human DNA testing for personal identification. Initial efforts are being concentrated on species of commercial interest or political importance.

References

Amato, I., Botanical witness for the prosecution, *Science,* 260, 894–895, 1993.
Clayton, B., Deputy County Attorney, Maricopa Co., personal communication, 1996.
Keim, P., Professor, Northern Arizona University, AZ, personal communication, 1996.

time in a county jail rather than a state facility. Further, some may be on parole or probation, and a parole officer will oversee collection of the sample. As a result, a wide variety of agencies must be prepared to collect and send samples to the state databank laboratory.

These agencies are required to collect samples in accordance with the needs of the laboratory. These requirements include collecting specific types of samples (either blood or buccal swabs), as well as demographic data about the offender, including, in some jurisdictions, the thumbprint of the offender to verify identity. There must be a uniform method of transporting the sample to the laboratory that minimizes container breakage and sample degradation . All of this effort requires funding, and a good databank program includes monies allocated to local agencies for the collection and transportation of the samples.

The databank must have a way of verifying the identity of the person contributing the sample, as well as a way of confirming that the felon has committed a qualifying offense. California provides a blood collection kit to agencies collecting samples for the databank. Included in this kit is a Genetic Marker Card (GMC) that contains a wide variety of demographic data obtained during the collection of the sample. Information such as the name, state identification number, place of collection, identity of the collector, date of collection, and the thumbprint of the offender is taken. The laboratory then matches the thumbprint to the name and state identification number in the criminal history records to confirm that this is the correct person. The next step confirms the offense committed by this individual, ensuring that it is included in the list of qualifying offenses. At least 5% of the samples collected are from non-qualifying offenders, and these samples must be removed from the databank.

The most efficient process collects the sample from the offender upon conviction. If the individual is committed to a state facility, he should be drawn upon entry to the department of corrections. If remanded to local custody, he should be drawn as soon as the conviction is obtained. This provides the laboratory sufficient time to analyze the sample and place the profile into the database for searching before the offender is released. This ensures that any subsequent violent crime committed by the offender has a reasonable chance of being solved.

2.   *Cases*

Historically, crime laboratories have been so overwhelmed with casework that managers had to make decisions about which cases to work. Criteria were set that outlined the types of cases the laboratory would even accept for analysis. This filter might be applied to the type of evidence that would be accepted (no soil cases, for example) or to the urgency of the case (it is going to trial tomorrow), or both.

For many laboratories, the main criterion for accepting cases with biological evidence was a court date. And a case would not be in court if there were no defendant. Hence, one important criterion for case acceptance was the existence of an identified suspect.

Recall that the purpose of the databank is to solve unsolved crimes. By definition, if a case has a suspect or a defendant, the detective thinks that it is solved. There existed a built-in bias against accepting the very types of cases that the databank was created to solve. This inertia had to be overcome in some fashion in order to maximize the potential of the databank.

The first cases to be solved with the databank were those in which DNA had eliminated the suspect identified by police. Because DNA eliminates between 15 and 20% of suspects as contributors to a biological sample, this created a reservoir of cases that could be searched against the databank of convicted offenders. After some initial successes, agencies began to craft coordinated strategies for submitting and accepting unsolved cases. These strategies must include re-educating detectives, who were told for 25 years that suspectless cases would not be worked.

One consequence of not working suspectless cases for over 25 years is a backlog of suspectless cases! Not only must laboratories struggle with changing policies and perceptions about current cases without suspects, they must come to grips with this huge inventory of unexamined evidence. This entails money and a plan, as well as involving all of the agencies that might have such cases. Local law enforcement agencies must create their own internal mechanisms for identifying eligible cases, and commit resources to reopening the case files and locating the evidence. This is but one of the ways in which DNA has changed the criminal justice system.

Detectives in England now approach cases with the databank as the primary means of connecting their suspect with the crime or crime scene. In many cases, even where the detective has identified suspects, the reference samples are submitted to the databank. The evidence is likewise submitted to the databank, and a blind search connects the suspect with the case. From this approach, virtually every case is a databank case, and many hits are obtained daily.

At this writing, a few states within the United States have dedicated resources to address the issue of old and current suspectless cases. Other states are just beginning a coordinated effort, while the remaining states are struggling with no increase in funding. This is clearly the next step requiring concerted action on the part of the criminal justice system in the United States.

C.   Analysis of Samples

1.   Choice of Markers

For the databank to be useful on a national or international level, several standards must be established and enforced. First among these is a decision about the technology and a set of markers to be used. In the early development of DNA, RFLP was the only technology widely available. In the early 1990s, DQA1 became more widely accepted but this marker (and its subsequent mate, polymarker) lacked the power to distinguish between the large numbers of people in the populations of interest. Thus, the first U.S. and European databanks were based on RFLP. One decision to be made centered on the combination of restriction enzyme and loci to be used. Europe settled on the enzyme *Hin*f1, while the

---

Sidebar 12

A Cold Hit in Minnesota
(or, the database in winter)

On November 17, 1991, police were called to a first-floor, four-bedroom apartment in South Minneapolis, where the body of Jean Broderick had been found in her bedroom. The cause of death was asphyxiation due to airway obstruction and strangulation, and the medical examiner found evidence that Broderick had been sexually assaulted. This included a finding of semen on the inner side of her buttocks. Several bloodstained items and a pubic hair were also collected at the crime scene. Although several eyewitnesses later identified the assailant, he was not immediately apprehended.

The Minnesota Bureau of Criminal Apprehension (BCA) received the evidence approximately 2 weeks later, and immediately began RFLP analysis of the semen swab, along with reference samples from the victim and her male roommate. The roommate was excluded immediately. However, because no suspect had yet been detained, there was no other reference sample to compare with the evidence. The one locus sample profile from the first autorad was entered into the Minnesota CSO database, and all but 6 of the 1700 individuals contained in the database were eliminated. A second locus was probed, and the two locus profile again compared to the six questioned profiles from the database. Using only two probes, the lab was able to exclude all but one individual. A conventional blood marker, PGM, also linked the evidence to the now-suspect individual.

Based on the typing results, probable cause was established to obtain a fresh sample from the suspect, Martin Estrada Perez. He was immediately located by the Minneapolis Police Department. By December 23, BCA criminalists had received an early Christmas present: a known blood sample to compare to the evidence. DNA from the reference sample was extracted, along with fresh extractions of the evidentiary semen swab and the CSO sample. A total of six different loci were eventually tested, producing RFLP profiles that were indistinguishable between all three samples. Additionally, a bloody tan jacket yielded a mixture of types. The now-defendant could not be excluded as a contributor to this mixture. The pubic hair found at the scene was also found to be indistinguishable from that of Mr. Perez.

The trial court admitted the DNA evidence but excluded the introduction of statistics relating to the significance of the matching genetic profiles. In this, the court took judicial notice of the *Kim* ruling, based on a composite of several previous Minnesota Supreme Court rulings regarding the admissibility of statistics relating to scientific evidence (*State v. Carlson*, 1978; *State v. Boyd*, 1983; *State v. Kim*, 1987). The state's witnesses were permitted to testify that a six-locus RFLP match is extremely rare, that there was not a significant chance that another person was the source of the evidence, and that to a reasonable medical/scientific certainty the defendant was the source of the unknown DNA samples found at the scene. The profile was also searched against a different database containing 3500 individuals, and no other sample was found that had the same profile at more than two loci. After considering the physical evidence as well as additional personal and eyewitness testimony, the trial court jury found Martin Perez guilty of first-degree murder. He was sentenced to life in prison without possibility of parole.

The defendant appealed his conviction and the case went before the appellate court in April 1994. In the meantime, however, the Supreme Court of Minnesota had reconsidered, jointly, the cases of *State v. Bloom*, *State v. Bauer*, and *State v. Perez*, and partially reversed its decision regarding the admissibility of statistics. In fact, based on the NRC I report and its recommendation of the "interim ceiling method" for calculating composite genotype frequencies, the court made a specific exception for DNA evidence. In a decision filed April 29, 1994, the Appellate Court relied entirely on the new Supreme Court position and denied the appeal.

United States decided to standardize on *Hae*III. Other countries also decided on one or the other of these systems.

While RFLP was a good choice at the time, it suffered from some disadvantages. It required a reasonable amount of high-quality DNA, and this virtually precluded the analysis of evidence that was degraded. In the early days, it required the use of radioactive phosphorus (^{32}P), which was expensive, hazardous, and regulated. Chemiluminescent alternatives appeared in the early to mid-1990s, but by this time many laboratories had decided to forego RFLP and use PCR-based markers.

PCR-based markers could successfully be examined even on small or degraded samples. When STR markers were discovered, the low discrimination power associated with the AmpliType® PM+DQA1 loci ceased to be an issue. Numerous STRs are scattered throughout the genome, and many of them exhibit moderate levels of heterozygosity. The overall power is achieved using several markers in combination. In the United States, the Scientific Working Group in DNA Analysis Methods (SWGDAM, see Chapter 10) decided to designate 13 core STR loci for use in the national database. In Great Britain, six STR markers were first used, and a third-generation kit that includes ten markers is the current standard.

2. Offenders

The analysis of offender samples posed new challenges for the forensic science community. For the first time, large numbers of samples required analysis under uniform standards and protocols. Samples, in large part, could be considered similar in nature and therefore amenable to mass analysis. This contrasted with the usual analysis of evidence and reference samples that has always proceeded in a slow and individualized manner. These protocols were ill-suited to large-scale production of results.

Two solutions to this problem exist. The first is to hire a lot of technicians and use the old protocols. The second is to automate the procedure as much as possible, taking advantage of the technology of robotic handling and analysis. Laboratories have adopted one or the other of these approaches. Great Britain adopted the former, while many U.S. states and private laboratories have adopted the latter. California and Florida, among others, have invested heavily in the robotic analysis of samples. The use of robots has, by default, resulted in changes to standard casework protocols.

Whatever procedure is adopted for offender analysis, protocols and standards must be consistent with those adopted for casework. Here, standards mean that results must comport with minimum levels of quality assurance and quality control. Results must be consistent from sample 1 to sample 100,000, and must also agree with results obtained from similar casework protocols. However, because the samples are of known provenance and can be considered unlimited in most cases, the standards for analysis, interpretation, and acceptance of data are different than for casework. To achieve the large-scale production of which robots are capable, more bumps in the data are accepted than is the situation for evidence samples. Of primary concern are sample switches and contamination, rather than mixtures of two or more unknown people. For case samples, peak height ratios of 70% are required to conclude that two alleles are from the same individual. For databank samples, the robot cannot achieve this standard at all times, and peak height ratios of 40% are tolerated as proof of heterozygosity at a locus. This is somewhat controversial. Key to the analysis is the understanding that once a hit occurs with an offender sample, a new reference is taken from the now-suspect and retyped using the same protocol as the evidence. In this way, problems that might accrue from these "relaxed" standards are overcome.

Timeliness of the analysis of offender samples is important to the success of the databank. It seems obvious that an offender's sample should be analyzed and placed in the database prior to his release from prison. Examining the records of the first hits in California shows that many felons re-offend within the first 3 months of their release from prison, and one even re-offended within the first 3 days of his release. The databank is most effective when habitual offenders are profiled and in the database. In the first years of DNA databanks, this was difficult to achieve because funds were limited and the technology of scale had not yet been implemented. Over the past 5 years, significant increases in funding and deployment of robotic analysis have brought the backlog of offender samples into a reasonable range.

3.   Cases

As stated previously, the markers used for casework evidence must be the same as those used for offenders samples. In Great Britain, all cases, whether solved or not, are databank cases, and so the same loci are used for all reference and evidence items.

In the United States, the practical effect of choosing 13 core STR loci for the databank is that most laboratories have also adopted these for all casework, whether or not the case might involve the databank. Again, standards for analysis and acceptance of data must be uniform, enforced, and yield the same results as protocols from the offender side of the equation.

Because case evidence samples are unknown, greater expertise and training is required of the analyst. Evidence may be refractory to analysis, either because it is mixed with some other component of the world or because it is old. Additionally, reference samples are required from the victim and perhaps other witnesses, which may be difficult to obtain if the case is old. Together, these factors mean that analysis of case samples takes longer and is more complicated than the analysis of offender samples.

However, as already discussed, there is renewed interest in examining unsolved cases dating back two or more decades. Tens of thousands of cases await analysis throughout the United States, which in turn begs for an automated analytical scheme. The solution to this problem (either through increased numbers of trained analysts or the use of automation) will occupy the field for the next 3 to 5 years.

D.   Transforming Analyzed Data into a Database

Once the samples have been analyzed, there must be a method that takes the relevant portion of each sample profile and makes it available for searching against the other sample profiles. In addition, other demographic information must be added to the database so that the identity of the case and the offender can be obtained once a hit has been made. All of these goals are achieved through the use of a computer program common to those performing this work.

1.   The Computer Program

Many of the standards established for the acceptance of data into the databank are reflected in the computer program used to hold the sample profiles. The number and identity of the loci are examples of such standards. Because no detail is trivial in the construction of a database, every piece of data must be correct, or it may be rejected as invalid by the computer. One example of this kind of detail is the spelling of the locus TH01. Is it TH01, where the 0 is a zero; or THO1, where the O is a capital letter O? The computer cares about such details (or at least the person programming the computer did). Another example of such mind-numbing detail is the names of the alleles themselves. For example, the typing system from different manufacturers may call the same allele a different name. One may call an allele a "20," while another may call it a ">19." Both are correct, but the computer must be able to resolve these discrepancies. While the computer must be able to keep track of the demographic data from each profile, its primary function is to search an evidence profile against several offender profiles. This becomes very complicated when tens of thousands of evidence profiles must be searched against hundreds of thousands (or even millions) of offender profiles. The search algorithm must be capable of searching these samples in a short time frame, and relaying results to all of the affected parties. The program must keep track of the number of times each profile has been searched, and whether the profile has been matched to another sample.

One of the difficulties involved in matching evidence and offender profiles is establishing match criteria. Because evidence can be limited by degradation or quantity, full profiles are not always developed. How will the computer handle profiles when fewer than the full complement of 13 loci are present, or when only one allele meets the threshold criterion to be called a true allele? The computer must have rules that govern these situations, but it is important to establish that the computer is merely a tool that the analyst uses to do the heavy lifting of searching through thousands of profiles. The role of the computer program is to identify candidate matches and present these to the analyst for a more refined evaluation. The analyst makes the final determination as to what constitutes a match, and whether more work should be performed on either the evidence or offender profile to confirm or refute the candidate match. We cover additional details about matching evidence to offender profiles later in the chapter. Here we only emphasize that the computer is a tool for the analyst and does not substitute for judgment on the part of the scientist.

Different countries have developed software for performing this task of profile housekeeping and matching. In the United States, this program is called CODIS, which stands for Combined DNA Index System.

2.   Communication Between Laboratories

When more than one laboratory is submitting profiles to the database, communication between them is an essential part of the overall system. First and foremost, communication must be secure. The information must be protected from unauthorized use, both from within and from outside the laboratory. The software must include provisions that prevent snooping or hijacking when information is transmitted. In the United States, the Criminal Justice Information System (CJIS), a part of the Department of Justice, oversees security.

Use of the same software by all parties is essential to standardized communication; and again, in the United States, this is accomplished by the use of CODIS and the accompanying communications hardware. The national coordination of communication enables everyone with a CODIS terminal to send profiles and messages either directly to the national database, or to specific laboratories for directed searching. This standardized and secure communication is the backbone of the flow of profile information within the CODIS network of laboratories.

3.   Privacy

The privacy of personal data concerns many in our culture, and DNA data has not escaped this scrutiny. Most state laws and federal legislation clearly enunciate how DNA data can be used and, more important, how it cannot be used.

The names of offenders included in the offender databank are never loaded into the database. Instead, they are kept in a separate file. The only link between the offender name and the profile is the submission number. This submission number accompanies the sample throughout processing, and only in the case of a hit against an evidence profile is the name made available.

More important to some civil rights groups, no medical or physical identifying information is found in the loci used. This means that no demographic or personal identification data about an individual can be inferred strictly from the DNA profile contained in the database. All of the data (demographic and DNA) is kept on a computer server that has both physical and software security systems to prevent unauthorized access. The sample itself is protected by normal crime laboratory security procedures. All samples are kept in a locked evidence vault, and only individuals with appropriate background clearance have access to them.

4. Flow of Offender Data into the Databank

It may be useful at this point to track a sample through the databank from reception through analysis to inclusion in the searchable database. The specific mechanisms and protocols vary from state to state and country to country, but the general outline is the same.

a. Receipt of samples. Samples may be sent to the laboratory via U.S. Mail or by special delivery. Biological samples should be packaged so that leaks or spills are contained and do not endanger anyone handling the container.

Once received by the laboratory, each sample is opened and examined for integrity of the seal and the sample itself. The sample (whether blood or a buccal swab) may be accompanied by demographic data about the person sampled. This generally includes name, date of birth, a criminal identification number, the place where the sample was taken, who took it, the date taken, and any witnesses to the sampling. In some jurisdictions, the thumbprint of the offender is also taken to verify the identity of the individual. All of this information is recorded into either an electronic or physical logbook, and a unique accession number is assigned to the sample.

b. Analysis of samples. The sample is now processed and analyzed. The DNA is extracted using any of the techniques discussed earlier in this book. Next, assuming that the laboratory is using a panel of STR markers, the sample may be quantitated, or it may be amplified directly. Typically, a laboratory uses one of several commercially available kits to type the sample. The samples are typed by separating the alleles by an electrophoretic technique, and then, depending on the kit used, detecting the separated alleles by silver staining or by a laser/CCD instrument (see Chapter 6). The analyst interprets the data and determines types for the samples. The profile is then exported to the database.

For laboratories analyzing tens or hundreds of thousands of offender samples, automated analysis protocols allow for the simultaneous examination of up to 96 samples at one time. This requires the adaptation of quality assurance measures for large-scale handling. This may include multiple reagent blanks and quality control samples. It may also include multiple analyses of the same sample or samples, depending on the criteria for acceptance of data.

c. Flow of case data into the databank. Cases are still generally analyzed one at a time, although research efforts are underway to automate the simultaneous analysis of multiple cases. Currently, if more than one case is worked at a time, the analytical scheme involves processing evidence samples in batch mode, rather than in an automated fashion. This simply means that multiple samples are processed simultaneously using manual methods.

The only difference between preparing an evidence sample for comparison to a known reference and preparing it for inclusion in the databank is that national standards for analysis and naming alleles must be observed, and mixtures must be addressed. While most algorithms can search profiles with more than two alleles over multiple loci (indicating a mixture), it is better to determine whether genotypes can be resolved. Otherwise, the computer program will match all offender profiles containing any of the alleles found. Of course, for some evidence samples, this may not be possible.

It is important that both solved and unsolved cases be entered into the databank. Not all offenders are sampled and analyzed immediately upon conviction and incarceration, and many offenders plead guilty to offenses that are lesser than or different from a qualifying offense. Entering solved cases increases the number of potential matches to unsolved cases.

5. Import of Profiles into the Database

Once the analyst is satisfied that the samples are typed correctly, the profiles must be moved into the database. This may be accomplished by software developed in conjunction with the database itself, or by third-party software that properly prepares the data for import into the database. The complexities of this process will not be discussed here; suffice it to say that several intermediate steps are required before the data is safely ensconced in the database. If the laboratory is remote from the repository of the state or national databases, then the data must be moved electronically to these databases in a secure fashion.

The integrity of the data as it passes through these steps is vital; if the types are somehow changed between typing by the analyst and final inclusion in the database, the integrity of the entire databank is suspect. To address this issue, laboratories have methods of checking the data contained in the database against the profiles documented during the typing phase of the analysis.

By the time data is first entered into the database, all of the standards and conventions have been implemented, and the samples are available for the next step: the creation of indexes.

6. Categories and Indexes

There exists a multiplicity of sample types, including evidence, offender, victim, and suspect samples. It would be inefficient to search the evidence samples first against the offender samples and then against the suspect profiles. Before searching one sample against many others, some order and rules are necessary. First, sample types are divided into *categories*, and categories are then later combined into *indexes*. Table 9.1 specifies the different specimen categories into which a sample can be placed.

Table 9.1   Specimen Categories

Alleged Father
Biological Mother
Convicted Offender
Elimination, Known
Forensic Unknown
Missing Person
Population
Suspect, Known
Unidentified Person
Victim, Known

Table 9.2 CODIS Indexes

Indexes	Specimen Categories
Population	Population
Convicted Offender	Convicted Offender
Casework	Forensic Unknown
	Unidentified Person
	Suspect, Known (in some cases)

Not all specimen categories can be placed into indexes for searching. Currently, only Forensic Unknown, Unidentified Person, Convicted Offender, Population, and, in some jurisdictions, Suspect Known specimens can be placed into searchable indexes. Further restrictions also apply to these specimens, in that they can only be placed into specific indexes. Table 9.2 shows the relationship between these categories and the allowed indexes.

An index groups specimen categories together for simplifying searches. When the Casework Index is searched against the Convicted Offender Index, then both the Forensic Unknown as well as the Unidentified Person specimens are searched. In addition, the Casework Index can be searched against itself. This allows all unsolved cases to be searched against other unsolved and solved cases This maximizes the potential of the databank to resolve unsolved cases. At this time, U.S. law precludes the searching of Forensic Unknown specimens against Suspect Profiles.

7. *Searching Profiles*

At the outset of this section, we emphasize that the computer does not declare a match; only a trained analyst can do that. The task of the computer program is to present the analyst with a reasonable number of candidate matches to evaluate further. The analyst then uses her judgment to decide if a candidate match warrants further work.

Once the database has been properly populated with profiles from both cases and offenders, a search is performed of one against the other. For the simplest cases, matching profiles is a trivial matter. Where all of the alleles at all of the loci have been detected in the evidence and offender samples, there should be a one-to-one correspondence of alleles at all tested loci for samples from the same source (Figures 9.1 and Figure 9.2). Difficulties arise when the evidence is limited in some way, for example, through degradation or small sample size. For these types of evidence samples, not all alleles at each locus are patent, and a search of offender profiles using the simplistic criteria outlined above will not show a match even if the source is present in the database.

Therefore, search criteria are needed that allow for explainable differences between the evidence and reference profiles, but that do not allow clearly erroneous candidate matches to be made. To address this issue, CODIS has flexible rules that allow the analyst to choose specific match criteria for the computer to follow during a search. These criteria are defined in the following sections.

a. Stringency.   This refers to the rules used to compare alleles at a locus between two samples. At *high stringency*, the number of alleles and the allelic values must be the same. If the evidence sample has two alleles at one locus, the matching sample must have two alleles of the same value. At *moderate stringency*, the sample with the fewest number of alleles determines the number of alleles that must match. If one sample has two alleles and the other has one allele, then only one allele must match to be considered a moderate

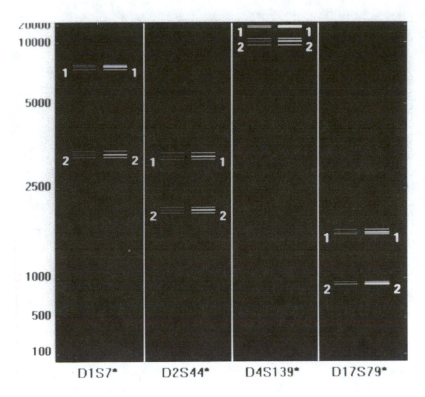

Figure 9.1 The computer screen generated when a potential cold hit is scored from RFLP profiles. Each of the four vertical panels is a comparison of the alleles at one locus in the profile of interest to the equivalent alleles in a database profile. The computer calculates windows of uncertainty for the band sizes of the profile entered and a putative matching database sample, and then compares them for overlap. The middle band of each triplet is the actual band size; the lower and upper bands define the uncertainty window (see also Chapter 8; Appendix E).

stringency match. At *low stringency*, there must be at least one allele with the same value in both samples.

The stringency rules give an analyst the requisite flexibility when searching incomplete evidence profiles against the offender databank. For example, assume that a highly degraded evidence sample is analyzed and shows a single allele at each of four loci. A reasonable possibility exists that at least one of these loci is a true heterozygote, where the other band is lost due to degradation. If this is the case, searching at high stringency will miss the true source of the sample, even if the source is in the database. Searching at moderate stringency, however, will hit the true source, as well as some other non-source samples (Figure 9.3). The analyst is now in a position to evaluate the totality of the data to determine if the match should be reported.

b. Minimum Number of Loci Required to Report a Match. For loci of medium heterozygosities, such as the STR loci, the analyst may want to specify a minimum number of loci required to match before considering the samples to be a true match. This eliminates adventitious hits that will occur over four or more loci when the number of offenders in the database is large. It would be unusual (but not impossible!) to have more than seven STR loci matching at high stringency between two unrelated individuals.

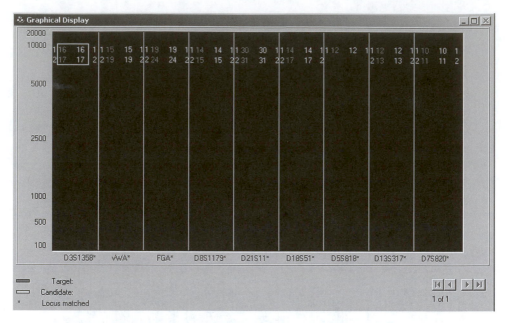

Figure 9.2 The computer screen generated when a potential cold hit is scored from STR profiles. Note that in contrast to the RFLP hit screen, the matching profiles are displayed along the top of the screen with the concordant alleles adjacent to each other. The white square highlights matching alleles at locus D3S1358. No attempt is made to graphically display the migration of the bands or peaks. The allele calls for each of the two samples are identical in the nine loci.

c. Include Candidate Specimens that Match on All but [X] Loci. This rule allows the analyst to consider candidate matches where one or more loci are reported as misses. This enlarges the number of candidates for an analyst to evaluate.

d. Indexes to Search. Once the stringency parameters have been set, the analyst will choose the indexes to search. Typically, the Casework Index will be searched against itself and the Convicted Offender Index. The computer will then take each profile in one index and search it against the profiles in the other index using the rules set by the analyst.

When the stringency parameters are satisfied between a target and a candidate profile, the computer declares them a candidate match and presents them to the analyst for evaluation. The analyst then examines each candidate match and decides whether it is a non-match, a match, or possible but not conclusive. If it is a match, no further work is performed. If it is possible but not definitive, the analyst may decide that more work should be performed to confirm or refute the match. This may include, for example, analyzing more loci or using a different DNA typing system. If the match appears legitimate, a confirmation process begins.

8. Confirmation of a Match

Because many agencies handle tens or hundreds of thousands of offender samples, there exists the possibility of a sample switch or a clerical error. One way to handle this issue is to analyze every sample in duplicate; however, given the limited resources normally available, this is an impractical solution. Another way of addressing the possibility of errors is

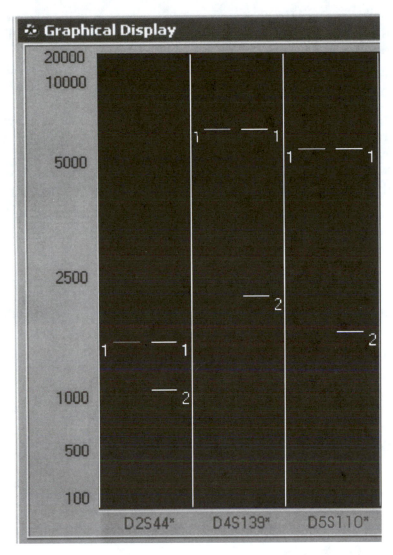

Figure 9.3 A moderate stringency database match for RFLP profiles. The match screen is arranged to show the matching bands at each locus between the evidence and felon reference samples. Three RFLP loci are shown: D2S44, D4S139, and D5S110. The bands from the evidence sample are located on the left within each locus, while the felon reference sample is on the right. Note that the evidence profile has only one band at each locus, while the reference profile has two. This would typically not be a match; however, by setting the search parameter to *moderate stringency*, the computer matches the sample with the fewest number of bands (in this case, the evidence sample) to any candidate (felon) sample containing a band matching the band(s) present in the evidence sample. The analyst must analyze the results of this match and determine if there is reason to believe that this could be a real match, although one band appears to be missing from each of the tested loci. In this case, the DNA profile was derived from sperm recovered from a vaginal swab of a woman who had been murdered and placed into the trunk of a car that was then set on fire. The casework analyst saw faint bands in the evidence autorad in the regions matching the felon reference, but decided that they were too weak to be called. More evidence remained from the vaginal swab, and the casework and databank laboratories reanalyzed the evidence and the felon reference samples using PCR-STR technology. Results showed genetic concordance between the evidence and felon reference samples at all nine loci tested.

to focus on those samples identified as matches to casework profiles. Because the number of matches is much lower than the number of offender samples, it is possible to confirm these profiles before reporting the match to the relevant agencies.

Several ways exist to achieve this goal. One is to retrieve the sample and reanalyze it, including the samples that flanked it during original receipt and analysis. If a sample switch has occurred, this reanalysis should detect it. Alternatively, an offender may have contributed more than one sample to the databank. In this case, a true duplicate sample is available and may already be analyzed. By whatever method, the profile of the offender sample is confirmed before reporting the match. The last step in the confirmation process is to obtain a new sample from the offender for the casework laboratory to type. This ensures that the evidence and offender samples are analyzed by the same laboratory using the same methods. The hit now makes the offender a suspect. Rather than this being the end of the case, it becomes a new beginning. Significant old-fashioned shoe leather is needed before an arrest can be made and the case prosecuted.

9. *United States Statistics*

As of September 2001, 116 laboratories in 37 U.S. states were participating in NDIS. Over 500,000 offender samples and 25,000 casework samples have been typed and entered into the national database. These have resulted in 791 offender hits, 519 case-to-case hits, and over 1600 cases solved using the national databank.

IV. Summary

The DNA databank has changed the way the criminal justice system conducts its work. The databank has changed the role of forensic science from confirming the work of the detective who has identified the assailant, to the process of providing the identity of the assailant to the detective. It thus joins fingerprints as an investigative tool, rather than merely a confirmatory tool.

Further References

DNA Identification Act of 1994 (the Act), (Public Law 103-322).

Federal Bureau of Investigation (FBI) *NDIS Standards for the Acceptance of DNA Data*, Jan. 4, 1999, <http://www.ncjrs.org/pdffiles1/nij/sl413apb.pdf>.

Sidebar 13

A False Database Hit
(or, it was my evil twin)

Early in February 2000, the British press reported the news of an erroneous DNA database hit. Public reaction to this event ranged from anger to disbelief. The FBI's Stephen Niezgoda, custodian of the American national DNA database, was quoted as exclaiming, "This is mind-blowing." Was this coincidental match really unexpected, and what are the implications for the expanding databank programs around the world? A closer look at the actual circumstances may shed some light on what actually happened, and whether an error occurred.

In 1999, police in Manchester, England, recovered a biological sample from the scene of a burglary. The evidence was typed using a six-locus STR system, and the DNA profile was submitted to the national database. The British convicted offender database had recently grown to include approximately 660,000 profiles. The computer reported a match to a sample in the database; it was estimated that the likelihood of this profile occurring at random among unrelated individuals was about 1 in 37 million. Based on the apparent strength of this evidence, the donor of the database sample was arrested for the burglary.

However, the suspect, a man with advanced Parkinson's disease who could barely dress himself, could not drive, and lived 200 miles from the site of the burglary, insisted that he had not committed the crime. He also provided an alibi that he had been babysitting a sick daughter at the time. His blood sample had landed in the database after it was collected following an arrest for hitting a daughter in a family dispute.

Only when the suspect's solicitor demanded a retest using additional markers, after the suspect had been in jail for months, was further testing performed. In this second analysis, a newer typing system, called SGM Plus was used. This STR system tests a total of nine autosomal loci as well as the gender identification locus. The suspect's DNA now failed to match that from the questioned sample at the additional loci, and he was therefore unequivocally excluded as a possible source of the crime scene evidence.

Was the "match" reported after the analysis of only six STR loci an "error"? Was the suspect falsely included as a possible donor to the sample? No. That all the loci matched was exactly the correct result. The very definition of a coincidental match is that another person with the same DNA profile who is not the source of the sample exists. What was erroneous was the inference that only the suspect could be the source of the sample.

First, it must be understood that the calculated profile frequency is an estimate, and can be off by an order of magnitude in either direction. Second, it is not only unsurprising, but expected, that the larger the database, the greater chance of a coincidental match. As databases grow, greater numbers of more discriminating loci are required to reduce the possibility of an adventitious hit. For example, in the United States, 13 STR loci are required to enter a sample into the national DNA database. Additionally, a profile frequency of 1 in 37 million does not mean that the six loci cannot match more than 1 person in 37 million. Formally, it can be said that, on average, 37 million unrelated individuals must be sampled to find one instance of the profile. It does not mean there cannot be two, and it also does not exclude the possibility of finding two of the same six-locus profiles in the first 660,000 people tested.

The Forensic Science Service Laboratory has acknowledged that when this incident occurred, its database had outgrown the marker system. The additional markers included in the updated STR typing system do not preclude another coincidental hit, but they do reduce the chance. However, not only can adventitious matches occur, but the mass analysis and automated nature of constructing DNA databanks leaves some "wiggle room" for other types of errors, such as sample switches or incorrect sample identifications. Because of these considerations, it is critical to regard a database hit as nothing more than probable cause to look further at the individual whose DNA has been matched to a sample. A new sample, independently obtained directly from the suspect, should be analyzed before any report is even released from the lab. Just as important, careful investigative work should complement the physical evidence analysis in attempting to link a source to a sample. An unlimited number of STR loci cannot compensate for a thoughtless investigation.

References

Willing, R., Mismatch calls DNA tests into question, *USA Today*, Feb. 8, 2000.
Moenssens, A.A., *A Mistaken DNA Identification? What Does It Mean?* 2000,
    <http://www.forensic-evidence.com/site/EVID/EL_DNAerror.html>.

Quality Assurance 10

I. Certification and Accreditation

Formal external review of both a forensic laboratory and the individuals performing work in that venue is useful for a number of reasons. Internally, the results provide the laboratory and its personnel with valuable information that can be used to detect and correct deficiencies and improve performance. The intent of impartial assessment provides judicial officers, the court, and other interested parties with information regarding the laboratory's credibility and fitness to reliably and accurately perform forensic testing.

A. Certification

Certification deals with the qualifications of an individual criminalist. In the United States, certification is not currently required to perform forensic testing, but is regarded as highly favorable. The trend is toward encouraging certification in at least an analyst's field of specialization. Certification examinations are provided by the American Board of Criminalistics (ABC), a group governed by a rotating quorum of qualified workers in the field who have an interest in upholding a self-imposed standard within their own ranks. Written examinations are offered in both general knowledge of forensic science, as well as in the various specialties. A passing score on the General Knowledge Examination qualifies the individual as a **Diplomate** of the ABC. To obtain **Fellow** status, the criminalist must pass a written specialty examination, then submit the results of a hands-on proficiency test within 1 year and annually thereafter. A DNA specialist must pass both the general biology exam and DNA specialty examinations. If a Fellow fails more than one proficiency test in a 4-year period, his status is temporarily revoked. It can only be reinstated when the deficiency is remedied to the satisfaction of the ABC review committee and a successful re-test completed. A **Technical Specialist** examination in DNA has recently been introduced by the ABC. This examination combines the specialist examination with a subset of questions from the generalist examination. The introduction of Technical Specialist examinations by the ABC has generated some debate within the forensic science community.

B. Accreditation

Accreditation pertains to the qualification of a laboratory that provides forensic testing services. This service, provided by the American Society of Crime Laboratory Directors

(ASCLD), is also at present voluntary and self-regulated. The program is managed and the standards established by the ASCLD Laboratory Accreditation Board (ASCLD/LAB), which is responsible to a delegate assembly composed of the directors of all accredited laboratories. Accreditation is also offered by the National Forensic Science and Technology Center (NFSTC). Similar to individual certification, an inspection serves to identify criteria that can be used by a laboratory to assess its level of performance and improve its operations. It is also an impartial means by which those that depend on the laboratory's services, as well as the general public, can ascertain that a particular lab meets established standards. To qualify for accreditation, a laboratory must demonstrate that it meets the standards for management, operations, personnel, procedures, equipment, physical plant, security, and health and safety procedures. The laboratory analysts must also participate in regular proficiency testing programs. Accreditation is granted for 5 years, provided that a laboratory continues to meet the standard during this period. Both the initial accreditation and reaccreditation on a 5-year cycle require a full review of the laboratory, including an on-site inspection. To remain in compliance, the laboratory must also conduct an internal audit every year and requisition an external audit on alternate years.

II.   SWDGAM (Formerly TWGDAM)

TWGDAM, the Technical Working Group on DNA Analysis Methods, was originally formed in 1988 at the behest of the FBI. Its self-assigned functions were to provide a forum for forensic DNA laboratories to discuss issues, conduct studies, and reach a consensus as to the DNA methodologies to be used in North American crime laboratories. In 1999, the name was changed to the Scientific Working Group on DNA Analysis Methods (SWGDAM). SWGDAM provides a medium for the different laboratories throughout the country to exchange DNA testing data, and has played a particularly important role in establishing guidelines for working forensic DNA laboratories. Members of SWGDAM include forensic scientists from public laboratories throughout the United States. Various subcommittees have been established to deal with specific issues such as quality assurance, quality control, database developments, and new systems as they are considered for use. The group has established and continues to update guidelines for quality assurance, proficiency testing, and interpretation, and has also sponsored several inter-laboratory studies.

SWGDAM has also issued several consensus statements regarding the validity and reliability of various DNA techniques and calculations, including the ill-fated ceiling calculation, guidelines for statistical treatment of forensic DNA data, and responses to DNA testing challenges. Although criticized by some as being too exclusive, particularly in the early stages of decision-making, and also as potentially biased in developing standards in which it has a vested interest, SWGDAM has nevertheless emerged as a nucleus around which the forensic community can assemble as the DNA typing explosion continues.

III.   NRC I and II

DNA was first used in forensic casework in the United Kingdom in 1985. By 1986 it was instituted in commercial laboratories in the United States, and in 1988 the FBI began casework testing. By the summer of 1989, important questions had begun to surface regarding scientific, legal, societal, and ethical issues brought forth by this new technology. These questions had as much to do with public perception of the reliability and validity of DNA evidence as with the dependability of laboratory analyses.

The National Research Council (NRC) of the National Academy of Sciences volunteered to shoulder the difficult task of addressing the general applicability and appropriateness of DNA technology to forensic science. In addition, they addressed issues of standardization and data management as well as legal, societal, and ethical considerations. In January 1990, the Committee on DNA Technology in Forensic Science held its first meeting, and in 1992 its report and recommendations were released and published.

Contrary to the news release printed by the *New York Times* on April 14, 1992, and retracted the next day, the committee recommended that the use of DNA analysis for forensic purposes be continued. However, this recommendation was contingent on the implementation of suggested improvements and changes in relatively short order. Their suggestions included many that were well-grounded in scientific principle and common sense. A few points, however, instigated even more controversy among the forensic and legal communities, engendering a second gathering of experts under the continuing auspices of the NRC.

We summarize the important, some of them controversial, points in the 1992 report, and then review and compare the report of the second committee, published in 1996. The exact text of the specific recommendations of both committees is found in Appendix I.

A. NRC I

The first NRC Committee on *DNA Technology in Forensic Science*, chaired by Victor McKusick, put forth recommendations in six separate areas: technical considerations, statistical interpretation, laboratory standards, databanks and privacy, legal considerations, and societal and ethical issues.

The technical recommendations encompassed the basics of good scientific research and testing. Particular to forensic science are the invocations to establish pattern identification and comparison criteria and to challenge and understand the limits of each particular typing system. Many of the technical concerns prevalent at that time have been remedied by both research and experience and have ceased to be issues even in court. The committee also suggested the establishment of a national committee on forensic DNA typing under the auspices of an appropriate government agency.

A hot item up for consideration was the statistical basis for interpretation of a DNA profile. The committee's recommendation in this area sparked some heated discussion and generated the most compelling impetus for the formation of the second committee. A calculation named the "ceiling principle" was invented, ostensibly to ensure that the rareness of any particular profile in the population was not underestimated. Unfortunately, the calculation was neither a principle, nor constituted a ceiling, and had no scientific basis. To further confuse the issue, an "interim ceiling principle," specifying even more conservative allele frequencies in the calculation, was recommended until enough population sampling could be completed to provide a sound genetic and statistical basis for the use of actual allele frequencies.

The controversial issue of laboratory error rates was also addressed. The committee's recommendation was that "Laboratory error rates should be measured with appropriate proficiency tests and should play a role in the interpretation of results of forensic DNA typing." Unfortunately, an "error" was never defined, nor was any specification for an acceptable or unacceptable risk of error put forth (see Chapter 8).

The committee called for standardization in the field and the assessment and assurance of quality in forensic DNA work. This challenge has been met by practicing laboratories and individuals, in large part by voluntary submission to the accreditation and certification programs outlined above. The spotlight on DNA has, in fact, forced the entire forensic profession to move toward providing proof of quality services. This trend has served to not only improve actual laboratory operations and criminalist proficiency, but has given users of forensic laboratory services, as well as the courts, juries, and general public, a higher confidence level in the validity and reliability of forensic testing in general and DNA analysis in particular.

The NRC I committee recommended that the courts take judicial notice of the basic underlying scientific validity of DNA typing and the fundamental soundness of the methods in use by the forensic community. They also supported the adjudication of DNA admissibility on a case-by-case basis, at least in the interim. This was a generally reasonable suggestion for that time, although many would argue that the specifics suggested pertaining to methodology and standardization should more correctly be applied to the weight of the evidence rather than its admissibility.

The creation of a national databank of DNA profiles was affirmed, along with an admonishment not to lock the format into technologies that were sure to become quickly outdated (see Chapter 9). Finally, cautions regarding the privacy of DNA information, the overselling of DNA evidence in court, and the influence of parties with vested interests in the accreditation process of laboratories were enumerated.

During the process of organizing the National Committee on Forensic DNA Typing recommended by the NRC I committee (eventually called the DNA Advisory Board (DAB), see Chapter 10.IV), an interesting sidelight emerged: Who is qualified to comment about DNA technology as applied to forensic analysis in general, and would different standards qualify someone to render an opinion regarding specific cases? Of the original 14 members on the NRC I committee, only two were working forensic scientists, and one more had extensive academic knowledge of the subject. The others, although considered outstanding in their various related expertises in DNA technology, had no experience with forensic applications. Two others, who had just begun to venture into forensic DNA applications, were pressured to resign because of "vested interests."

Was this an appropriate composition for a body entrusted with the promulgation of standards for the discipline of DNA testing in the profession of forensic science? If the forensic scientist is highly informed, involved in the field, and perhaps recognized as an outstanding contributor, is she necessarily biased and closed-minded? On the other hand, is a "disinterested" expert in molecular biology, biotechnology, or statistics with no forensic background really the appropriate person to render an opinion about a field in which he has no experience? On the surface, it might seem that an "outside opinion" from a "disinterested party" is more trustworthy. But if it is based on an incomplete body of knowledge, of what worth is it?

Forensic scientists are uniquely qualified to render opinions on the reliability of a technology as used for the analysis of physical evidence. Because they routinely encounter evidence that comes from real-world environments, they are able to devise experiments that test the validity and reliability of new techniques that may have forensic utility under such conditions. The result of this work and experience also puts the criminalist in an ideal position to interpret results from casework samples. This does not imply that forensic scientists carry out their work in a vacuum with blatant disregard for the seminal literature or the opinions of academic scientists. On the contrary, these are resources that should be, and in most cases are, used in the process of understanding and testing new technologies. Judgments regarding the use of a technology are best rendered by those most familiar with its advantages, limitations, and consequences. Although fresh ideas and critical review are always welcome, and indeed should be solicited, "disinterested outside experts" are just that, and their opinions should not be given undue weight in the misguided fear of bias from those who perform the work on an everyday basis.

B.   NRC II

In April 1993, Judge William Sessions, then Director of the FBI, requested that the NRC do a follow-up study to resolve, in particular, the statistical controversies generated by NRC I, and also to incorporate new data on population substructure that had been accumulating. Dr. James Crow was asked to chair the second committee, and the first meeting was held in September 1994. The NRC II report, entitled *The Evaluation of Forensic DNA Evidence*, was published in November 1996. The report is of a much narrower scope than the previous one and primarily addresses population statistic issues along with some additional considerations of laboratory operations and risk of laboratory errors.

The members of the new committee freely acknowledged the blunder incurred in the recommendation of both the "ceiling principle" and the "interim ceiling principle," and further submitted that some of the supporting statements had been misinterpreted or misapplied in the courts. They concluded that those calculations were not only unnecessary but, in fact, inadvisable. In their place, they recommended standard statistical procedures based on population genetics, with suggestions for some of the special circumstances that arise in forensic applications. In particular, they fully endorsed the multiplication of allele frequencies from genetically independent loci (i.e., use of the **product rule**) when applied with the appropriate caveats and a modicum of common sense.

With regard to the estimation of risk of error, the NRC II committee severely discouraged any attempt to adjust the estimation of a profile frequency by combining it with an "error rate." Among other things, they recognized that the number of proficiency tests required to give an accurate estimate of an acceptable error rate would be outlandishly expensive and disruptive. They suggested that such efforts would be better applied to raising laboratory standards. Additionally, they emphasized that it is the current practice, not the past record of a laboratory that is relevant, particularly with rapidly evolving technology. We would additionally suggest that the only relevant question is whether an error occurred in the case at hand. (The questions of "what is an error?" and "is there a rate?" are addressed in Chapter 8.) In addition to the proper use of standards and controls, a rigorous technical review process is the best way to avoid issuing reports containing errors. Further review by an independent expert provides an additional level of confidence that no substantive errors remain. As a final check, the committee recommended the time-honored and reasonable practice of saving out a portion of the sample for a future independent test.

The NRC II committee concluded that, overall, "The technology for DNA profiling and the methods for estimating frequencies and related statistics have progressed to the point where the reliability and validity of properly collected and analyzed DNA data should not be in doubt."

IV. Federal DNA Advisory Board

In 1994, the DNA Identification Act was passed by Congress. One consequence of this legislation was the formation of a DNA Advisory Board (DAB). Members were appointed by the FBI from nominations submitted by the National Academy of Sciences (NAS) and other organizations. The duties of the DAB were originally scheduled to revert to the TWGDAM group in 1999, but the mandate was extended through 2000 to allow the DAB to complete certain tasks. During its tenure, this board has provided guidelines for both forensic DNA testing and DNA database typing on a wide variety of quality control issues. In October, 1998, the director of the FBI issued *Quality Assurance Standards for Forensic DNA Testing Laboratories;* and in April 1999, a separate but overlapping set of standards, *Quality Assurance Standards for Convicted Offender DNA Databasing Laboratories,* was provided for groups performing DNA databasing.

The DAB has also seen fit to weigh in on the subject of objective audit standards. Laboratory audits to document compliance with DAB-established standards are performed by forensic scientists, either internal or external to the laboratory. Typically, such audits are performed by inspectors from ASCLD/LAB, or more recently the NFSTC. However, it immediately became clear that the differences in interpretation of various standards by the audit teams (in all disciplines, not just DNA) may have exceeded the differences in implementation of those same standards between laboratories. Laboratories were putting more energy into trying to second-guess the expectations of their audit team than into the creation of a quality program. In an effort to clarify the intent of various standards, and to minimize interpretation variability, the FBI, reportedly with input from multiple forensic DNA laboratories and in collaboration with ASCLD/LAB and NFSTC, set about to develop a comprehensive audit document. This document, *Quality Assurance Audit for Forensic DNA and Convicted Offender DNA Databasing Laboratories*, was published in December 2000. It remains to be seen how this document will be used by inspection teams and what its impact will be on the overall standard of DNA testing laboratories.

The power of the DAB has been substantial, primarily because any agency requesting federal development funds for forensic DNA testing or DNA databasing must demonstrate compliance with the standards set by this group. As with the original TWGDAM guidelines, standards promulgated by the DAB have become *de facto* for any laboratory providing DNA services to courts. This is true regardless of whether the laboratory is formally accredited and irrespective of whether it receives federal monies. We expect that this tradition will continue as DAB is phased out and the now SWGDAM group once again assumes responsibility for setting quality assurance standards for the forensic DNA community.

Further References

Bär, W., Brinkmann, B., Budowle, B., Carracedo, A., Gill, P., Lincoln, P., Mayr, W., and Olaisen, B., DNA recommendations. Further report of the DNA Commission of the ISFH regarding the use of short tandem repeat systems. International Society for Forensic Haemogenetics, *Int. J. Legal Med.*, 110(4), 175–176, 1997.

Carracedo, A., Bär, W., Lincoln, P., Mayr, W., Morling, N., Olaisen, B., Schneider, P., Budowle, B., Brinkmann, B., Gill, P., Holland, M., Tully, G., and Wilson, M., DNA Commission of the International Society for Forensic Genetics: guidelines for mitochondrial DNA typing, *Forensic Sci. Int.*, 110(2), 79–85, 2000.

Duewer, D.L., Gary, K.T., and Reeder, D.J., RFLP Band size standards: cell line K562 values from 1991–1997 proficiency studies, *J. Forensic Sci.*, 45(5), 1106–1118, 2000.

Duewer, D.L., Gary, K.T., and Reeder, D.J., RFLP band size standards: NIST standard reference material 2390, *J. Forensic Sci.*, 45(5), 1093–1105, 2000.

DNA Commission of the ISFG, 1991 report concerning recommendations of the DNA commission of the, International Society for Forensic Haemogenetics Relating to the use of DNA, Polymorphism, *Vox Sang.*, 63(1), 70–73, 1992.

DNA Commission of the ISFG, DNA recommendations — 1992 report concerning recommendations of the DNA Commission of the International Society for Forensic Haemogenetics relating to the use of PCR-based polymorphisms, *Int. J. Legal Med.*, 105(1), 63–64, 1992.

DNA Commission of the ISFG, Statement by DNA Commission of the International Society for Forensic Haemogenetics concerning the National Academy of Sciences report on DNA Technology in Forensic Science in the USA., *Forensic Sci. Int.*, 59(1), 1–2, 1993.

DNA Commission of the ISFG, Recommendations of the DNA Commission of the International Society for Forensic Haemogenetics relating to the use of PCR-based polymorphisms, *Forensic Sci. Int.*, 55(1), 1–3, 1992.

DNA Commission of the ISFG, Second DNA recommendations. 1991 report concerning recommendations of the DNA commission of the International Society for Forensic Haemogenetics relating to the use of DNA polymorphisms, *Int. J. Legal Med.*, 104(6), 361–364; *Forensic Sci. Int.*, 52(2), 125–130, 1992.

DNA Commission of the ISFG, Recommendations of the Society for Forensic Haemogenetics concerning DNA polymorphisms, *Forensic Sci. Int.*, 43, 109–111, 1989

DNA Identification Act of 1994; Public Law 103-322.

Federal Bureau of Investigation (FBI), Quality assurance audit for forensic DNA and convicted offender DNA databasing laboratories, *Forensic Sci. Commun.*, 3(1), 2001, <http://www.fbi.gov/hq/lab/fsc/current/backissu.htm>.

Koehler, J.J., Chia, K., and Lindsey, A., The random match probability (RMP) in DNA evidence: irrelevant and prejudicial?, *Jurimetics J.*, 35, 1995.

Koehler, J.J., Error and exaggeration in the presentation of DNA evidence at trial, *Jurimetics J.*, 34, 1993.

Morton, N.E. and Collins, A.E., Statistical and genetic aspects of quality control for DNA identification, *Electrophoresis*, 16(9), 1670–1677, 1995.

National Research Council, *The Evaluation of Forensic DNA Evidence*, National Academy Press, Washington, D.C., 1996.

National Research Council, *DNA Technology in Forensic Science*, National Academy Press, Washington, D.C., 1992.

Olaisen, B., Bär, W., Brinkmann, B., Budowle, B., Carracedo, A., Gill, P., Lincoln, P., Mayr, W.R., and Rand, S., DNA recommendations 1997 of the International Society for Forensic Genetics, *Vox Sang*, 74(1), 61–63, 1998.

Technical Working Group on DNA Analysis Methods (TWGDAM), Established guidelines for a quality assurance program for DNA testing laboratories; including RFLP and PCR technologies, *Crime Lab. Dig.*, 18, 44–75, 1995.

Technical Working Group on DNA Analysis Methods (TWGDAM), Established guidelines for DNA proficiency test manufacturing and reporting, *Crime Lab. Dig.*, 21, 27–32, 1994.

Technical Working Group on DNA Analysis Methods (TWGDAM), Established guidelines for conducting a DNA quality assurance audit, *Crime Lab. Dig.*, 20, 8–18, 1993.

Technical Working Group on DNA Analysis Methods (TWGDAM), Established guidelines for a proficiency testing program for DNA analysis, *Crime Lab. Dig.,* 17, 59–64, 1990.

Technical Working Group on DNA Analysis Methods (TWGDAM), Guidelines for a proficiency testing program for DNA restriction fragment length polymorphism analysis, *Crime Lab. Dig.,* 17(2), 50–60, 1990.

Technical Working Group on DNA Analysis Methods (TWGDAM), Statement of the Working Group on Statistical Standards for DNA Analysis, *Crime Lab. Dig.,* 17(3), 53–58, 1990.

Technical Working Group on DNA Analysis Methods (TWGDAM), Guidelines for a quality assurance program for DNA restriction fragment length polymorphism analysis, *Crime Lab. Dig.,* 16(2), 40–59, 1989.

Admissibility Standards: Science on Trial in the Courtroom

11

I.   Frye, Daubert, and the Federal Rules of Evidence

 DNA evidence is not the first scientific evidence to be presented in a court of law, although it may well be the most highly scrutinized. Often, basic scientific procedures are adapted specifically for use in forensic science, or sometimes completely new techniques are developed to address a particular question. For all generally accepted testing procedures, there was once a first instance when a judge made the decision to allow a specific type of scientific evidence to be presented at trial. Typically, when a new technique is applied to criminal investigation, an admissibility hearing is held by the trial court to determine if the evidence should be heard by the jury. If the ruling is confirmed by an appellate court and eventually by a supreme court, legal precedent is established for the admissibility (or inadmissibility) of a general category of scientific evidence. Lower courts are then bound by this precedent and a pre-trial admissibility hearing is unnecessary.

One of the confusions that confounds the acceptance of scientific evidence is the existence of three different standards of admissibility at the federal level: one statutory and the other two grounded in case law. Individual states have adopted one of these standards, often adding their own variations and restrictions.

A.   The *Frye* Standard

The oldest precedent relies on *Frye v. United States* (1923). The science being presented in this case was the theory underlying the "lie-detector", or polygraph, test. In *Frye*, it was ruled that

> "… the thing from which the deduction is made must be sufficiently established to have gained ***general acceptance*** in the particular field in which it belongs" [emphasis added]

The motion to exclude the evidence was granted by the District of Columbia Trial Court and affirmed by the D.C. Appellate Court the same year; polygraph testing remains inadmissible to this day. This federal ruling, codifying the concept of *general acceptance*, has come to be known as the ***Frye* Standard**. Until recently, the majority of federal decisions

183

relied on *Frye* and a majority of states had adopted various iterations of it, also incorporating their own additional requirements.

The corollary ruling to *Frye* on the admissibility of scientific evidence (voice prints) in California is *People v. Kelly* (1976), which consists of three parts:

1. Reliability must be established by experts.
2. Experts must be properly qualified.
3. Correct procedures must be used.

Several adjunct rulings are often quoted in the State of California. In *People v. Guerra* (1984), *general acceptance* was equated with *consensus* or *clear majority*. *People v. Reilly* (1987) defines the *field in which it belongs*, or *relevant scientific community*, as:

1. Forensic scientists
2. Scientists in broader disciplines who are knowledgeable in the technique
3. Well-credentialed analysts

The states of Hawaii and Oregon also stand out as having specifically enumerated their guidelines for the admissibility of novel scientific evidence to the trial court. The Hawaii Rules of Evidence, which are layered on top of *Frye*, state that:

1. The evidence will assist the trier of fact to understand the evidence or to determine a fact in issue.
2. The evidence will add to the common understanding of the jury.
3. The underlying theory is generally accepted as valid.
4. The procedures used are generally accepted as reliable if performed properly.
5. The procedures were applied and conducted properly in the present instance.

They then add that, "The court should then consider whether admitting such evidence will be more probative than prejudicial", giving due to the Federal Rules of Evidence.

The state of Oregon also combines elements of both *Frye* and Relevancy. *State v. Brown* (1984) reads, "The salutary aspect of the *Frye* general acceptance test is retained, not as a prerequisite to admissibility, but as one of seven steps in the screening process. To determine the relevance or probative value of proffered scientific evidence ... the following seven factors are to be considered as guidelines:"

1. The technique's general acceptance in the field
2. The expert's qualifications and stature
3. The use which has been made of the technique
4. The potential rate of error
5. The existence of specialized literature
6. The novelty of the invention
7. The extent to which the technique relies on subjective interpretation of the expert

B.   The Federal Rules of Evidence

The **Federal Rules of Evidence** were originally promulgated by the Supreme Court of the United States under its authority to proscribe the general rules for federal, civil, and criminal proceedings. They were enacted by Congress in 1975 and have been amended several times since then. These rules (specifically 702 and 403) may be summarized to say that, if findings are reliable, relevant, and more probative than prejudicial, they may be admitted for the jury to consider. The Federal Rules of Evidence are generally regarded as a somewhat looser standard than *Frye* and certainly relegate a wide breadth of discretion to the court. As of the mid-1990s, a number of states had also co-opted the Relevancy Standard based on the Federal Rules of Evidence, sometimes in addition to their own statutory Rules of Evidence. A couple of states had drawn from both decisions. and a few relied only on their own internal standards, often citing "reliability" and individual State Rules of Evidence or the more recent federal *Daubert* decision.

C. The *Daubert* Standard

Most recently, in 1993, the U.S. Supreme Court rejected use of the *Frye* general acceptance test in those jurisdictions governed by the Federal Rules of Evidence. The new federal decision, *Daubert et ux. v. Merrell Dow* (1993), gives the trial judge great discretion in determining the admissibility of scientific evidence. The Court set the following guidelines for use by trial courts in determining admissibility:

1. Whether the theory or technique in question can be (and has been) tested
2. Whether it has been subjected to peer review and publication
3. Its known or potential error rate, and the existence and maintenance of standards controlling its operation
4. Whether it has attracted widespread acceptance within a relevant scientific community

The assumed role of the trial court judge as a "gatekeeper" of scientific evidence has generated controversy among both the scientific and legal communities, as has the comment about "error rates" (see Chapter 8). Interestingly, the decision has had more impact on the admission of "technical but not scientific" evidence, including the definition of the foregoing, than on scientifically based analyses such as DNA (see *Kumho Tire Co., Ltd., v. Carmichael*).

Initially, state courts apparently paid this ruling little heed and continued to rely on *Frye* and, to a lesser extent, on the Relevancy Standard. For example, in a 1994 California Supreme Court decision (*People v. Leahy*), Chief Justice Malcolm Lucas held that California's standard for admissibility of new scientific evidence would be the *Kelly* test, rather than the new federal standard adopted in *Daubert*. The case involved the horizontal gaze nystagmus test, a field sobriety test. Judge Lucas wrote, "… it may be preferable to let admissibility questions regarding new scientific techniques be settled by those persons most qualified to assess their validity" (i.e., those with scientific rather than legal expertise).

While some states, including California, continue to uphold the *Frye* Standard[1], other states have been moving toward the standard promulgated by the *Daubert* decision. It remains to be seen what, if any, effect this swing will have on the admissibility of DNA evidence at the state and federal levels.

---

[1] Alaska, Arizona, California, Colorado, District of Columbia, Florida, Illinois, Kansas, Maryland, Michigan, Minnesota, Mississippi, Nebraska, New Jersey, New York, Pennsylvania, and Washington.

D. Past Admissibility

Typically, an appellate admissibility decision is regarded as precedent within the judicial system. Relying on such a decision, a court might exercise its discretion to admit evidence without an evidentiary hearing through a process called judicial notice. At this writing, there have been more than 150 reported state appellate decisions regarding DNA analysis; the vast majority opined admission. Initially, these rulings represented mostly RFLP cases, and subsequently the early PCR-based systems of PM+DQA1 and D1S80 also found judicial approval. However, just as state supreme courts were beginning to generate rulings regarding the general admissibility of DNA profiling, the more recently developed STR systems and also mitochondrial DNA (mtDNA) analysis generated challenges anew at the trial court level. To date, 13 states have passed legislation mandating the admission of DNA evidence. (*Appendix I*) In the previous edition of this book, we made the statement that, "It is probable that, in the future, DNA testing will come to be as easily accepted as traditional fingerprints." Interestingly, while DNA testing will likely come to be accepted as fingerprint comparison once *was*, it is fingerprinting and other comparative evidence that are now being challenged, as the scientific standards required of DNA testing permeate the consciousness of the legal and judicial systems.

II.   DNA: Some Landmark Cases

A.   RFLP

The use of DNA typing in criminal cases in the United States got off to a somewhat inauspicious start. Virgin molecular biologists were running the show and were unacquainted with, and uninitiated in, the intricacies and adversarial nature of the legal system. They were also naiive to the nature of the special problems presented by forensic evidence. The first use of DNA in a criminal trial was in Florida in 1987 during the sexual assault case of *Andrews v. State* (see *Sidebar 14*). The first trial resulted in a hung jury; however, a retrial resulted in a conviction of Andrews. Both the ruling and the conviction were upheld at the appellate level. For the next couple of years, DNA testing of forensic evidence in general, and RFLP analysis in particular, was admitted at trial almost without question. This set the stage for the first case in which DNA was seriously challenged.

The year was 1987, the locale a New York State Trial Court, presided over by the Honorable Judge Gerald Sheindlin. Joseph Castro was accused of stabbing Vilma Ponce and her 2-year-old daughter to death. The evidence submitted for DNA analysis was a spot of blood, allegedly Vilma Ponce's, on his watch. RFLP analysis was performed by a private company, Lifecodes, that had just entered the forensic market. The autorads submitted would not have met today's critical standards. The lanes were dark with nonspecific background, and a number of extra, unexplainable bands were present. Of equal concern, the results were outside the match criteria established by their own lab. Despite this, the scientist nevertheless chose to render an opinion that the blood on the watch came from Vilma Ponce.

In an unprecedented move, and to their credit, four of the expert witnesses, representing both the prosecution and the defense, met to review the scientific evidence after they had already testified. The result of this meeting was a two-page consensus statement that addressed the inadequacy of the scientific evidence and the legal procedures for assessing

Sidebar 14

The First RFLP Case
(State of Florida versus Tommy Lee Andrews)

For the police in Orlando, Florida, the year of 1986 was marked by over 20 cases of prowling, breaking and entering, and attempted sexual assault. In each case, the man would stalk his victim for weeks, prowling around her house, and peeping through her windows. When he attacked his victims, the assailant always managed to arrange things so that he was not directly observed for any length of time. Tommy Lee Andrews was finally arrested, based mostly on composite drawings extracted from fleeting glimpses by his many victims.

Hal Uhrig, a private defense attorney, was appointed council for Andrews. Little did he know that he was about to become involved in the first criminal case in the United States in which DNA evidence would be introduced. The prosecuting attorney had read an advertisement for DNA testing by Lifecodes Corp., and decided to employ their services. RFLP testing was performed on some of the sexual assault evidence, and the first DNA admissibility hearing commenced. Although the results from the Lifecodes tests were admitted, the trial ended in a hung jury.

Jeffrey Ashton was the prosecuting attorney for the retrial of Tommy Lee Andrews, and this time Andrews was convicted. Both the conviction and the introduction of DNA evidence were upheld at the appellate level.

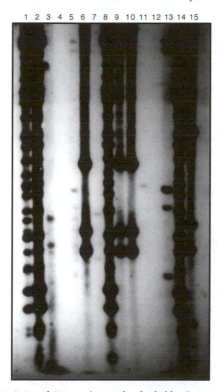

One autorad from the case. Lanes 1, 2, 8, and 14 contain a molecular ladder. Lane 3 contains a victim reference sample and Lane 5 contains the sexual assault evidence from a vaginal swab; the sperm and non-sperm fractions were not separated in this case. Lane 13 contains the reference blood sample from Andrews. The other lanes contain various control samples. Both bands from Andrews and the single band from the victim are clearly present in the mixed evidentiary sample, at least on the original autorad. The restriction enzyme used was *Pst*I, and the probe was PAC 256. Neither are currently in common use. (Courtesy of the District Attorney's Office, Orlando, Florida.)

scientific evidence. The court chose to render inadmissible the RFLP DNA evidence indicating that the blood on Castro's watch came from the victim; however, results were admitted to support an exclusion (it was not *Castro's* blood). Judge Sheindlin later quipped that Joseph Castro and the analyst were the only two people in the courtroom who knew that it was indeed Vilma Ponce's blood on the watch. Joseph Castro was convicted on the basis of other evidence and later confessed to the crime.

Thus, in *People v. Castro* (1989), the admissibility and reliability of DNA evidence was seriously challenged for the first time. In the process of considering its determination of the admissibility of the RFLP results, the court set out a three-prong test criterion extending the *Frye* Standard.

1. Is there a sound theory behind DNA testing?
2. Are the techniques for testing capable of producing reliable results?
3. Were the tests performed properly in this case?

In *Castro*, concordant results linking the suspect to the crime were ultimately excluded from trial because they failed to meet the third prong of this standard, although an exclusionary result was admitted. While the inherent reliability of DNA typing was acknowledged, the inadequacy exhibited in this case prevented full admission of the DNA evidence. Since then, many courts have taken judicial notice of this decision and admissibility standard. The *Castro* decision was a major factor in the increased focus on issues of accreditation, certification, quality assurance, and standardization by DNA laboratories and ultimately by the entire profession.

United States v. Yee et al. (1990) was the first case in which the FBI accepted evidence for RFLP DNA analysis. On February 27, 1988, at approximately 9:30 p.m., David Hartlaub's body was found outside the night depository at a bank in Perkins Township, Ohio. Hartlaub had been shot in or near his van at least six times by gunmen who quickly fled the scene after completing the brutal and unprovoked murder (the crime was a murder for hire, and Hartlaub was mistaken for the intended victim). There were no eyewitnesses to the actual shooting, but fresh blood was found inside Hartlaub's van that was driven from the scene by one of the group of Hell's Angels who had perpetrated the attack. It was this blood from the van that was submitted to the FBI lab for testing and subsequently showed the same genetic pattern as a sample obtained from the defendant, John Ray Bonds.

A contentious legal battle erupted between the scientific opponents and proponents of DNA testing. Richard Lewontin and Daniel Hartl led the attack on DNA in general, and the FBI analysis in particular, for the failure to account for possible population substructure that might have caused ambiguities in assessing the estimated frequency of the DNA profile in the population. Nevertheless, the judge in this federal trial court ruled in favor of the prosecution in allowing the DNA evidence at trial. This hearing called to the front issues regarding the interpretation of DNA results in the context of population genetics.

In *United States v. Jakobetz* (1990), a federal appellate court upheld the admissibility of RFLP DNA evidence, including statistical calculations to assess the significance of the results. The defendant had abducted a woman from an Interstate 91 rest area in Westminster, Vermont, and forced her into the back of a tractor-trailer truck. She was then driven to an unknown location, raped, and ultimately released in the New York City area. Although RFLP DNA evidence was admitted and linked the defendant to the crime, Jakobetz was ultimately convicted only of kidnapping.

In *People v. Axell* (1991), Linda Axell was accused of killing the owner of a convenience store. Left behind in the grasp of the victim were several strands of hair containing roots. Depending on the number of hairs, and the amount and condition of cellular material attached to the root end, hairs can occasionally be analyzed by RFLP. In this case, the RFLP testing was successful and, in fact, genetic concordance was demonstrated between the hair and Axell. A long-term and long-distance admissibility hearing was held, in which many experts from throughout the country testified (the testimony of some witnesses took place outside of court, usually in the experts' office or laboratory). The hearing focused on both the molecular biology and population issues. The judge allowed the DNA to be admitted, including the use of statistics.

The decision on *Axell* was filed in October of 1991. In December 1991, the beginnings of a controversy over the use of population statistics erupted in the pages of one of the foremost scientific journals, *Science*. At the heart of the debate was the effect of possible substructure in the population on the assumption of statistical independence of the genetic loci used for forensic analysis. The practical consequence of this assumption is that the frequencies for each allele can be multiplied together to give a reliable estimate for the frequency of the composite DNA profile.

In 1992, the National Research Council (NRC) Committee on DNA Technology in Forensic Science published a set of recommendations addressing this topic and others. The committee's suggestion was to employ a calculation called the "ceiling principle," which put an artificial limit on the rareness of a particular genetic profile (see Chapter 10). Although the judicial system initially regarded the "ceiling principle" as a long-awaited solution, many scientists rebelled against it as an artificial construct with no scientific foundation. The original NRC Committee itself was plagued with intrigue and dissent, so much so that in 1994 a new committee was convened in an attempt to clarify the many misunderstandings that resulted from the original publication.

However, in the meantime, two more landmark cases came before the 1st Appellate District of California in 1992. In each of the cases, *People v. Barney* and *People v. Howard,* the County of Alameda Superior Court had ruled RFLP evidence admissible. In opposition to the *Axell* decision, the appellate court ruled that in the intervening time a controversy about the use of population statistics had surfaced in the scientific community. On the basis of this new information, the court barred the use of DNA until the controversy had been resolved. However, the error in admitting DNA was judged harmless, and both convictions were upheld based on other evidence. The irony of the situation can be summed up in a footnote of the decision:

> "We recognize the irony in finding a frequency estimate of 1.2 in 1,000 (from conventional typing) to be significant while excluding DNA evidence which would have to be in error by five or six orders of magnitude — a degree of error not even claimed by Lewontin and Hartl — to approach a reduced equivalence ..."

In the face of apparent dissension and controversy, two more California appellate decisions on the admission of RFLP evidence followed in the tracks of *Barney-Howard*. In *People v. Pizarro* (1992), the decision was remanded back to trial court for evidence on frequency estimates. Soon after, RFLP DNA analysis in *People v. Wallace* (1993) was rejected, also based on the perceived lack of consensus concerning the method for estimating profile frequencies. A 1994 decision from the Fourth District Court of Appeals,

People v. Soto reversed this trend. The case was an attempted rape of a 78-year-old woman in Orange County that occurred in 1989. Sexual assault evidence was obtained, and RFLP results associated Frank Soto with the crime scene. A *Kelly* hearing was held, and the court of appeals ruled that the procedures used to estimate the frequency of the DNA profile were considered reliable and valid by the relevant scientific community. Further, the judge's ruling stated that the DNA results were too relevant and probative to be ignored.

Since then, not only have several other California appellate courts held DNA typing to be admissible, the California Supreme Court rendered a ruling regarding the admissibility of RFLP DNA evidence (*People v. Venegas*, 1995). In this ruling, the court opined that all of the molecular biology procedures used were generally accepted and legally admissible, but that the FBI had erred in a statistical calculation. The conviction was overturned and the case remanded for retrial based on this one issue alone. The case was retried in 1999 and Sergio Venegas was easily convicted of sexual assault. However, because of the scope of this particular supreme court decision, it did little to forestall admissibility hearings relating to STRs in California. In addition, it also specified that, "… due to the inherent complexity of DNA typing, trial courts must first determine whether correct procedures were utilized by the testing laboratory in the particular case at issue", generating lifetime job security for independent experts.

Two states in particular have a history of admitting DNA testing results, while specifically barring any numerical statements regarding the strength of a pattern match. In Arizona, this includes *State v. Hummert* and *State v. Hale* (1991), as well as a case dealing with analysis of plant DNA, *State v. Bogen* (1995) (see Sidebar 11). The Arizona Supreme Court finally ruled in *State v. Johnson* (1996) that a variety of statistical estimates might be admissible, although it left to the trial courts to decide exactly which those might be in any particular case. Similarly, the Supreme Court of the State of Minnesota had, since the late 1970s, issued rulings precluding the introduction of statistics pertaining to any scientific evidence, not just DNA specifically. However, in 1994 while considering *State v. Bloom*, along with *State v. Bauer* and *State v. Perez*, they partially reversed themselves. In their decision, they state that:

> "National Research Council's adoption of a conservative 'interim ceiling method' for computation of probability that a randomly selected person would have same DNA profile as that of a sample found at crime scene justifies creation of a **DNA exception** to the rule against admission of statistical probability evidence in criminal prosecution to prove identity; moreover, a properly qualified expert may, if the evidentiary foundation is sufficient, give an opinion that, to a reasonable degree of scientific certainty, the defendant is (or is not) the source of the bodily evidence found at the crime scene."

We discuss the most recent developments with regard to the expression of an opinion of source determination in Chapter 8.

B.   PCR: DQα/A1, Polymarker, D1S80

Since being introduced in the United States in 1986, PCR testing initially enjoyed a higher success rate in the trial courts, although it was a newer technique than RFLP at the time. Ironically, part of the reason was that the HLA DQα test, which was the only one available for many years, was not nearly as powerful as RFLP, so the comfort level was greater. Also, for the original DQα system and also for D1S80, only one locus was tested, so arguments about combining the results from several different loci in a frequency estimate did not come into play. This began to change as additional PCR markers were introduced, in particular the AmpliType® PM+DQA1 kit and various multi-locus STR systems. Although, in most instances, the polymarker loci combined with the DQα locus (renamed DQA1) were readily admitted, the STR systems and mtDNA testing brought new issues to the fore. In general, PCR DNA analysis has encountered different challenges than RFLP. While the issues in RFLP focused primarily on population genetics, challenges to PCR-based testing have also included the specific application of the methodology, the electronics and software of the automated systems, and disclosure of developmental validation and proprietary reagents.

Pennsylvania v. Pestinikas was the first U.S. case in which *any* DNA evidence was employed. Two autopsies were performed on the same body at different times. Formalde-hyde-preserved tissues taken from each of the autopsies were compared by DNA typing to test the possibility that they were from different people. HLA DQα results confirmed the notion that both sets of samples in question were from Pestinikas, and the evidence was accepted by the civil court.

PCR-based DNA testing, starting with HLA DQα, has garnered much public attention as a powerful tool to free men wrongly convicted of rape. PCR-based systems are more likely to produce interpretable results in these cases, because the biological evidence being tested is often old and therefore limited or degraded. In a number of these cases the victims had identified their alleged assailants in a lineup, leading to convictions of the suspects. Interestingly, no resistance has come from any corner concerning the use of DNA analysis for post-conviction testing.

One of the first examples of this use of DNA typing was *People v. Dotson*. In 1977, Gary Dotson was accused of raping Cathleen Webb. Although conventional serological typing was inconclusive, he was convicted in 1979, primarily on the basis of her eyewitness identification. Eight years later, in 1985, the victim recanted her identification and admitted to having had consentual intercourse with her boyfriend. Eleven years later, HLA DQα typing clearly eliminated Dotson as the semen donor of the evidence; moreover, the boy-friend was included. The judge, however, refused to believe either the victim's recantation or the corroborating DNA evidence and would not release Dotson. Ultimately, the governor of Illinois did grant clemency to Gary Dotson, although he was never pardoned. *Dotson* is an example of a common use of early PCR-based systems as an exclusionary tool. As with all genetic marker tests, regardless of the power of inclusion, exclusion is absolute.

In *People v. Martinez* (1989), one of a small number of early rejections of PCR-based DNA typing occurred. On post-conviction review, HLA DQα analysis showed a pair of panties from a child molestation victim to contain semen from someone other than the defendant. Testimony was offered by a single defense expert (the analyst who performed the test) whose results did not convince the judge to overturn the conviction. It seemed that the technique was simply too new at that time for the majority of forensic scientists to have had an opportunity to use it, much less endorse it. Dr. Edward Blake, a pioneer in the use of HLA DQα, was one of the few forensic scientists using the technique at the time, although PCR, in general, was already well-accepted in the general scientific community.

Another case in which HLA DQα evidence failed admissibility was *People v. Mack* (1990). This was a Sacramento, California, case in which it was alleged that semen found on the panties of the deceased victim was from the defendant. As in *Martinez*, Judge Tochterman found that PCR had not yet achieved a reasonable level of acceptance in the forensic community, and that more validation was needed. An interesting aside is that

Mack confessed on the stand to having had intercourse with the victim the last time she was seen alive.

In *People v. Quintanilla* (1991) (see Sidebar 4), PCR-based typing was successfully advanced. In this case, HLA DQα typing was used to both exclude the original suspect and subsequently include a different suspect. The evidence was admitted by the trial court and the second suspect was ultimately convicted. As in several other cases involving PCR in California, when the case came before them, the appellate court refused to rule on the admissibility issue, saying any finding would constitute harmless error.

C. PCR: STRs

Although many courts throughout the United States have admitted DNA evidence typed using various STR systems (Appendix L), trial courts in three states have recently declined to admit such evidence.

The first of these rulings emerged from a San Francisco trial court in the Spring of 1999. The analysis of some apparent bloodstains in the trunk of a car was performed by the local crime laboratory. In *People v. Bokin*, the court rejected STR results obtained using the PE-ABD[2] AmpF*l*STR® Green™ I kit and detected on their ABI PRISM® 310 Genetic Analyzer using capillary electrophoresis and fluorescent detection. The AmpF*l*STR® Green I™ kit was an intermediate version of one of the multiplex STR systems and included three loci that were subsequently incorporated into a larger megaplex system (COfiler™). The main obstruction to general acceptance, and hence admissibility, was that no peer-reviewed scientific papers had been published using this exact combination of reagents and detection system. Lengthy testimony was given by an employee of PE-ABD who had played a large part in developing the system. However, because the company refused to allow discovery of the supporting validation studies (including the primer sequences) upon which the scientist relied in forming her opinion, the judge concluded that:

> "The sum of this record is the government has not provided the Court with enough to conclude that STRs identified by using Green one with ABD genetic analyzer 310 satisfies TWGDAM requirements pertaining to developmental validation."

Using the *Frye* admissibility standard, Judge Dondero denied introduction of the STR results, although DNA results using other systems were admitted. The defendant, Jack

---

[2] Much confusion arises from the ever-changing corporate identity of one of the main manufacturers of forensic DNA products. The following is a brief historical summary to help the reader sort out the various names. However, we do not promise that the information will be current by the time this edition sees print. *Cetus Corporation* developed and produced the DQα typing kit. After *Roche Molecular Systems* bought *Cetus* in 1991 (which mostly meant purchasing worldwide rights to the *Taq* polymerase patent, a claim that has been vigorously challenged in court ever since), the same group of people developed the PM+DQA1 DNA typing system. However, the kit was then manufactured by the *Perkin-Elmer Corporation*, which, in 1993, merged with *Applied Biosystems Inc. (ABI)* The now *Applied Biosystems Division* of *Perkin Elmer (PE-ABD)* continued the development of the gel-based semi-automated instrumentation and multiplex fluorescently labeled STR reagent systems. In 1998, Perkin Elmer consolidated its life science technologies, including Applied Biosystems into the PE Biosystems division. Also in 1998, *Perkin-Elmer* established *Celera Genomics*. The *Perkin-Elmer Corporation* was recapitalized under the name *PE Corporation* in 1999, retaining the *Applied Biosystems Group* and the *Celera Genomics Group*. The company sold its analytical instruments division and the *Perkin Elmer* name. In 2000, The *PE Biosystems Group* was renamed the *Applied Biosystems Group* and *PE Corporation* changed its name to *Applera Corporation*. We will attempt to be more or less historically accurate throughout this book, consequently the reader may see any of the following monikers, all of which refer more or less to the same development and manufacturing group: *Perkin-Elmer, PE, Applied Biosystems, ABI, ABD*.

Bokin, was nevertheless convicted of serial rape and attempted murder, and was sentenced to 231 years to life in prison.

A year later, in April 2000, Judge Michael Kupersmith, in Vermont District Court, denied introduction of certain STR results, while admitting others, in the quarter-century-old murder trial of *State v. Pfenning*. Several hairs found on the body of a deceased schoolteacher were analyzed using a number of different DNA systems, including multiplex and megaplex STR systems from two different manufacturers. Cellmark Diagnostics used both the CTT system from Promega Corporation and the Profiler Plus™ kit from PE-ABD. The CTT system is similar to the Green I™ system described in the *Bokin* case except that Cellmark detected the result using silver-staining of a manually run acrylamide gel. The Profiler Plus™ system, which detects ten loci simultaneously, was run on a 310 Genetic Analyzer. Genelex Corporation used a slightly different system to analyze the same evidence. This system, the PowerPlex® 1.1 kit offered by Promega Corporation, examined eight loci simultaneously and the results were detected using a laser scanner after electrophoresis gels were run. Under the *Daubert* criteria adopted by the State of Vermont, Judge Kupersmith opined that neither of the newer systems met the requirements of general acceptance, again because of the lack (for Profiler Plus™) or dearth (PowerPlex® 1.1) of peer-reviewed published material, and also because of both manufacturers' failure to disclose the primer sequences. The court seemed particularly annoyed at the change in TWGDAM guidelines that no longer required publication of primer sequences:

> "The State's experts never explained why the TWGDAM guideline was not followed. Current guidelines, issued by the DNA Advisory Board, no longer require publication of primer sequences. Again, no explanation of the modification was offered; the Court infers it was done in order to bring the guideline into compliance with practice."

Despite the physical evidence provided by several other DNA typing systems that the court ruled admissible, Michael Pfenning was acquitted of the murder of Lyda Jameson.

Later the same year, Judge Daniel Hale, in Colorado District Court, denied admission of STR results under both *Frye* and *Daubert* in *People v. Shreck*. The state crime laboratory had analyzed semen-containing samples from a rape kit using both the Profiler Plus™ system described above and a companion system, also developed by PE-ABD, called COfiler™. Again, based on the lack of formal publication and PE-ABD's failure to release validation studies and primer sequences,

> "… the Court finds that, at this point in time, the multiplex technique employed by the Profiler Plus and COfiler kits has not been generally accepted in the scientific community."

Nevertheless, based on several non-STR DNA analysis systems that were admitted, Michael Eugene Shreck was convicted of the rape of a University of Colorado student, and the conviction was upheld on appeal. However, on April 23, 2001, the Colorado Supreme Court vacated the trial court's original ruling. They opined that all STR systems should be admissible under the *Daubert* Standard based on Federal Rule of Evidence 702.

The contradictions between decisions in the same state, and even within the same jurisdiction, have created confusion among the legal community. Almost simultaneously with the *Bokin* decision in San Francisco Superior Court, several conflicting decisions were rendered in California (*People v. Bertsch and Hronis, People v. Hill, People v.*

Hackney, People v. Elizarraras, and *People v. Hunt*), including two in the same jurisdiction (*People v. McClanahan,* and *People v. Moevao*). Even more strangely, a California Court of Appeals had already, in 1999, issued a very broad ruling that STR testing had achieved general acceptance in the relevant scientific community (*People v. Allen*)[3]. Similarly, in 2000, a Colorado district court issued a contradictory ruling in *Shreck,* admitting the DNA results obtained using the Profiler Plus™ system on a 310 Genetic Analyzer (*People v. Flores*).

In the three criminal cases in which a trial court originally denied admissibility of an STR system, disclosure and publication were the two main issues. Although much work had been performed by the manufacturers of the various STR kits and instrumentation platforms (developmental validation) and by the forensic laboratories using the products (internal validation), and much of the data had been presented at scientific meetings, key studies had not yet been published in any peer-reviewed journals. Publication in a peer-reviewed journal means that the work has been reviewed by the authors' scientific peers, that the reviewers (typically two or three) have agreed that the data supports the conclusions, and that the body of work is of interest to the relevant scientific community. Two problems existed with publication. One of the manufacturers, PE-ABD, was unwilling to release the scientific data underlying its developmental validation studies (see *People v. Bokin*). Although the conclusions to the studies had been publicized in PE-ABD's protocols manual (as opposed to being published in a peer-reviewed journal), neither the scientists relying on the kits nor the defense experts reviewing the cases could independently assess the data. Promega Corporation, manufacturer of a competing STR system, had published a developmental validation study and was more cooperative about providing access to the underlying data. Hence, those using the Promega systems encounter fewer problems with court acceptance. An additional problem encountered when the FBI laboratory attempted to publish its extensive internal validation in *Forensic Science International* was that the study was deemed to provide no novel information, and therefore was not worthy of publication. Thus, the forensic laboratories were stuck in between a journal editor who was not interested in publishing a mundane validation study and a court system that relied on such publication as a *pro forma* prerequisite for admissibility. These articles and several others were ultimately published in the May 2001 issue of the *Journal of Forensic Sciences.* This should go a long way toward reassuring the courts that the various STR systems are, in fact, generally accepted by the relevant scientific community; and that the results obtained from them are reliable when performed in laboratories that have undertaken comprehensive internal validation studies and when said results are analyzed and interpreted by trained, experienced analysts.

An additional problem lay in the proprietary rights each company exerted regarding the sequence of the specific DNA primers used in the PCR-STR amplification reactions. Although PE-ABD and Promega were legally within their rights to withhold such information, the defense successfully used their lack of access to this information in their bid to exclude the evidence in the three cases mentioned above. Recently, Promega has decided to publicly release their primer sequences, and PE-ABD has released them under protective order in several cases.

---

[3] The work in this case was performed by Cellmark, using an early version of STR testing, the CTT triplex, and was detected using simple silver staining of the polyacrylamide gel.

D.   Mitochondrial DNA

As the previous edition of this book went to press in 1996, we added a note in proof that the very first mtDNA typing evidence had been admitted at the trial court level in the United States. Based on several hairs that were ultimately associated with the suspect, a Chattanooga, Tennessee, jury convicted a man of raping and murdering a 4-year-old girl. The decision in *State v. Ware* was upheld by an appellate court, as was a second Tennessee decision, *State v. Scott*. Trial courts in at least 18 states have now admitted mtDNA evidence[4] and appellate courts in Tennessee, North Carolina, and South Carolina have affirmed. A Maryland appellate court is now considering a double-murder case.

At least one instance exists in which mtDNA typing was excluded from a trial court. In *State of Florida v. James Deward Crow*, the Honorable Judge O.C. Eaton ruled that the results of a mtDNA test did not meet the *Frye* Standard and were inadmissible as evidence. He based his opinion on his understanding that the FBI database was too small and was insufficient to provide reliable statistical conclusions. Judge Eaton further found that the "counting method" failed to provide meaningful comparison that would assist, rather than confuse, the jury.

As described in more detail in Chapter 7, the capabilities and limitations, and hence the issues, are somewhat different for mtDNA as compared to nuclear DNA testing. A number of different questions have been raised by opponents of mtDNA testing, including contamination, population genetics, and methodology. The most prominent issue, however, is the interpretation of evidence samples that exhibit heteroplasmy (an authentic mixture of types). How do we compare the hypotheses that a particular suspect is either included (with some degree of rarity) or the alternate hypothesis that the suspect is excluded? As mtDNA testing becomes more common, we expect to see these issues contested in court. Certainly, there will be more to say about the progress and acceptance of mtDNA typing in the next revision of this book.

III.   The State of the Debate

In October 1994, Eric Lander of the Whitehead Institute and Bruce Budowle of the FBI published a joint letter in the journal *Nature* in which they declared the DNA wars over. Lander had been one of the main detractors of the particular application of statistics to DNA analysis and was a member of the original NRC Committee. Lander and Budowle wrote that the extensive scientific literature, existing quality assurance (QA) guidelines, and the NRC I Report had resolved all of the issues preventing the admissibility of DNA in court. They further indicated that the NRC I Report had been misinterpreted by both the forensic community and the legal system. The "ceiling principle" had never been intended to replace an estimate obtained by multiplying the frequencies of alleles contained in a DNA profile; rather, it was to provide a conservative limit value as a secondary alternative. In the meantime, the data on population substructure was accumulated and now most scientists agree that (1) substructure is present in human populations, and (2) the level at which it is present has little effect on estimating the rareness of a particular

---

[4] Alabama, California, Connecticut, Florida, Georgia, Hawaii, Indiana, Louisiana, Maryland, Michigan, Mississippi New Mexico, North Carolina, Ohio, Pennsylvania, South Carolina, Tennessee, and Texas.

DNA profile in the general population. It will be interesting to watch as the evolving forensic science of mtDNA typing follows a similar, if foreshortened, path.

In 1996, the second committee gathered by the NRC published its report, *The Evaluation of Forensic DNA Evidence* (see Chapter 10). It even more fully endorses DNA typing for forensic use. Interestingly, the NRC II committee agreed with the dissenters regarding the lack of merit of the "ceiling principle," and has dropped support of its use in estimating profile frequencies. Instead, the committee suggests several alternative procedures, based on population genetics and statistics, for providing an estimate of the strength of indistinguishable genetic profiles. In the Executive Summary of the NRC II Report, they conclude that:

> "The technology for DNA profiling and the methods for estimating frequencies and related statistics have progressed to the point where the reliability and validity of properly collected and analyzed DNA should not be in doubt."

One of the main issues pervading the current state of the debate is the issue of source attribution (see Chapter 8). Now that profile frequency estimates for unrelated individuals routinely exceed the world's population, should a DNA analyst provide an opinion that this evidence sample came from that person? Some laboratories, including the FBI, routinely provide such statements; others maintain staunch objections based on either precedent or statistics. In a sense, we have come full circle, from Alec Jeffreys' "DNA fingerprints" to STR megaplexes. Add to the mix the current debate regarding the scientific merits of dermal ridge prints and you have the makings of a paradigm shift in forensic science.

In 1997, we wrote, "Although, as with all forensic evidence, each case must be considered on its own merits, it seems hopeful that a consensus regarding the general reliability of DNA analysis is at least within grasp." This prediction seemed reasonable at the time; however, it has not proved to be the case in all jurisdictions. With many objections to the use of population statistics out of the way, detractors are free to seek new challenges, in particular to STR systems. Keeping optimism firmly in mind, we try again in the year 2001: With the long-awaited publication of studies validating the use of megaplex STR systems for forensic DNA typing, and the trend toward release of the underlying data and PCR primer sequences, challenges in typical cases should subside, and most STR evidence should be admitted as a routine matter. Moreover, older and wiser by several years, we also predict that emerging technologies for DNA typing will endure a similar period of vigorous challenge before they are accepted by the judicial system. Furthermore, we expect that the door opened by DNA will swing wide to admit intense scrutiny of other kinds of forensic testing, such as is already being seen with fingerprint comparisons.

Perhaps the most painful lesson learned from our decade-long battle for admissibility of DNA evidence is that progress rarely occurs without substantial challenge. Forensic scientists tend to be insular and self-reliant to a fault; academicians tend to believe that the graduate thesis under which they became "Piled Higher and Deeper" qualifies them as instant experts. Good-faith input from both groups, as well as law enforcement and legal professionals, contributes to the best interests of forensic science and is essential to its role in the judicial system.

Further References

American Prosecutors Research Institute (APRI), *Silent Witness*, 5(2), 2000.

Bernstein, D.E., Frye, Frye, again: the past, present, and future of the general acceptance test, *Jurimetrics J.*, in press, 2001, <http://www.law.gmu.edu/faculty/papers/docs/01-07.pdf>.

Blake, E., Mihalovich, J., Higuchi, R., Walsh, P.S., and Erlich, H., Polymerase chain reaction (PCR) amplification and human leukocyte antigen (HLA)-DQ alpha oligonucleotide typing on biological evidence samples: casework experience, *J. Forensic Sci.*, 37(3), 700–726, 1992.

Budowle, B. and Sprecher, C.J., Concordance study on population database samples using the PowerPlex®16 kit and AmpF*l*STR® Profiler Plus™ kit and AmpF*l*STR® COfiler™ kit, *J. Forensic Sci.*, 46(3), 637–641, 2001.

Budowle, B. and Lander, E.S., DNA fingerprinting dispute laid to rest, *Nature*, 371, 735–738, 1994.

Concordance study on population database samples using the PowerPlex®; 16 kit and AmpF*l*STR® Profiler Plus™; kit and AmpF*l*STR® COfiler™ kit, *J. Forensic Sci.*, 46(3), 637–641, 2001.

Devlin, B., Risch, N., and Roeder K., Statistical evaluation of DNA fingerprinting: a critique of the NRC's report, *Science*, 259, 748–750, 1993.

Devlin, B., Risch, N., and Roeder, K., Comments on the statistical aspects of the NRC's report on DNA typing, *J. Forensic Sci.*, 39(1), 28–40, 1994.

Devlin, B., Technical Comments, *Science*, 253, 1039–1041, 1991.

Evett, I.W., Buckleton, J.S., Raymond, A., and Roberts, H., The evidential value of DNA profiles, *J. Forensic Sci. Soc.*, 33(4), 243–244, 1993.

Frank, W.E., Llewellyn, B.E., Fish, P.A., Riech, A.K., Marcacci, T.L., Gandor, D.W., Parker, D., Carter, R.R., and Thibault, S.M., Validation of the AmpF*l*STR® Profiler Plus™ PCR amplification kit for use in forensic casework, *J. Forensic Sci.*, 46(3), 642–646, 2001.

Hartl, D.L., Forensic DNA typing dispute, *Nature*, 372(6505), 398–399, 1994.

Jeffreys, A.J., 1992 William Allan Award address, *Am. J. Human Genet.*, 53(1), 1–5, 1993.

Jeffreys, A.J., DNA typing: approaches and applications, *J. Forensic Sci. Soc.*, 33(4), 204–211, 1993.

Kaye, D.H., Bible Reading: DNA Evidence in Arizona, *Arizona State Law J.*, 28(4), 1035–1077, 1997, <http://www.law.asu.edu/kaye/pubs/dna/bible.htm>.

Kaye, D.H., DNA Identification in criminal cases: some lingering and emerging evidentiary issues, *Proc. 7th Int. Symp. Human Identification*, Promega Corporation, 1996, <http://www.promega.com/geneticidproc/ussymp7proc/0702.html>.

Kisluik, B., Court spurns federal 'Junk Science' ruling, *The Recorder*, Oct. 1994.

Lander, E.S., DNA fingerprinting on trial, *Nature*, 339, 501–505, 1989.

Lewontin, R. and Hartl, D., Population genetics in forensic DNA analysis, *Science*, 254, 1745–1750, 1991.

Lewontin, R. and Hartl, D., Statistical Evaluation of DNA Fingerprinting: a critique of the NRC's report, *Science*, 259, 748–750, 1993.

Micka, K.A., et al., TWGDAM validation of a nine-locus and a four-locus fluorescent STR multiplex system, *J. Forensic Sci.*, 44(6), 1243–1256, 1999.

Monckton, D.G. and Jeffreys, A.J., DNA profiling, *Curr. Opin. Biotechnol.*, 4(6), 660–664, 1993.

Moretti, T.R., Baumstark, A.L., Defenbaugh, D.A., Keys, K.M., Brown, A.L., and Budowle, B., Validation of STR typing by capillary electrophoresis, *J. Forensic Sci.*, 46(3), 661–676, 2001.

Moretti, T.R., Baumstark, A.L., Defenbaugh, D.A., Keys, K.M., Brown, A.L., and Budowle, B., Validation of STR typing by capillary electrophoresis, *J. Forensic Sci.*, 46(3), 661–676, 2001.

Moretti, T.R., Baumstark, A.L., Defenbaugh, D.A., Keys, K.M., Smerick, J.B., and Budowle, B., Validation of short tandem repeats (STRs) for forensic usage: performance testing of fluorescent multiplex STR systems and analysis of authentic and simulated forensic samples, *J. Forensic Sci.*, 46(3), 647–660, 2001.

National Research Council, *DNA Technology in Forensic Science*, National Academy Press, Washington, D.C., 1992.

National Research Council, *The Evaluation of Forensic DNA Evidence*, National Academy Press, Washington, D.C., 1996.

Reinhart, C., *Admissibility of DNA Evidence*, <http://www.cga.state.ct.us/2001/rpt/olr/htm/2001-r-0047.htm>.

Robertson, B. and Vignaux, G.A., DNA evidence: wrong answers or wrong questions?, *Genetica*, 96(1–2), 145–152, 1995.

Rothwell, T. J., DNA profiling and crime investigation — the European context, *J. Forensic Sci. Soc.*, 33(4), 226–227, 1993.

Sheilds, W.M., The validation of novel DNA typing techniques for forensic use: Peer review and validity of the FBI's validation studies of PCR amplification and automated sequencing of mitochondrial DNA, unpublished draft, 1998.

Technical Working Group on DNA Analysis Methods (TWGDAM), Guidelines for a proficiency testing program for DNA restriction fragment length polymorphism analysis, *Crime Lab. Dig.*, 17(2), 50–60, 1990.

Technical Working Group on DNA Analysis Methods (TWGDAM), Guidelines for a quality assurance program for DNA restriction fragment length polymorphism analysis, *Crime Lab. Dig.*, 16(2), 40–59, 1989.

Technical Working Group on DNA Analysis Methods (TWGDAM), Statement of the Working Group on Statistical Standards for DNA Analysis, *Crime Lab. Dig.*, 17(3), 53–58, 1990.

Van Derbeken, J., Bokin gets 231 years in S.F. Rapes; Attacker made escape attempt last week, *San Francisco Chronicle*, Jan. 20, 2000.

Wooley, J. and Harmon, R.P., The forensic DNA brouhaha: science or debate?, *Am. J. Human Genet.*, 51(5), 1164–1165, 1992.

Cases

Adams v. Missisipi, No. 200-KA-00242-COA, Miss. App., 2001.

Anderson v. State, 718 N.E.2d 1101, Ind., 1999.

Andrews v. State, 533 So. 2d 841, Fla. Dist. Ct. App., 1988.

Commonwealth v. Dillon, CC# 97-CR-1575, Lackawanna Co., 1998.

Commonwealth v. Rorrer, PICS Case No. 98-0320, Lehigh Co., 1998.

Connecticut v. Pappas, CC# CR10-246884, New London, 1999.

Crow v. State, Case No. 96-1156-CFA, 1996.

Daubert et ux. v. Merrell Dow Pharmaceuticals, Inc., 509 U.S. 579, 1993.

Florida v. Bolin, CC# 90-11832, 13th Judicial D., 1999.

Frye v. United States, 293 F. 1013, D.C. District Court, 1923; 54 App. DC 46, 293 F.2d 101, 1923.

Kumho Tire Co., Ltd. v. Carmichael, et al., 526 US 137, 1999.

Magaleti v. State, No. 00-17574-CF, Flo. Cir. Ct., 2001.

Pennsylvania v. Pestinikas, 1986.

People v. Allen, 72 Cal. App. 4th 1093, 1999.

People v. Axell, 235 Cal. App. 3d 836, 1991.

People v. Barney; *Howard*, 8 Cal. App. 4th 798, 1992.

People v. Bertsch and Hronis, 94F07295, Cal. Super. Ct., Sac. Co., 1999.

People v. Bokin, No. SCN 168461. Cal. Sup. Court, San Francisco Co., 1999.

People v. Castro, 144 Misc.2d 956, 545 N.Y.S. 2d 985, Sup. Ct., 1989.

People v. Dotson, 516 N.E.3d 718, Ill. App. Ct., 1987.

People v. Elizarraras, No. 50651 Cal. Sup. Court, Tulare Co., 2000.

People v. Flores, No. 99-CR2022, Co. District Court, Adams Co., 2000.

People v. Guerra, 37 Cal. 3d. 385, 418, 1984.

People v. Hackney, No. 97F02466 Cal. Sup. Court, Sacramento Co., 1999.

People v. Hill, No. 232982, Cal. Sup. Court, Santa Barbara Co., 2000.

People v. Hunt, et. al., No. SA034500, Cal. Sup. Court, Los Angeles Co., 2000.

People v. Kelly, 17 Cal. 3d 24, 1976.

People v. Klinger, No. 0849/00, 713 NYS.2d 823, NY.Co.Ct., 2000.

People v. Leahy, 8 Cal. 4th 587, 1994.

People v. Mack, No. 89-25, Super. Ct., Sacramento County, 1990.

People v. Martinez, No. A70932, Super. Ct., Los Angeles County, 1989.

People v. McClanahan, No. 162412, Cal. Sup. Court, San Francisco Co., 1998.

People v. Moevao, No. 162412, Cal. Sup. Court, San Francisco Co., 2000.

People v. Pizarro, 10 Cal. App. 4th 57, 1992.

People v. Quintanilla, A054959 [non pub.opn.], 1994.

People v. Reilly, 196 Cal.App.3d 1127, 1134, 1987.

People v. Shreck, No. 98CR2475, Co. District Court, Boulder County, 2000; Reversed, Case No. 00SA105, Co. Supreme Court, 2001.

People v. Soto, 30 Cal. App. 4th 340, 1994.

People v. Venegas, 31 Cal.App.4th 234, 246, 250, 1995.

People v. Wallace, 14 Cal. App. 4th 651, 1993.

State v. Bauer, 516 N.W. 2d 174 (Minn. 1994) affirming 512 N.W.2d 11, Minn. Ct. App., 1994.

State v. Bloom, 516 N.W.2d 15, Minn., 1994.

State v. Bogen, 905 P.2d 515 (Ariz Ct. App. 1995).

State v. Brown, 297 Or. 404, 687 P.2d 751, 759, Or., 1984.

State v. Council, 515 S.E.2d 508, 516-19, S.C., 1999.

State v. Hummert; Hale, 905 P.2d 493 Ariz. Ct. App. 1994; 933 P.2d 1187 Ariz. Supreme Ct., 1997.

State v. Johnson, *922 P.2d 294*, Az., 1996.

State v. Perez, 516 N.W.2d 175, Minn., 1994 (see *State v. Bloom*).

State v. Pfenning, Case No. 57-4-96 GiCr, Vermont District Court, Grand Isle County, 2000.

State v. Scott, Tenn. Crim. App. (unpublished), 1999.

State v. Smith, Wash. Ct. App. (unpublished), 2000.

State v. Underwood, 518 S.E.2d 231, N.C. Ct. App., 1999.

State v. Ware, Tenn. Crim. App. (unpublished), 1999.

State v. Williams, Anne Arundel County Circuit Court for Maryland, 1998; affirmed Court of Special Appeal of Maryland, April 12, 2000.

United States v. Jakobetz, 747 F. Supp 250, D. Vt., 1990.

United States v. Turns, United States District Court (Southern District of Ohio-Eastern division), 2000.

United States v. Yee et al., ND, Ohio 129 FRD 692, 1990.

Epilogue: The New Millennium 12

The last chapter in the first edition of this book was entitled, "Epilogue — Moving into the Next Millennium." We were fortunate that the publication date was close to the dawn of the new millennium because almost everything mentioned came to fruition before the year 2000 closed. Automation in DNA laboratories is common, samples are analyzed in days rather than weeks, source determination of a sample to a reference is routinely claimed by some workers, mtDNA is a common tool used on small samples, laboratories are being accredited and individuals are being certified in increasing numbers, and a national DNA databank is a reality. What's next?

! The Crime Scene !

DNA analysts and criminalists alike recoil in horror at the thought of performing DNA analysis in the field. Most DNA analysts have never been to a crime scene, having toiled in the cloistered halls of the laboratory for several years. Criminalists are skeptical that persons with only an academic background could venture into the field without losing their cookies. Both would agree that the crime scene is a cesspool of contamination that mocks efforts at keeping analyses clean of extraneous substances.

However, the move of DNA from the lab to the field is inexorable. Several disparate facts combine to support this contention. First, cases not solved within the first 24 to 48 hours have little chance of resolution at a later time. Second, DNA-on-a-chip technologies will soon make the analysis of miniscule biological samples a virtually instantaneous proposition. Third, national and state databases contain data from over 500,000 convicted felons; and fourth, the continuing emergence of global communications means that contact with the DNA database from the field is possible. Thus, the analysis of DNA at a crime scene can provide investigative leads to a detective, potentially solving a case within the precious 24- to 48-hour window.

Some company will make a device for the examination of DNA in a field setting, and some detective or law enforcement agency will want to try it. This is certain. What detective would not be delighted with the opportunity of obtaining the name of his suspect before adjourning for breakfast? It is true that access to the database is severely restricted, so that unauthorized searching is unlikely. However, the possibility of field-testing the evidence and suspect's DNA is equally enticing. DNA will screen the suspects, rather than interrogation. In any case, neither a detective nor an evidence technician should perform this work. The field of criminalistics must be prepared to reclaim its roots as primarily a field science, not strictly a laboratory science.

We consider forensic DNA analysis to be a part of criminalistics, and therefore subject to the principles and practices governing that discipline. The questions to be asked of biological physical evidence are not DNA questions, they are criminalistics questions. These questions are concerned with common source between an evidence and reference, questions of contact between two or more objects, and questions of crime scene reconstruction.

The ramifications of this perspective is that DNA analysts must be trained as criminalists, that criminalists must control the introduction of DNA analysis for use at the crime scene, and that criminalists must interpret and report DNA results. We make a light-hearted attempt at making this point in another publication (Inman and Rudin, 2000). Assuming that DNA analysis becomes, at times, a field test, then allowing other disciplines, industries, or professions to introduce and oversee it would be an abdication of our professional responsibility.

Further References

Inman, K. and Rudin, N., *Principles and Practice of Criminalistics*, CRC Press, Boca Raton, FL, 2000, chap. 13.

Glossary

9477A	Name of the positive control used in STR forensic DNA analysis in the United States.
A	Single-letter designation of the base adenine; one of the four building blocks of DNA (*see also* **adenine**).
ABC	American Board of Criminalistics, the oversight body for certification of criminalists.
Accreditation	Crime laboratories can be accredited for forensic testing. Accreditation of a crime laboratory means that the lab meets minimum professional standards for general operations.
Acrylamide	(*See* **polyacrylamide**)
Adenine	One of the four chemical building blocks of DNA (*see also* **A**).
AFIS	Automated Fingerprint Identification System.
Agarose	Gel medium used for separation of DNA fragments in a variety of tests, including yield gels, digest gels, PCR product gels, and RFLP analytical gels.
Allele	One of two or more alternative forms of a gene or genetic marker.
Allele frequency	The relative occurrence of a particular allele, or gene form, in a population.
Amelogenin	The locus at which gender can be determined in forensic typing systems.
AMP-FLP, AFLP, AMFLP	Amplified Fragment Length Polymorphism; a length polymorphism (VNTR) analyzed using PCR. D1S80 is analyzed as an AMP-FLP.
Artifact	A spurious result caused by or during the analysis; extrinsic to the sample itself.
ASCLD	American Society of Crime Laboratory Directors.
ASCLD/LAB	American Society of Crime Laboratory Directors/Laboratory Accreditation Board.
ASO	Allele-specific oligonucleotide. A technically incorrect name for a short synthetic probe used to pinpoint a specific sequence using hybridization. (*see also* **SSO**)
Association	Concept used in crime scene reconstruction; description of relationship between two objects, items, or people.
Autoradiogram, Autoradiograph, Autorad	An X-ray film on which radioactively or chemiluminescently labeled probes have left a mark determining the positions of particular DNA fragments; (*see* **Lumigraph**).

Autosome	Any chromosome other than the sex chromosomes X and Y.
Band	The visual image representing a particular DNA fragment on an autorad.
Band shift	The phenomenon in which DNA fragments in one lane of a gel migrate at a rate different from that of identical fragments in other lanes of the same gel.
Base	A subunit of a nucleic acid. Technically, the base is the portion of a nucleotide that makes it an **A**, **G**, **T**, **C**, etc. The term is often used informally in discussing the nucleotide "residues" in a DNA or RNA molecule.
Base pair (bp)	Two complementary bases held together by chemical bonds; complementary base pairing occurs between **A** and **T** and between **G** and **C**.
Baye's Theorem	A formal theory of probability used to evaluate competing hypotheses in the context of specific information. It incorporates but is not wholly defined by a likelihood ratio.
Biallelic, Diallelic	A locus at which only two alleles are found.
Binning	A method used to assign allele frequencies in constructing a population database. All the alleles in a bin take on the frequency of the entire group. Also, one of the steps used in assigning an allele designation to an STR product based on fragment length.
C	Single-letter designation of the base cytosine; one of the four building blocks of DNA (*see also* **Cytosine**).
CACLD	California Association of Crime Laboratory Directors.
Capillary electrophoresis (CE)	A method used to separate DNA fragments of different sizes using a liquid polymer inside of a very narrow length of tubing.
Ceiling Principle	A now-defunct calculation, originally endorsed by the NRC I Committee, to multiply allele frequencies to determine the strength of a genetic concordance. It states that for each allele in a product calculation, the highest frequency among the groups sampled, or 5%, must be used, whichever is larger (*see also* **Interim ceiling principle**).
Cell	The basic building block of an organism.
Centromere	The central element of a chromosome.
Certification	Forensic scientists (criminalists) can be certified for DNA testing. Certification in Molecular Biology of a forensic scientist (criminalist) means that the analyst has demonstrated the minimum professional knowledge, skills, and abilities to perform DNA testing.
Chelex	Chemical used in DNA extraction.
Chelex extraction	One method of isolating DNA from cells.
Chromosome	The structure by which hereditary information is physically transmitted from one generation to the next; the organelle that carries the genes.

Circumstantial evidence	Any evidence in a case for which an inference is needed to relate it to the crime. Not observed by an eyewitness. Most physical evidence, with the exception of blood alcohol determination and drug identification, is circumstantial. DNA evidence is circumstantial.
Class characteristic	A characteristic of an item that puts it in a class with other similar items.
Coding region	A region of DNA that has the capability of producing a protein.
CODIS	<u>C</u>ombined <u>D</u>NA <u>I</u>ndex <u>S</u>ystem: a series of local, state, and national computer applications and databases.
Complementary base pairing	(*See* **Base pair**)
Conservative estimate	An estimate designed to deliberately overestimate the occurrence of any particular profile in the population. Depending on the circumstances of the case, this may or may not "favor the defendant."
Controls	Tests performed in parallel with experimental or evidence samples and designed to demonstrate that a procedure worked correctly.
Cytosine	One of the four chemical building blocks of DNA (*see also* **C**).
D1S80	A VNTR locus used in forensic DNA typing. D1S80 is typed using PCR.
D-loop	A hypervariable region of DNA sequence located on mitochondrial DNA (mtDNA). It is the region that is typed in mtDNA analysis for forensic purposes.
DNA database	A computer repository of DNA profiles.
DNA databank	Specifically in the context of an offender databank, an infrastructure that includes enabling legislation, specifications for sample collection, analysis and search parameters, specifications for processing hits, and a database of DNA profiles.
Degradation	The breakdown of DNA into smaller fragments by chemical or physical means.
Denaturation	The separation of double-stranded DNA into single-stranded DNA by heat or chemical means.
Deoxynucleotides	The specific type of nucleotides that comprise DNA.
Deoxyribonucleic acid (DNA)	The genetic material of organisms. It is composed of two complementary chains of nucleotides in the form of a double helix.
Dideoxynucleotides	A synthetic DNA nucleotide analogue, they are missing the portion that allows linkage to the next nucleotide in a chain, and therefore terminate DNA chains into which they become incorporated.
Differential extraction	DNA extraction procedure in which sperm cells are separated from the DNA of other cells before their DNA is isolated.

Digest gel	Diagnostic step in the RFLP DNA typing procedure that measures completeness of restriction enzyme digestion.
Diploid	Having two sets of chromosomes, in pairs; people are diploid organisms.
Diplomate of the ABC	A criminalist who has passed a general knowledge test in forensic science given by the American Board of Criminalistics.
Discrete alleles	Any allele in a genetic typing system in which the detection method can clearly distinguish between the variants being tested.
DNA	Deoxyribonucleic acid (*see also* **Deoxyribonucleic acid**).
DNA amplification	Process of making multiple copies of a particular region of DNA using the polymerase chain reaction (PCR).
DNA band	(*See Band*)
DNA fingerprint	A misnomer (*see* **DNA profile**; **DNA type**).
DNA polymerase	An enzyme that synthesizes new DNA from an existing template.
DNA probe	A short segment of DNA labeled with a radioactive or chemical tag that is used to detect the presence of a particular DNA sequence or fragment.
DNA profile	Profile compiled from the results of DNA testing of one or more genetic markers.
DNA replication	The synthesis of new DNA from existing DNA.
DNA type, Genetic type	(*See* **DNA profile**)
DOJ	Department of Justice.
Double helix	Native form of DNA in which single strands are held together by complementary base pairing and twined around each other in the form of a double helix.
Double-stranded DNA	Form of DNA in which single strands are held together by complementary base pairing.
DQα	(*See* **HLA DQα**)
DQA1	(*See* **HLA DQA1**)
Electropherogram	A representation of alleles in the form of peaks after separation by electrophoresis and electronic detection.
Electrophoresis	A technique in which molecules are separated by their rate of movement in an electric field; in the case of DNA, the fragments are separated according to size.
Enzyme	A protein that is capable of speeding up a specific biochemical reaction but which itself is not changed or consumed in the process; a biological catalyst.
Epithelial cells (e. cells)	Cells such as skin cells, vaginal cells, or other cells normally found on an inner or outer body surface (*see also* **Non-sperm cells**).
Error	In the context of forensic DNA typing, the *reporting* of an incorrect inclusion or exclusion (genetic concordance or discordance) between two samples.

Error rate	A specious concept that has become associated with the admissibility of forensic evidence, in large part because of some language in the *Daubert* decision. Although an error may occur in any particular case, no reliable way exists to determine any sort of rate (implies a constant over time).
Ethidium bromide	Chemical dye that binds to double-stranded DNA and renders it visible in the presence of ultraviolet light.
Eukaryote; Eukaryotic	A type of cell that contains a nucleus and various organelles, or an organism composed of such cells. Humans are eukaryotes.
Evidence sample	Sample for which the origin is unknown; usually taken from the crime scene or people or objects associated with it.
Exclusion	Two samples that could not share a common origin, frequently a reference sample and an evidence sample.
Extension	In the polymerase chain reaction (PCR), the addition of nucleotides to form a new DNA strand from a primed template.
FBI	Federal Bureau of Investigation.
Federal Rules of Evidence	An admissibility standard for scientific evidence that relies on Federal Rules 702 and 403. The criteria are reliability, relevancy, and more probative than prejudicial.
Fellow of the ABC	A criminalist who has passed a general knowledge test in forensic science, and also a specialty exam given by the American Board of Criminalistics. A Fellow must also pass a proficiency test given by an approved provider.
Frye Standard	An admissibility standard for scientific evidence that relies on the federal decision of *Frye v. United States*. General acceptance in the relevant scientific community is the main criteria.
G	Single-letter designation of the base guanine, one of the four building blocks of DNA (*see also* **Guanine**).
Gamete	A haploid reproductive cell; sperm or egg.
Gel	Semisolid matrix (usually agarose or acrylamide) used in electrophoresis to separate molecules.
Gene	The basic unit of heredity; a sequence of DNA nucleotides on a chromosome.
Gene frequency	(*See* **Allele frequency**)
Genetic concordance	When genetic profiles show the same types at all loci tested and no unexplainable differences exist (*see also* **Match**).
Genetic linkage, Linkage	Used to describe genetic markers that are often inherited together. They may or may not be physically linked (close together on the same chromosome).
Genetic marker, Marker	A defined location on a chromosome having known genetic characteristics.
Genome	The total genetic makeup of an organism.

Genotype	The genetic makeup of an organism, as distinguished from its physical appearance or phenotype. It may pertain to one locus or many loci.
Guanine	One of the four chemical building blocks of DNA (*see also* **G**).
*Hae*III	A restriction enzyme used in RFLP analysis. The standard enzyme used in the United States.
Haploid	Having one set of chromosomes (*compare* **Diploid**).
Hardy-Weinberg Equilibrium	The condition, for a particular genetic locus and a particular population, with the following properties: allele frequencies are constant in the population over time and no statistical correlation exists between any two alleles possessed by individuals in the population; such a condition is approached in large randomly mating populations in the absence of selection, migration, and mutation.
Hemizygous	The situation in which a chromosomal element has no complement. This is normal for haploid organisms, and for some genetic elements such as mtDNA in diploid organisms.
Heredity	The transmission of genetic characteristics from parent to offspring.
Heteroplasmy	In particular reference to mtDNA, the situation in which two populations of hemizygous molecules exist in an individual.
Heterozygote	A diploid organism that carries different alleles at one or more genetic loci on each of the paired chromosomes.
Heterozygous	Having different alleles at a particular locus. This is manifest by the presence of two bands or peaks at the locus in question.
Heterozygosity	The proportion of the population that has two different alleles (heterozygous) at a particular locus. It is preferable for loci used in forensic typing to exhibit a relatively high heterozygosity.
*Hin*fI	Restriction enzyme use in RFLP analysis. Most European labs use this enzyme.
HLA DQα	The historical name for a locus used in forensic DNA typing. It also refers to the first iteration of the commercial kit available for its analysis (*see also* **HLA DQA1**).
HLA DQA1	The current name for a locus used in forensic DNA typing. It also refers to the second iteration of the commercial kit available for its analysis (*see also* **HLA DQα**).
HMW, High Molecular Weight	Use to describe DNA that is in large pieces, and has not been significantly broken down or degraded by physical or chemical means.
Homozygous	Having the same allele on both chromosomes at a particular locus. This is manifest by the presence of one band or peak at the locus in question.

HRP, Horseradish peroxidase	Enzyme used in some forensic PCR typing systems, it produces a blue color that marks the presence of a particular allele on a typing strip.
Human Genome Project	International project to decipher and catalog all the information in the human genome; completed in 2000.
Human leukocyte antigen (HLA)	Cell structures that differ among individuals and are important for acceptance or rejection of tissue grafts or organ transplants; the DNA locus of one particular class, HLA DQA1, is used for forensic analysis with PCR.
Hybridization	Detection of particular DNA fragments or sequences by complementary base pairing of tagged probes.
Hypervariable	A DNA locus that shows extreme variation between individuals.
Hypervariable Region I (HVI)	In mtDNA, one of the two highly polymorphic areas in the control region in the D-loop.
Hypervariable Region II (HVII)	In mtDNA, one of the two highly polymorphic areas in the control region in the D-loop.
In vitro	Literally "in glass," it refers to biochemical reactions that take place out of the body, usually in a test tube or other laboratory apparatus.
Inclusion	Two samples that could share a common origin; frequently a reference sample and an evidence sample.
Independent segregation	Offspring inherit one homologous chromosome of a pair from each parent, never two from the same parent.
Individualization	Two samples that share a common unique source or origin.
Interim ceiling principle	A now-defunct calculation, originally endorsed by the NRC I Committee, to multiply allele frequencies to determine the significance of a genetic concordance. It states that for each allele in a product calculation, the highest frequency among the groups sampled, or 10%, must be used, whichever is larger (*see also* **Ceiling principle**).
Isotope	An alternative form of a chemical element; used particularly in reference to the radioactive alternative forms, or radioisotopes.
K562	Name of the standard sample used in RFLP forensic DNA analysis in the U.S.
Kilobase pair (kb)	One thousand base pairs.
Length polymorphism	A locus that exhibits variations in length when cut with restriction enzymes or amplified with PCR primers. In forensic DNA analysis, variable number tandem repeat (VNTR) loci and short tandem repeat (STR) loci are used. Polymorphism within the restriction enzyme site produces another kind of length polymorphism.
Likelihood ratio	The direct comparison of the probabilities of two competing hypotheses. When the evaluation is complete, the conclusion is phrased as: "The evidence is X times more likely under proposition A than under proposition B."

Linkage Equilibrium (LE)	When two or more genetic loci appear to segregate randomly in a given population. The genotypes appear randomly with respect to each other.
Locus (pl., Loci)	The specific physical location of a gene on a chromosome.
Lumigraph	An X-ray film on which chemiluminescently labeled probes have left a mark determining the positions of particular DNA fragments (*see also* **Autoradiograph**).
Match	When genetic profiles show the same types at all loci tested and no unexplainable differences exist. (also see *Genetic Concordance*)
Match criteria	A set of empirically derived, laboratory-specific data that is used to set limits on the amount of difference within which two DNA fragments can be considered the same size in RFLP analysis.
Membrane	The support (usually nylon) to which DNA is transferred during the Southern blotting procedure.
Mitochondrial DNA (mtDNA)	The small, numerous, circular DNA molecules found in mitochondria.
Mitochondrion (pl., Mitochondria)	An organelle found in eukaryotes, including humans. Specific hypervariable regions of mtDNA are typed in forensic testing.
MO	*Modus operandi* (Latin). The operational elements of a crime.
Molecular weight	Refers to the molecular mass of a molecule. In DNA analysis, "molecular weight" and "band size" are often used interchangeably.
Molecular-weight size marker	DNA fragments of known size, from which the size of an unknown DNA sample can be determined.
Monoclonal	A group of chromosomes or cells derived respectively from one chromosome or cell, and thus are identical.
Monomorphic probe	A DNA probe that detects an allele that is the same in everyone, and hence shows the same pattern. Used as a diagnostic standard in RFLP analysis to check for sample-to-sample variation due to causes other than genetic polymorphism, such as environmental and experimental factors.
Multi-locus probe	A DNA probe that detects genetic variation at multiple sites; an autoradiogram of a multi-locus probe yields a complex, stripe-like pattern of 30 or more bands per individual. This pattern was originally called a "DNA fingerprint" by its originator Alec Jeffreys. It was never used in the United States for forensic typing (*see also* **Single-locus probe**).
MVR	Minisatellite variant repeat.
NDIS	National DNA Index System
NIH	National Institutes of Health.
NIJ	National Institute of Justice.
NIST	National Institute of Standards and Technology.

Noncoding	A region of DNA that lacks the capacity to produce a protein.
Non-sperm cells	Any cell not derived from a male gamete.
Non-sperm cell fraction	In a differential extraction, the portion of a sample containing DNA isolated from non-sperm cells.
Nuclear DNA	The DNA contained within the nucleus of a cell. It constitutes the vast majority of the cell genome.
Nucleic acid	A general class of molecules that are polymers of nucleotides. DNA is a nucleic acid.
Nucleotide	A unit of nucleic acid. Technically, nucleotides are the raw building blocks of DNA or RNA. The term is often used informally in discussing the nucleotide "residues" left after the molecule is strung together.
Nucleus	An organelle found in the vast majority of eukaryotic cells, including most in the human body. It contains most of the cell's genome.
Organelle	Any of the subcellular structures found in eukaryotic cells.
Organic extraction	One method of isolating DNA from cells.
Partial, Partial digest	The result of incomplete digestion by restriction enzymes. In RFLP analysis, this may confound interpretation of the result.
PCR	(*See* **Polymerase chain reaction**)
PCR product	The DNA amplified as a result of the polymerase chain reaction (PCR).
P_d	(*See* **Power of discrimination**)
Peak	The visual image representing an allele on an electropherogram.
Phenotype	The physical appearance or functional expression of a trait.
Physical evidence	Any evidence in a case that can be subjected to physical analysis.
Point mutation	An alteration of one complementary nucleotide pair in chromosomal DNA that consists of addition, deletion, or substitution of paired nucleotides.
Polyacrylamide	A polymer that is used to separate relatively small DNA fragments. In forensic DNA analysis, used in AMP-FLP and STR analyses.
Polymarker	Common usage for a commercial kit called *AmpliType* PM; group of five different bi- and tri-allelic loci exhibiting sequence variation. Available as a kit for forensic DNA analysis.
Polymerase	A category of enzymes that catalyzes the addition of subunits into a polymer (*see* **DNA polymerase**)
Polymerase chain reaction (PCR)	A process mediated by a DNA polymerase that can yield millions of copies of a desired DNA sequence.
Polymorphism	The presence of multiple alleles of a gene in a population.
Population	A group of individuals occupying a given area at a given time.

Population substructure, Subpopulations	The existence of smaller mating groups within a larger community.
Power of discrimination (P_d)	Used in reference to a genetic marker or combination of markers. Defines the potential power of a system to differentiate between any two people chosen at random. Can be calculated from the allele frequencies in a defined population.
Probe	A short segment of synthetic, tagged DNA used to detect a particular DNA fragment or sequence.
Product gel	Diagnostic tool used in PCR analysis to determine if a DNA sample has been successfully amplified.
Product Rule	A calculation based on population genetics that allows individual allele frequencies and genotype frequencies to be multiplied together to generate an overall profile frequency.
Proficiency test	The analysis of material provided by an outside agency or laboratory to determine whether an analyst can accurately and reliably perform DNA typing. In open tests, the analysts are aware that they are being tested; in blind tests, they are unaware of being tested. Internal proficiency tests are conducted by the laboratory itself; external tests are conducted by an independent agency.
Prokaryote	A cell lacking a nucleus or any other subcellular organelles. Prokaryotes are all bacteria.
Protein	A class of biological molecules made up of amino acids, proteins provide much of the body's structure and function. Enzymes are a subclass of proteins that perform specific biochemical functions.
Pull-up	Specifically related to ABD Genescan software, a peak (*see also* **Peak**) seen in one color that is not due to the presence of DNA, but to incorrect compensation for the spectral overlap of the four dyes used in detecting multiple loci in one reaction.
Quality assurance (QA)	The plan by which a laboratory can ensure that minimum professional standards for general operations are met.
Quality control (QC)	The program used to monitor the quality of laboratory reagents, supplies, and equipment. The operational part of quality assurance (QA).
Random assortment	Describes the behavior of non-homologous chromosomes in the generation of gametes; either chromosome of a homologous pair can associate randomly with either from another pair.
Reannealing	The process of complementary single strands of DNA binding together (*see also* **Hybridization**).
Reference sample	A sample (often blood) taken from a known person, against which an evidence sample is compared.
Relevancy Standard	(*See* **Federal Rules of Evidence**)

Restriction enzyme, Restriction endonuclease
An enzyme that cuts DNA at specific locations determined by the DNA sequence.

Restriction fragment length polymorphism (RFLP)
Variation in the length of DNA fragments produced by a restriction endonuclease (an enzyme) that cuts at a polymorphic locus. The polymorphism can be either in the restriction enzyme site or in the number of tandem repeats between the cut sites. Variable Number Tandem Repeat (VNTR) loci are used in forensic DNA analysis [*see also* **Variable number tandem repeat (VNTR)**].

Reverse dot blot
A specific method used to detect DNA, it is employed in the AmpliType® PM+DQA1 kit. The probe is bound to the typing strip and challenged with the PCR product from the samples.

RFLP
(*See* **Restriction fragment length polymorphism (RFLB)**)

RFLP analysis
A technique that uses probes to detect length variation in a specific region of DNA. The variation is caused by differences in the number of tandemly repeated DNA sequences between restriction enzyme cut sites.

Sequence polymorphism
Variation in specific base pairs at a particular locus. May include addition, deletion, or substitution of base pairs.

Sequence-specific oligonucleotide
Sequence-Specific Oligonucleotide. A short synthetic probe used to pinpoint a specific sequence using hybridization. SSOs are sometimes incorrectly referred to as ASOs (*see also* **SSO**).

Serology
The discipline concerned with the immunologic study of the body fluids.

Serum
The liquid that separates from blood after coagulation.

Sex chromosomes (X and Y)
Chromosomes that are different between the two sexes; in humans, females are XX and males are XY.

Short tandem repeat (STR)
Repeating units of an identical (or similar) DNA sequence, where the repeat sequence unit is 2 to 5 base pairs (bp) in length. The repeat units are arranged in direct succession of each other, and the number of repeat units varies between individuals.

Single-locus probe
A DNA probe that detects genetic variation at only one site in the genome; an autorad produced using one, single-locus probe usually displays one band in homozygotes and two bands in heterozygotes.

Single-stranded DNA
A form of DNA in which the two strands that normally make up the double helix are separated.

Slot blot
A diagnostic tool used in DNA analysis to determine how much human (higher primate) DNA has been extracted from a sample. Useful in making decisions about how much sample to use for various typing procedures.

Southern blot
The technique for transferring DNA fragments that have been separated by electrophoresis from the gel to a nylon membrane.

Sperm (cell) fraction	In a differential extraction, the portion of a sample containing DNA from the sperm cells.
Spike	A peak in an electropherogram caused by electrical fluctuations in the current (an artifact).
SSO	Sequence-Specific Oligonucleotide. A short synthetic probe used to pinpoint a specific sequence using hybridization. SSOs are sometimes incorrectly referred to as ASOs.
Standards	Criteria established for quality control and quality assurance; or established or known test reagents, such as molecular-weight standards.
State of the DNA	The condition of a DNA sample. It may be poor in quality or quantity, particularly after exposure to environmental conditions commonly encountered in crime scene samples (*see also* **Short tandem repeat (STR)**).
STR	(*See* **Short tandem repeat (STR)**)
Streptavidin	Protein molecule used in the detection of amplified DNA on a reverse dot blot. Binds tightly to the protein biotin.
Stringency	Specific conditions used in the hybridization of DNA. Also refers to a specific parameter used when searching a DNA database.
Stutter	A minor band appearing one repeat unit smaller than a primary STR allele. Occasionally, the repeat unit is larger than the primary allele.
Subpopulation, Substructure	(*See* **Population substructure**)
SWGDAM	Scientific Working Group on DNA Analysis and Methods, formerly TWGDAM.
T	Single-letter designation of the base thymine; one of the four building blocks of DNA (*see also* **Thymine**).
Tandem repeats	Repeating units of an identical (or similar) DNA sequence arranged in direct succession in a particular region of a chromosome.
Taq DNA polymerase	The enzyme used to copy DNA in the polymerase chain reaction (PCR) reaction.
Taq polymerase	(*See* **Taq DNA polymerase**)
Thymine	One of the four chemical building blocks of DNA (*see also* **T**).
Transfer theory	The theory attributed to Edmond Locard regarding the transfer of trace evidence between two objects.
Variable number tandem repeat (VNTR)	Repeating units of an identical (or similar) DNA sequence, arranged in direct succession in a particular region of a chromosome, for which the number varies between individuals.
VNTR	(*See* **Variable number tandem repeat (VNTR)**)

Yield gel   Diagnostic tool in DNA analysis. Aids in determining the
                                       quality and quantity of DNA extracted from a sample.
                                       Affects decisions about how much to use in various typing
                                       procedures.

DNA: Some Key Phrases

- DNA is the genetic material that determines physical traits.
- Every individual, with the exception of identical twins, is believed to have unique DNA.
- Except for identical twins, who share the same genetic material, siblings share the most genetic material.
- The use of DNA for identification is called "DNA typing" or "DNA profiling."
- Several different kinds of DNA typing tests are available; they fall into two general categories called length polymorphisms and sequence polymorphisms.
- RFLP is a length polymorphism system that does not depend on PCR amplification before detection.
- PCR is a method that is used to amplify selected portions of DNA containing either length or sequence polymorphisms before detection.
- Both RFLP and PCR-based typing systems are accurate, reliable, and valid.
- RFLP loci, taken individually, exclude a greater number of people as potential donors of the sample than individual PCR-based loci.
- The power of exclusion is increased by adding additional loci in either RFLP- or PCR-based tests.
- RFLP requires a greater amount of sample and better-quality DNA.
- PCR-based systems often yield results for a tiny sample of relatively poor quality.
- PCR-based tests have included HLA DQα/A1, polymarker (PM), D1S80, and STRs.
- The final result in RFLP analysis looks like a simplified supermarket bar code.
- The final result in HLA DQα/A1 or polymarker (together known as PM+DQA1) is seen as blue dots on a white strip.
- The final result in D1S80 or manual STRs looks like a simplified supermarket bar code.
- The final result in automated STRs looks like an arrhythmic electrocardiogram.
- A similar pattern of bands, dots, or peaks leads to an inference of common source of varying strength.
- Poor-quality DNA can result from exposure to sunlight, chemicals, soil, micro-organisms.
- Poor-quality DNA can result from cells that have been outside of a living person for a long time.
- The strength of similar DNA types is usually expressed as the rarity of that type in the population.
- The greater the number of genetic markers tested, the stronger the inference of a common source for matching profiles.
- Usually 100 to 500 or more people are sampled from a population to see how common or rare the DNA alleles are.

- DNA can link a suspect or victim to the scene of a crime with varying degrees of certainty.
- Most body fluids, organs, and other physiological materials will give a DNA type.
- From one person, all body fluids and organs will show the same type for nuclear DNA.
- It is not possible to tell the race or ethnicity of a person by looking at the markers currently used in forensic DNA testing.
- A criminalist is an expert who examines and analyzes physical evidence used in criminal investigation.
- A forensic scientist is an expert who examines and analyzes the physical evidence used in criminal investigation.
- A criminologist is an expert who analyzes sociological and psychological factors involved in criminal investigation.
- Crime laboratories can be accredited.
- Accreditation of a crime laboratory means that the laboratory meets minimum professional standards for laboratory operations.
- Forensic Scientists (Criminalists) can be certified for DNA testing.
- Certification of a Forensic Scientist (Criminalist) in Molecular Biology means that the analyst has the minimum professional knowledge, skills, and abilities to perform DNA testing.
- Proficiency testing is the analysis of material provided by an outside agency or laboratory to determine whether an analyst can accurately and reliably perform DNA typing.

Assessment Tools

1.   Slot Blot

The slot blot technique is used to obtain information about the quantity of human DNA recovered from a sample. A small portion of each sample is applied to a nylon membrane. A set of standard samples, for which the quantities are known, is also applied for comparison. After permanently fixing the samples to the membrane, they are probed with a small fragment of synthetic DNA that has been selected to hybridize only to higher primate DNA. If the gorilla did it, you may be in trouble; but otherwise, this probe adequately detects DNA of human origin. Because bacterial DNA often makes up a significant portion of a forensic sample, it is critical to have this information to make appropriate decisions regarding subsequent analysis. A slot blot does not yield information regarding the state of degradation of DNA. The probe used in this case is tagged with an enzyme that interacts with a certain chemical to produce a discharge of light. This effect is called **chemiluminescence**. When the probed membrane is soaked in the chemical and exposed to X-ray film, a black band corresponding to the region detected by the probe is produced, just as

slot blot

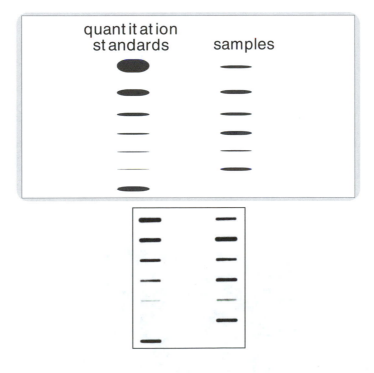

with X-rays. This provides a permanent record that can be analyzed visually, as well as with computer-aided imaging systems.

Source: Walsh, P.S., Varlaro, J., and Reynolds, R., A rapid chemiluminescent method for quantitation of human DNA, *Nucleic Acids Res.*, 20, 19, 1992.

2.   Yield Gel

A yield gel is a miniature agarose gel. Its purpose is to aid in assessing the amount of total DNA recovered from a sample, as well as the state of degradation of the DNA. A tiny slab of agarose is prepared and a small portion of each sample loaded into separate wells. Standard samples of known quantity are run along side the questioned samples to provide a comparison. The run is complete in less than an hour and the gel is stained with the dye **ethidium bromide**, which binds to double-stranded DNA. It binds to single-stranded DNA only poorly, and thus cannot be used to quantify Chelex-extracted DNA. The ethidium bromide fluoresces under ultraviolet light and marks the place where the DNA has migrated to in the gel. DNA viewed in this way is seen as a blob or smear, depending on its state of degradation. Large, intact DNA molecules will form a compact band near the origin of the gel, similar in placement and shape to the standards. Degraded DNA will form more of a smear and migrate further through the gel, depending on the average size of the pieces. Extremely degraded DNA may not be visible at all. Sometimes, but not always, evidence of bacterial DNA may be detected as a bright blob near the bottom of the yield gel. It is important to realize that staining with ethidium bromide dye detects all the DNA in the genome(s) present, and does not give any information about species or specific loci. The result is recorded using standard photographic techniques.

yield gel

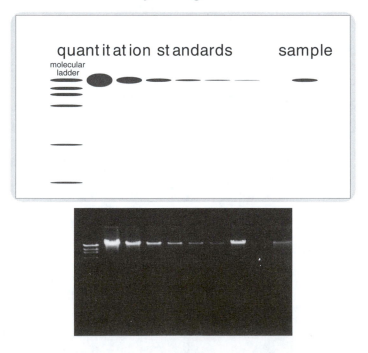

3.   Digest Gel

The digest gel is prepared in the same way as a yield gel. It is used in assessing the completeness of restriction enzyme digestion before proceeding to a RFLP analytical gel. A small portion of DNA that is thought to be digested is removed and loaded into a well on the gel. Standards that are known to be either uncut or completely cut are loaded alongside for comparison. The gel is run for approximately an hour and stained with ethidium bromide like a yield gel. Uncut DNA will form a compact band near the origin of the gel, similar in placement and shape to the uncut standard. A complete digest is evidenced by a uniform smear composed of different-sized fragments running down the length of the lane, similar in placement and shape to the fully digested standard. The result is recorded using standard photographic techniques.

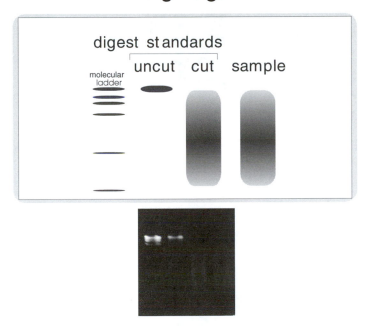

4.   Product Gel

The product gel is used as a tool to assess the efficiency of amplification by *Taq* polymerase. It is prepared in much the same way as the yield and digest gels in RFLP analysis. After PCR amplification, a small sample is removed and loaded on the gel alongside a molecular ladder containing bands of known sizes. The gel is run for about an hour and stained with ethidium bromide. A band, or lack thereof, in a product lane gives an indication of the success of amplification. The bands are compared with the ladder to check that a band of the correct size has been generated; this is a check on the fidelity of the amplification. The result is recorded using standard photographic techniques.

product gel

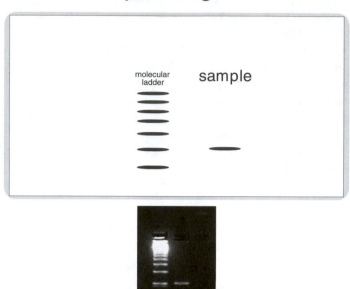

Chromosomal Locations

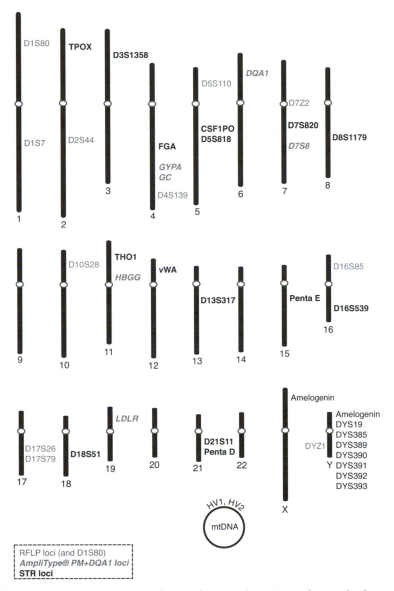

Appendix D. Chromosomal location of some forensic loci. Note that each chromosome, identified by the number below, has two arms extending from a central element called a centromere. The shorter arm is conventionally called **P** and the longer arm is called **Q**. Neither the exact location of a locus nor its order relative to other loci on the same chromosome arm should be considered accurate. It is important to realize that although two markers may be on the same chromosome, or even on the same chromosome arm, the distances between them are still quite large when considered on a molecular level, and the loci may be completely unlinked; that is, they show no tendency to be inherited together. See Chapter 8 for a further discussion of this topic.

Sample Frequency Calculation

In this example, we consider the results of a series of DNA tests performed on an evidence sample, and compare the results to reference samples taken from two individuals. We then estimate the frequency of the evidence DNA profile in a hypothetical population. Two RFLP loci, one sequence polymorphic locus (which will be referred to as an sequence specific oligonucleotide, or SSO) and one STR locus are used to illustrate various aspects of the procedures. For the purposes of this exercise, we will assume that the evidence sample represents only one individual.

We first consider the RFLP result. The analyst inspects the autorad to determine whether the evidence and either or both of the reference samples appear to be visually concordant. If none of the band patterns are similar, both reference donors are excluded from having contributed to the evidence sample. If, in the analyst's trained judgment, the patterns are indistinguishable, the next step in determining the significance of the genetic concordance is to calculate the band sizes, usually with the aid of a computer.

The SSO locus is analyzed next. Again, comparisons are made between the dot patterns in the evidence and reference samples (see Chapter 8) to determine if genetic concordance exists between any of them. If the patterns are clearly different, both the reference donors are excluded; if the patterns are similar, the strength must be determined.

An STR locus is analyzed next, using yet another portion of the DNA. This is followed by visualization using any of the various methods detailed in Chapter 7. Band or peak patterns are compared between the evidence and reference samples; either the patterns are different, in which case analysis stops with an exclusion, or they are indistinguishable and the strength must be determined. Alleles are assigned either by visual comparison to an appropriate ladder or by a computer algorithm.

The following results are obtained:

	Evidence Stain	Individual 1	Individual 2
RFLP Locus A	3500 bp	3490 bp	2750 bp
	2100 bp	2050 bp	1640 bp
SSO Locus	3,3	3,3	2,5
STR Locus	4,7	4,7	5,5

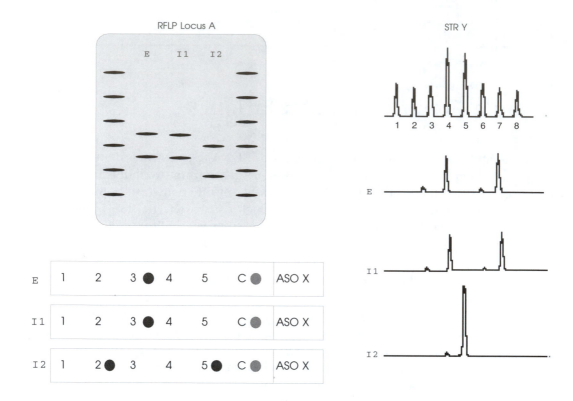

Discrete Allele Systems

We first examine the discrete allele systems (the SSO and STR loci). Individual 2 clearly shows different types than the evidence at both loci, so he is eliminated as a possible donor. However, the genotypes for Individual 1 and the evidence stain are the same (SSO:3,3; STR: 4,7), so this individual is included as a possible donor of the evidence.

Continuous Allele Systems

We next evaluate the RFLP locus. The elimination of Individual 2 by the other two systems is confirmed by the RFLP analysis. However, Individual 1 shows a band pattern that is visually indistinguishable from that of the evidence. In this situation, it is necessary to perform a proscribed set of statistical calculations to either confirm or refute the visually established concordance.

Assume that laboratory validation has established that, when analyzed repeatedly, RFLP bands from the same source generally fall within ±1.8% of their average value. We must check the evidence and reference band sizes to see if they fit within this match criteria, or window of uncertainty. The measurment uncertainty for any band is calculated by adding and subtracting 1.8% of its measured size. For example, the uncertainty window for band 1 of locus A spans the range from 3437 (−1.8%) below to 3563 (+1.8%) above the measured value. Similar calculations for band 1 of the reference sample produce an uncertainty window that measures from 3427 to 3553 bp. Notice that these two ranges overlap; when this occurs for all (usually both) bands in a profile, the samples are considered genetically indistinguishable. The following chart gives the values for the RFLP loci in this example:

RFLP Locus A		Size (bp)	Range of Uncertainty (bp)
Band 1	Evidence	3500	3437–3563
	Individual 1	3490	3427–3553
Band 2	Evidence	2100	2062–2138
	Individual 1	2050	2013–2087

Both RFLP bands show an overlap in the range of uncertainty between the evidence sample and the reference sample from Individual 1. This leads to the conclusion that the samples show genetic concordance at the RFLP loci tested, confirming our conclusion from analysis of the PCR-amplified loci. The results from both the continuous and discrete allele systems tested establish genetic concordance between the evidence profile and the profile from Individual 1.

Estimation of the Profile Frequency

Having determined that the DNA profiles of the evidence stain and Individual 1 are indeed the same, we need to evaluate the probability of this match if someone other than Individual 1 is the donor. We do this by estimating the frequency of this profile in a population.

A survey of the appropriate population is required to estimate profile frequencies. The usable form of this survey is a table of allele frequencies that are then used to calculate genotype frequencies for the profile of interest. For RFLP loci, all the alleles from each locus sampled in a population survey are grouped into arbitrarily designated "bins" down the length of the autorad; each bin contains a range of allele sizes. A hypothetical table of RFLP allele frequencies for use in this example is given here:

RFLP Bin Table

Bin #	Locus A		
	Size Range	Allele Counts	Frequency
1	0–500	0	0.000
2	501–1000	0	0.000
3	1001–1500	5	0.005
4	1501–2000	8	0.008
5	**2001–2500**	**13**	**0.013**
6	2501–3000	29	0.030
7	3001–3500	38	0.039
8	**3501–4000**	**58**	**0.059**
9	4001–4500	126	0.13
10	4501–5000	77	0.079
11	5001–5500	86	0.088
12	5501–6000	92	0.094
13	6001–6500	110	0.11
14	6501–7000	100	0.10
15	7001–7500	95	0.097
16	7501–8000	66	0.067

RFLP Bin Table *(Continued)*

Bin #	Locus A Size Range	Locus A Allele Counts	Locus A Frequency
17	8001–8500	42	0.043
18	8501–9000	28	0.029
19	9001–9500	5	0.005
20	9501–10000	0	0.000

Allele frequencies in discrete allele systems, such as SSOs and STRs, may be used directly without any additional steps. Hypothetical tables for these systems are given below.

SSO Allele Frequency Table

Allele	Count	Frequency
1	45	0.17
2	62	0.24
3	37	0.14
4	16	0.062
5	41	0.16
6	57	0.22

STR Allele Frequency Table

Allele	Count	Frequency
1	34	0.13
2	53	0.21
3	26	0.10
4	34	0.13
5	5	0.02
6	78	0.30
7	13	0.05
8	15	0.058

Note: Assume that these population surveys have been tested for H-W and LE within and between loci and have been accepted for use in calculating profile frequencies.

Continuous Allele Loci (RFLP)

For every band, we determine the uncertainty of the size measurement and compare the resulting size range to the bin frequency table. For locus A, we know that the uncertainty spans the range from 3437 to 3563 bp. Inspection of the bin table reveals that this range actually spans two allele bins: bin 7, which includes alleles ranging from 3001 to 3500 base pairs, and bin 8, which includes alleles ranging from 3501 to 4000 bp. When the potential size range of an evidence allele spans one of the arbitrarily designated bin boundaries, the bin that has the higher frequency is chosen for use in the frequency estimate. This potentially overestimates the occurrence of the allele in the population, and is one of the devices used to ensure a conservative estimate. Bin 7 has a frequency of 0.039, and bin 8 has a frequency of 0.059. Therefore, the frequency of bin 8 (0.059) is chosen for use in the calculation. For the alleles at locus A, the results are below.

Locus A	Bin #	Frequency
Band 1	Bin 8	0.059
Band 2	Bin 5	0.013

Calculating Genotype Frequencies

Now that we have decided which allele frequencies to use, we can calculate the genotype frequency for the locus by applying the following formulae:

For heterozygous loci (locus A), the genotype frequency is given by:

$$2 \times \text{(Frequency of band 1)} \times \text{(Frequency of band 2)}$$

which, for locus A gives:

$$2 \times 0.059 \times 0.013 = 0.0015$$

Discrete Allele Loci (PCR)

The frequency tables for each locus are used to find the allele frequencies as follows:

The SSO locus has two type 3 alleles.

SSO Locus

Allele	Frequency
3	0.14

The frequency table for this SSO locus shows the frequency of the 3 allele to be 0.14.

STR Locus

Allele	Frequency
4	0.13
7	0.05

The frequency table for this STR locus shows the frequency of the 4 allele to be 0.13 and the frequency of the 7 allele to be 0.05.

The following formulae are used to determine the genotype frequencies for discrete allele loci.

1. For heterozygous loci, the genotype frequency is given by:

$$2 \times \text{(Frequency of allele 1)} \times \text{(Frequency of allele 2)}$$

which, for the STR locus, is

$$2 \times (0.13) \times (0.05) = 0.013$$

2. For homozygous loci (SSO locus), the genotype frequency is given by:

(Frequency of allele)^2 + correction factor $(p(1 - p)\theta)$, where θ helps to correct for any effect of population substructuring, recommended by NRC II as 0.01 for most U.S. populations.
For the SSO locus this is:

$$(0.14)^2 + (0.14)(1 - 0.14)(0.01) = 0.021$$

The last step is to estimate the frequency of the entire profile, incorporating the frequency estimates for each of the individual loci. Use of this formula is predicated on the assumption that the loci involved are in linkage equilibrium with each other in the population under consideration (see Chapter 8).

RFLP locus A × SSO locus × STR locus

which for this example gives:

$$0.0015 \times 0.013 \times 0.021 = 4 \times 10^{-7}$$
(about 1 in 2.4 million people)

Likelihood Ratio and Probability of Exclusion

1. Assuming the presence of the boyfriend

The probability of the profile is this many times more likely if the boyfriend and suspect are the donors than if the boyfriend and a random man of the indicated race are the donors

$$\frac{P(E \mid \text{Boyfriend} + \text{Suspect})}{P(E \mid \text{Boyfriend} + \text{Random man})}$$

$$\text{AfAm} = \frac{1}{5.7\text{E-}10} = 1{,}700{,}000{,}000$$

$$\text{Cauc} = 6.6\text{E-}10 = 1{,}500{,}000{,}000$$

$$\text{Hisp} = 7.7\text{E-}11 = 13{,}000{,}000{,}000$$

2. Assuming neither donor is identified

The probability of the profile is this many times more likely if the suspect and a random man are the donors than if two random men of the indicated race are the donors

$$\frac{P(E \mid \text{Suspect} + \text{Random man})}{P(E \mid 2 \text{ Random men})}$$

$$\text{AfAm} = \frac{4.0\text{E-}09}{1.2\text{E-}16} = 33{,}000{,}000$$

$$\text{Cauc} = \frac{4.1\text{E-}08}{9.1\text{E-}16} = 45{,}000{,}000$$

$$\text{Hisp} = \frac{2.7\text{E-}07}{1.3\text{E-}15} = 200{,}000{,}000$$

3. Assuming neither race, number, nor identity of donors

RMNE

$$\text{Freq} = 5.4\text{E-}07 = 1 \text{ in } 1{,}800{,}000$$

Quality Assurance Standards for Forensic DNA Testing Laboratories

DNA Advisory Board 1998

<http://www.for-swg.org/swgdamin.htm>

Preface

Throughout its deliberation concerning these quality standards, the DNA Advisory Board recognized the need for a mechanism to ensure compliance with the standards. An underlying premise for these discussions was that accreditation would be required to demonstrate compliance with the standards and therefore assure quality control and a quality program. Accordingly, the Board recommends that forensic laboratories performing DNA analysis seek such accreditation with all deliberate speed. Additionally, the Board strongly encourages the accrediting bodies to begin positioning themselves to accommodate the increasing demand for accreditation.

Proposed Mechanism to Recommend Changes to Standards Once the Director of the FBI has issued standards for quality assurance for forensic DNA testing, the DNA Advisory Board may recommend revisions to such standards to the FBI Director, as necessary. In the event that the duration of the DNA Advisory Board is extended beyond March 10, 2000 by the FBI Director, the Board may continue to recommend revisions to such standards to the FBI Director. In the event that the DNA Advisory Board is not extended by the FBI Director after March 10, 2000, the Technical Working Group on DNA Analysis Methods (TWGDAM) may recommend revisions to such standards to the FBI Director, as necessary.

Effective Date

These standards shall take effect October 1, 1998.

Introduction

This document consists of definitions and standards. The standards are quality assurance measures that place specific requirements on the laboratory. Equivalent measures not outlined in this document may also meet the standard if determined sufficient through an accreditation process.

References

American Society of Crime Laboratory Directors-Laboratory Accreditation Board (ASCLD-LAB), ASCLD-LAB Accreditation Manual, January 1994, and January, 1997.

International Standards Organization (ISO)/International Electrotechnical Commission (IEC), ISO/IEC Guide 25-1990, (1990) American National Standards Institute, New York.

Technical Working Group on DNA Analysis Methods, "Guidelines for a Quality Assurance Program for DNA Analysis," Crime Laboratory Digest, April 1995, Volume 22, Number 2, pp. 21-43. 42 Code of Federal Regulations, Chapter IV (10-1-95 Edition), Health Care Financing Administration, Health and Human Services.

1.   Scope

The standards describe the quality assurance requirements that a laboratory, which is defined as a facility in which forensic DNA testing is performed, should follow to ensure the quality and integrity of the data and competency of the laboratory. These standards do not preclude the participation of a laboratory, by itself or in collaboration with others, in research and development, on procedures that have not yet been validated.

2.   Definitions

As used in these standards, the following terms shall have the meanings specified:

(a) Administrative review is an evaluation of the report and supporting documentation for consistency with laboratory policies and for editorial correctness.

(b) Amplification blank control consists of only amplification reagents without the addition of sample DNA. This control is used to detect DNA contamination of the amplification reagents.

(c) Analytical procedure is an orderly step-by-step procedure designed to ensure operational uniformity and to minimize analytical drift.

(d) Audit is an inspection used to evaluate, confirm, or verify activity related to quality.

(e) Calibration is the set of operations which establish, under specified conditions, the relationship between values indicated by a measuring instrument or measuring system, or values represented by a material, and the corresponding known values of a measurement.

(f) Critical reagents are determined by empirical studies or routine practice to require testing on established samples before use on evidentiary samples in order to prevent unnecessary loss of sample.

(g) Commercial test kit is a pre-assembled kit that allows the user to conduct a specific forensic DNA test.

(h) Examiner/analyst is an individual who conducts and/or directs the analysis of forensic casework samples, interprets data, and reaches conclusions.

(i)   Forensic DNA testing is the identification and evaluation of biological evidence in criminal matters using DNA technologies.

(j)   Known samples are biological material whose identity or type is established.

(k)   Laboratory is a facility in which forensic DNA testing is performed.

(l)   Laboratory support personnel are individual(s) who perform laboratory duties and do not analyze evidence samples.

(m)   NIST is the National Institute of Standards and Technology.

(n)   Polymerase Chain Reaction (PCR) is an enzymatic process by which a specific region of DNA is replicated during repetitive cycles which consist of (1) denaturation of the template; (2) annealing of primers to complementary sequences at an empirically determined temperature; and (3) extension of the bound primers by a DNA polymerase.

(o)   Proficiency test sample is biological material whose DNA type has been previously characterized and which is used to monitor the quality performance of a laboratory or an individual.

(p)   Proficiency testing is a quality assurance measure used to monitor performance and identify areas in which improvement may be needed. Proficiency tests may be classified as:
   (1)   Internal proficiency test is one prepared and administered by the laboratory.
   (2)   External proficiency test, which may be open or blind, is one which is obtained from a second agency.

(q)   Qualifying test measures proficiency in both technical skills and knowledge.

(r)   Quality assurance includes the systematic actions necessary to demonstrate that a product or service meets specified requirements for quality.

(s)   Quality manual is a document stating the quality policy, quality system, and quality practices of an organization.

(t)   Quality system is the organizational structure, responsibilities, procedures, processes, and resources for implementing quality management.

(u)   Reagent blank control consists of all reagents used in the test process without any sample. This is to be used to detect DNA contamination of the analytical reagents.

(v)   Reference material (certified or standard) is a material for which values are certified by a technically valid procedure and accompanied by or traceable to a certificate or other documentation which is issued by a certifying body.

(w)   Restriction Fragment Length Polymorphism (RFLP) is generated by cleavage by a specific restriction enzyme and the variation is due to restriction site polymorphism and/or the number of different repeats contained within the fragments.

(x)   Review is an evaluation of documentation to check for consistency, accuracy, and completeness.

(y)   Second agency is an entity or organization external to and independent of the laboratory and which performs forensic DNA analysis.

(z)   Secure area is a locked space (for example, cabinet, vault or room) with access restricted to authorized personnel.

(aa)   Subcontractor is an individual or entity having a transactional relationship with a laboratory.

(bb)   Technical manager or leader (or equivalent position or title as designated by the laboratory system) is the individual who is accountable for the technical operations of the laboratory.

(cc) Technical review is an evaluation of reports, notes, data, and other documents to ensure an appropriate and sufficient basis for the scientific conclusions. This review is conducted by a second qualified individual.

(dd) Technician is an individual who performs analytical techniques on evidence samples under the supervision of a qualified examiner/analyst and/or performs DNA analysis on samples for inclusion in a database. Technicians do not evaluate or reach conclusions on typing results or prepare final reports.

(ee) Traceability is the property of a result of a measurement whereby it can be related to appropriate standards, generally international or national standards, through an unbroken chain of comparisons.

(ff) Validation is a process by which a procedure is evaluated to determine its efficacy and reliability for forensic casework analysis and includes:

   (1) Developmental validation is the acquisition of test data and determination of conditions and limitations of a new or novel DNA methodology for use on forensic samples.

   (2) Internal validation is an accumulation of test data within the laboratory to demonstrate that established methods and procedures perform as expected in the laboratory.

3.   Quality Assurance Program

STANDARD 3.1 The laboratory shall establish and maintain a documented quality system that is appropriate to the testing activities.

3.1.1   The quality manual shall address at a minimum:
   (a) Goals and objectives
   (b) Organization and management
   (c) Personnel qualifications and training
   (d) Facilities
   (e) Evidence control
   (f) Validation
   (g) Analytical procedures
   (h) Calibration and maintenance
   (i) Proficiency testing
   (j) Corrective action
   (k) Reports
   (l) Review
   (m) Safety
   (n) Audits

4.   Organization and Management

STANDARD 4.1 The laboratory shall:

(a) Have a managerial staff with the authority and resources needed to discharge their duties and meet the requirements of the standards in this document.

(b) Have a technical manager or leader who is accountable for the technical operations.

(c) Specify and document the responsibility, authority, and interrelation of all personnel who manage, perform or verify work affecting the validity of the DNA analysis.

5. Personnel

STANDARD 5.1 Laboratory personnel shall have the education, training, and experience commensurate with the examination and testimony provided. The laboratory shall:

5.1.1 Have a written job description for personnel to include responsibilities, duties, and skills.

5.1.2 Have a documented training program for qualifying all technical laboratory personnel.

5.1.3 Have a documented program to ensure technical qualifications are maintained through continuing education.

    5.1.3.1 Continuing education — the technical manager or leader and examiner/analyst(s) must stay abreast of developments within the field of DNA typing by reading current scientific literature and by attending seminars, courses, professional meetings, or documented training sessions/classes in relevant subject areas at least once a year.

5.1.4 Maintain records on the relevant qualifications, training, skills, and experience of the technical personnel.

STANDARD 5.2 The technical manager or leader shall have the following:

5.2.1 Degree requirements: The technical manager or leader of a laboratory shall have at a minimum a Master's degree in biology-, chemistry-, or forensic science-related area and successfully completed a minimum of 12 semester or equivalent credit hours of a combination of undergraduate and graduate course work covering the subject areas of biochemistry, genetics, and molecular biology (molecular genetics, recombinant DNA technology), or other subjects which provide a basic understanding of the foundation of forensic DNA analysis as well as statistics and/or population genetics as it applies to forensic DNA analysis.

    5.2.1.1 The degree requirements of section 5.2.1 may be waived by the American Society of Crime Laboratory Directors (ASCLD) or other organization designated by the Director of the FBI in accordance with criteria approved by the Director of the FBI. This waiver shall be available for a period of two years from the effective date of these standards. The waiver shall be permanent and portable.

5.2.2 Experience requirements: A technical manager or leader of a laboratory must have a minimum of three years of forensic DNA laboratory experience.

5.2.3 Duty requirements:

    5.2.3.1 General: manages the technical operations of the laboratory.

    5.2.3.2 Specific duties:

        (a) Is responsible for evaluating all methods used by the laboratory and for proposing new or modified analytical procedures to be used by examiners.

(b) Is responsible for technical problem solving of analytical methods and for the oversight of training, quality assurance, safety, and proficiency testing in the laboratory.

5.2.3.3 The technical manager or leader shall be accessible to the laboratory to provide onsite, telephone, or electronic consultation as needed.

STANDARD 5.3 Examiner/analyst shall have:

5.3.1   At a minimum a BA/BS degree or its equivalent degree in biology-, chemistry-, or forensic science-related area and must have successfully completed college course work (graduate or undergraduate level) covering the subject areas of biochemistry, genetics, and molecular biology (molecular genetics, recombinant DNA technology) or other subjects which provide a basic understanding of the foundation of forensic DNA analysis, as well as course work and/or training in statistics and population genetics as it applies to forensic DNA analysis.

5.3.2   A minimum of six (6) months of forensic DNA laboratory experience, including the successful analysis of a range of samples typically encountered in forensic case work prior to independent casework analysis using DNA technology.

5.3.3   Successfully completed a qualifying test before beginning independent casework responsibilities.

STANDARD 5.4 Technician shall have:

5.4.1   On-the-job training specific to their job function(s).

5.4.2   Successfully completed a qualifying test before participating in forensic DNA typing responsibilities.

STANDARD 5.5 Laboratory support personnel shall have:

5.5.1   Training, education, and experience commensurate with their responsibilities as outlined in their job description.

6.   Facilities

STANDARD 6.1 The laboratory shall have a facility that is designed to provide adequate security and minimize contamination. The laboratory shall ensure that:

6.1.1   Access to the laboratory is controlled and limited.

6.1.2   Prior to PCR amplification, evidence examinations, DNA extractions, and PCR setup are conducted at separate times or in separate spaces.

6.1.3   Amplified DNA product is generated, processed, and maintained in a room(s) separate from the evidence examination, DNA extractions, and PCR setup areas.

6.1.4   The laboratory follows written procedures for monitoring, cleaning, and decontaminating facilities and equipment.

7.   Evidence Control

STANDARD 7.1 The laboratory shall have and follow a documented evidence control system to ensure the integrity of physical evidence. This system shall ensure that:

7.1.1   Evidence is marked for identification.
7.1.2   Chain of custody for all evidence is maintained.
7.1.3   The laboratory follows documented procedures that minimize loss, contamination, and/or deleterious change of evidence.
7.1.4   The laboratory has secure areas for evidence storage.

STANDARD 7.2 Where possible, the laboratory shall retain or return a portion of the evidence sample or extract.

7.2.1   The laboratory shall have a procedure requiring that evidence sample/extract(s) are stored in a manner that minimizes degradation.

8.   Validation

STANDARD 8.1 The laboratory shall use validated methods and procedures for forensic casework analyses.

8.1.1   Developmental validation that is conducted shall be appropriately documented.
8.1.2   Novel forensic DNA methodologies shall undergo developmental validation to ensure the accuracy, precision, and reproducibility of the procedure. The developmental validation shall include the following:
   8.1.2.1 Documentation exists and is available which defines and characterizes the locus.
   8.1.2.2 Species specificity, sensitivity, stability, and mixture studies are conducted.
   8.1.2.3 Population distribution data are documented and available.
      8.1.2.3.1 The population distribution data would include the allele and genotype distributions for the locus or loci obtained from relevant populations. Where appropriate, databases should be tested for independence expectations.
8.1.3   Internal validation shall be performed and documented by the laboratory.
   8.1.3.1 The procedure shall be tested using known and non-probative evidence samples. The laboratory shall monitor and document the reproducibility and precision of the procedure using human DNA control(s).
   8.1.3.2 The laboratory shall establish and document match criteria based on empirical data.
   8.1.3.3 Before the introduction of a procedure into forensic casework, the analyst or examination team shall successfully complete a qualifying test.
   8.1.3.4 Material modifications made to analytical procedures shall be documented and subject to validation testing.
8.1.4   Where methods are not specified, the laboratory shall, wherever possible, select methods that have been published by reputable technical organizations or in rele-

vant scientific texts or journals, or have been appropriately evaluated for a specific or unique application.

9. Analytical Procedures

STANDARD 9.1 The laboratory shall have and follow written analytical procedures approved by the laboratory management/technical manager.

9.1.1 The laboratory shall have a standard operating protocol for each analytical technique used.
9.1.2 The procedures shall include reagents, sample preparation, extraction, equipment, and controls which are standard for DNA analysis and data interpretation.
9.1.3 The laboratory shall have a procedure for differential extraction of stains that potentially contain semen.

STANDARD 9.2 The laboratory shall use reagents that are suitable for the methods employed.

9.2.1 The laboratory shall have written procedures for documenting commercial supplies and for the formulation of reagents.
9.2.2 Reagents shall be labeled with the identity of the reagent, the date of preparation or expiration, and the identity of the individual preparing the reagent.
9.2.3 The laboratory shall identify critical reagents and evaluate them prior to use in casework. These critical reagents include but are not limited to:
  (a) Restriction enzyme
  (b) Commercial kits for performing genetic typing
  (c) Agarose for analytical RFLP gels
  (d) Membranes for Southern blotting
  (e) K562 DNA or other human DNA controls
  (f) Molecular weight markers used as RFLP sizing standards
  (g) Primer sets
  (h) Thermostable DNA polymerase

STANDARD 9.3 The laboratory shall have and follow a procedure for evaluating the quantity of the human DNA in the sample where possible.

9.3.1 For casework RFLP samples, the presence of high molecular weight DNA should be determined.

STANDARD 9.4 The laboratory shall monitor the analytical procedures using appropriate controls and standards.

9.4.1 The following controls shall be used in RFLP casework analysis:
    9.4.1.1 Quantitation standards for estimating the amount of DNA recovered by extraction.

9.4.1.2 K562 as a human DNA control. (In monitoring sizing data, a statistical quality control method for K562 cell line shall be maintained.)

9.4.1.3 Molecular weight size markers to bracket known and evidence samples.

9.4.1.4 Procedure to monitor the completeness of restriction enzyme digestion.

9.4.2 The following controls shall be used for PCR casework analysis:

9.4.2.1 Quantitation standards which estimate the amount of human nuclear DNA recovered by extraction.

9.4.2.2 Positive and negative amplification controls.

9.4.2.3 Reagent blanks.

9.4.2.4 Allelic ladders and/or internal size makers for variable number tandem repeat sequence PCR based systems.

STANDARD 9.5 The laboratory shall check its DNA procedures annually or whenever substantial changes are made to the protocol(s) against an appropriate and available NIST standard reference material or standard traceable to a NIST standard.

STANDARD 9.6 The laboratory shall have and follow written general guidelines for the interpretation of data.

9.6.1 The laboratory shall verify that all control results are within established tolerance limits.

9.6.2 Where appropriate, visual matches shall be supported by a numerical match criterion.

9.6.3 For a given population(s) and/or hypothesis of relatedness, the statistical interpretation shall be made following the recommendations 4.1, 4.2, or 4.3 as deemed applicable of the National Research Council report entitled "The Evaluation of Forensic DNA Evidence" (1996) and/or court-directed method. These calculations shall be derived from a documented population database appropriate for the calculation.

10.   Equipment Calibration and Maintenance

STANDARD 10.1 The laboratory shall use equipment suitable for the methods employed.

STANDARD 10.2 The laboratory shall have a documented program for calibration of instruments and equipment.

10.2.1 Where available and appropriate, standards traceable to national or international standards shall be used for the calibration.

10.2.1.1 Where traceability to national standards of measurement is not applicable, the laboratory shall provide satisfactory evidence of correlation of results.

10.2.2 The frequency of the calibration shall be documented for each instrument requiring calibration. Such documentation shall be retained in accordance with applicable federal or state law.

STANDARD 10.3 The laboratory shall have and follow a documented program to ensure that instruments and equipment are properly maintained.

10.3.1 New instruments and equipment, or instruments and equipment that have undergone repair or maintenance, shall be calibrated before being used in casework analysis.

10.3.2 Written records or logs shall be maintained for maintenance service performed on instruments and equipment.

Such documentation shall be retained in accordance with applicable federal or state law.

11. Reports

STANDARD 11.1 The laboratory shall have and follow written procedures for taking and maintaining case notes to support the conclusions drawn in laboratory reports.

11.1.1 The laboratory shall maintain, in a case record, all documentation generated by examiners related to case analyses.

11.1.2 Reports according to written guidelines shall include:
  (a) Case identifier
  (b) Description of evidence examined
  (c) A description of the methodology
  (d) Locus
  (e) Results and/or conclusions
  (f) An interpretative statement (either quantitative or qualitative)
  (g) Date issued
  (h) Disposition of evidence
  (i) A signature and title, or equivalent identification, of the person(s) accepting responsibility for the content of the report.

11.1.3 The laboratory shall have written procedures for the release of case report information.

12. Review

STANDARD 12.1 The laboratory shall conduct administrative and technical reviews of all case files and reports to ensure conclusions and supporting data are reasonable and within the constraints of scientific knowledge.

12.1.1 The laboratory shall have a mechanism in place to address unresolved discrepant conclusions between analysts and reviewer(s).

STANDARD 12.2 The laboratory shall have and follow a program that documents the annual monitoring of the testimony of each examiner.

13. Proficiency Testing

STANDARD 13.1 Examiners and other personnel designated by the technical manager or leader who are actively engaged in DNA analysis shall undergo, at regular intervals of not to exceed 180 days, external proficiency testing in accordance with these standards. Such external proficiency testing shall be an open proficiency testing program.

13.1.1 The laboratory shall maintain the following records for proficiency tests:
  (a) The test set identifier.
  (b) Identity of the examiner.
  (c) Date of analysis and completion.
  (d) Copies of all data and notes supporting the conclusions.
  (e) The proficiency test results.
  (f) Any discrepancies noted.
  (g) Corrective actions taken.

  Such documentation shall be retained in accordance with applicable Federal or state law.

13.1.2 The laboratory shall establish at a minimum the following criteria for evaluation of proficiency tests:
  (a) All reported inclusions are correct or incorrect.
  (b) All reported exclusions are correct or incorrect.
  (c) All reported genotypes and/or phenotypes are correct or incorrect according to consensus genotypes/phenotypes or within established empirically determined ranges.
  (d) All results reported as inconclusive or uninterpretable are consistent with written laboratory guidelines. The basis for inconclusive interpretations in proficiency tests must be documented.
  (e) All discrepancies/errors and subsequent corrective actions must be documented.
  (f) All final reports are graded as satisfactory or unsatisfactory. A satisfactory grade is attained when there are no analytical errors for the DNA profile typing data. Administrative errors shall be documented and corrective actions taken to minimize the error in the future.
  (g) All proficiency test participants shall be informed of the final test results.

14. Corrective Action

STANDARD 14.1 The laboratory shall establish and follow procedures for corrective action whenever proficiency testing discrepancies and/or casework errors are detected.

14.1.1 The laboratory shall maintain documentation for the corrective action. Such documentation shall be retained in accordance with applicable Federal or state law.

15. Audits

STANDARD 15.1 The laboratory shall conduct audits annually in accordance with the standards outlined herein.

15.1.1 Audit procedures shall address at a minimum:
  (a) Quality assurance program

    (b) Organization and management
    (c) Personnel
    (d) Facilities
    (e) Evidence control
    (f) Validation
    (g) Analytical procedures
    (h) Calibration and maintenance
    (i) Proficiency testing
    (j) Corrective action
    (k) Reports
    (l) Review
    (m) Safety
    (n) Previous audits

15.1.2 The laboratory shall retain all documentation pertaining to audits in accordance with relevant legal and agency requirements.

STANDARD 15.2 Once every two years, a second agency shall participate in the annual audit.

16. Safety

STANDARD 16.1 The laboratory shall have and follow a documented environmental health and safety program.

17. Subcontractor of Analytical Testing for which Validated Procedures Exist

STANDARD 17.1 A laboratory operating under the scope of these standards will require certification of compliance with these standards when a subcontractor performs forensic DNA analyses for the laboratory.

17.1.1 The laboratory will establish and use appropriate review procedures to verify the integrity of the data received from the subcontractor.

DNA Advisory Board Recommendations

Forensic Science Communications, 2(3), July 2000
<http://www.fbi.gov/hq/lab/fsc/backissu/july2000/dnastat.htm>

Statistical and Population Genetics Issues
Affecting the Evaluation of the Frequency of Occurrence of DNA Profiles
Calculated From Pertinent Population Database(s)

Introduction

When a comparison of DNA profiles derived from evidence and reference samples fails to exclude an individual(s) as a contributor(s) of the evidence sample, statistical assessment and/or probabilistic reasoning are used to evaluate the significance of the association. Proper statistical inference requires careful formulation of the question to be answered, including, in this instance, the requirements of the legal system. Inference must take into account how and what data were collected, which, in turn, determine how the data are analyzed and interpreted.

Previously, the DNA Advisory Board (DAB; June 21, 1996, New York, New York) endorsed the recommendations of the National Research Council's Report (1996; henceforth NRC II Report):

> The DAB congratulates Professor Crow and his NRC (National Research Council) Committee for their superb report on the statistical and population genetics issues surrounding forensic DNA profiling. We wholeheartedly endorse the findings of the report in these substantive matters.

As the NRC II Report (1996) describes, there are alternate methods for assessing the probative value of DNA evidence. Rarely is there only one statistical approach to interpret and explain the evidence. The choice of approach is affected by the philosophy and experience of the user, the legal system, the practicality of the approach, the question(s) posed, available data, and/or assumptions. For forensic applications, it is important that the statistical conclusions be conveyed meaningfully. Simplistic or less rigorous approaches are often sought. Frequently, calculations such as the random match probability and probability of exclusion convey to the trier of fact the probative value of the evidence in a straightforward fashion. Simplified approaches are appropriate, as long as the analysis is conservative or does not provide false inferences. Likelihood ratio (LR) approaches compare mutually exclusive hypotheses and can be quite useful for evaluating the data. However, some LR calculations and interpretations can be complicated, and their significance to the case may not be apparent to the practitioner and the trier of fact.

Bayesian inference, which accounts for information other than the DNA evidence, also could be applied. Bayesian approaches sometimes require knowledge of circumstances beyond the domain of the DNA scientist and have not been addressed in U.S. criminal courts for DNA analysis. The DAB believes it is for the courts to decide whether or not Bayesian statistics are solely the responsibility of the trier of fact. The DAB recognizes that these different approaches can be applied, as long as the question to be answered and the assumptions underlying the analyses are clearly conveyed to the trier of fact. We have been charged with clarifying issues that arise for the following special cases:

- Source attribution or identity;
- Cases where relatives may be involved;
- Interpretation of mixtures; and
- The significance of a match derived through a felon database search.

Source Attribution

According to *Webster's Third New International Dictionary* (Merriam-Webster 1961; henceforth *Webster's Third*), the term unique can convey several meanings, including the only one, unusual, and some [circumstance] that is the only one of its kind. Those who question the concept of assigning source attribution for DNA evidence often dwell on the former (e.g., Balding 1999). In their argument against source attribution, some critics say that it is difficult to establish, beyond doubt, that a DNA profile is carried by only one individual in the entire world. Within that context, their argument can be compelling, especially if the profile consists of a fairly small number of loci. Their conclusion, however, is problematic because source attribution should be evaluated within the context defined by the case, and the world's population rarely would be the appropriate context. Because source attribution can only be meaningful within the context of the instant case, *Webster's Third* definition of uniqueness comes closest to that required by the legal setting: a circumstance that is the only one of its kind.

By contrast to the world's population, examples of limiting, case-specific contexts are more common. Suppose, for example, the presence of a small group of individuals at the crime scene is stipulated. However, the identity of the single individual who sexually assaulted the victim is at issue. DNA evidence on the victim matches a DNA profile from only one of the named defendants. In this instance, it is simple to assign source because all other individuals are excluded. Now suppose the identities of some individuals at the crime scene are unknown, yet the DNA profile matches one of the defendants. Further suppose this defendant has no close relatives aside from parents. Source attribution is not challenging in this setting. While the answer depends on the number and kind of loci examined, in most instances the source can be assigned with a very high degree of scientific certainty. Suppose, instead, the defendant has multiple siblings, one of whom may have been the assailant and whose profiles are not available for some reason. Even then source can be assigned with a high degree of scientific certainty when a sufficient number of highly polymorphic loci are typed.

Inference regarding source attribution should always be based on the facts in the case. Arguments against source attribution based on premises having nothing to do with the case at hand should not be compelling.

Another set of questions arises when commentators fail to distinguish between source attribution and guilt. Some commentators, for example, set up the following scenario: Suppose inculpating DNA evidence appears to come from the defendant with high probability, yet all the non-DNA evidence is exculpatory (e.g., Balding 1999). In this instance, they say, source attribution is impossible. We do not agree. If, to a high degree of scientific certainty, the DNA evidence appears to come from the defendant, then the only reasonable conclusion is that the DNA did indeed come from the defendant. The trier of fact, however, has a different question to ponder: What value is source attribution if the preponderance of the evidence suggests the defendant cannot be the perpetrator? The trier of fact should seek other explanations for the data, some or all of which may exculpate the defendant.

As described above, the possible source of the DNA depends on the context of the case, and thus calculations for source attribution must reflect the appropriate reference population. If relatives are potential contributors, the calculations for source attribution must reflect that fact. If relatives are not potential contributors, the calculations for source attribution should be based on a defined population; that population could be as small as two unrelated individuals or an entire town, city, state, or country. The DNA analyst should take great care with evidence presentation, with two important facts in mind:

- Inference about source attribution is a probabilistic statement, and its degree of uncertainty is governed by the genetic information contained in the profile; and
- Inference about source attribution is distinct from inference regarding guilt.

One way to develop criteria to assess the question of source attribution is to let p_x equal the random match probability for a given evidentiary profile X. The random match probability is calculated using the NRC II Report (1996) Formulae 4.1b and 4.4a for general population scenarios or Formula 4.10 under the assumption that the contributor and the accused could only come from one subgroup. The value q is 0.01, except for estimates for isolated subgroups, where 0.03 is used. The rarity of the estimate is decreased by a factor of 10 (NRC II Report 1996).

$$\text{Then } (1 - p_x)^N$$

is the probability of not observing the particular profile in a population of N unrelated individuals. We require that this probability be greater than or equal to a $1 - a$ confidence level

$$(1 - p_x)^N = 1 - a$$

or

$$p_x \leq 1 - (1 - \alpha)^{1/N}$$

Specifying a confidence level of 0.95 (0.99; i.e., an a of 0.05 or 0.01) will enable determination of the random match probability threshold to assert with 95% (99%) confidence that the particular evidentiary profile is unique, given a population of N unrelated individuals.

In practice, p_x is calculated for each of the major population groups residing in the geographic area where the crime was committed (i.e., typically African American, Caucasian, and Hispanic). When there is no reason to believe a smaller population is relevant, the FBI, for example, has set N to 260 million, the approximate size of the U.S. population. For smaller, defined populations, N should be based on census values or other appropriate values determined by the facts of the case. The source attribution formula advocated here is simple and likely to be conservative, especially when N is larger than the size of the population that would inhabit a geographic area where a crime is committed.

Relatives

As described previously in the Source Attribution section, the possibility of a close relative (typically a brother) of the accused being in the pool of potential contributors of crime scene evidence should be considered in case-specific context. It is not appropriate to proffer that a close relative is a potential contributor of the evidence when there are no facts in evidence to suggest this instance is relevant. However, if a relative had access to a crime scene and there is reason to believe he/she could have been a contributor of the evidence, then the best action to take is to obtain a reference sample from the relative. After all, this scenario should be sufficient probable cause for obtaining a reference sample. Typing with the same battery of short tandem repeat (STR) loci will resolve the question of whether or not the relative carries the same DNA profile as the accused.

When a legitimate suspected relative cannot be typed, a probability statement can be provided. Given the accused DNA profile, the conditional probability that the relative has the same DNA profile can be calculated. Examples of methods for estimating the probability of the same DNA profile in a close relative are described in the NRC II Report (1996) and Li and Sacks (1954).

Mixtures

Mixtures, which for our purposes are DNA samples derived from two or more contributors, are sometimes encountered in forensic biological evidence. The presence of a mixture is evident typically by the presence of three or more peaks, bands, dots, and/or notable differences in intensities of the alleles for at least one locus in the profile. In some situations, elucidation of a contributor profile is straightforward. An example would be the analysis of DNA from an intimate swab revealing a mixture consistent with the composition of the perpetrator and the victim. When intensity differences are sufficient to identify the major contributor in the mixed profile, it can be treated statistically as a single source sample. At times, when alleles are not masked, a minor contributor to the mixed profile may be elucidated. Almost always in a mixture interpretation, certain possible genotypes can be excluded. It may be difficult to be confident regarding the number of contributors in some complex mixtures of more than two individuals; however, the number of contributors often can be inferred by reviewing the data at all loci in a profile.

Interpretation of genotypes is complicated when the contributions of the donors is approximately equal (i.e., when a major contributor cannot be determined unequivocally) or when alleles overlap. Also, stochastic fluctuation during polymerase chain reaction (PCR) arising from low quantity of DNA template can make typing of a minor contributor complicated. When the contributors of a DNA mixture profile cannot be distinguished, two calculations convey the probative value of the evidence.

The first calculation is the probability of exclusion (PE; Devlin 1992 and references therein). The PE provides an estimate of the portion of the population that has a genotype composed of at least one allele not observed in the mixed profile. Knowledge of the accused and/or victim profiles is not used (or needed) in the calculation. The calculation is particularly useful in complex mixtures, because it requires no assumptions about the identity or number of contributors to a mixture. The probabilities derived are valid and for all practical purposes are conservative. However, the PE does not make use of all of the available genetic data.

The LR provides the odds ratio of two competing hypotheses, given the evidence (Evett and Weir 1998). For example, consider a case of sexual assault for which the victim reported there were two assailants. A mixture of two profiles is observed in the "male fraction," and the victim is excluded as a contributor of the observed mixed profile. Two men are arrested, and their combined profiles are consistent with the mixture evidence. A likelihood calculation logically might compare the probability that the two accused individuals are the source of the DNA in the evidence versus two unknown (random men) are the source of the evidence. Various alternate hypotheses can be entertained as deemed appropriate, given the evidence. Calculation of a LR considers the identity and actual number of contributors to the observed DNA mixture. Certainly, LR makes better use of the available genetic data than does the PE.

Interpretation of DNA mixtures requires careful consideration of factors including, but not limited to, detectable alleles; variation of band, peak, or dot intensity; and the number of alleles. There are a number of references for guidance on calculating the PE or LR (Evett and Weir 1998; NRC II Report 1996; PopStats in CODIS). The DAB finds either one or both PE or LR calculations acceptable and strongly recommends that one or both calculations be carried out whenever feasible and a mixture is indicated.

Database Search

As felon DNA databases develop in all 50 states, searches for matches between evidentiary and database profiles will become increasingly common. Two questions arise when a match is derived from a database search: (1) What is the rarity of the DNA profile? and (2) What is the probability of finding such a DNA profile in the database searched? These two questions address different issues. That the different questions produce different answers should be obvious. The former question addresses the random match probability, which is often of particular interest to the fact finder. Here we address the latter question, which is especially important when a profile found in a database search matches the DNA profile of an evidence sample.

When the DNA profile from a crime scene sample matches a single profile in a felon DNA database, the NRC II Report (1996) recommended the evaluation of question number

2 be based on the size of the database. They argued for this evaluation because the probability of identifying a DNA profile by chance increases with the size of the database. Thus this chance event must be taken into account when evaluating value of the matching profile found by a database search. Those who argue against NRC II's recommended treatment (e.g., Balding and Donnelly 1996; Evett and Weir 1998; Evett et al. in press) say the NRC II Report's formulation is wrong and undervalues the evidence. In fact, they argue that the weight of the evidence (defined in terms of a likelihood ratio) for a DNA database search exceeds the weight provided by the same evidence in a "probable cause" case — a case in which other evidence first implicates the suspect and then DNA evidence is developed.

When other evidence first implicates the suspect, the DNA evidence can be evaluated using the probability p_x of randomly drawing the profile X from the (appropriate) population, which expresses the degree of surprise that the suspect and evidentiary profiles match. Equivalently, we can express it as a LR for two competing hypotheses, namely the likelihood of the evidence when the data come from the same individual (H_s) versus the likelihood of the evidence when the data come from two different individuals (H_d). The LR in this instance is

$$\text{Lik}(\text{Profile} \mid H_s)/\text{Lik}(\text{Profile} \mid H_d) = p_x/(p_x * p_x) = 1/p_x$$

For the DNA database search, the NRC II Report recommended the calculation (defined in terms of a LR) to be evaluated as $1/(N\, p_x)$, where N is the size of the database. While justification for this calculation is given in their report, it is often misunderstood. Stockmarr (1999) rederives this result in a way that should be more comprehensible. As a special case, assume only one profile in the database matches the evidentiary profile; we can consider that individual is a suspect. Now consider two competing hypotheses, namely the source is or is not in the database (H_{in} versus $H_{not\,in}$). These likelihoods are relevant because we wish to identify whether the suspect is likely to be the source of the sample (H_{in}) or if it is more likely he was identified merely by chance ($H_{not\,in}$). What is the LR for these hypotheses?

$$\text{Lik}(\text{Profile} \mid H_{in})/\text{Lik}(\text{Profile} \mid H_{not\,in}) = 1/\,(N\, p_x)$$

Stockmarr (1999) argues this formulation is the appropriate treatment of the data, as did the NRC II Report (1996) before him. Both recognize an intuitive counter example. Suppose we had a DNA database of the entire world's population (size N), except one individual (N − 1). A DNA profile from a crime scene is found to match one and only one profile in the database, and its frequency is 1/N. According to critics (e.g., Balding 1997), this example demonstrates the fallacious nature of the NRC II Report's proposed evaluation of the evidence for a database search, because the value of the evidence appears to be nil (the likelihood ratio is essentially one instead of a large number). Both Stockmarr (1999) and the NRC II Report recognize this interesting result; however, by treating the problem from a Bayesian perspective and invoking prior probabilities that are a function of the size of the database, they argue the example is irrelevant. In essence, the prior probability of H_{in} rises as N rises. This approach is coherent, from the statistical perspective, but it may not be particularly helpful for the legal system. Without the use of prior probabilities, it should be apparent that the treatment of the database search recommended by the NRC II Report can be conservative when the database is extremely large.

It is important to consider the treatment proposed by Balding and Donnelly (1996) and recently endorsed by Evett, Foreman, and Weir (in press). By their line of reasoning, the LR is no different whether other evidence first implicates the suspect or the suspect is identified by a database search. In fact, they argue the true weight of the evidence is actually larger for the latter, albeit the increase is small unless N is large. This argument has some intuitive appeal, especially in light of the example given above, and it is true that their LR is unaffected by sampling.

Both camps appear to present rigorous arguments to support their positions. Indeed the proper treatment superficially appears to rest in the details of arcane mathematics (Balding and Donnelly 1996; NRC II Report 1996; Stockmarr 1999). We believe, however, there is a way to see which of the two treatments is better for the legal setting without resorting to mathematical details. Consider the following scenario:

> A murder occurs, and the only evidence left at the crime scene is a cigarette butt. DNA analysis types five loci from the saliva on the cigarette butt. The probability of drawing the resulting profile X from a randomly selected individual is $p_x = 1/100,000$. A search of the DNA database, which contains $N = 100,000$ profiles, reveals a single match. No other evidence can be found to link the "suspect," whose profile matches, to the murder.

If we follow Balding and Donnelly (1996), the message for the investigators is that the evidence is 100,000 times more likely if the suspect is the source than if he is not. Alternatively, by the NRC II Report (1996) recommendations, the evidence is not compelling because the likelihood the profile, *a priori*, is/is not in the database is the same. In probabilistic terms, it is not surprising to find a matching profile in the database of size 100,000 when the profile probability is 1/100,000. Curiously, the mathematics underlying both approaches are correct, despite the apparently divergent answers. It is the foundations of the formulations that differ, and they differ substantially.

At present there are about 20,000 known, variable STR loci in the human genome. Of these, forensic scientists use a little more than a dozen, which is sufficient for most forensic analyses. Although not strictly accurate, let us think of the selection of STR loci as random and return to our case. The forensic scientists who worked on the cigarette butt could assay only five loci of the dozen they might type. Suppose they were to type five different loci and generate a new profile based on only these additional five loci? If our suspect were the true source of the sample, a match at those loci would be obtained; however, if he were not the source, a match would be highly unlikely. If the new (i.e., second) profile probability were again on the order of 1/100,000, someone else may have been selected. If our suspect is not the source, no one else in the database is, and yet we can easily imagine selecting a set of five loci (out of the thousands possible) to single out each individual therein. This seems like an unsatisfactory state in light of the LR espoused by Balding and Donnelly (1996).

Thus we are left with an interesting dilemma. Within a Bayesian context, the NRC II Report's LR and Balding and Donnelly's (1996) LR could be interpreted to yield a coherent evaluation of the evidence. Unfortunately, Bayesian logic has not been considered by the U.S. criminal legal system for DNA analysis. Clearly, what is required is a formulation of the LR that transparently conveys its import without resorting to Bayesian statistics. In this setting, the treatment of the database search recommended by the NRC II Report can be conservative, but only for the unlikely scenario of a very large N is it very conservative. Apparently the treatment of the database search recommended by Balding and Donnelly

(1996) is not conservative when the number of loci genotyped is small and remains so until the number of loci becomes large enough to essentially ensure uniqueness. To put it another way, without the Bayesian framework, the Balding and Donnelly (1996) formulation is easily misinterpreted in a fashion unfavorable to the suspect. Stockmarr's (1999) formulation, which is a more formal exposition of what originally appeared in the NRC II Report (1996), communicates value of a database search far better, and it is always conservative. Thus, we continue to endorse the recommendation of the NRC II Report for the evaluation of DNA evidence from a database search.

Conclusion

Statistical analyses are sometimes thought to yield automatic rules for making a decision either to accept or reject a hypothesis. This attitude is false in any setting and should be especially avoided for forensic inference. One rarely rests his/her decisions wholly on any single statistical test or analysis. To the evidence of the test should be added data accumulated from the scientist's own past work and that of others (Snedecor and Cochran 1967). Thus, in this light, statistical analyses should be thought of as useful guides for interpreting the weight of the DNA evidence.

References

Balding, D.J., Errors and misunderstandings in the second NRC report, Jurimetrics (1997) 37:603–607.

Balding, D.J., When can a DNA profile be regarded as unique?, Science & Justice (1999) 39:257–260.

Balding, D.J., and Donnelly, P. Evaluating DNA profile evidence when the suspect is identified through a database search, Journal of Forensic Sciences (1996) 41:603–607.

Devlin, B., Forensic inference from genetic markers, Statistical Methods in Medical Research (1992) 2:241–262.

Evett, I. W., Foreman, L. A. and Weir, B. S. Biometrics, in press.

Evett, I. W., and Weir, B. S. Interpreting DNA Evidence. Sinauer, Sunderland, Massachusetts, 1998.

Li, C.C. and Sacks, L., The derivation of joint distribution and correlation between relatives by the use of stochastic matrices, Biometrics (1954) 10:347–360.

Merriam-Webster, Incorporated. Webster's Third New International Dictionary.

Merriam-Webster, Incorporated, Springfield, Massachusetts, 1961.

National Research Council Committee on DNA Forensic Science. An Update: The Evaluation of Forensic DNA Evidence. National Academy Press, Washington, D.C., 1996.

Snedecor, G.W. and Cochran, W.G., Statistical Methods (6th ed.). Iowa State University Press, Ames, 1967, p. 28.

Stockmarr, A., Likelihood ratios for evaluating DNA evidence when the suspect is found through a database search, Biometrics (1999) 55:671–677.

NRC I and NRC II Recommendations

Recommendations of NRC I

Technical Considerations

- Any new DNA typing method (or substantial variation of an existing method) must be rigorously characterized in both research and forensic settings, to determine the circumstances under which it will yield reliable results.
- DNA analysis in forensic science should be governed by the highest standards of scientific rigor, including the following requirements:
  - Each DNA typing procedure must be completely described in a detailed, written laboratory protocol.
  - Each DNA typing procedure requires objective and quantitative measures for identifying the pattern of a sample.
  - Each DNA typing procedure requires a precise and objective matching rule for declaring whether two samples match.
  - Potential artifacts should be identified by empirical testing, and scientific controls should be designed to serve as internal checks to test for the occurrence of artifacts.
  - The limits of each DNA typing procedure should be understood, especially when the DNA sample is small, is a mixture of DNA from multiple sources, or if contaminated with interfering substances.
  - Empirical characterization of a DNA typing procedure must be published in appropriate scientific journals.
  - Before a new DNA typing procedure can be used, it must have not only a solid scientific foundation, but also a solid base of experience.
- The committee strongly recommends the establishment of a National Committee on Forensic DNA Typing (NCFDT) under the auspices of an appropriate government agency or agencies to provide expert advice primarily on scientific and technical issues concerning forensic DNA typing.
- Novel forms of variation in the genome that have the potential for increased power of discrimination between persons are being discovered. Furthermore, new ways to demonstrate variation in the genome are being developed. The current techniques are likely to be superseded by others that provide unambiguous individual identification and have such advantages as automatability and economy. Each new method should be evaluated by the NCFDT for use in the forensic setting, applying appropriate criteria to ensure that society derives maximal benefit from DNA typing technology.

Statistical Basis for Interpretation

- As a basis for the interpretation of the statistical significance of DNA typing results, the committee recommends that blood samples be obtained from 100 randomly selected persons in each of 15-20 relatively homogeneous populations; that the DNA in lymphocytes from these blood samples be used to determine the frequencies of alleles currently tested in forensic applications; and that the lymphocytes be "immortalized" and preserved as a reference standard for determination of allele frequencies in tests applied in different laboratories or developed in the future. The collection of samples and their study should be overseen by a National Committee on Forensic DNA Typing.
- The ceiling principle should be used in applying the multiplication rule for estimating the frequency of particular DNA profile. For each allele in a person's DNA pattern, the highest allele frequency found in any of the 15-20 population or 5% (whichever is larger) should be used.
- In the interval (which should be short) while the reference blood samples are being collected, the significance of the findings of multilocus DNA typing should be presented in two ways: (1) If no match is found with any sample in a total databank of N persons (as will usually be the case), that should be stated, thus indicating the rate of a random match. (2) In applying the multiplication rule, the 95% upper confidence limit of the frequency of each allele should be calculated for separate U.S. "racial" groups and the highest of these values or 10% (whichever is the larger) should be used. Data on at least three major "races" (e.g., Caucasians, Blacks, Hispanics, Asians, and Native Americans) should be analyzed.
- Any population databank used to support DNA typing should be openly available for scientific inspection by parties to a legal case and by the scientific community.
- Laboratory error rates should be measured with appropriate proficiency tests and should play a role in the interpretation of results of forensic DNA typing.

Standards

Although standardization of forensic practice is difficult because of the nature of the samples, DNA typing is such a powerful and complex technology that some degree of standardization is necessary to ensure high standards

- Each forensic science laboratory engaged in DNA typing must have a formal, detailed quality-assurance and quality-control program to monitor work, on both an individual and a laboratory-wide basis.
- The technical Working Group on DNA Analysis and Methods (TWGDAM) guidelines for a quality-assurance program for DNA RFLP analysis are an excellent starting point for a quality-assurance program, which should be supplemented by the additional technical recommendations of this committee.
- The TWGDAM group should continue to function, playing a role complementary to that of the National Committee on Forensic DNA Typing (NCFDT). To increase its effectiveness, TWGDAM should include additional technical experts from outside the forensic community who are not closely tied to any forensic laboratory.
- Quality-assurance programs in individual laboratories alone are insufficient to ensure high standards. External mechanisms are needed, to ensure adherence to the

practices of quality assurance. Potential mechanisms included individual certification, laboratory accreditation, and state or federal regulation.

- One of the best guarantees of high quality is the presence of an active professional-organization committee that is able to enforce standards. Although professional societies in forensic science have historically not played an active role, the American Society of Crime Laboratory Directors (ASCLD) and the American Society of Crime Laboratory Director-Laboratory Accreditation Board (ASCLD-LAB) recently have shown substantial interest in enforcing quality by expanding the ASCLD-LAB accreditation program to include mandatory proficiency testing. ASCLD-LAB must demonstrate that it will actively discharge this role.

- Because private professional organizations lack the regulatory authority to require accreditation, further means are needed to ensure compliance with appropriate standards.

- Courts should require that laboratories providing DNA typing evidence have proper accreditation for each DNA typing method used. Any laboratory that is not formally accredited and that provides evidence to the courts — e.g., a nonforensic laboratory repeating the analysis of a forensic laboratory — should be expected to demonstrate that it is operating at the same level of standards as accredited laboratories.

- Establishing mandatory accreditation should be a responsibility of the Department of Health and Human Services (DHHS), in consultation with the Department of Justice (DOJ). DHHS is the appropriate agency, because it has extensive experience in the regulation of clinical laboratories through programs under the Clinical Laboratory Improvement Act and has extensive expertise in molecular genetics through the National Institutes of Health. DOJ must be involved, because the task is important for law enforcement.

- The National Institute of Justice (NIJ) does not appear to receive adequate funds to support proper education, training, and research in the field of forensic DNA typing. The level of funding should be re-evaluated and increased appropriately.

Databanks and Privacy of Information

- In the future, if pilot studies confirm its value, a national DNA profile databank should be created that contains information on felons convicted of particular violent crimes. Among crimes with high rates of recidivism, the case is strongest for rape, because perpetrators typically leave biological evidence (semen) that could allow them to be identified. Rape is the crime for which the databank will be of primary use. The case is somewhat weaker for violent offenders who are most likely to commit homicide as recidivist offense, because killers leave biological evidence only in a minority of cases.

- The databank should also contain DNA profiles of unidentified persons made from biological samples found at crime scenes. These would be samples known to be of human origin, but not matched with any known persons.

- Databanks containing DNA profiles of members of the general population (as exist for ordinary fingerprints for identification purpose) are not appropriate, for reasons of both privacy and economics.

- DNA profile databanks should be accessible only to legal authorized persons and should be stored in a secure information resource.

- Legal policy concerning access and use of both DNA samples and DNA databank information should be established before widespread proliferation of samples and information repositories. Interim protection and sanctions against misuse an abuse of information derived from DNA typing should be established immediately. Policies should explicitly define authorized uses and should provide for criminal penalties for abuses.

- Although the committee endorses the concept of a limited national DNA profile databank, it doubts that existing RFLP-based technology provides an appropriate wise long-term foundation for such a databank. We expect current methods to be replaced soon with techniques that are simpler, easier to automate, and less expensive — but incompatible with existing DNA profiles. Accordingly, the committee does not recommend establishing a comprehensive DNA profile databank yet.

- For the short term, we recommend the establishment of pilot projects that involve prototype databanks based on RFLP technology and consisting primarily of problems of violent sex offenders. Such pilot projects could be worthwhile for identifying profiles and issues in the creation of databanks. However, in the intermediate term more efficient methods will replace the current one, and the forensic community should not allow itself to become locked into an outdated method.

- State and federal laboratories, which have a long tradition and much experience in the management of other types of basic evidence, should be given primary responsibility, authority, and additional resources to handle forensic DNA testing and all the associated sample-handling and data-handling requirements.

- Private-sector firms should not be discouraged from continuing to prepare and analyze DNA samples for specific cases or for databank samples, but they must be held accountable for misuse and abuse to the same extent as government-funded laboratories and government authorities.

DNA Information in the Legal System

- Courts should take judicial notice of three scientific underpinnings of DNA typing:
  - The study of DNA polymorphism can, in principle, provide a reliable method for comparing samples.
  - Each person's DNA is unique (except that of identical twins), although the actual discriminatory power of any particular DNA test will depend on the sites of DNA variation examined.
  - The current laboratory procedure for detecting DNA variation (specifically, single-locus probes analyzed on Southern blots without evidence of band shifting) is fundamentally sound, although the validity of any particular implementation of the basic procedure will depend on proper characterization of the reproducibility of the system (e.g., measurement variation) and inclusion of all necessary scientific controls.

- The adequacy of the method used to acquire and analyze samples in a given case bears on the admissibility of the evidence and should, unless stipulated by opposing parties, be adjudicated case by case. In this adjudication, the accreditation and certification status of the laboratory performing the analysis should be taken into account.

- Because of the potential power of DNA evidence, authorities should make funds available to pay for expert witnesses, and the appropriate parties must be informed of the use of DNA evidence as soon as possible.
- DNA samples (and evidence likely to contain DNA) should be preserved whenever that is possible.
- All data and laboratory records generated by analysis of DNA samples should be made freely available to all parties. Such access is essential for evaluating the analysis.
- Protective orders should be used only to protect the privacy of individuals.

DNA Typing and Society

- In the forensic context as in the medical setting, DNA information is personal, and a person's privacy and need for confidentiality should be respected. The release of DNA information on a criminal population without the subjects' permission for purposes other than law enforcement should be considered a misuse of the information, and legal sanctions should be established to deter the unauthorized dissemination or procurement of DNA information that was obtained for forensic purposes.
- Prosecutors and defense counsel should not oversell DNA evidence. Presentations that suggest to a judge or jury that DNA typing is infallible are rarely justified and should be avoided.
- Mechanisms should be established to ensure accountability of laboratories and personnel involved in DNA typing and to make appropriate public scrutiny possible.
- Organizations that conduct accreditation or regulation of DNA technology for forensic purposes should not be subject to the influence of private companies, public laboratories or other organizations actually engaged in laboratory work.
- Private laboratories used for testing should not be permitted to withhold information from defendants on the ground that trade secrets are involved.
- The same standards and peer-review processes used to evaluate advances in biomedical science and technology should be used to evaluate forensic DNA methods and techniques.
- Efforts at international cooperation should be furthered, in order to ensure uniform international standards and the fullest possible exchange of scientific knowledge and technical expertise.

Recommendations of NRC II

Admissibility of DNA Evidence (Chapter 2)

DNA analysis is one of the greatest technical achievements for criminal investigation since the discovery of fingerprints. Methods of DNA profiling are firmly grounded in molecular technology. When profiling is done with appropriate care, the results are highly reproducible. In particular, the methods are almost certain to exclude an innocent suspect. One of the most widely used techniques involves VNTRs. These loci are extremely variable, but individual alleles cannot be distinguished, because of intrinsic measurement variability, and the analysis requires statistical procedures. The laboratory procedure involves radio-activity and requires a month or more for full analysis. PCR-based methods are prompt, require only a small amount of material, and can yield unambiguous identification of individual alleles.

The state of the profiling technology and the methods for estimating frequencies and related statistics have progressed to the point where the admissibility of properly collected and analyzed DNA data should not be in doubt. We expect continued development of new and better methods and hope for their prompt validation, so that they can quickly be brought into use.

Laboratory Errors

The occurrence of errors can be minimized by scrupulous care in evidence-collecting, sample-handling, laboratory procedures, and case review. Detailed guidelines for QC and QA (quality control and quality assurance), which are updated regularly, are produced by several organizations, including TWGDAM. ASCLD-LAB is established as an accrediting agency. The 1992 NRC report recommended that a National Committee on Forensic DNA Typing (NCFDT) be formed to oversee the setting of DNA-analysis standards. The DNA Identification Act of 1994 gives this responsibility to a DNA Advisory Board appointed by the FBI. We recognize the need for guidelines and standards, and for accreditation by appropriate organizations.

Recommendation 3.1: Laboratories should adhere to high quality standards (such as those defined by TWGDAM and the DNA Advisory Board) and make every effort to be accredited for DNA work (by such organizations as ASCLD-LAB).

Proficiency Tests

Regular proficiency tests, both within the laboratory and by external examiners, are one of the best ways of assuring high standards. To the extent that it is feasible, some of the tests should be blind.

Recommendation 3.2: Laboratories should participate regularly in proficiency tests, and the results should be available for court proceedings.

Duplicate Tests

We recognize that no amount of care and proficiency testing can eliminate the possibility of error. However, duplicate tests, performed as independently as possible, can reduce the risk of error enormously. The best protection that an innocent suspect has against an error that could lead to a false conviction is the opportunity for an independent retest.

Recommendation 3.3: Whenever feasible, forensic samples should be divided into two or more parts at the earliest practicable stage and the unused parts retained to permit additional tests. The used and saved portions should be stored and handled separately. Any additional tests should be performed independently of the first by personnel not involved in the first test and preferably in a different laboratory.

Population Genetics

Sufficient data now exist for various groups and subgroups within the United States that analysts should present the best estimates for profile frequencies. For VNTRs, using the 2p rule for single bands and HW for double bands is generally conservative for an individual locus. For multiple loci, departures from linkage equilibrium are not great enough to cause errors comparable to those from uncertainty of allele frequencies estimated from databases.

With appropriate consideration of the data, the principles in this report can be applied to PCR-based tests. For those in which exact genotypes can be determined, the 2p rule should not be used. A conservative estimate is given by using the HW relation for heterozygotes and a conservative value of $\bar{\theta}$ in Equation 4.4a for homozygotes.

Recommendation 4.1: In general, the calculation of a profile frequency should be made with the product rule. If the race of the person who left the evidence-sample DNA is known, the database for the person's race should be used; if the race is not known, calculations for all racial groups to which possible suspects belong should be made. For systems such as VNTRs, in which a heterozygous locus can be mistaken for a homozygous one, if an upper bound on the genotypic frequency at an apparently homozygous locus (single band) is desired, then twice the allele (bin) frequency, 2p, should be used instead of p^2. For systems in which exact genotypes can be determined, $p^2 + p(1 - p)\theta$ should be used for the frequency at such a locus instead of p^2. A conservative value of θ for the U.S. population is 0.01; for some small, isolated a populations, a value of 0.03 may be more appropriate. For both kinds of systems, $2p_ip_j$ should be used for heterozygotes.

A more conservative value of $\theta = 0.03$ might be chosen for PCR-based systems in view of the greater uncertainty of calculations for such systems because of less extensive and less varied population data than for VNTRs.

Evidence DNA and Suspect from the Same Subgroup

Sometimes there is evidence that the suspect and other possible sources of the sample belong to the same subgroup. That can happen, e.g., if they are all members of a an isolated village. In this case, a modification of the procedure is desirable.

Recommendation 4.2: If the particular subpopulation from which the evidence sample came is known, the allele frequencies for the specific subgroup should be used as described in Recommendation 4.1. If allele frequencies for the subgroup are not available, although data for the full population are, then the calculations should use the population structure equations 4.10 for each locus, and the resulting values should then be multiplied.

Insufficient Data

For some groups — and several American Indian and Inuit tribes are in this category — there are insufficient data to estimate frequencies reliably, and even the overall average might be unreliable. In this case, data from other, related groups provide the best information. The groups chosen should be the most closely related for which adequate databases exist. These might be chosen because of geographical proximity, or a physical anthropologist might be consulted. There should be a limit on the number of such subgroups analyzed to prevent inclusion of more remote groups less relevant to the case.

Recommendation 4.3: If the person who contributed the evidence sample is from a group or tribe for which no adequate database exists, data from several other groups or tribes thought to be closely related to it should be used. The profile frequency should be calculated as described in Recommendation 4.1 for each group or tribe.

Dealing with Relatives

In some instances, there is evidence that one or more relatives of the suspect are possible perpetrators.

Recommendation 4.4: If the possible contributors of the evidence sample include relatives of the suspect, DNA profiles of those relatives should be obtained. If these profiles cannot be obtained, the probability of finding the evidence profile in those relatives should be calculated with Formula 4.8 or 4.9.

Statistical Issues (Chapter 5)

Confidence limits for profile probabilities, based on allele frequencies and the size of the database, can be calculated by methods explained in this report. We recognize, however, that confidence limits address only part of the uncertainty. For a more realistic estimate, we examined empirical data from the comparison of different subpopulations and of subpopulations within the whole. The empirical studies show that the differences between the frequencies of the individual profiles estimated by the product rule from different adequate subpopulation databases (at least several hundred persons) are within a factor of about 10 of each other, and that provides a guide to the uncertainty of the determination for a single profile. For very small estimated profile frequencies, the uncertainty can be greater, both because of the greater relative uncertainty of individually small probabilities and because more loci are likely to be multiplied. But with very small probabilities, even a larger relative error is not likely to change the conclusion.

Database Searches

If the suspect is identified through a DNA database search, the interpretation of the match probability and likelihood ratio given in Chapter 4 should be modified.

Recommendation 5.1: When the suspect is found by a search of DNA databases, the random-match probability should be multiplied by N, the number of persons in the database.

If one wishes to describe the impact of the DNA evidence under the hypothesis that the source of the evidence sample is someone in the database, then the likelihood ratio should be divided by N. As databases become more extensive, another problem may arise. If the database searched includes a large proportion of the population, the analysis must take that into account.

In the extreme case, a search of the whole population should, of course, provide a definitive answer.

Uniqueness

With an increasing number of loci available for forensic analysis, we are approaching the time when each person's profile is unique (except for identical twins and possibly other close relatives). Suppose that, in a population of N unrelated persons, a given DNA profile has probability P. The probability (before a suspect has been profiled) that the particular profile observed in the evidence sample is not unique is at most NP.

A lower bound on the probability that every person is unique depends on the population size, the number of loci, and the heterozygosity of the individual loci. Neglecting population structure and close relatives, 10 loci with a geometric mean heterozygosity of 95% give a probability greater than about 0.999 that no two unrelated persons in the world have the same profile. Once it is decided what level of probability constitutes uniqueness, appropriate calculations can readily be made.

We expect that the calculation in the first paragraph will be the one more often employed.

Matching and Binning

VNTR data are essentially continuous, and, in principle, a continuous model should be used to analyze them. The methods generally used, however, involve taking measurement uncertainty into account by determining a match window. Two procedures for determining match probabilities are the floating-bin and the fixed-bin methods. The floating-bin method is statistically preferable but requires access to a computerized database. The fixed-bin method is more widely used and understood, and the necessary data tables are widely and readily available. When our fixed-bin recommendation is followed, the two methods lead to very similar results. Both methods are acceptable.

Recommendation 5.2: If floating bins are used to calculate the random-match probabilities, each bin should coincide with the corresponding match window. If fixed bins are employed, then the fixed bin that has the largest frequency among those overlapped by the match window should be used.

Ceiling Principles

The abundance of data in different ethnic groups within the major races and the genetically and statistically sound methods recommended in this report imply that both the ceiling principle and the interim ceiling principle are unnecessary.

Further Research

The rapid rate of discovery of new markers in connection with human gene-mapping should lead to many new markers that are highly polymorphic, mutable, and selectively neutral, but which, unlike VNTRs, can be amplified by PCR and for which individual alleles can usually be distinguished unambiguously with none of the statistical problems associated with matching and binning. Furthermore, radioactive probes need not be used with many other markers, so identification can be prompt and problems associated with using radioactive materials can be avoided. It should soon be possible to have systems so powerful that no statistical and population analyses will be needed, and (except possibly for close relatives) each person in a population can be uniquely identified.

Recommendation 5.3: Research into the identification and validation of more and better marker systems for forensic analysis should continue with a view to making each profile unique.

Legal Issues

In assimilating scientific developments, the legal system necessarily lags behind the scientific world. Before making use of evidence derived from scientific advances, courts must scrutinize the proposed testimony to determine its suitability for use at trial, and controversy within the scientific community often is regarded as grounds for the exclusion of the scientific evidence. Although some controversies that have come to closure in the scientific literature continue to limit the presentation of DNA evidence in some jurisdictions, courts are making more use of the ongoing research into the population genetics of DNA profiles. We hope that our review of the research will contribute to this process.

Our conclusions and recommendations for reducing the risk of laboratory error, for applying human population genetics to DNA profiles, and for handling uncertainties in estimates of profile frequencies and match probabilities might affect the application of the rules for the discovery and admission of evidence in court. Many suggestions can be offered to make our recommendations most effective: for example, that every jurisdiction should make it possible for all defendants to have broad discovery and independent experts; that accreditation, proficiency testing, and the opportunity for independent testing (whenever feasible) should be prerequisites to the admission of laboratory findings; that in resolving disputes over the adequacy or interpretation of DNA tests, the power of the court to appoint its own experts should be exercised more frequently; and that experts should not be barred from presenting any scientifically acceptable estimate of a random-match probability. We have chosen, however, to make no formal recommendations on such matters of legal policy; we do, however, make a recommendation concerning scientific evidence — namely, the need for behavioral research that will assist legal decision makers in developing standards for communicating about DNA in the courtroom.

Recommendation 6.1: Behavioral research should be carried out to identify any conditions that might cause a trier of fact to misinterpret evidence on DNA profiling and to assess how well various ways of presenting expert testimony on DNA can reduce such misunderstandings.

The full texts of both NRC reports are available from:
National Academy Press, Washington, D.C., 1-800-624-6242.

DNA Statutes

Offender database; Admissibility; Statute of Limitations; Admissibility, Post-conviction
Most of this information kindly provided by the American Prosecutors Research Institute

Additional information taken from *Admissibility of DNA Evidence*, Christopher Reinhart
<http://www.cga.state.ct.us/2001/rpt/olr/htm/2001-r-0047.htm>

ALABAMA
§ 12-15-102 — Fingerprints, photographs, blood or other samples; Taken from a child
§ 15-20-21 — Convicted sex offenders; Law enforcement notification of residence following incarceration
§ 36-18-20 through 36-18-39 — DNA Database
§ 36-18-30 — Admits DNA evidence if it meets general requirements for use of expert testimony as set by the U.S. Supreme Court
§ 9.25.051 — Admits DNA evidence if it is scientifically valid

ALASKA
§ 09.25.051 — Admissibility of DNA profiles; Civil proceeding
§11.56.760 — Violating an order to submit to DNA testing
§ 12.45.035 — Admissibility of DNA profiles; Criminal proceeding; Only scientific validity (and not general acceptance) is required
§22.20.200 — DNA evidence information; Judicial council to give periodic info. about DNA to judge
§44.41.035 — DNA identification system

ARIZONA
§ 31-281 — Deoxyribonucleic acid identification; Sexual offenses; Applicable to sex offenders, parolees, and probationers
§41-2418 — Arizona deoxyribonucleic acid identification system

ARKANSAS
§ 9-27-342 — Proceedings concerning illegitimate juveniles
§ 12-12-1101 through § 12-12-1120
§ 19-6-447 — Establishing the DNA Detection Fund

CALIFORNIA
Cal Gov Code § 76104.5 — Counties may establish funds for financing DNA identity programs and equipment

Cal Pen Code § 290.3 — Establishes a fee schedule for repeat sexual offenders; fees are paid into the DNA Testing Fund

Cal Penal Code § 290.7 — Provision of blood & saliva samples to county in which inmate is to be released

Cal Penal Code § 295, § 295.1, §§ 296 through 296.2, §§ 298 through 298.1, § 299, §§ 299.5 through 299.7, § 300 — DNA and Forensic Identification Data Base and Data Bank Act of 1998

Cal Penal Code § 11170(7)(C) — Fees paid as a result of habitual child sexual assaults go to the DNA Testing Fund

COLORADO
None

CONNECTICUT
§ 54-86K — Admissibility of DNA analysis

§ 54-102g through 54-102l, § 54-102r — DNA analysis and registration of sexual offenders

DELAWARE
11 § 3515 — Admissibility of DNA profiles

16 §§ 1220 through 1222, § 1224 — Informed Consent and Confidentiality

29 § 4713 — DNA analysis and data bank

DISTRICT OF COLUMBIA
None

FLORIDA
§ 760.40 — Genetic testing; informed consent; confidentiality

§ 943.325 — Blood specimen testing for DNA analysis

§ 947.1405 — Conditional release program; Required to supply two blood samples for data bank

§ 948.03 (5)(a)(8) — Court must require donation of blood sample to databank as condition of probation where crime committed after October 1, 1995

GEORGIA
§§ 24-4-60 through 24-4-65 — DNA analysis upon conviction of certain sexual offenses

HAWAII
§ 706-603 — Mental and medical examination; deoxyribonucleic acid collection

IDAHO
§§ 19-5501 through 19-5509, §§ 19-5511 through 19-5516 — Idaho DNA Database Act of 1996

ILLINOIS
§ 30 ILCS 105/5.457 — State Offender DNA Identification System Fund

§ 705 ILCS 405/5-601 — Trial; Court may postpone trial for 120 days waiting for DNA tests if State diligently tried to obtain the results in time for trial

§725 ILCS 5/103-5 — Speedy Trial (see above)

§ 725 ILCS 5/116-3 — Motion for postconviction fingerprint or forensic testing not available at trial regarding actual innocence

§ 730 ILCS 5/5-4-3 — Persons convicted of, or found delinquent for, sexual offenses or institutionalized as sexually dangerous; Blood specimens; Genetic marker groups

Rule

Criminal Proceedings in Trial Court Rule 413 — Disclosure to Prosecution; Medical and scientific reports

INDIANA

§§ 10-1-9-1 through 10-1-9-22 — Indiana DNA Data Base

§ 16-18-2-99 — DNA test; Hospital regulation

§ 16-37-2-10 — DNA test defined; Paternity cases

§§20-12-34.5-1 through 20-12-34.5-6 — Databank for DNA population statistics

§ 35-37-4-13 — Forensic DNA analysis — admissibility as evidence

IOWA

§ 13.10 — Physical criminal evidence; DNA profiling; AG must promulgate rules regarding the collection of DNA samples

§ 901.2 — Presentence investigation; Once a verdict or plea of guilty is entered, the court may order the person to give DNA samples, regardless of what rules the AG may have promulgated under § 13.10

§ 906.4 — Standards for release on parole or work release; Once a person is deemed eligible for parole, the parole board may order the person to give DNA samples, regardless of what rules the AG may have promulgated under § 13.10

KANSAS

§ 21-2511 — Collection of specimens on fingerprints, blood, and saliva from certain persons; Kansas bureau of investigation, powers and duties

§ 22-4907 — Information required in registration; DNA profile required for sex offender registration

KENTUCKY

§ 17.170 — Blood sampling for DNA law enforcement identification purposes; Cost; Penalty for tampering with blood samples

§ 17.175 — Centralized database for DNA identification records; Penalty for unlawful use

LOUISIANA

15 § 441.1 — Relevant evidence; DNA, blood, and saliva testing relevant to prove identity in a criminal setting

15 §§ 601 through 605, §§ 607 through 612, § 614, §§ 617 through 619 — DNA Detection of Sexual and Violent Offenders

MAINE

7 § 232 — Definition; Genetic engineering; Commission on Biotechnology

25 §§ 1571 through 1578 — DNA Data Base and Data Bank Act

MARYLAND
Md. Courts and Judicial Proceedings § 10-915 — Admissibility of DNA profiles
Art. 88B, § 12A — DNA database system and repository

MASSACHUSETTS
Chap. 22E, § 1 through 15 — State DNA Database

MICHIGAN
MSA § 4.475(7) — Sex offenders registration act
MSA §§ 4.484(1) through 4.484(4), §§ 4.484(6)
MSA §§ 25.399(57a), 25.399(255a) — Discharge from wardship and placement in the community of neglected children; requirement of submission of DNA sample prior to placement
MSA § 27.3178(598.18k) — DNA identification profiling; providing samples for chemical testing; Convicted juveniles
MSA § 28.788(13) — Collection of DNA sample from person convicted of criminal sexual conduct
MSA § 28.2303(5) — Samples for chemical testing; DNA testing of incarcerated convicts, parolees, and probationers

MINNESOTA
§ 299C.11 — Identification data furnished to bureau
§ 299.155 — Standardized evidence collection; DNA analysis data and records; Protocols for collection and database storage
§ 590.01(1a) — Motion for postconviction fingerprint or forensic testing not available at trial
§ 609.3461 — DNA analysis of sex offenders required
§ 609A.03 — Petition to expunge criminal records
§ 628.26 — Limitations
§ 634.26 — Statistical evidence; Probability of random match at tested markers admissible in criminal or civil trial

MISSISSIPPI
§ 45-33-15 — DNA identification system; Convicted sex offender to provide blood sample for purposes of DNA identification analysis

MISSOURI
§ 650.050 — DNA profiling system to be established in department of public safety, purpose
§ 650.052 — Consultation with crime laboratories; DNA system, powers and duties; Expert testimony
§ 650.055 — Felony conviction for violent or sex offenses to have biological samples collected, when — use of sample — highway patrol and department of corrections, duty
§ 650.057 — Local law enforcement agencies not to operate system, exceptions — rules authorized — DNA evidence in court use by local law enforcers

MONTANA
§§ 44-6-101 through 44-6-103, §§ 44-6-106 through 44-6-108, § 44-6-110 — DNA Index

§ 46-18-202 — Judge may require defendant to submit DNA sample to DNA Index as an additional condition of sentencing

NEBRASKA
§§ 29-4101 through 29-4115 — DNA Detection of Sexual and Violent Offenders Act

NEVADA
§ 176.0911, § 176.0913, § 176.0915, § 176.0917 — Genetic Marker Testing

NEW HAMPSHIRE
§§ 632-A:20 through 632-A:24 — DNA Testing of Sexual Offenders

NEW JERSEY
§§ 53:1-20.17 through 53:1-20.30 — DNA Database and Databank Act of 1994

NEW MEXICO
§ 29-16-1, §§ 29-16-3 through 29-16-13 — DNA Identification

NEW YORK
Civil Rights § 79-l — Confidentiality of records of genetic tests; Including DNA profile for identity purposes

Criminal Procedure Law § 440.30 (1-a) (1994) — Moving party can request DNA testing in connection with a motion to vacate judgment (postconviction)

Executive Law, Article 49-B § 995, §§ 995-a through 995-f — Commission on forensic science and establishment of DNA identification index

NORTH CAROLINA
§ 15A-266, §§ 15A-266.1 through 15A-266.12 — DNA Database and Databank Act of 1993

NORTH DAKOTA
§§ 31-13-01 through 31-13-09 — DNA Analysis

OHIO
§ 109.573 — DNA laboratory and database; Unidentified person database; Relatives of missing person database

§ 109.99 — Penalties for improper use of database under § 109.573

§ 149.43 — Availability of public records; DNA records held in the database are excluded from the definition of public record

§ 313.08 — Coroner's duties where decedent is not identified; Required to forward DNA sample and fingerprints of deceased to bureau of criminal identification and investigation

§ 2151.315 — DNA testing of adjudicated delinquents

§ 2901.07 — DNA testing of offenders sentenced to incarceration

§ 2929.13(H) — Court must require donation of DNA sample for database as part of sentence for person convicted of violent sexual assault

OKLAHOMA
20 § 1313.2 — Fee; Any person that the DNA Offender Database statute requires to donate a DNA sample once convicted must also pay a $150 Laboratory Analysis Fee

22 § 751.1 — DNA profile — use as evidence — notification of defendant

22 § 991a — Sentencing powers of court; Order to participate in alcohol and drug substance abuse evaluation program; Limitations on availability of suspended sentence; Consideration of victim impact statement; Probation; Administration of restitution and service programs; County community service sentencing programs; Definitions; Submission to DNA testing

57 §§ 584 — Sex Offender Registration Act; Registration may include DNA sample

74 §§ 150.2, 150.27, 150.27a, 150.28 — State Bureau of Investigation

OREGON

§ 137.076 — Blood sample of certain convicted defendants required; Application

§ 181.085 — Authority over blood samples and analyses; Disclosure; Inspection by subject person; Destruction of sample

§ 419C.473 — Authority to order blood testing of juvenile offenders

PENNSYLVANIA

35 Penn. Stat. §§ 7651.101 through 7651.103, §§ 7651.301 through 7651.312, §§ 7651.501 through 7651.506, §§ 7651.1101 through 7651.1102 — DNA Detection of Sexual and Violent Offenders Act

RHODE ISLAND

§ 12-1.5-1 through 12-1.5-18 — DNA Detection of Sexual and Violent Offenders

SOUTH CAROLINA

§§ 23-3-600 through 23-3-700 — State DNA Identification Record Database Act

SOUTH DAKOTA

None

TENNESSEE

§ 24-7-117 — DNA analysis; Admissibility in evidence

§ 38-6-113 — DNA analysis; Procedures for collection and preservation of human biological specimens

§ 40-28-407 — Transfer of persons convicted of sexual offenses; Biological specimens

§ 40-28-409 — Sex offender treatment program

§ 40-35-321 — Collection of biological specimens for DNA analysis; Persons convicted of certain offenses; Condition of release from imprisonment

TEXAS

Tex. Gov't Code §§ 411.141 through 411.154 — DNA Database System

Tex. Code of Crim. Proc. art. 42.12 § 11(a)(22) — Court may require defendant to submit a blood sample to the database as a term of community supervision

UTAH

§ 53-10-406 — Blood analysis; Bureau responsibilities

VERMONT

20 V.S.A. §§ 1931 through 1945 — State DNA Database and State Data Bank

VIRGINIA
§ 9-196.1 — Division of Forensic Science
§ 16.1-299.1 — Blood sample required for DNA analysis upon conviction or adjudication of felony; Juvenile offender
§ 19.2-270.5 — DNA profile admissible in criminal proceeding
§ 19.2-310.2, § 19.2-310.7 — DNA Analysis and Data Bank
§ 19.2-387 — Exchange to operate as a division of Department of State Police; Authority of Superintendent of State Police
§ 32.1-286 — Exhumations

WASHINGTON
§ 43.43.752, § 43.43.754, § 43.43.756, § 43.43.758, and § 43.43.759 — DNA identification system

WEST VIRGINIA
§§ 15-2B-1 through 15-2B-13 — DNA Data

WISCONSIN
§ 165.76 — Submission of human biological specimen
§ 973.046 — Deoxyribonucleic acid analysis surcharge

WYOMING
§ 7-19-305 — Sex offender registration; Duties of registering entities; Notice to persons required to register
§§ 7-19-401 through 7-19-406 — DNA Identification Record System

FEDERAL
42 U.S.C. §§ 14131 through 14133 — DNA Identification

CANADA
§§ 487.04 through 487.09, § 487.091 — Forensic DNA Analysis

Summary of STR and mtDNA Decisions in United States Courts

Through July 2001
Some of this was information kindly provided by the American Prosecutors Research Institute

Additional information was obtained from the Denver District Attorney's Office Web site
<http://denverda.org/legalResource/legalresource.htm>

STR Decisions

Court	Accepted	Denied	Total
Federal Supreme Courts	0	0	0
Federal Appellate Courts	0	0	0
Federal Trial Courts	0	0	0
State Courts of Last Resort	1	0	1
State Appellate Courts	2	0	2
State Trial Courts	24	3[1]	27
Total STR Decisions	**31**	**3**	**34[2]**

mtDNA Decisions

Court	Accepted	Denied	Total
Federal Supreme Courts	0	0	0
Federal Appellate Courts	0	0	0
Federal Trial Courts	0	0	0
State Courts of Last Resort	0	0	0
State Appellate Courts	4	0	4
State Trial Courts	4	1	5
Total STR Decisions	**8**	**1**	**9**

[1] One of these three decisions, *Colorado v. Shreck,* was subsequently overturned by the Colorado Supreme Court. This event is represented as the one case listed under State Courts of Last Resort.
[2] Shreck is counted only once in the total.

STR and mtDNA Decisions in United States Courts

Through July 2001
Some of this was information kindly provided by the American Prosecutors
Research Institute

Additional information was obtained from the Denver District Attorney's Office
Web site
<http://denverda.org/legalResource/legalresource.htm>

STR Decisions

FEDERAL COURTS

None

STATE COURTS

Arizona
State v. Lynch, No. CR 98-11390 (Ariz. Super. Ct. Aug. 17, 1999)

California
People v. Allen, 85 Cal. Rptr.2d 655 (Cal. App. 2 Dist., 1999)
People v. Bertsch and Hronis, No. 94F07255 (Cal. Super. Ct. Oct. 20, 1999)
People v. Hill, No. 232982 (Cal. Super. Ct. Apr. 18, 2000)
People v. Bokin, No. 168461 (Cal. Super Ct. May 6, 1999)
People v. Moveo, No. 168277 (Cal. Super Ct. Jul. 25, 2000)
People v. Hackney, No. 97F02466 (Cal. Super Ct. Jul. 16, 1999)
People v. Elizarraras, No. 50651 (Cal. Super Ct. Oct. 13, 2000)
People v. Hunt, No. SA034500 (Cal. Super Ct. Oct. 24, 2000)
People v. Baylor, No. INFO29736 (Cal. Super Ct. Dec. 5, 2000)

Colorado
Shreck v. People, 00SA105 (Co. Sup. Ct. Apr. 23, 2001)
*Flores v. Peopl*e, 99 CR2022 (Co. Dist. Ct. Oct. 20, 2000)
Shreck v. People, 98 CR 2475 (Co Dist. Ct. Apr. 2000)

Delaware
State v. Roth, No. 9901000330 (Del. Super. Ct. May 12, 2000)

Florida
Yisrael v. State, No. 99-20176CF10A (Fl. Dist. Ct. Aug. 8, 2000)

Maryland
Commonwealth v. Rosier, 685 N.E.2d 739, 743 (Mass. Sup. Ct., Aug. 25, 1997)
Commonwealth v. Gaynor, No. 98-0965-0966 (Mass. Super. Ct. Apr. 13, 2000)

Michigan
People v. Phillips, No. 00-02025-FC (Mich. Dist. Ct. Oct. 20, 2000)
People v. Cavin, No. 00-4395-FY (Mich. Dist. Ct. Oct. 18, 2000)
People v. Kopp et al., No. 00-04014-FH (Mich. Dist. Ct. Oct. 20, 2000)

Minnosota
State v. Dishmon, No. 99047345 (Minn. Dist. Ct. Mar. 3, 2000)
State v. Kirkendahl, No. 00044987 (Minn. Dist. Ct. Jan. 16, 2001)

Mississippi
Watts v. State, No. 96-DP-01030-SCT 733 So.2d 214 (Miss. Sup. Ct. 1999)

Missouri
State v. Boyd, No. 991-3613 (Mo. Dist. Ct. Apr 24, 2000)
State v. Staples, No. CR1999-03841 (Mo. Dist. Ct. Nov. 15, 2000)

Nebraska
State v. Jackson, No. S-97-522. 82 N.W.2d 317, 325 (Neb. App., 1998)
State v. Champ, No. A-00-617 (Neb. App., Mar. 20, 2001)

New York
People v. Owens, No. IND 547/99 (N.Y. Sup. Ct. Apr. 11, 2001)

Rhode Island
State v. Motyka, No. N1-1999-0341A (R.I. Super. Jan. 23, 2001)

South Dakota

Utah
State v. Butterfield, No. 990654 (2001 UT 59) Supreme Court

Vermont
State v. Pfenning, No. 57-4-96 (Vt. Dist. Ct. Apr. 6, 2000)

mtDNA Decisions

Connecticut
State v. Pappas, No. CR10-246884 (Conn. Super. Ct. July 21, 1999)

Florida
Crow v. State, No. 96-1156-CFA (Fl Super. Ct.)

Indiana
Anderson v. State, 718 N.E.2d 1101 (Ind. 1999)

New York
People v. Klinger, No. 0849/00 713 N.Y.S.2d 823, 2000 N.Y. Slip Op. 20450 (N.Y. Co. Ct. Sept. 5, 2000)

North Carolina
State v. Underwood, No. COA98-648 134 N.C. App. 533 518 S.E.2d 231 (N.C. App., Aug. 17, 1999)

South Carolina
State v. Council, No. 24932515 S.E.2d 508, 516-19 (S.C., Apr. 5, 1999)

Tennessee
State v. Scott, 1999 Tenn. Crim. App. (Tenn. Crim. App. 1999) (unpublished)
State v. Ware, No. 03C01-9705CR00164 1999 Tenn. Crim. App. 1999 (Tenn. Crim. App., Apr. 20, 1999)

Washington
State v. Smith, No. 23406-8-II 2000 100 Wash. App. 1064. (Wash. App. Div. 2, May 26, 2000) (unpublished)

Vancouver, British Columbia
R. v. Murrin, No. CC971114 B.C.J. No. 2715 (B.C. Sup. Ct. Nov. 17, 1999)

Plant Decisions

Arizona
State v. Bogan, 905 P.2d 515, 519-20 (Ariz. Ct. App. 1995), *app. dismissed,* 920 P.2d 320 (Ariz. 1996)

Animal Decisions

Federal District Court (Alabama)
United States v. Guthrie, No. 93 6508 50 F.3d 936, 944 (11th Cir. 1995)

Forensic Science Internet Resources

Forensic science mailing list: http://statgen.ncsu.edu/majordomo/forens.html
Comprehensive link pages
    Zeno's Forensic Page   http://forensic.to/forensic.html
    Reddy's Forensic Page   http://haven.ios.com/~nyrc/homepage.html#Private Labs
    Kruglick's Forensic Resource   http://www.kruglaw.com
    Carpenter's Forensic Science Resources   http://www.tncrimlaw.com/forensic
    Moenssen's Forensic Evidence Site   http://forensic-evidence.com
Forensic DNA information
    Denver District Attorney's office (PDF   http://denverda.org/legalResource/legalresource.htm
      downloads of DNA admissibility decisions)
    STRbase   http://www.cstl.nist.gov/div831/strbase
    Forensic Education and Consulting   http://www.forensicdna.com
Forensic science organizations
    American Academy of Forensic Science   http://www.aafs.org
    American Society of Crime Laboratory   http://www.ascld.org
      directors
    California Association of Criminalists (CAC)   http://www.cacnews.org
    American Board of Criminlistics (ABC)   http://www.criminalistics.com/ABC
Government publications
    The Future of Forensic DNA Testing   http://www.ojp.usdoj.gov/nij/pubs-sum/183697.htm
      Predictions of the Research and
      Development Working Group
    What Every Law Enforcement Officer Should   http://www.ojp.usdoj.gov/nij/pubs-sum/000614.htm
      Know about DNA Evidence
    Postconviction DNA Testing   http://www.ojp.usdoj.gov/nij/pubs-sum/177626.htm
      Recommendations for Handling Requests
    Convicted by Juries, Exonerated by Science   http://www.ojp.usdoj.gov/nij/for96.htm
      (Case Studies in the Use of DNA Evidence
      to Establish Innocence After Trial)
Online journals
    Forensic Science Communications: (Online   http://www.fbi.gov/programs/lab/fsc/current/descript.htm
      journal of the FBI)
Statistics in DNA
    Charles Brenner's Forensic Mathematics Page   http://dna-view.com

Index

A

ABC, *see* American Board of Criminalistics
ABI PRISM®
    DNA Sequencer, 85
    310 Genetic Analyzer, 86, 192
ABO blood
    group system, 8, 9
    types, 34
Accreditation, 25, 262
ACSLD, *see* American Society of Crime Laboratory
         Directors
Adenylate kinase (AK), 8
Administrative review, 234
Admissibility
    hearing, pre-trial, 183
    past, 186
Admissibility standards, 183–200
    cases, 198–200
    DNA landmark cases, 186–195
        mitochondrial DNA, 195
        PCR DQα/A1, polymarker, D1S80, 190–192
        RFLP, 186–190
    Frye, Daubert, and Federal Rules of Evidence,
        183–186
        Daubert standard, 185
        Federal Rules of Evidence, 184–185
        Frye standard, 183–184
        past admissibility, 186
    PCR STRs, 192–194
    state of debate, 195–196
AFDIL, *see* Armed Forces DNA Identification Labo-
        ratory
AFLPs, *see* Amplified fragment length polymor-
        phisms
Agarose gel, 71
AK, *see* Adenylate kinase
Allele(s), 34, 50
    continuous, 140
    discrete, 140, 141
    dropout, 119
    on each chromosome, 92

    frequencies, 143
    ladder, 50
    -specific probes (ASO), 78
    system, continuous, 110
    typing, 86
AluQuant™, 70
Ambiguity, 141
Amelogenin, 52
    locus, structure of, 55
    use of in static detection system, 85
American Board of Criminalistics (ABC), 175
American Society of Crime Laboratory Directors
        (ASCLD), 175–176, 237, 255
Amplification, 118
    blank control, 234
    differential, 126
    PCR, 222
    preferential, 119
    primers, 119
    robot, 89
    tube, 119
Amplified fragment length polymorphisms (AFLPs),
        49–50
AmpliType® PM+DQA1 system, 48, 80, 99, 127
Analytical procedure, 234
Andrews v. State, 186
Animal geneticists, 23
Annealing, 77, 120
Applied Biosystems, 70
Armed Forces DNA Identification Laboratory
        (AFDIL), 22
ASCLD/LAB, *see* ASCLD Laboratory Accreditation
        Board
ASCLD Laboratory Accreditation Board
        (ASCLD/LAB), 176
ASO, *see* Allele-specific probes
Assessment tools, 219–221
    digest gel, 221
    product gel, 222
    slot blot, 219
    yield gel, 220
Association, 2, 6